T0317601

J.K. LASSER PRO™
EXPERT FINANCIAL PLANNING

The *J.K. Lasser Pro* Series

J.K. Lasser Pro Expert Financial Planning: Investment Strategies from Industry Leaders Robert C. Arffa

J.K. Lasser Pro Wealth Building: Investment Strategies for Retirement and Estate Planning David R. Reiser and Robert L. DiColo with Hugh M. Ryan and Andrea R. Reiser

J.K. Lasser Pro Fee-Only Financial Planning: How to Make It Work for You John E. Sestina

J.K. Lasser Pro Preparing for the Retirement Boom Thomas Grady

The *Wiley Financial Advisor* Series

Tax-Deferred Investing: Wealth Building and Wealth Transfer Strategies Cory Grant and Andrew Westhem

Getting Clients, Keeping Clients Dan Richards

Managing Family Trusts: Taking Control of Inherited Wealth Robert A. Rikoon with Larry Waschka

Advising the 60+ Investor: Tax and Financial Planning Strategies Darlene Smith, Dale Pulliam, and Holland Tolles

Tax-Smart Investing: Maximizing Your Client's Profits Andrew D. Westhem and Stewart J. Weisman

J.K. LASSER PRO™

EXPERT FINANCIAL PLANNING

Investment Strategies from Industry Leaders

Robert C. Arffa
Editor

John Wiley & Sons, Inc.
New York • Chichester • Weinheim • Brisbane • Singapore • Toronto

This book is printed on acid-free paper. ⊚

Copyright © 2001 by Robert Arffa. All rights reserved.

Published by John Wiley & Sons, Inc.

Published simultaneously in Canada.

This publication is designed to provide accurate and authoritative information in regard to the subject matter covered. It is sold with the understanding that the publisher is not engaged in rendering legal, accounting, or other professional services. If legal advice or other expert assistance is required, the services of a competent professional person should be sought.

Designations used by companies to distinguish their products are often claimed as trademarks. In all instances where John Wiley & Sons, Inc. is aware of a claim, the product names appear in initial capital or all capital letters. Readers, however, should contact the appropriate companies for more complete information regarding trademarks and registration.

Library of Congress Cataloging-in-Publication Data:
Expert financial planning: investment strategies from leaders / [edited by] Robert C. Arffa.
     p. cm. – (The J.K. Lasser pro series)
     Includes bibliographical references and index.
     ISBN 0-471-39366-5 (cloth : alk. paper)
     1. Finance, Personal. 2. Investments. I. Arffa, Robert C.
II. Title. III. Series.
HG179 .E958 2001
332.024'01—dc21   00-051371

10 9 8 7 6 5 4 3 2 1

Contents

Section VI. Financial Planning

About the Contributors

Harold Apolinsky

Harold I. Apolinsky, Esq., EPLS, is a board-certified estate planning attorney (1 of 12 out of 120 lawyers) with the law firm Sirote & Permutt, P.C., in Birmingham, Alabama. Harold is an adjunct professor of estate planning at the Cumberland School of Law (1976 to present); he taught at the University of Alabama School of Law (1975 to 1997).

Robert Arffa, M.D.

Dr. Robert Arffa is an ophthalmologist who specializes in the treatment of corneal diseases and refractive surgery. He is director of the Cornea Division of Allegheny General Hospital, Adjunct Associate Professor of Ophthalmology at Allegheny University of the Health Sciences, Clinical Assistant Professor at the University of Pittsburgh, Medical Director for Eyes at the Center for Organ Recovery and Education, and Medical Director for TLC-Pittsburgh. He has written numerous original research articles and book chapters about corneal diseases and has authored two editions of Grayson's Diseases of the Cornea, a widely read ophthalmology text. Dr. Arffa was selected by his peers as one of the "Best Doctors in America" and one of the "Top Doctors." This is his first non-medical text.

Sharon Arffa, Ph.D.

Dr. Sharon Arffa is a psychologist in private practice in Pittsburgh. She is Clinical Assistant Professor of Psychology at MCP/Hahnneman University.

Lisa Blonkvist

Lisa Blonkvist, a certified investment management analyst, is a senior vice president and a senior investment management consultant at Salomon Smith Barney, Inc. She is recognized as a leader in the consulting services process—the selection and evaluation of money managers. She is the San Antonio, Texas, branch coordinator for the Consulting Group of Salomon Smith Barney. She has been published in *Barron's* and has contributed to articles in various publications.

John C. Bogle

John C. Bogle has spent his entire 42-year career in the mutual fund business. In 1974 he founded The Vanguard Group, Inc., and until recently was chairman and chief executive officer of each of the mutual funds in the $100 billion Vanguard Group of Investment Companies. Mr. Bogle is the author of *Bogle on Mutual Funds: New Perspectives for the Intelligent Investor*, which has sold over 250,000 copies. Mr. Bogle is also a director and chairman of the Corporate Objectives Committee of The Mead Corporation, a director and member of the Executive Committee of the General Accident Group of Insurance Companies, and a director of the Princeton University Investment Company.

Jonathan Clarke

Jonathan Clarke is a Ph.D. candidate in finance at the University of Pittsburgh.

Gregory D. Curtis

Mr. Curtis is chief executive officer of Greycourt & Co., Inc., an Internet-based, open-architecture wealth advisory firm. He is a nationally known investment adviser whose column, "Right on the Money," appears in the *Pittsburgh Business Times*. Prior to forming Greycourt, Mr. Curtis was the principal financial adviser to Pittsburgh's Mellon family for 15 years. Since forming his own company, Mr. Curtis has advised many of the world's wealthiest families and largest institutions. Mr. Curtis chairs the board of directors of Foundation Advisors, Inc, the investment adviser to The Investment Fund for Foundations, and also chairs the board of visitors and governors of St. John's College. He received his A.B. degree, cum laude, from Dartmouth College and a J.D. degree, cum laude, from Harvard Law School, and is a graduate of The Endowment Institute at Harvard Business School.

Robert Deckey

Robert E. Deckey, director, joined the Salomon Smith Barney Investment Banking Division's Real Estate and Lodging Group from J.P. Morgan Securities, where he was responsible for providing investment banking expertise to domestic and international real estate companies. Mr. Deckey currently focuses on providing corporate finance to global real estate companies and has extensive transaction experience in debt and equity capital markets, raising in excess of $6 billion in the last five years. Prior to J.P. Morgan Securities, Mr. Deckey was with AEW Capital Management in Boston, MA, where he was responsible for both new real estate investments and portfolio management. Mr. Deckey graduated from Brown University with a B.A. in Engineering and Economics and from the Wharton School with an M.B.A. in Finance.

Richard H. Driehaus

Richard H. Driehaus is founder, chief investment officer, CEO and chairman, Driehaus Capital Management, Inc.; CEO and chairman, Driehaus Securities Corporation; president and chairman of the Board of Trustees, Driehaus Mutual Funds; lead portfolio manager, Driehaus Small Cap Growth and Driehaus Mid Cap Growth; and co-portfolio manager, Small Cap Recovery Growth.

Mr. Driehaus is widely regarded within the investment industry as an expert in the specialty of aggressive growth investing. He is the architect of Driehaus Capital Management's investment philosophy and has overall responsibility for the firm's investment process and style. He is primarily responsible for all domestic portfolio management and investment analysis within the firm. In early 2000, Mr. Driehaus was named to Barron's "All-Century" team of the 25 individuals who have been the most influential within the mutual fund industry over the past 100 years.

Mr. Driehaus holds a B.S.C and an M.B.A. from DePaul University.

Charles Gradante

Mr. Gradante is cofounder and codirector of the Hennessee Group. He has held executive positions in banking and securities, including at Drexel Burnham Lambert, Citibank, and Union Chelsea National Bank where he served as President and CEO.

Mr. Gradante has cohosted and made guest appearances on CNN and CNBC for his expertise on hedge funds and global financial markets. He appears monthly on Bloomberg, and is often quoted by financial publications regarding the hedge fund industry.

Gerald A. Guild

Gerald Guild is a nationally recognized bond expert. He has served as senior vice president and chief fixed-income strategist and director for Advest, Inc. He also writes a regular column for *Financial World*.

E. Lee Hennessee

Ms. Hennessee cofounded Hennessee Group LLC with Charles Gradante in 1997. She focuses on manager selection and client services, sharing overall management with Mr. Gradante. Prior to forming the Hennessee Group she directed the Hedge Fund Advisory Group as a division of Weiss, Peck & Greer. Ms. Hennessee is one of the most widely sourced consultants in the hedge fund industry. She has published articles in and is often quoted by major financial publications, has spoken at numerous conferences, and has made guest television appearances concerning hedge funds. Her pioneering efforts in 1987 created the first hedge fund manager database.

David Hillman

David McL. Hillman, partner and executive vice president of PNC Equity Management Corp., joined the management training program of PNC's affiliate, PNC bank, in 1976. He subsequently held several positions in the Corporate Banking Division. In 1982 he joined PNC's newly formed Equity Management Corp. as its cofounder and was named executive vice president in 1983. David is a director of Via Source Communications, Deka Medical, Inc., and LDMI Telecommunications, Inc., and is an advisory board director of Arlington Capital Partners, Prime New Ventures, and Sentinel Capital Partners. He is a former member of the board of governors and executive committee of the National Association of Small Business Investment Companies (NASBIC). He earned his B.A. from Williams College in 1976 and his M.B.A. from the University of Virginia in 1982.

Tomas Jandik

Tomas Jandik is assistant professor of finance at the University of Arkansas.

Peter Katt

Peter Katt is a nationally recognized life insurance expert. He has had published some 100 articles as a contributing editor and columnist for the *Journal of Financial Planning* and *AAII Journal* and as a contributor to such publications as *Money* magazine, *Consumers Research*, *Louis Rukeyser's Wall Street*, *Personal Advantage/Financial*, and *Executive Wealth Advisory*. Mr. Katt was one of three judges for *Money* magazine's life insurance agents test and has been featured in articles in *Newsweek* and *Consumer's Research*. He appeared regularly on CNBC's *$mart Money* show and was a featured guest on an *Oprah Winfrey* show. Mr. Katt has been a life insurance adviser since 1979 and is a pioneer in fee-only life insurance advising.

Gershon Mandelker

Dr. Mandelker earned an M.B.A. and Ph.D. in finance and economics at the University of Chicago. He was on the faculty of Carnegie-Mellon University during 1973–1977. He has been on the University of Pittsburgh faculty since 1977, where he is the Katz Alumni Professor of Finance. Dr. Mandelker's research involves testing economic hypotheses related to corporate finance and the securities markets. His research papers have dealt with issues such as corporate mergers and acquisitions, executive compensation, the efficiency of financial markets, the impact of inflation on financial securities, the determinants of risk, and the long-term returns on stock involved in mergers and takeovers. He has published articles in various journals in finance, economics, and accounting, which have generated citations in more than 600 scholarly journals.

James Meredith

Jim Meredith is the Financial Expert of the popular radio program Hefren-Tillotson's "Your Money and You" heard every Sunday morning on KDKA-AM 1020. As an executive vice president of the firm and the president of Masterplan, Inc., Hefren-Tillotson's parent company, Mr. Meredith has been a leader on the Hefren-Tillotson team since 1977.

Jim Meredith has also earned the prestigious Personal Financial Specialist (PFS) designation. The American Institute of Certified Public Accountants (AICPA), a national professional organization of CPAs has only granted the PFS accreditation to 2,700 CPA's nationwide.

Jim Meredith received his B.S. degree in Accounting and his M.B.A. in Finance from the University of Dayton.

Jay N. Mueller

Jay N. Mueller, CFA, joined Strong Funds in September 1991 as a securities analyst and portfolio manager. For four years prior to that, he was a securities analyst and portfolio manager with R. Meeder & Associates of Dublin, Ohio. Jay received his B.A. in economics in 1982 from the University of Chicago. He has managed the Strong Heritage Money Fund since its inception in June 1995, the Strong Money Market Fund since September 1991, and the Strong Investors Money Fund since January 1998.

Bernard Newman

Dr. Bernard D. Newman has been a licensed chiropractor in the Commonwealth of Pennsylvania since 1983. In addition to private practice, Dr. Newman received his Certified Financial Planner (CFP) license from the CFP Board of Standards in Denver, Colorado, in 1994. Since that time, Dr. Newman has been consulting with health-care practitioners about financial matters specific to them.

Larry Swedroe

Larry Swedroe is a principal of Buckingham Asset Management and BAM Adviser Services, St. Louis, Missouri. He was vice chairman of Prudential Home Mortgage, the nation's second largest home mortgage lender, and also held positions at Citicorp as senior vice president and regional treasurer, responsible for treasury, foreign exchange, and investment banking activities, including risk management strategies. Larry has an M.B.A. in finance and investment from New York University, and a B.A. in finance from Baruch College. His book, *The Only Guide to a Winning Investment Strategy You'll Ever Need*, has been published by Truman Talley Dutton, an imprint of Penguin Publishing.

Peter Tanous

Peter Tanous is president of Lynx Investment Advisory, Inc., in Washington, D.C. and a director of Cedars Bank in Los Angeles. He is the author of *Investment Gurus* and *The Wealth Equation*. Previously he held positions as executive vice president and director of Bank Audi (USA), chairman of Petra Capital Corp., and first vice president and international director of Smith Barney, Inc. Mr. Tanous lives in Washington, D.C., with his wife Ann.

Gary S. Weinstein

Gary S. Weinstein, M.D., is an oculoplastic surgeon practicing in Pittsburgh, Pennsylvania. He is a diplomate of the American Board of Ophthalmology and a fellow of the American Academy of Ophthalmology, the American Society of Ophthalmic Plastic and Reconstructive Surgery, and the American College of Surgeons. He has published clinical research papers and chapters in prominent textbooks of oculoplastic surgery. Dr. Weinstein is a clinical assistant professor of ophthalmology at the University of Pittsburgh School of Medicine.

Weston J. Wellington

Weston J. Wellington is a vice president with Dimensional Fund Advisors, Inc. Prior to joining Dimensional in 1995, Mr. Wellington was director of research at LPL Financial Services, Inc. in Boston, and has twenty-five years of experience in the investment industry. He holds a B.A. in History from Yale University (1973).

David Winters

David Winters, CFA, is portfolio co-manager of Mutual Beacon Fund and a senior vice president of Franklin Mutual Advisers. Previously, David was a trader for Herzog, Heine, Geduld, Inc., and a financial analyst for KMS Investment Adviser, Inc. He earned his bachelor's degree in economics from Cornell University. David has been with Mutual Series since 1988 and offers expertise in a variety of industries, including railroads, beverages, candy, timber, media, and consumer goods, both domestically and abroad. He was featured in *Outstanding Investors Digest* in 1996 and 1997.

Preface

Let me first tell you a little about myself. I am an ophthalmologist, specializing in corneal transplants, cataract surgery, and refractive surgery. While I am primarily a clinician, I also am a teacher and researcher. I am on the faculty of Allegheny University of the Health Sciences and the University of Pittsburgh School of Medicine. I have published many research and review articles and write a commonly used textbook on diseases of the cornea. While the subject matter of this book has nothing to do with my professional interests, my approach to finances and investment is rooted in my medical and scientific background.

Sitting in the surgeons' lounge or the doctors' dining room I often hear my colleagues discuss their investments. Many of these bright, highly educated, and high-income professionals admittedly have very little knowledge of personal financial management or investment strategy. Our decades of education never included a course on accounting, finance, investment, or business management.

The types of investments most frequently discussed are highly speculative, such as fledgling companies, pre–public offerings, and new medications in Food and Drug Administration (FDA) trials, and my colleagues are investing $25,000, $50,000, or even $100,000 in them. At the same time I would hear from my advisers—my investment adviser, insurance agent, and estate attorney—that my fellow physicians were not amassing large savings. I would also discuss investments with a friend, Gershon Mandelker, who is an academician specializing in the financial markets. I was surprised how little agreement there was between what the research indicated and professionals recommended, and what my colleagues were doing.

Even in the bookstores there really wasn't a good independent and unbiased source of information. Very little is aimed at those with higher incomes, where the issues are often different. Also, few resources include the findings of the large volume of academic research that has been amassed over the past 50 years.

I decided to put together such a source, for the relatively bright and educated who have good income but are ignorant of personal finance and investment. With some advice, I made an outline of the major financial questions all of us face, and the major types of investments and investment styles. In each of these areas I sought out experts with a national reputation and an ability to communicate their knowledge.

The contributors include many of the highly regarded professionals in their fields. While the material cannot be comprehensively covered in so short a volume, this book does provide a sound overview to the key subject areas.

Acknowledgments

I owe thanks to several who provided assistance in this project. Debra Englander, who saw the potential and provided guidance; Gershon Mandelker, who has always been a good sounding board and source of research; Steven Hesky, who helped ignite my financial interests and encouraged me to write this book; Peter Tanous, who has been a source of contacts and advice; George Vahanian, for his practical experience; and John Bogle, who agreed to participate early, and thereby facilitated enlisting others.

J.K. LASSER PRO™

EXPERT FINANCIAL PLANNING

CHAPTER 1

Developing a Financial Plan

Jim Meredith and Robert Arffa

Why Do You Need a Financial Plan?

Most of us make our way day by day. Our society has conditioned us to think and react with a short-term perspective. Occasionally we can become overwhelmed when we think about future commitments like paying for the kids' education or our retirement. However, it is the rare person who determines exactly what it is going to take to reach his or her goals, and follow through the necessary steps. But planning makes it much more likely that you will be able to accomplish your goals.

A major part of this process is determining your own set of values and goals. You and your spouse or companion must reach a consensus. There is little that is more important than for a couple to sit down and talk about their respective life goals. Most goals and life events involve finances. Marriage, change in job, relocation, starting your own business, number of children, caring for aged parents, age of retirement—these are a few examples of life decisions that affect your finances. Reaching a consensus with your spouse on your goals, their relative priorities, and the use of your financial resources to reach them is essential for your relationship as well as your financial security.

1

Financial planning helps you both to balance the constant trade-off between spending on what you want today and saving for what you want in the future.

Making a financial plan is not a one-time or static decision. It is as dynamic as life itself. Your financial situation changes over time, and so may your goals. Often life will throw you curves, and a good plan will prepare you and protect you as much as possible from what life may bring. Developing an emergency fund can help you cope with unexpected expenses or financial setbacks. You can estimate the size of such a reserve, and where those funds should be placed. You can also determine what types and amounts of insurance you need to protect your family from catastrophic financial losses.

The Planning Process

The first step in developing a financial plan is to *make a commitment to the process*. It takes time, and often difficult or uncomfortable decisions must be made. You have to think about and discuss with your spouse your financial situation, goals, and priorities. You must review your spending, savings, investments, and insurance. You may have to work out compromises with your spouse on some important issues. However, in the long run the time spent will be profitable.

There is no way to come to conclusions quickly. Designing a long-term plan follows the same path as building a home. Plan the size, shape, number of rooms, cost, and so on before breaking ground. Many of us rush to pick out wallpaper before we've determined the size and shape of the room and locations of doors and windows. Instead of following a plan, many people patch together a poorly designed house, frequently changing directions in the middle of the project.

The next step is to *set your goals*. You begin with a simple list of your needs and dreams, and through the planning process (Figure 1.1.) they are prioritized, revised, and refined. The most common goals are buying a (first/larger/nicer/more expensive) home, children's education, and retirement. Many other goals are listed in Table 1.1. Generally goals fall into two categories: accumulation goals and income replacement goals. With an accumulation goal you are aiming to have a certain amount of money by a given date. College funding is one example. An income replacement goal is a need to generate a stream of cash flow starting at some point and continuing into the future, such as for retirement. Retirement funding is often the most challenging goal, because retirement can be so far in the future, and it involves such a large amount of savings.

Once you have a tentative list of goals, you and your spouse should *priori-*

The Planning Process
1. Commit to the process.
2. Develop a list of goals.
3. Prioritize your goals.
4. Assess your current financial status:
   Current resources/balance sheet.
   Cash flow analysis.
5. Make projections for each goal.
6. Revise/refine your goals.
7. Devise a strategy to achieve all goals:
   Spending/savings plan.
   Investment plan.
8. Review risk management.

FIGURE 1.1   The Planning Process

tize them. For example: Is it more important to retire at a younger age or move into a larger home? Should you purchase a larger home or a vacation home? Should you leave more investments in your names for retirement, or gift them to the children?

The next step is to *assess your current financial status.* Create a portrait of your family's finances from a business perspective. Three different types of assessments must be performed: a balance statement, a cash flow statement, and future projections. A balance statement is a summary of (1) your assets,

TABLE 1.1 Planning Goals	
An emergency fund	An expensive car
Starting a business	Jewelry
Relocating	Charitable gifts
Changing occupations	Family gifts
Obtaining further education	Providing for aged parents
Repaying education loans	Disabled child needs
Repaying a mortgage	Closely held business planning
A second home	Divorce-remarriage issues

such as investments, pension plans, your home, and other possessions; and (2) your debts or liabilities, such as mortgage, education loans, and car loans. Your net worth is the difference between your assets and your liabilities (Table 1.2). The cash flow statement is an itemized list of annual income, expenditures, and savings (Table 1.3).

If your net worth is negative, it means that either you are early in your earnings phase or your household is operating like the federal government—borrowing money to make ends meet. The cash flow statement will tell you which of these applies. Are you saving money, repaying loans, and accumulating investments, or is your debt growing?

Together these two statements will give you a good idea of how you have used your resources. Even if you are making progress, most likely you are saving and accumulating less wealth than you might have expected.

Information from these two statements is then used to *make projections*, and determine whether you are likely to meet your goals, given your present course. A financial planner (person or software) can calculate the funds required for each of your goals, and whether you can expect to accumulate those funds, based on your current assets and savings rate.

Making these projections entails assumptions about several important variables:

- Your future income, spending, and savings rate
- Rates of inflation (for consumer products in general, for real estate, for college expenses, etc.)
- Rate of return on your investments
- Your life span(s)
- Tax rates

Which numbers you choose for each of these have a significant effect on the results of the projections. Here's one example: Your child will enter college in 15 years, and current total annual private college expenses are $30,000. If you predict the rate of inflation of college expenses will be 6%, you will need $314,500. But if you predict that expenses will rise at only 4% per year, you need to save only $230,000. Let's say that you have $25,000 saved now. If you invest this amount, what will it be worth in 15 years? If you assume a return of 11%, it should amount to $119,500 when your child enters college. If you assume a return of 8% you would expect to have $79,000.

Therefore, even if you hire someone to do this analysis for you, it is important to review the assumptions to make sure that they are realistic. Some rea-

TABLE 1.2 Family Balance Statement

Date: / /

Assets

Cash and Bank Accounts   Balance

_____   _____

_____   _____

_____   _____

_____

Total Cash and Bank Accounts   _____

Investments

    Tax-Deferred Accounts   Balance

        Pension Plan/401(k) 1   _____

        Pension Plan/401(k) 2   _____

        IRA/Keogh 1   _____

        IRA/Keogh 2   _____

        Annuity   _____

        Other   _____

    Taxable Accounts

      _____   _____

      _____   _____

      _____   _____

      _____   _____

      _____   _____

Total Investments   _____

Other Assets   Value

    House 1   _____

    House 2   _____

    Car 1   _____

    Car 2   _____

    Jewelry   _____

    Home furnishings   _____

    Computer/Audio Equipment   _____

    Other   _____

    Total Other Assets   _____

Total Assets   _____

(Continued)

TABLE 1.2 Continued

Liabilities	
Credit card balances	_____
Mortgage 1	_____
Mortgage 2	_____
Home equity loan	_____
Education loans	_____
Automobile loan/lease	_____
Other debts	_____
Total Liabilities	_____
Net Worth (Total Assets Less Total Liabilities)	_____

---

sonable assumptions will be discussed in later chapters. Generally it is better to be a little conservative on your assumptions, to make it more likely that you will achieve your goals. We recommend using a general inflation rate of 4%, a life expectancy of 95 years, and current tax rates. Investment returns depend on your asset mix, which, in turn, will vary with the time span and your risk tolerance. Try to err a little on the conservative side in estimating your future income as well.

Using these assumptions, you then determine how much cash you would need to save each year to meet each of your goals. From this, you add up the total savings required each year, and determine whether you can achieve it. Are you currently saving enough, or can you increase income or cut back spending enough to accumulate the savings? If not, you must revise one or more goals.

Once you have decided on a set of goals that you think you can achieve, you must *devise a strategy*. How much money will you put away each month? Into what accounts and investments will those funds go? What is the asset allocation (mix of investment assets) for each goal?

Tracking Your Finances

Owners of businesses, whether large or small, must regularly close their account books to review their progress and tally their assets. Building a positive net worth requires the same discipline. Sitting down once every one or two years and trying to analyze your finances is next to impossible without thor-

TABLE 1.3 Family Cash Flow Statement

Period: One year beginning   /   /

Inflows

    Salary 1   _____

    Salary 2   _____

    Other income source 1   _____

    Other income source 2   _____

    Investment income

       Interest   _____

       Dividends   _____

       Capital gains   _____

    Pension plans   _____

Total Inflows   _____

Outflows

    Accounting   _____

    Alimony/child support   _____

    Automobile/transportation

       Fuel   _____

       Repairs/maintenance   _____

       Lease/loan payments   _____

    Charity   _____

    Children

       Child care   _____

       School   _____

       Other classes   _____

    Clothing   _____

    Dining out   _____

    Education   _____

    Entertainment   _____

    Gifts   _____

    Groceries   _____

    Home repair   _____

    Household furnishings   _____

    Miscellaneous household expenses   _____

    Insurance   _____

    Loan payments   _____

    Medical expenses   _____

(Continued)

TABLE 1.3 Continued

Mortgage/Rent	_____
Recreation	_____
Taxes	
Federal income	_____
Medicare	_____
FICA	_____
State income	_____
City income	_____
Property	_____
Travel	_____
Utilities	_____
Wines and spirits	_____
Other	_____
Total Outflows	_____
Overall Total (Inflows Less Outflows)	_____

Note: Bold print indicates relatively fixed expense.

ough records. We strongly encourage use of a home computer with personal financial software. There are several excellent personal finance programs, such as Quicken (Intuit) and Money (Microsoft). Also, many web sites offer simpler versions. Any of these will help you track income and spending, monitor the performance of your investments, and keep track of tax-related information. However, in our experience they work only if you enter all your data regularly, at least monthly. Currently it is possible for the programs to download personal bank, credit card, and investment account information via telephone or the Internet. Use of these programs is of great assistance in creating and monitoring your financial plan. They also facilitate setting up a monthly or annual budget and tracking your adherence to it.

The best way to figure out how you can save more is to track your spending carefully, and find the fat. Table 1.3 suggests how to categorize your spending. This makes it easier to see where your money is going and to identify categories of discretional spending that can be trimmed. Chapter 2 contains statistics about the spending of typical American families for comparison.

Table 1.4 lists recommendations for which types of records to retain, where to keep them, and how long you should keep them.

TABLE 1.4 Records You Should Retain

Type	Where	For How Long
Household bills paid	File by year	Three years
Checks/account statements	File by year	Seven years
Credit card statements	File by year	Seven years
Investment account statements	File by account	Seven years after account closed
Major equipment receipts/ manuals	File	Until disposed of
Home records (purchase, repair, improvements)	File	Until after house sold
Tax returns and related documents	File by year	Seven years
Insurance policies and statements (life, health, disability, auto, homeowner)	File by policy	Three years after expired
Inheritance documents	Safe-deposit box	Indefinitely
Gift tax returns	File	Indefinitely
Copies of your will, living will, durable power of attorney, and inventory or important papers and documents	Safe-deposit box	Indefinitely
Stock certificates	Safe-deposit box	Indefinitely
Deeds, mortgages, and other real estate title documents	Safe-deposit box	Indefinitely
Inventory, receipts, and photos or video of valuable possessions	Safe-deposit box	Indefinitely, regularly update
Automobile titles	Safe-deposit box	Indefinitely

Risk Management

Risk management is protecting yourself and your family from large, unexpected financial events. Yes, insurance is boring or depressing, but it is essential to have adequate coverage. Many of us realize this, but partly because we dislike it so much, we don't take the care to make sure that we are properly insured. The National Insurance Consumer Organization reports that more than 9 of 10 Americans carry the wrong types and amounts of insurance coverage (according to Eric Tyson, *Personal Finance for Dummies*, Chicago: IDG Books, 1995, p. 333).

Giving sound insurance advice does not necessarily mean selling another insurance policy. Insurance is nothing more than transferring a risk for a price. Avoid in-house or captive agents. With only one tool available such as a hammer, every need starts to look like a nail. Good insurance is not and will never be a good investment. Remember that you are paying someone to assume your risk. If the insurers do not make a profit from your business, they may not stay in business long enough to be there when you need them.

What Do You Need?

The simple answer is to buy coverage for all possible financial catastrophes. Don't consider how remote the possibility of the disaster. If the risk is very low, the insurance will not be expensive. Insurance companies are very accurate at calculating risks, and almost the entire insurance premium goes toward that risk. (Most of the money they make is from investing the funds while they have them.)

Everyone must have health insurance. If you have any dependents (spouse/children/aged parents) you probably need life insurance to support them when you cannot. The only circumstances in which life insurance is not necessary are (1) if either spouse can earn enough to provide for your dependents, or (2) if you have accumulated sufficient wealth to provide for them.

If you own a home, you need homeowners insurance. If you live in an area where flooding is possible, separate flood insurance must be purchased. Anyone who earns money used for living expenses should have disability insurance. Anyone who drives a car is required by law to have automobile insurance.

Chapter 25 goes into more detail about purchasing life and disability insurance, determining your needs, and how to obtain coverage. Health insurance is a complicated subject and is currently in a state of evolution, so it will not be covered in this book. We would just like to make some general insurance recommendations here.

Insure Only Against Catastrophic Expenses

Don't purchase insurance that reimburses you for expenses you could easily pay yourself. Whenever possible, be your own insurer. Don't purchase small insurance policies, such as extended warranties or other product insurance, dental insurance, or rental car insurance. Take the highest deductible you can on your automobile, homeowners, and medical insurances. In the long run, you'll save more than you spend.

Shop Around, and Buy Direct

There are significant pricing differences among insurance policies, and price is poorly correlated with the quality of the company and the policy. It is possible to find lower-cost, high-quality policies by shopping around. The most likely source of these policies is directly from the company itself. By eliminating the insurance agent, you are less likely to have a more expensive policy or more coverage than you need. However, coverage issues can be more complex than you realize, so thorough research or professional advice can be valuable.

Also, take advantage of group membership. Group policies (other than life insurance) tend to be lower in price than policies you can buy on your own. Make sure that you check out the insurance company before purchasing a policy. Obtain its financial rating from several rating agencies, and find out what other policy owners' experiences have been in dealing with the company.

Generally Avoid Add-on Riders

Companies and agents push add-on riders because they have high profit margins. They are usually not worth purchasing. Riders are additions to the standard policy that provide further benefits or special features. The most common riders are waiver of premium in the event of the policyholder's disability, options to purchase additional insurance in the future without a new health examination, and additional benefits in the event of accidental death.

Emergency Fund

An important part of risk management is to have a fund of cash or other liquid assets to fall back on in case of emergency. Most financial advisers recommend cash or cash-equivalent investment equal to three to six months of earned income. However, this depends on your situation. If your employee benefits include disability insurance that begins at 90 days, and you are certain that if you were laid off you could start another job within three months, you may need a reserve of only two to three months' expenses.

In actuality, your money earns less if you keep funds in cash rather than higher-returning investments like stocks. For example, if your current annual earned income is $100,000, keeping $50,000 in a money-market account for 20 years will yield $132,000 (at 5%, before taxes) versus $336,000 in the stock market (assuming 10% return, before taxes). Therefore, if it is unlikely that you will need the funds, a more profitable liquid investment such as a mutual fund can be used.

Planning for Other Needs

Anyone with assets or dependents needs a *will*. If you do not have a will, the state will appoint someone to determine what happens to your assets and dependents. It will take the state a long time to decide, and the state and federal governments probably will keep a large portion of your assets in the process. A will names a guardian to oversee the interests of minor children, and an executor to administer your estate. Your property is transferred more rapidly and smoothly, and to whom you intend.

A *living will* declares your wishes regarding medical measures that could be taken in the event of grave illness or injury. If you are incapacitated and unable to make decisions or communicate your wishes, your family and doctors can use this document to guide their decisions regarding treatment.

You should designate someone to make decisions for you in the event that you become incapacitated or mentally incompetent. Such *durable power of attorney* is usually given to your spouse or an adult child. You can indicate which decisions this person has the authority to make, such as writing checks, paying bills, selling your property, or designating gifts to your loved ones. (A word of caution: Avoid contingent or springing powers events, or medical conditions that are not clearly defined.)

A *health care proxy* designates an attorney-in-fact to make health-care decisions for you if you are incapacitated. This document may contain a living will, but the powers can be broader.

You should also make an inventory of important information and documents for your survivors. This contains detailed information about your personal property, financial assets, and advisers who may assist in settling your estate. It should list all bank and investment accounts, pension and employee benefit plans, mortgages, and other loans. Information about insurance policies, stock certificates, certificates of deposit, buy-sell agreements, tax records and returns, real estate deeds, and legal documents such as birth and marriage certificates and wills should be recorded.

Conclusion

This chapter outlines the value of making a personal financial plan and the most crucial issues. Most of the important topics—investment vehicles, asset allocation, expected returns on investments, insurance, retirement planning, estate planning—are covered in later chapters.

Don't forget that it is your plan. You are the final arbiter of all decisions.

Achieving Financial Security

Sharon Arffa and Robert Arffa

Sixty-seven percent of Americans are more concerned about their financial security than their physical security, and 56% say they think about money more often than about sex.[1] How do people achieve financial security? Surprisingly, doing so is not primarily dependent on income level. Above a certain minimum income to meet basic needs, financial security is mainly an attitude or state of mind. It is an approach to personal finances that involves planning, and some sacrifice of immediate pleasure for long-term goals. As professionals, nearly all of us planned ahead and sacrificed for many years during our education and training. However, the evidence is that most of us do not continue the same philosophy once having achieved our professional positions.

Each of us would probably have a different definition of financial security. Almost none of us will have so much money that we would never have to worry about what we spent, or enough to insulate us from the possibility of becoming disabled or losing our positions. We will never have enough to protect our family from sickness or injury, or (if they occur) from the effects of war, famine, or the collapse of financial markets.

One reasonable way to define financial security would be as an absence of great concern about having enough income to meet your family's needs, being wealthy enough to retire in comfort, and being able to protect your family in the event of your premature death. Such security is obtained through management and planning of your financial life. Achieving a good income is helpful, but not sufficient.

However, such security is rarely achieved in America today. There is instead a pervasive atmosphere of consumerism. We succumb to the highly persuasive marketing and peer pressures that increase our desires to have the latest and best products.

Only 52% of Americans have money saved outside of a work-related savings or retirement plan.[2] Approximately 25% to 30% of American households live from paycheck to paycheck.[3] Borrowing has steadily increased over the past four decades. The typical American household is $38,000 in debt.[4] There are more than 840,000 personal bankruptcy filings annually.

It's not the less educated and those with low incomes who are living beyond their means. In 1995 one-third of households headed by college-educated did *no* saving.[5] The largest increase in debt in the 1990s occurred in households with annual incomes of $50,000 to $100,000. Sixty-three percent of these houses now carry credit card debt. A study of personal bankruptcies found that the typical filer was a "well-educated, middle-class baby boomer with big-time credit card debt."[6]

The main characteristic of American families that achieve wealth is their ability to resist the culture of consumerism. Thomas Stanley and William Danko are professors of marketing who have spent 20 years studying wealthy Americans. In their 1996 book *The Millionaire Next Door: The Surprising Secrets of America's Wealthy*, they concluded that: "It is seldom luck of inheritance or advanced degrees or even intelligence that enables people to amass fortunes. Wealth is more often the result of a lifestyle of hard work, perseverance, planning, and, most of all, self-discipline." (See Figure 2.1.)

Very few people become wealthy or financially secure just by having sufficient income. It is rare to have enough income to be able to spend what you want and have enough left over to accumulate a stockpile sufficient to meet future needs. Yes, it is true that the higher your income, the more likely you will reach $1 million of net worth. However, the median total annual taxable income of millionaires is approximately $131,000, and only 13% of millionaires have taxable incomes of more than $500,000 per year.[7]

So how do they amass a net worth of over $1 million, on average over 12 times their annual taxable income? Saving. The average American millionaire has saved approximately 20% of their total annual taxable income each year.

Common Denominators of the Wealthy
1. Live well below their means.
2. Allocate their time, energy, and money productively.
3. Chose the right occupation.
4. Believe that financial security is more important than displaying high social status.
5. Were not indulged economically by their parents.
6. Can identify and take advantage of market opportunities.

FIGURE 2.1 Common Denominations of the Wealthy
Source: The Millionaire Next Door.

Millionaires have accumulated their wealth by planning, making a conscious decision to live below their means, and investing their savings.

American families save less than families in other countries. The typical American family saves 4.5% of their income each year. This is half of the savings rate 15 years ago, and about one-third of what the average Japanese, French, German, or Italian family saves.[8] Of American immigrants, in general, the longer the average member of an ancestry group has been in the United States, the less likely that the group produces a disproportionately large percentage of millionaires.[9] This is because they are more likely to become fully socialized to the high-consumption U.S. lifestyle.

Starting to save while relatively young maximizes the likelihood of achieving wealth. The amount you accumulate for retirement is highly dependent on how early you start saving. Table 2.1 compares two savers. The first invests $2,000 annually for 10 years beginning at age 25, and then invests nothing further. The second waits until age 35 to begin investing, and invests $2,000 annually to age 65. As you can see, the savings procrastinator never catches up with the early starter.

Insuring Your Success

Insurance is an important part of financial security. You must make sure that your family will not suffer financially if you or your spouse dies or becomes disabled. Adequate life and disability insurance, homeowners insurance, medical insurance, and wills are essential.

Are You Spending Wisely?

How much do we have to spend to meet our basic needs? How much money does it take to live comfortably? Obviously this depends on our requirements

TABLE 2.1 Effect of Early Start on Savings

	Early Saver		Late Saver	
Age	Contribution	Cumulative Value	Contribution	Cumulative Value
25	$2,000	$2,200	$0	$0
26	$2,000	$4,620	$0	$0
27	$2,000	$7,282	$0	$0
28	$2,000	$10,210	$0	$0
29	$2,000	$13,431	$0	$0
30	$2,000	$16,974	$0	$0
31	$2,000	$20,872	$0	$0
32	$2,000	$25,159	$0	$0
33	$2,000	$29,875	$0	$0
34	$2,000	$35,062	$0	$0
35	$0	$38,569	$2,000	$2,200
36	$0	$42,425	$2,000	$4,620
37	$0	$46,668	$2,000	$7,282
38	$0	$51,335	$2,000	$10,210
39	$0	$56,468	$2,000	$13,431
40	$0	$62,115	$2,000	$16,974
41	$0	$68,327	$2,000	$20,872
42	$0	$75,159	$2,000	$25,159
43	$0	$82,675	$2,000	$29,875
44	$0	$90,943	$2,000	$35,062
45	$0	$100,037	$2,000	$40,769
46	$0	$110,041	$2,000	$47,045
47	$0	$121,045	$2,000	$53,950

(Continued)

TABLE 2.1 Continued

Age	Early Saver		Late Saver	
	Contribution	Cumulative Value	Contribution	Cumulative Value
48	$0	$133,149	$2,000	$61,545
49	$0	$146,464	$2,000	$69,899
50	$0	$161,110	$2,000	$79,089
51	$0	$177,222	$2,000	$89,198
52	$0	$194,944	$2,000	$100,318
53	$0	$214,438	$2,000	$112,550
54	$0	$235,882	$2,000	$126,005
55	$0	$259,470	$2,000	$140,805
56	$0	$285,417	$2,000	$157,086
57	$0	$313,959	$2,000	$174,995
58	$0	$345,355	$2,000	$194,694
59	$0	$379,890	$2,000	$216,364
60	$0	$417,879	$2,000	$240,200
61	$0	$459,667	$2,000	$266,420
62	$0	$505,634	$2,000	$295,262
63	$0	$556,197	$2,000	$326,988
64	$0	$611,817	$2,000	$361,887
65	$0	$672,998	$2,000	$400,276

Note: Assumes 10% annual return.

and attitudes. Our spending patterns are very complex behaviors that are a function of (1) our motives and values; (2) our relationships with our spouses, children, other family members, coworkers, and neighbors; as well as (3) our susceptibility to marketing and sales techniques. In the process of exploring how our purchasing decisions are shaped, this chapter will try to sort out rational from emotional behaviors, and to point out how to better understand and resist those external pressures that lead us to overspending.

Why, for example, are some people moved to buy $3,000 bedsheets made from exotic Egyptian cotton? Why do people proudly sport clothing with corporate logos, thus paying a premium for the privilege of providing advertising for the company? Why are some of us embarrassed to be seen shopping in a discount store? Why do generic products rarely achieve sales equal to those of brand-name products, in spite of their comparable quality and lower price?

We need to assess our personal habits. How much "stuff" do we really need? Is the stuff that we own making our lives better? Wouldn't life actually be simpler if we owned less stuff? How much of our time is spent maintaining our possessions—purchasing them, caring for them, repairing them, cleaning them?

We also need to consider the economic impact of our purchases: How much are we paying in interest on our mortgages, credit cards, and other debts? What is the opportunity lost by our spending? How much would the money have grown to if we had put it to work in investments instead of spending it?

Projected living expenses dramatically affect the capital required for funding retirement and your likelihood of amassing that capital. For example, let's assume that you are 49 years old, earning $300,000 a year, and spending $200,000 (all of your after-tax income) on living expenses. If you would like to retire at age 65, you will need approximately $5,600,000 to continue your current lifestyle. However, if your annual living expenses are going to be $100,000 you would require only $2,600,000 for retirement.

You can compare your spending with those of other American families. The Bureau of Labor Statistics has accumulated data on the average percentage of income expended on food, clothing, and so on (Table 2.2). You can obtain data more appropriate for your situation at the following web site: http://cgi.pathfinder.com/cgi-bin/Money/instant.cgi.

However, to emulate the millionaires, you'll have to spend much less than average. As a guide, Stanley and Danko determined the maximum amount the millionaires ever spent on some common items. Fifty percent of them never spent more than $400 for a dress suit, and only 10% ever spent $1,000 or more. The 50th percentile (median) for spending on a pair of shoes was $140, a watch $235, and a car $30,000.

TABLE 2.2 Typical Spending Habits, Based on Annual Income

Category	$50,000	$75,000	$100,000 +
Total Annual Expenditures	107.1%	100.8%	93.3%
Food	13.2%	13.4%	10.3%
Food at home	7.7%	8.1%	5.5%
Dining out	5.5%	5.3%	4.8%
Housing	28.7%	25.9%	22.6%
Mortgage interest and charges	9.8%	9.5%	8.2%
Property taxes	2.7%	2.6%	2.3%
Maintenance/repairs	1.2%	1.0%	0.6%
Utilities/services	6.1%	5.0%	4.0%
Insurance	0.6%	0.5%	0.5%
Household furnishings	4.5%	3.4%	3.1%
Household operations/supplies	2.9%	2.9%	2.5%
Clothing	4.5%	5.6%	4.9%
Transportation	20.5%	15.8%	16.2%
Vehicle purchases	9.6%	7.0%	7.9%
Fuel	3.6%	2.7%	2.3%
Maintenance/repairs	2.5%	1.7%	1.6%
Auto insurance	2.3%	2.0%	1.8%
Other	1.3%	1.5%	1.8%
Vehicle finance charges	1.1%	0.8%	0.8%
Health Care	4.9%	3.7%	3.3%
Insurance	2.0%	1.5%	1.3%
Medical services	2.0%	1.4%	1.5%
Medications/supplies	0.9%	0.8%	0.6%

TABLE 2.2 Continued

Category	$50,000	$75,000	$100,000 +
Entertainment	6.2%	5.1%	4.4%
Electronic equipment (e.g., TV, sound)	1.7%	1.6%	1.4%
Pets/toys	0.9%	1.0%	0.6%
Other	3.6%	2.6%	2.5%
Personal Care Products	1.2%	1.1%	1.0%
Reading Materials	0.5%	0.5%	0.4%
Education	1.8%	1.7%	2.0%
Tobacco Products	0.8%	0.5%	0.4%
Alcoholic Beverages	0.6%	0.6%	0.5%
Charitable Contributions	2.4%	2.6%	1.9%
Life Insurance	1.3%	1.2%	1.3%
Social Security and Pensions	10.3%	10.9%	11.0%
Income Taxes	8.8%	10.8%	11.7%
Federal income tax	6.1%	7.8%	8.9%
State, local, and other taxes	2.7%	3.0%	2.8%
Miscellaneous	1.4%	1.4%	1.5%

Source: Bureau of Labor Statistics, based on head of household aged 35–50, four or more living in household, own home, and two wage earners.

Are You Saving Appropriately?

The first step in the evaluation process is to analyze your current spending and saving habits. You can estimate how much you should be worth from your age and your annual income:

1. Multiply your age by your total taxable annual income—your pretax income from all sources except inheritances. (It should include investment

income as well as earned income.) If your income varies considerably from one year to the next, average the past three to five years' incomes.

2. Divide by 10.

For example, if you are 40 years of age, your salary was $75,000 last year, and you earned $5,000 in dividends from your investments, $320,000 is your expected net worth (40 × 80,000 = 3,200,000; divided by 10 = $320,000).

You should subtract any inherited wealth from your actual net worth before comparing with this figure. You are considered a wealth accumulator if your net worth is approximately double this figure, and an underaccumulator if your net worth is half of this amount.

Another way to determine how you are doing is to calculate your annual savings rate by dividing your annual invested savings by your total income. You should save at least 15% of your income.

You should also size up your debt load. Divide your debt into productive and nonproductive debt. Productive debt is used to finance an investment. Education loans, business loans, and primary home mortgages can be considered investments rather than expenditures. Nonproductive debt is used to finance expendable or depreciating items, such as a vacation, car, boat, clothing, and jewelry. Most wealth accumulators incur little or no nonproductive debt. Usually they purchase these items only with money they have already accumulated. The total of your nonproductive debt should not amount to more than 25% of your annual income.

Professional Spenders

The financial habit of high expenditure dooms many professionals to poor savings. The average income of a physician is $140,000, versus $33,000 for the average American household. However, physicians tend not to be wealth accumulators. Partly this is because they start earning late and often have large loans to repay, but physicians also are inclined to be spenders rather than savers. Their expenses are higher than others with equal incomes in part because they are expected to live a little better—live in better neighborhoods, own more expensive homes, wear better clothes, and drive more expensive cars. Physicians tend to contribute a higher percentage of their incomes to charity, and they are less likely to inherit money (their parents favor the non-physician siblings). Also, since they spend so much time working, many may not have time to look after their own economic well-being.

As if this weren't bad enough, physicians are known to make particularly poor investment decisions. They don't investigate investments as thoroughly as they should, they take excessive risks, and they look for quick killings rather than consistent returns.

Although this information was gathered about physicians, it probably applies to many other professionals. High expenses, inadequate financial planning, and poorly designed investment strategies counterbalance a comfortable income and impede progress toward financial security.

Why We Buy

Buying is a very complex behavior, affected by our individual needs, our psychological makeup, cultural influences, our past experiences, relationships with our spouse and children, and our susceptibility to marketing messages. To understand what motivates each of us to buy, and to learn how we might be able to change our buying patterns, we must look at our personalities, our values, our relationships with our families and our neighborhoods, and our reaction to marketing efforts.

Basically, we buy to satisfy our needs. While today the goods may be more sophisticated and varied, we still experience the same joy that our primitive ancestors received from a successful hunt. However, we are no longer content with satisfying our basic needs for food, clothing, and shelter. Now we also buy to satisfy our needs for security, self-fulfillment, intellectual stimulation, belonging, and diversion.

Our personalities strongly influence our buying habits. Myers and Briggs divided personalities into 16 types, based on individual reactions to stressful events, relationships with others, and general philosophy toward life.[10] They observed significant differences among the personality types in people's attitudes toward money. The most conservative spenders are introverts whose aims are more pragmatic than lofty, and who make decisions based more on intellect than emotion. Big spenders are extroverts and risk takers. They may buy impulsively or only after concentrated reasoning and comparison.

Our experiences and our relationships with family members also greatly influence spending patterns. For example, when Sharon's father was young, he experienced prolonged periods of deprivation after being orphaned at age 14. As an adult, although he was conservative in his business spending, he periodically made impulsive purchases of surprise gifts. These may have been in part a response to the feelings of deprivation he had as a child.

Someone we know grew up with every need fulfilled and most whims indulged. However, her parents were not warm or supportive, and she came to use buying sprees as comforts when feeling stressed or deprived in some way. Another woman, married to a man with a modest income, uses expensive purchases to punish him when she perceives he has slighted her. When he complains about her extravagances, she points out his inadequacy as a provider.

From research, it appears that the most significant reason for spending is that it's what the people we admire and respect do. As Juliet Schor, a professor of the economics of leisure, wrote in *The Overspent American*: "Unlike the millionaires next door, who are not driven to use their wealth to create an attractive image of themselves, many of us are continually comparing our own lifestyle and possessions to those of . . . people we respect and want to be like, people whose sense of what's important in life seems close to our own." For many of us, our reference group consists of people whose incomes are three, four, or five times our own. They may be television or movie families, celebrities, or owners of homes featured in magazines, not just our circle of families and coworkers.

Characteristics associated with low savings rates have been statistically identified. Controlling for other factors, the more education a person has, the less he or she saves. Time spent shopping is also related to education level; women with graduate degrees spend the most time shopping of any group. Number of hours spent watching TV is inversely related to savings rate. However, the factor with the greatest impact is how your income relates to the average income of your reference group. The lower your income is in relation to the others, the less you save.

Americans feel that they need more than ever before. It may not be surprising that 50% of families with incomes between $25,000 and $35,000 feel that they cannot afford to buy everything they really need.[11] But 27% of families with incomes over $100,000 feel the same way. Between 1979 and 1995 the average American's spending increased between 30% and 70%. In less than 50 years, the size of the average American house has doubled.

Our concept of necessities has clearly changed. Thirty-seven percent require a second car, 41% auto air-conditioning, and 51% home air-conditioning. These rates are approximately double the percentages in 1973.[12] Also, in 1996 we rated a lot of things "necessities" that didn't exist in 1973: microwave 32%, home computer 26%, answering machine 26%, basic cable 17%, and VCR 13%. Our view of "the good life" has changed. We are twice as likely to include a vacation home, swimming pool, second color TV, and "a lot of money."

Yet, spending is not all selfishness or greed. There are practical reasons for spending. Professionals, managers, salespeople, and business owners must present an image to others that meets their expectations. Appearance, car, home, and consumption are perceived as reflections of our ability and success. Socializing requires money as well. Many social activities and entertainments have expenses tied to them, such as dining out.

Extreme buying patterns can be associated with psychiatric disorders. People with manic-depressive disorder can spend indiscriminately and far beyond their resources when in their manic phase. Individuals with impulse control disorders are also prone to shopping sprees, in addition to poor investments, chronic overspending, and gambling. They may not lose their life savings in a week, as could a manic-depressive, but their poor control of spending and their lack of savings lead to lives fraught with financial crises. Fortunately, effective pharmacological and behavioral treatments are now available for these disorders.

Resisting Marketing

We are constantly bombarded with marketing messages. Companies spend billions of dollars trying to persuade us to buy their products or to use their services. It is not surprising, with this much money involved, that a lot of sophisticated study has been applied to consumer behavior and marketing techniques. The savvy consumer needs to be resistant to modern marketing ploys.

As one marketing text stated, "Marketing is perception, and *quality* is a nebulous characteristic alive only in the eyes of the buyer."[13] Companies strive to endow their brand names with an image of quality or status. Pinnacle brands such as Rolex, Armani, and BMW are symbols, the possession of which often fulfills a fantasy of ultimate wealth begun in childhood. Premium brands such as Nike, Chivas Regal, and Lexus hold higher status than brands such as Gillette, Ford, and Sears that are perceived as "middle-class."

However, there is often little relationship between perceived and true quality. The best way to objectively determine quality is through "blind" testing, such as performed by *Consumer Reports* or government agencies. For example, one such testing of hair shampoos found that a dishwashing liquid was just as effective as the most expensive hair products, at a fraction of the price. There is no reason why we can't perform small "blind" tests at home. Why not put a store-brand cereal in the box of the nationally sold taste-alike, and see if anyone notices?

We should determine what qualities we are looking for in a product, and evaluate those without regard to the brand label. Don't ignore less-known or so-called middle-class brands. Also, be honest with yourself. If you want a BMW because it is a costly status symbol, don't say you bought it because of the engineering.

Resist the pressures to acquire the symbols of success. It is much easier to purchase products associated with wealth and status than to achieve either. Spending time and money in the pursuit of looking superior often results in inferior economic achievement.

Even small savings add up. We may be paying only 60 cents a can for our favorite soft drink, versus 40 cents for a less-known brand. However, if we drink two cans a day from 25 to 65 years of age, we are looking at an expense of nearly $3,000. For a family of five, with 10 products of equal savings, you could save $150,000, before investment.

Shopping as Hobby

Many women love to shop. They view shopping as entertainment or avocation. The theme of one bat mitzvah we attended was shopping. Each table was decorated as a different department store, such as Bloomingdale's or Saks Fifth Avenue, with large plastic credit cards. Yes, shopping can be fun, but if you're really a good shopper you should probably be at T. J. Maxx, Marshalls, or J. C. Penney. Being a good shopper takes knowledge and skills. Researching products, determining desirable qualities, and obtaining them at the lowest possible price are accomplishments of which we can be proud.

Controlling Spending

Understanding the motivations, emotions, or disorders underlying spending behavior is necessary in order to make a change. We must discuss with our spouses our attitudes toward spending, gift giving, control of money, splurging, and conserving, and our financial goals and values. A couple must reach some consensus in order for both partners to be content, and for financial goals to be met.

Controlling our desire for more is not an easy task. Here are some suggestions:

- Focus on what really matters in your life.

- Separate needs from wants.

- When shopping, emphasize durability over novelty.

- Don't shop for entertainment. Avoid malls and other places where you are more likely to spend.

- Throw away catalogs that come in the mail.

- Spend less time with big spenders.

- Spend more time in church or synagogue.
- Try to see the symbolism (hidden fantasy) in advertising.
- Don't buy on impulse. Make yourself wait for something you want.
- Coordinate thrift with friends and coworkers. Get together to put spending limits on gifts, nights out together, or children's sneakers.

Allocating Our Resources

According to Stanley and Danko, "There is an inverse relationship between the time spent purchasing luxury items such as cars and clothes and the time spent planning one's financial future."[14]

As busy professionals, our most precious resource is often time. We are constantly forced to make choices about how to spend our limited time away from work. We won't discuss the difficult balance between our responsibilities to our patients or clients and our obligations to our family and community. However, some of the time we devote to ourselves and our families should be allocated to planning. It may be more fun to spend an evening in the jewelry store or test-driving a Mercedes, but it can be much more rewarding to spend that time planning for your financial success.

Those who accumulate wealth allocate much of their spare time to activities they hope will enhance their wealth, including studying about and planning investment strategies. The planning process is covered in Chapter 1. For most, a successful strategy involves developing a family budget and savings plan and frequently monitoring your adherence to it. A budget can be developed from past spending records and the guidelines in Table 2.2. Tracking your spending and saving and your financial progress is a good way of enhancing your feeling of financial security and making the attainment of wealth and security more likely.

Suggested Reading

Ramsey, Dave. *Financial Peace: Restoring Financial Hope to You and Your Family*. New York: Viking Penguin, 1997.

Ries, Al, and Jack Trout. *The 22 Immutable Laws of Marketing: Violate Them at Your Own Risk*. New York: Harper Collins, 1994.

Schor, Juliet B. *The Overspent American: Upscaling, Downshifting, and the New Consumer*. New York: HarperCollins, 1999.

Stanley, Thomas J., and William D. Danko. *The Millionaire Next Door: The Surprising Secrets of America's Wealthy.* Marietta, GA: Longstreet Press, 1996.

Notes

1. Bernice Kanner, Are you normal about money? (statistics on spending habits), *Ladies' Home Journal*, October 1998.
2. Bernice Kanner, Bloomberg Business News.
3. Dearborn Trade, Fast Facts on Consumer Credit Problems and Bankruptcy; Juliet B. Schor, *The Overspent American: Upscaling, Downshifting, and the New Consumer*, New York: Basic Books, 1998, p. 19.
4. *Consumer Reports Money Book.*
5. A. B. Kennickell, M. Starr-McCluer and A. E. Sunden, "Family Finances in the U.S.: Recent Evidence from the Survey of Consumer Finances," *Federal Feserve Bulletin* 80 (January 1997):1.
6. Wade Lambert, "The New Faces of Personal Bankruptcy: Baby Boomers," *Wall Street Journal* (October 7, 1993), B-1.
7. *The Millionaire Next Door.*
8. U.S. Department of Commerce, 1996.
9. *The Millionaire Next Door*, pp. 21-23.
10. Myers-Briggs Type Indicator, registered trademark of Consulting Psychologists Press, Inc.
11. Merck Family Fund poll, February 1995.
12. Roper Center, University of Connecticut.
13. Al Ries and Jack Trout, *The 22 Immutable Laws of Marketing: Violate Them at Your Own Risk*, New York: Harper Collins, 1994.
14. *The Millionaire Next Door*, p. 84.

Investment Vehicles: Description and Historic Performance

Robert Arffa

There is a vast array of investment opportunities available to the general public. I will describe the most common types (Table 3.1), and give some information about their historical behavior. Many will be covered in more detail in later chapters.

Financial Assets versus Real Assets

Real assets are the physical and human wealth of our society: land and other natural resources, buildings, machinery, and technology that produce marketable goods, and the people whose skills create these goods. Financial assets, such as stocks and bonds, are not productive in themselves, but are means of providing funds for productive enterprises. Real assets generate income and wealth, while financial assets serve to allocate this income among owners (investors).

Businesses need to raise money to finance their investments in real assets

TABLE 3.1 Investment Vehicles
Money market
Bonds
Treasury
Municipal
Corporate
Mortgages
Mortgage-backed securities
Common stock
Preferred stock
Futures
Options
Real estate
Precious metals
Collectibles (e.g., art, coins, stamps, antiques)
Commodities (e.g., grains, oil, pork bellies)
Venture capital
Limited partnerships

such as buildings, equipment, and technology. They can raise this money by borrowing it—by obtaining a loan from a bank or by issuing bonds (IOUs) to investors—or by selling shares of stock, which are ownership shares in the business. The government also needs funds, to finance its deficit spending. It borrows money from citizens by issuing bonds.

Individuals who wish to invest for their futures can acquire real assets or financial assets. Usually financial assets are easier to purchase and sell than are real assets. For example, it is much easier to purchase shares of IBM than to buy a computer company. Financial assets generate wealth for those who hold them, because they are claims to the income from real assets. The greater the production of income or increase in wealth of a company, the greater its attractiveness to investors, the easier it is for the company to acquire funds, and the more valuable its stock shares.

Fixed-Income Securities

Financial assets, also called *securities*, are generally divided into *fixed-income* and *equity*. When you invest in a fixed-income security, such as a bond, you are lending the issuer of that security your money in return for a fixed amount of interest for a specific amount of time. Therefore, they are also called *debt obligations*. Equity securities, also called *common stocks* or *equities*, represent shares of ownership in a corporation. Their value changes with the value of the corporation, and there is no time limit.

When you purchase a new bond issue, you are entitled to a specified income (interest) on the dates that the interest is due, and return of your initial investment (principal) when the bond matures (comes due). Even if issued by a corporation, you will not receive corporate reports, be invited to the company's annual meeting, or be asked to vote on corporate decisions. Your investment will not be altered by the success or failure of the corporation (except by bankruptcy).

Fixed-income securities vary according to several factors:

■ Issuer (corporation, state or federal government, bank)

■ Time before the security matures (90 days to 30 years)

■ Risk of bankruptcy of the issuer

■ Tax status of the interest (taxable or free from state and/or federal taxes)

■ How the interest is paid (at regular intervals or only at maturity)

If you hold onto a bond until maturity, the interest payments and return of principal are fixed. However, after purchase you can sell a bond to another investor. The price that you are offered for the bond may be more or less than the principal you paid. If interest rates are higher than when you bought the bond, the price that you will be offered will be lower, and if interest rates are lower, you will be offered more than you paid. The longer the time until maturity, the more the bond's price will react to fluctuations in interest rates. This is discussed in more detail in Chapter 19.

The *yield* is the return on your investment in the bond, and may be described in several ways. *Current yield* is the annual return at the bond's current price (interest payment per year divided by price of the bond). The *yield to maturity* takes into account the difference between the current price and the original principal (paid at maturity) and the number of years remaining until the bond matures. It is a more complicated calculation. A bond may be *callable*, which means that the issuer can repurchase the bond at its original price after a specified amount of time. You can also calculate the *yield to call*, which is the yield if the issuer redeems the bond at the first potential date.

If you purchase a previously issued bond, you may pay more or less than the initial principal amount, which is called the *par value*. However, the interest payments (the *coupon rate*) and payment of principal at maturity do not change.

For example, a $1,000 bond is issued with a 10% coupon rate and a 10-year maturity. It pays $100 a year in interest. If you purchase it two years later and interest rates have risen, you may be able to obtain the bond for $900. You still receive $100 a year in interest, which would make its current yield 11.1%. At maturity, in eight years, you will receive $1,000, and the yield to maturity is approximately 12.5%.

Money Market

The money market is a subsector of the fixed-income market. Money market instruments are highly marketable, very short-term loans. Individuals can purchase many of them, but very large investments may be necessary. Most investors purchase them through money market mutual funds. These funds pool the resources of many investors to purchase a variety of money market securities.

U.S. Treasury bills, commonly known as T-bills, are the most readily traded money market securities. Investors buy the bills at a discount from the stated maturity value. At maturity they receive their purchase price plus interest. Maturity can be 91 days, 182 days, or 52 weeks. The income earned on these bills is exempt from state and local taxes.

Certificates of deposit, or CDs, are timed deposits with a bank. Like T-bills, the bank pays interest and principal at the end of the term of the CD. Only CDs in denominations greater than $100,000 can be sold to another investor before maturity. The interest is fully taxable, and the Federal Deposit Insurance Corporation (FDIC) insures the principal (up to $100,000) against bank default.

Commercial paper is short-term notes issued by large, well-known companies. The companies issue these notes rather than borrow the money from a bank. The values of the notes are multiples of $100,000 and maturity can be up to 270 days. These are considered to be fairly safe.

Other components of the money market include banker's acceptances, Eurodollars, repurchase agreements, federal funds, and broker's calls. They are all low-risk, short-term debt obligations.

The yield of money market instruments is slightly greater than the yield of T-bills, because of slightly higher risk and reduced liquidity.

Fixed-Income Capital Market

The fixed-income capital market is composed of longer-term debt obligations. The market includes Treasury notes and bonds, corporate bonds, federal agency debt, mortgage securities, and municipal bonds.

Treasury Notes and Bonds

The federal government funds most of its deficit spending by selling Treasury notes (T-notes) and Treasury bonds (T-bonds). T-notes range in maturity from 1 to 10 years, and may be callable during part of this period. T-bonds are issued with maturities of 10 to 30 years, and are not callable. They are fully insured by the federal government, so are considered to be the safest bonds.

Corporate Bonds

Private corporations sell these as an alternative to raising funds by issuing stock or obtaining a loan from a bank. Like T-bonds, they pay interest semiannually and return the principal at maturity. They may be callable, or convertible into a stipulated number of shares of the corporation's stock.

Corporate bonds are riskier than T-bonds, because there is a risk of bankruptcy of the issuing company. Ratings of this risk can be obtained from several agencies. *Secured bonds* have specific collateral backing them in the event of company bankruptcy. *Unsecured bonds* are called debentures. *Subordinated debentures* are greater in risk, since they have a lower-priority claim to the firm's assets in the event of bankruptcy.

Convertible bonds can be exchanged for shares of stock. They pay a fixed rate of interest that is lower than the straight bonds of the same corporation. However, they can be converted into the corporation's stock if the price of the stock appreciates to a specified amount. The conversion price is typically between 15% and 50% above the price at the time of issuance. The market value of a convertible bond depends on its rate of return relative to current interest rates, and the market's assessment of the growth potential of the corporation.

Government Agency Securities

A variety of federal agencies issue bonds in order to finance their activities. These agencies usually are formed to channel credit to a particular sector of the economy, for political purposes (e.g., when Congress feels that the sectors might not receive adequate credit through private sources). Some of these agencies are federally owned, and others are federally sponsored.

They do not have the full faith and credit of the U.S. government behind them, but you can be fairly certain that Congress would find a way to make sure that these agencies would not default on their debts. Therefore, they generally pay only slightly higher yields than equivalent T-bonds. Like interest from Treasury securities, interest on these issues is exempt from state and local taxes.

Examples of government agencies that issue securities are: Export-Import Bank of the United States, Federal Farm Credit System, Federal Housing Administration, World Bank, Small Business Administration, Student Loan Marketing Association (Sallie Mae), Tennessee Valley Authority, and United States Postal Service. Several federal agencies issue mortgage-backed securities, which are covered in the next section.

Mortgages and Mortgage-Backed Securities

A *mortgage-backed security* is either a share of ownership in a pool of mortgages or an obligation that is secured by such a pool. Mortgage lenders originate loans and then sell packages of them to investors. The investors are entitled to the cash inflows from the mortgages, including interest and principal payments. The federal agency guarantees payments to investors, even if the mortgagees are late or default. Mortgage-backed securities are sold by the Government National Mortgage Association (GNMA or Ginnie Mae), Federal National Mortgage Association (FNMA, or Fannie Mae), and Federal Home Loan Mortgage Corporation (FHLMC, or Freddie Mac).

Municipal Bonds

These are bonds issued by state and local governments. Interest paid on these bonds is exempt from federal income taxation, and from state and local taxation in the issuing state. However, capital gains taxes must be paid if the bonds are sold for more than the investor's purchase price.

These bonds vary widely in maturity. They also vary in risk according to the financial strength of the state or municipality. The yield is lower than on equivalent T-bonds and corporate bonds, because of their tax-exempt status. The minimum denomination is usually $5,000.

Equity Securities

Common stocks, or equity securities, are ownership shares in a corporation. A board of directors elected by the shareholders controls the corporation. They select and monitor the chief officers of the corporation, who are responsible for day-to-day business decisions. The board ensures that the corporation acts in the best interests of the shareholders.

The common stock of most large corporations is publicly traded on one or more stock exchanges. Each share entitles the owner to one vote on any matter put to a vote by the corporation's board. The corporation sends all shareholders annual reports, and invites them to its annual shareholders' meeting. If the corporation's assets are liquidated, the stockholders are last in line of all those who have a claim on the assets and income of the corporation. On the other hand, stockholders have limited liability—the most they can lose in the event of bankruptcy of the corporation is their original investment. The creditors cannot lay claim to their other personal assets.

Preferred stock is closer to a bond than to equity. It promises to pay its holder fixed dividends each year, in perpetuity. It does not convey voting power. However, unlike a bond, failure to pay the dividend does not precipitate bankruptcy for the corporation. The dividends cumulate, and must be paid in full before any dividends are paid to holders of common stock. They rank after corporate bonds in the event of bankruptcy. However, their yields are often lower than those of corporate bonds.

Derivative Markets

Derivatives are securities whose payoffs are contingent upon the values of other assets. The most common types are *futures* and *options*.

A *call option* gives the holder the right to purchase an asset for a specified price, called the *exercise* or *strike price*, on or before a specified expiration date. For example, a June call option on Microsoft with an exercise price of $100 entitles its owner to purchase Microsoft stock for a price of $100 on or at any time before the expiration date in June. If the Microsoft price remains below $100, the option will expire without being exercised. In contrast, a *put option* gives the holder the right to sell an asset for a specified price on or before a specified expiration date. The purchaser pays a price, or *premium*, for the option.

A *futures contract* is an obligation to buy or sell a security at a stipulated price on a specified date. A futures contract can be entered into without any cost to either party. If you think that the security will decrease in value, you could hold a contract to sell the security for its current price on a future date (*short position*). If the security decreases in value, on that date you would purchase the security for the lower price, and sell it for its previous higher price. The investor holding the *long position* is counting on the security increasing in price. He or she commits to purchasing the security on a future date for its current (lower) price.

A futures contract is an obligation rather than an option. The long position taker must purchase the security at the specified price. In contrast, the holder of a call option has the right to purchase the security at the exercise price, but will do so only if it is profitable. Therefore, the signer of a futures contract can lose a lot of money if the security's price moves differently than desired, whereas the option holder loses only the cost of the option.

If you own a security, you can profit from selling options on it. For example, if you own 100 shares of Philip Morris at $34 a share, you can write a call option on your shares (e.g., at $36). You receive $4 a share, or $400, which is yours to keep no matter what happens to the stock price. However, if the price rises beyond $36, most likely you will have to sell your shares to the option buyer at $36.

Options and futures contracts can be pure bets on the direction of a security's price. However, they can also be used as insurance or hedging against losses in more conservative strategies. For example, a *protective put* strategy lowers the risk of stock ownership by purchasing a put option on stock you own. For example, if you would like to buy shares of IBM at its current price of $100, but are concerned about the possibility of a large drop in the stock price, you could purchase shares of the stock and a put option at $95. If the price of IBM shares stays the same or goes higher, you don't benefit from the price you paid for the option, but your stock has retained its value. If instead the price of IBM shares drops to $85, you can sell the IBM shares for $95. Thus you limit your potential loss without limiting your potential gain.

Real Estate

Most of us invest in real estate by purchasing a home. You can invest further by buying land, other homes, or commercial buildings. Real estate investments have appreciation potential, can pay rental income, and may have tax benefits. It is usually a leveraged investment, in that you can obtain a $100,000 property with $10,000 down. Real estate also provides good collateral for other loans, and for pyramiding wealth. However, in general large investments are required, a lot of time and considerable expertise are necessary, real estate is relatively illiquid, and it requires active management. Maintenance and tenants can drive you crazy. Buildings age and may require additional investment to stay rentable. New government regulations or increasing property taxes can reduce profitability.

Rather than purchasing and managing real estate yourself, you can invest in real estate investment trusts (REITs), in real estate mutual funds, or real estate limited partnerships. REITs are a relatively new approach to real estate investment. They are publicly traded companies that own and operate real estate properties. They have relatively predictable operating income and low debt, and are readily marketable. Real estate mutual funds invest in publicly traded real estate–oriented stocks. This can include REITs, stocks of home builders, or stocks of suppliers to the home-building industry.

Real estate limited partnerships are run by general partners, who pool limited partners' money to purchase and manage properties. In exchange, the general partners are paid management fees and a percentage of the profits. Unlike other types of partnerships, the limited partners are not liable for partnership debts beyond the amount of their investment.

Gold and Other Precious Metals

Gold and precious metals maintain value independent of governments and corporations. Even if our government was to collapse and its paper money become worthless, gold would retain some value. Traditionally, gold has been seen as a hedge against high inflation and financial and political turmoil. Its value tends to rise in times of rising inflation and declining stock and bond markets.

Silver, platinum, and palladium are other precious metals that can be viewed as inflation hedges. However, they have wider commercial and industrial uses, and their price is more dependent on industrial supply and demand.

Precious metals can be purchased as coins, bars, or certificates of ownership. You can also invest in publicly traded mining companies, or mutual funds that own mining stocks.

Antiques and Collectibles

No matter how well your stock and bond investments do, you're not going to put them up on your wall or ask your friends to admire them. That is the chief attraction of collectibles. Antiques, art, autographs, cars, comic books, gems, rare books, memorabilia, stamps, toys, and wines are some common collectibles.

They can appreciate tremendously in value, but it is very difficult to predict which collectibles will become popular. Investors feel that like other hard assets, such as gold and real estate, they will better retain their value when inflation is high or stocks and bonds prices are sinking. Also like other assets, their price is determined by supply and demand. It can be difficult to determine the value of a collectible. The ease with which you can sell a collectible is variable. Buying and selling of collectibles requires a lot of specific expertise, and sales commissions can be high.

Commodities

Commodities are industrial raw materials and consumer goods such as corn and wheat. Like futures in the securities market, contracts can be obtained for goods to be delivered at a certain price at a specific time. These contracts were created to allow developers and consumers of raw materials to lock in future prices at the time of delivery. However, pure speculators now conduct a large percentage of the daily trading volume.

Venture Capital

Venture capital is the main source of funds for start-up companies with high growth potential. Some of today's most successful companies were helped by venture funding, including Intel, Apple, Microsoft, Netscape, and Sun Microsystems. Wealthy private investors, pension funds, endowments, foundations, and corporations contribute capital. The venture capitalist selects investments, and often helps guide the start-up company's development. In recent years, venture capitalists have achieved high returns, which has attracted many new investors.

The venture capitalists realize that many of their start-ups will not come to fruition. They hope that they will make enough money on their winners to more than make up for their losers.

Unfortunately, the availability of funds has become so great that there is a relative shortage of good start-ups requiring investment, and the bargaining power has shifted from the venture capitalists to the entrepreneurs. As a result, the percentage of start-ups that issue stock (become IPOs) or become acquired by an established public company is shrinking.

Limited Partnerships

Limited partnerships allow investors to own most of the enterprise but limit their liability, usually to their cash investments. The general partners, who usually own 1% or less of the partnership, control the operations of the partnership and retain most of the liability. In exchange they receive management fees and/or a significant portion of the profits. The 1986 Tax Act reduced the attractiveness of this form of investment.

Historic Performance

A long-term analysis of capital market history uncovers the basic relationships between risk and return among the different classes of financial assets. Information about the returns of different assets is available from multiple sources. The most commonly used data is from Ibbotson Associates. They have accumulated data since 1926. This period includes times of war and peace, growth and decline, bull and bear markets, inflation and deflation.

Figure 3.1 depicts the growth of $1 invested in large-company stocks, small-company stocks, long-term government bonds, intermediate-term government bonds, Treasury bills, and a hypothetical asset returning the inflation rate over the period from the end of 1935 to the end of 1999. All results assume reinvestment of dividends on stocks or coupons on bonds, and do not re-

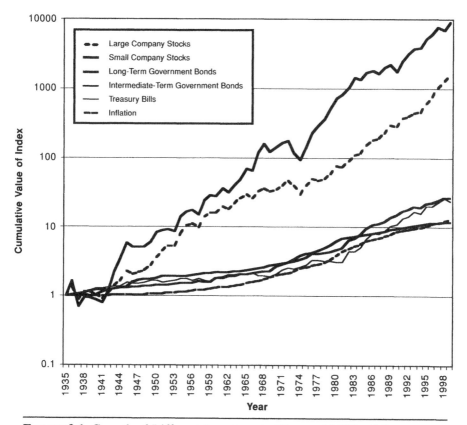

FIGURE 3.1 Growth of Different Investments (Year-end 1935 = $1)

Data Source: *Stocks, Bonds, Bills, and Inflation 2000 Yearbook*, Ibbotson Associates, Chicago, Illinois.

flect the effect of taxes. Transaction costs are not included, except in the small stock index starting in 1982.

The total annual returns are the sum of three components: capital appreciation, income, and reinvestment return. Capital appreciation is the change in the value of the asset. The income portion consists of interest payments for bonds, and dividends and capital gains for stocks. Reinvestment return reflects the return from income reinvested in the financial asset for the remainder of the year.

The graph clearly illustrates that large-company stocks and small-company stocks provided the greatest cumulative returns, while the return of lower-risk investments, such as Treasury bills, barely exceeded the rate of inflation.

Inflation

Next to taxes, inflation is the greatest consumer of our wealth. Each year, with very rare exceptions, our savings have less purchasing power. The U.S. Department of Commerce estimates the inflation rate by regularly measuring the cost of a mix of 400 different goods and services. From this they calculate the *consumer price index* (*CPI*). The index is imprecise, because the exact goods and services measured change over time, and little adjustment is made for substitutions cost-conscious consumers make when relative prices change. However, the CPI is probably the best estimate available. The goods and services that could be purchased for $1 at year-end 1925 cost $9.30 by year-end 1999. This represents a compound annual rate of inflation of 3.1% over the past 74 years.

The inflation rate varied considerably over this period, ranging from a high of 18.2% in 1946 to a low of –10.3% in 1932. There was substantial deflation from 1926 to 1933, reducing the CPI from $1 to $0.73. Since then prices have increased almost every year. In the 1970s inflation reached a pace previously unseen in peacetime, peaking at 13.3% in 1979.

Economists determine the difference between the return on an investment (nominal return) and the inflation rate over the same period, and call it the *real return*. Investors should be concerned with real returns, because they more accurately reflect the change in buying power obtained from an investment. If an investment's return is less than the rate of inflation, the investor is losing buying power, and the real return is negative.

Treasury Bills

Treasury bills are considered a risk-free investment. The expected return of such an investment should be greater than the expected rate of inflation by only a small expected real return. Since the actual rate of inflation may be different than predicted, the actual real return may be more or less than forecast. One dollar invested in T-bills in 1925 amounted to $15.64 in 1999, for an average compounded annual return of 3.8%. However, after adjusting for inflation, the real return was only a 0.7% compound annual return.

Over the entire period, an investor in T-bills (or similar money market securities) would have barely beaten inflation. Over shorter periods investors frequently ended up with less purchasing power than when they started. The real return was negative in 25 of the 74 years. However, most of these negative real rates of return were in the 1940s, when the federal government kept T-bill yields low during a period of higher inflation. Treasury bill yields were deregulated in 1951, and yields closely tracked inflation until 1973. Then, between 1974 and 1980 T-bill returns were consistently lower than inflation rates. Since 1981 real returns have been positive.

The yield of other money market instruments, such as certificates of deposit and commercial paper, average approximately 0.5% to 1.0% more than T-bills. Therefore, on average, their returns will slightly exceed the inflation rate. However, the difference in yields can become much greater in times of economic crisis.

These calculations do not take taxes into account. If the T-bill and money market returns were adjusted downward to cover payment of income taxes, their performance would have lagged considerably behind inflation. Thus, although these are considered risk-free investments, they entail a significant risk of loss of purchasing power. Many investors who fear the risks associated with equity investments choose what they perceive to be the safe return of short-term money market instruments, such as T-bills and CDs. However, they mistake the absence of the risk of loss of principal with the risk of loss of buying power.

Bonds

Ibbotson Associates' long-term government bond index is constructed from U.S. Treasury securities with an approximate 20-year maturity. Between year-end 1925 and year-end 1999, $1 invested grew to $40.22, for a compound annual return of 5.1%. However, if income returns were not reinvested, the value of the $1 index declined to $0.83 over this period. This does not take into account the decline in purchasing power due to inflation. Therefore, the total returns of these bonds depend on the regular investment of income over their 20-year duration, at the rates of return prevailing at the time of income distribution.

An intermediate-term government bond index is calculated from the returns of noncallable U.S. Treasury securities of approximately five-year maturity. Over the 1926–1999 period the cumulative return, with reinvestment of income, of $1 invested was $43.15, for a compound annual total return of 5.2%. Without reinvestment of income, $1 invested increased to $1.22.

Why is the return lower on longer-term bonds? The offered initial interest rate of intermediate and long-term bonds is based on investors' expectations about future (short-term) interest rates. However, the actual future rates are uncertain, and if they turn out to be higher than predicted, investors may have to sell their long-term bonds at a loss. Therefore, the value of the principal is at risk, and investors theoretically would expect to be compensated for bearing it by receiving a higher yield. However, this does not appear to be the case. (The extra yield for assuming risk is called a *risk premium*; in this specific case it is called a *liquidity premium*, because you do not know the price for which you will be able to sell the asset.)

The long-term corporate bond index grew from $1 to $61.34, a compound annual rate of 5.6%. This was greater than either category of government bond, as would be expected because of the additional risk from the possibility of default. Based on this data, the average annual return premium for this risk was 0.5%.

The relationship between the returns of T-bills and long-term bonds is not consistent. The yield of T-bills exceeded the yield of long-term bonds in 34 of the 74 years. The nominal rate of long-term bonds tends to be slower to rise in periods of inflation, and slower to fall in periods of deflation. As a result, T-bill yield tends to be greater during periods of rapid inflation, but when interest rates are steady or declining long-term bonds outperform.

One would expect the return of long-term bonds to be higher than the return of intermediate-term bonds, because they have greater interest-rate risk. The income of long-term bonds was greater, but long-term bonds experienced a capital loss due to rising interest rates over much of the period, while intermediate-term bonds experienced a net capital gain. This is related to the greater sensitivity of long-term bonds to rising interest rates.

Stocks

One dollar invested in large-company stocks[1] at year-end 1925, with dividends reinvested, grew to $2,845.63 by year-end 1999. This represents a compound annual growth rate of 11.3%. Annual returns ranged from a high of 54% in 1933 to a low of –43.3% in 1931. This does not take into account the effect of taxes.

The effect of compounding interest is evident. The annual compound rate of return for large stocks was 11.3%, versus 5.1% for long-term government bonds, yet the total return of large stocks was more than 70 times greater.

The small company stock index[2] grew over the period from $1 to $6,640.79, representing a compound annual return of 12.6%. Total annual returns ranged from a high of 142.9% in 1933 to a low of –58.0% in 1937.

The reason for the superior long-term performance of small-company stocks is a hotly debated topic. Some argue that small-company stocks are riskier, mainly due to a greater risk of going out of business. Others believe that the superior performance of small-company stocks results from investor bias in favor of large, well-known companies.

Comparisons

Table 3.2 presents the annual total returns of each asset class over the entire 74-year period of 1926–1999. It is clear that compound annual return and volatility of returns, indicated by standard deviation, are directly related. Small-company stocks were the most volatile asset class, with a standard deviation of 33.6%, but also provided the greatest reward to long-term investors, with a compound annual return of 12.6%. Large-company stocks, long-term government bonds, long-term corporate bonds, and intermediate-term government bonds are progressively less risky, and have correspondingly lower average returns. An exception to this general pattern is the return of intermediate-term government bonds, which was greater than the return of long-term government bonds, due to the rise in bond yields over the period.

Figure 3.2 shows histograms of the frequency distributions of returns in each asset class. The height of each bar is proportional to the number of years in the study period that the asset had a return in that range. From the distribu-

TABLE 3.2   Annual Returns of Different Asset Classes, 1926–1999

Asset	Total Returns		Inflation-Adjusted Returns
	Compound Annual	Standard Deviation	Compound Annual
Large-company stocks	11.3%	20.1%	8.0%
Small-company stocks	12.6%	33.6%	9.3%
Long-term corporate bonds	5.6%	8.7%	2.5%
Long-term government bonds	5.1%	9.3%	2.0%
Intermediate-term government bonds	5.2%	5.8%	2.1%
U.S. Treasury bills	3.8%	3.2%	0.7%
Inflation (compound annual rate)	3.1%	4.5%	—

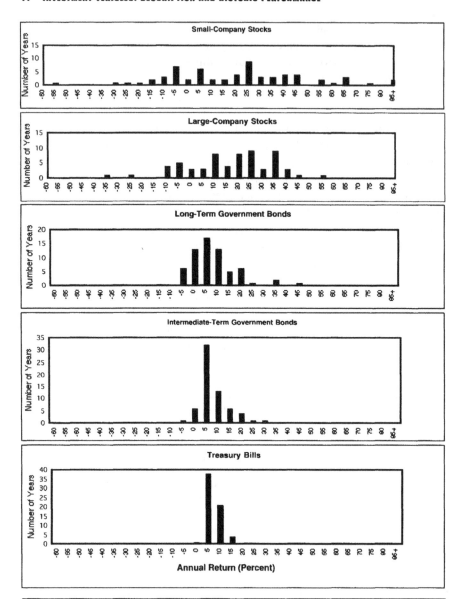

FIGURE 3.2 Frequency Distributions of Returns in Each Asset Class

tion patterns alone it is easy to recognize the difference in the spreads of returns of stocks from those of bonds and T-bills. The histogram of T-bill returns
is steep and one-sided, lying almost entirely to the right of the vertical line
representing a zero return.

Economists consider volatility a form of risk, because the risk of your investment declining in value in any one year is proportional to the volatility of
the investment's returns. Therefore, we see that volatility risk is rewarded by a
higher return over the long term.

How predictable is this higher return advantage? The first answer is that it
depends on how long a period you are going to invest. One can then rephrase
the question: Over a 1-, 5-, 10-, or 20-year period, how likely are the returns of
stocks to be greater than the returns of bonds or T-bills? Or, how long would
our investment term have to be to be assured of obtaining a better yield with
stocks than with T-bills or intermediate-term bonds?

There is no way to predict short- or long-term future returns. The best that
we can do is to look at the past behavior of these securities. Figure 3.3 graphically demonstrates the comparative volatility in annual returns of stocks, long-

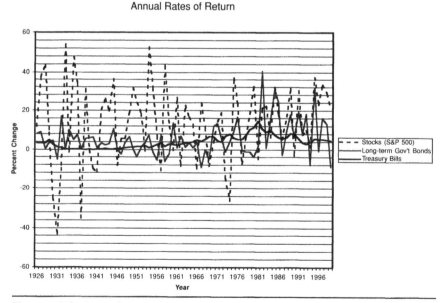

FIGURE 3.3 Annual Rates of Return

term government bonds, and T-bills. Figure 3.4 displays the range of average annual returns for different asset classes over 1-, 5-, 10-, and 20-year periods.

Over 74 one-year periods, large-company stocks were the best investment in 46 periods, intermediate-term government (I-T) bonds in 18, and T-bills in 10. However, an investment in large-company stocks lost money in 20 years, versus eight years for I-T bonds and only one year for T-bills. In the worst years you lost 43.34% in large-company stocks, 5.14% in I-T bonds, and 0.02% in T-bills.

Over 69 overlapping five-year periods (between 1926 and 1998), large-company stocks were the best investment in 53 periods, I-T bonds in 13, and T-bills in three. Large-company stocks lost money in seven periods, and I-T bond and T-bill returns were positive in all periods. In the worst periods large-company stocks lost 12.47% (1928–1932), while the lowest returns were 0.96% for I-T bonds and 0.07% for T-bills.

Over 64 overlapping 10-year periods, large-company stocks were the best

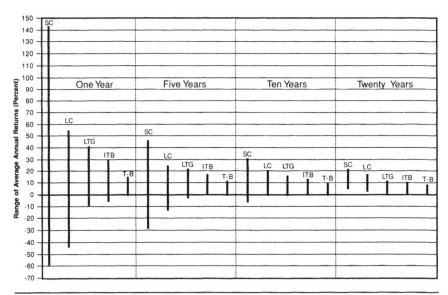

FIGURE 3.4 Asset Returns over Different Time Periods, 1926–1998

SC = Small company
LC = Large company
LTG = Long-term government bonds
ITB = Intermediate-term government bonds
T-B = Treasury bills

investment in 54 periods, I-T bonds in eight, and T-bills in two. Large-company stocks lost money in two periods, and I-T bond and T-bill returns were positive in all periods. In the worst period large-company stocks lost 0.89% (1929–1938), while the lowest returns were 1.25% for I-T bonds and 0.15% for T-bills.

If we extend the investment period to 20 years, large-company stocks were the best investment in 53 of 54 periods, and I-T bonds in one period. Between 1929 and 1948 large-company stocks returned 3.11%, versus 3.38% for I-T bonds. The returns of each of the types of securities were positive over all periods. The minimum returns were 3.11% for large-company stocks, 1.58% for I-T bonds, and 0.42% for T-bills.

Therefore, the longer the investment period, the more likely it was that your return would have been better in large-company stocks, and the less likely it was that your investment would decline in value.

Prediction of Future Returns

Using the mean and standard deviation of historical returns, future returns can be estimated. This can be applied to both individual asset types and mixtures (portfolios) of asset types. The following data was obtained from the Financial Engines web site (www.financialengines.com).

Table 3.3 and Figures 3.5–3.9 display the predicted values of $1,000 invested in T-bills, five-year government bonds, long-term government bonds, large-company stocks, and small-company stocks. Most students are surprised to learn that the range of possible total returns widens over longer investment periods, despite the narrowing of the range of compound annual returns. The reason for this is the effect of the order of returns. If you start your series of returns with two or three years of losses, the total return will be much lower than if you start off with two or three years of large gains, even if the average annual return over the entire period is the same.

Returns of Other Investments

Data on REIT returns is available from the National Association of Real Estate Investment Trusts (NAREIT). The average annual dividend yield between 1988 and 1999 was 7.64%. The average annual price change was +2.66%, and the average total return was 10.73%.

Venture Economics reports that for the period ended September 30, 1999, the average annual returns for venture funds were as follows: one-year—+ 62.5%; three-year—+33.7%; 10-year—+20.8%.

TABLE 3.3 Forecast Values of $1,000 Invested (Beginning 4/30/2000)

	Percentile	2000	2004	2009	2019
Large-company stocks[1]	95th	1,430	2,480	4,220	10,500
	50th	1,090	1,380	1,840	3,200
	5th	833	738	733	858
Small-company stocks[2]	95th	1,500	2,790	5,130	13,400
	50th	1,100	1,420	1,910	3,320
	5th	781	646	619	670
Intermediate-term government bonds[3]	95th	1,120	1,280	1,480	1,930
	50th	1,040	1,140	1,250	1,490
	5th	972	928	935	974
Treasury bills[4]	95th	1,070	1,170	1,290	1,550
	50th	1,030	1,100	1,180	1,350
	5th	998	989	1,010	1,080

[1]Predicted returns of the Vanguard Index 500 Fund.
[2]Predicted returns of the Dimensional Fund Advisors 6–10 Fund.
[3]Predicted returns of the Dimensional Fund Advisors 5-Year Government Bond Fund.
[4]Predicted returns of the Vanguard Money Market Fund: Federal.

Conclusion

There are myriad investment options, each with its specific potential risks and rewards. The investment choices you make can profoundly affect the total money that will be available to you when you need it. In general, over long periods, the returns are proportional to the risks you take. However, selecting a portfolio of investments is a complex individual decision influenced by your risk tolerance, goals, and time horizon. Modern portfolio theory has demonstrated that your choice must depend not only on the risk/reward relationship of any one investment, but also on the correlation between the performances of investment alternatives. You can maximize your predicted return for the risk that you are willing to take by selecting a mixture of investments with relatively low cross-correlations.

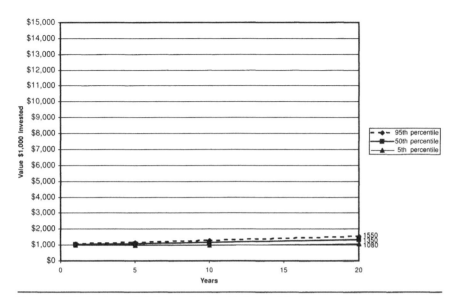

FIGURE 3.5 Projected Values—Federal Money Market

Source: Illustration provided by Wilentz, Goldman & Spitzer. For illustration purposes only.

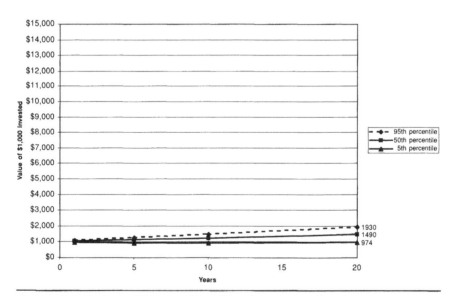

FIGURE 3.6 Projected Values—Five-Year Government Bonds

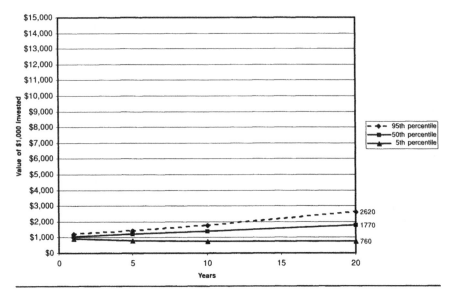

FIGURE 3.7 Projected Values—Long-Term Government Bonds

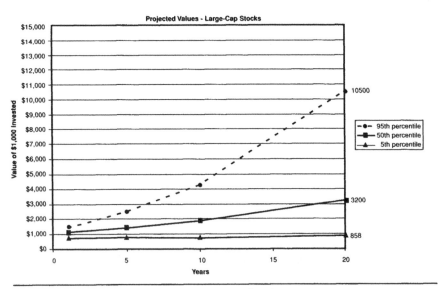

FIGURE 3.8 Projected Values—Large-Cap Stocks

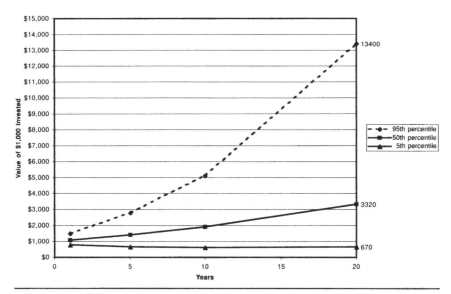

FIGURE 3.9 Projected Values—Small-Cap Stocks

The individual investment alternatives, including money market instruments, stocks, bonds, REITs, and venture capital, will be discussed in more detail in subsequent chapters. In addition, the process of creating a portfolio of investments will be covered in Chapter 22 "Asset Allocation."

Notes

1. Represented by the Standard & Poor's composite index (S&P 500, 1957 to present; S&P 90, 1926–1956).
2. Based on the fifth quintile of stocks on the New York Stock Exchange (NYSE), based on market capitalization, for 1926–1981. Based on the Dimensional Fund Advisors Small Company 9/10 Fund (invested in the fifth quintile of NYSE stocks, plus American Stock Exchange and over-the-counter stocks with the same or less capitalization), 1982 to present.

Earning Interest on Cash

Jay N. Mueller

Cash Is an Asset

Most of us can list cash among our personal assets. We have cash in checking accounts, cash in brokerage accounts, maybe even currency in a safe at home. Our cash may also reside in places that are not so obvious. Many people hold a portion of their retirement assets in a "stable value" option of a 401(k) plan, for example. Others have brokerage accounts that automatically sweep noninvested balances into some sort of cash vehicle. Broadly defined, cash may constitute a significant portion of one's total wealth and must be managed as carefully as any other asset. Approached properly, the investment of personal cash can result in higher returns, a comfortable risk posture, and favorable tax consequences. Recognizing that the investment of cash is an integral part of an overall personal financial strategy allows us to make decisions that fulfill our broader portfolio goals.

The process of investing cash has four steps: identifying the existing pockets of cash among your assets, analyzing your needs and constraints, selecting from a range of alternatives, and monitoring ongoing performance. The purpose of this chapter is to lead you through these steps, examining the choices that must be made along the way. In this process we shall find that not all cash is the same, that we have different motivations for holding various forms of cash, and that our expectations for these slices of the cash pie also vary. We will consider the factors that incline us toward some cash investment options over others, and set forth a structure for rational comparison of the alternatives. The methodology outlined here should help you to get the most from your cash consistent with your unique financial circumstances.

Identifying Cash on Your Personal Balance Sheet

What is cash and where do we find it? Willie Sutton explained his motivation for robbing banks very simply: "That's where the money is." So, like the famous thief, we shall start looking for cash in the bank. Nearly everyone has a checking account, and many investors also have savings accounts, certificates of deposit, or money market accounts.

Checking Accounts

Checking accounts are typically used for transactional purposes. We deposit paychecks or other income in our checking accounts, and draw that money out again to pay mortgages, utility bills, car loans, and other regular day-to-day expenses. Some people carry a checking account balance far in excess of predictable spending needs in order to have a cushion against surprise expenses. Checking accounts may pay interest on balances (often only above a certain minimum), allowing the depositor to earn at least some income for the use of his or her money by the bank. Checking accounts, like other bank deposit products, are insured by the Federal Deposit Insurance Corporation (FDIC) up to $100,000. By setting up accounts in different banks, depositors can accumulate deposits well in excess of the $100,000 per account limit. The rate of interest paid on a checking account is typically lower than rates available on alternative cash investments, such as money market funds, but checking account cash is instantly available for use.

Savings Accounts

Savings accounts also pay interest and are almost as liquid as checking accounts. The interest rate paid on savings accounts has typically been far below certificate of deposit and money market fund rates in recent years, but savings accounts, like checking accounts, benefit from FDIC insurance.

Bank Money Market Accounts

Bank money market accounts are a lot like savings accounts for larger balances. These accounts are covered by FDIC insurance up to the same $100,000 limit, and typically pay a higher interest rate than either savings or checking accounts. Account minimums vary, and some banks limit the number of transactions permitted in a given period. Interest rates paid on bank money market accounts tend to float with market rates of interest, in many cases tied to a specific formula such as the level of three-month Treasury bills or some other widely recognized benchmark.

Certificates of Deposit

Certificates of deposit (CDs) tend to be the most competitive bank offerings from a yield standpoint. The depositor gives up a certain degree of liquidity in order to earn a higher yield, though, as CD investment typically involves penalties for early withdrawal. Certificates of deposit generally pay a fixed rate of interest for a fixed term, typically between three months and five years. While a depositor in a bank money market account receives a rate of interest that may change every month, the CD depositor knows what yield will be accrued each month until the termination of the deposit. If market interest rates are falling, therefore, the CD holder will benefit from locking in a fixed rate for a specific term. In a rising rate environment, though, the CD holder must be content to receive a fixed return while those investing in money market accounts and money market mutual funds see their monthly interest accruals rise with market rates. The fixed term of a CD, therefore, can be a benefit or a curse.

Beyond Banks

Investors often have significant cash holdings beyond the readily identifiable bank deposit accounts. *Brokerage accounts*, for example, typically involve some provision for cash that is not currently invested in securities. In general, brokerage accounts automatically transfer or sweep uninvested dollars into a money market mutual fund, very often a fund sponsored by the brokerage firm itself. Similarly, investors who have all-in-one account relationships with a broker or mutual fund company often have their excess cash swept into a money market fund.

Many of us have employer-sponsored *retirement plans* that allow some degree of participant direction. In particular, 401(k) plans typically offer a variety of investment options including one or more cashlike vehicles such as money market funds or guaranteed investment contract pools. Industry research indicates that a high percentage of employee-directed assets in such plans is invested in cash or near-cash options. Such holdings should be examined in the context of a complete investment strategy. They may be lumped together with other cash holdings for some purposes, and considered separately for others.

For example, a money market mutual fund investment made through a 401(k) plan should be considered together with other cash holdings to develop an assessment of total portfolio asset allocation. That is, the risk reduction afforded by a money market investment in a 401(k) plan is economically equivalent to that afforded by cash swept into a money fund in a nonretirement brokerage account. The two must be added together to get an accurate picture of total risk exposure.

On the other hand, access to cash in a 401(k) plan is limited prior to retirement, so it should not be considered part of your emergency cash reserve. The purpose for which one holds cash, then, becomes important when evaluating how much to have and in what form it should be held.

Purposes of Holding Cash

People hold cash and cashlike investments for three basic reasons: to make transactions, to maintain a cushion against significant unanticipated expense, and to reduce the overall risk level of aggregate portfolio investments. I describe the monies set aside for these three functions as transactional cash, reserve cash, and core cash.

Transactional cash is typically found in something like a checking account, though a money market mutual fund that provides checking services may also fill this role, at least in part. *Reserve cash* may be thought of as rainy-day money—the cushion that allows us to handle a significant financial setback, such as the loss of a job, or major damage to a house or car not covered by insurance. A reserve of three to six months' earnings is generally considered a decent cushion against adverse surprises.

Core cash is held for completely different reasons. We may dedicate a certain portion of our assets to cash purely for the purpose of mitigating the risks inherent in our other investments. For example, an individual may be comfortable with the risk level generated by an asset allocation of 60% stocks and 40% bonds. If that investor believes that stocks are likely to outperform bonds for some extended period of time, but does not wish to increase his or her overall risk level, the investor could consider shifting to an allocation of, say, 70% stocks, 20% bonds, and 10% cash. Such a mix might have the same degree of expected risk as measured by volatility of returns, but promises a greater total return.

Similarly, an investor with a 70% commitment to large-capitalization stocks and 30% to long-term bonds who wishes to shift a portion of assets to higher-volatility equity alternatives such as small-cap or emerging-market stocks could keep overall risk down by holding some portion of assets in cash. It should be noted that the efficacy of any particular asset allocation trade-off depends on the accuracy of the expected return and expected volatility forecasts for each asset class.

Decision Factors

Having identified the three general purposes for which an investor holds cash, we can now explore in greater detail the factors that determine how much cash ought to go into each bucket and what cash investment vehicles might be appropriate for a particular investor's needs. The major influences affecting these decisions are time horizon, risk tolerance, return expectations, and tax status. Other factors are magnitude of assets, legal constraints, and in some cases the wishes of other interest parties, such as family members or beneficiaries.

Time Horizon

An investor's time horizon is a crucial piece of the investment decision process for all asset classes. Time horizon is simply a succinct way of saying how long you can wait before you need your money back. If in January you put aside a quantity of cash that you will need to pay your property tax bill in December, your time horizon for that cash is 11 months. If you are saving for the college expenses of a 16-year-old child, your time horizon for that investment is about two years. Putting aside your Christmas bonus for a down payment on a new car in the spring involves a time horizon of about three months. Some form of cash investment might be employed for any or all of these scenarios, but given the disparate time horizons the type of cash appropriate for each may vary considerably. A 12-month CD, for example, might work quite well for the tax payment, but would make little sense in planning for the new car purchase, if your time horizon is less than one year.

Risk Tolerance and Return Expectations

Time horizon is tightly bound up with the twin concepts of risk tolerance and return expectations. At its simplest level, the phrase "risk tolerance" is a proxy for the question, "How much of this money can you afford to lose?" If you can't take the chance of losing even a penny of your initial investment—whether over a day, a week, a month, or five years—your risk tolerance is zero. If you can afford to lose your entire investment, you have a 100% risk tolerance.

Risk tolerance requires self-assessment. Determining how much of a loss a person can sustain without threat to his or her standard of living is reasonably simple, but no one can determine for you how much psychic discomfort you'll suffer from an investment loss. Some millionaires do not consider themselves able to afford the loss of a thousand dollars. One the other hand, there are some people of comparatively modest means but great entrepreneurial spirit who are willing to bet everything they own to start up their own enterprises.

A useful concept of risk tolerance, though, is more complex than this formulation. In the investment world, most risk analyses involve calculations of the probabilities of gain or loss over a particular time period. (This is usually expressed in terms of standard deviation, a statistical measure of variability.) For example, over long periods of history, the average annual return of the U.S. stock market has been about 10%, with most years falling within the range of a 10% loss and a 20% gain. Though less frequent, gains and losses significantly larger than these values have also been recorded. If this historic pattern remains in place, an investor in stocks faces the distinct possibility of a substantial loss in any given year.

Highly important to the measurement of risk is the probability that an investment loss of a certain magnitude will be recouped over the long haul. Stock investors generally take comfort from the fact that though any particular year may produce losses, measured over a period of many years the stock market has nearly always produced positive returns; indeed, returns that comfortably exceed those of less volatile investment alternatives.

We see, then, that the concept of time horizon must come into play in the assessment of risk tolerance. I am much more willing to accept the risk of a 10% loss in any given year if I am convinced that the probabilities of a net gain at the end of five years are very high. At least, I am more willing to accept such a risk if I have five years to wait! If I do not, I have a shorter time horizon, and (if I am thinking rationally) a lower risk tolerance.

We do not have the same degree of risk tolerance for every investment we make. I must pay my property taxes at the end of the year or face legal consequences, so I have a low risk tolerance for the cash I set aside for that purpose. Young workers have many years of productive earning power ahead of them, so when they invest for retirement they can afford to have a higher risk tolerance in the sense that short-term variations in the value of their accumulated retirement savings are largely irrelevant. Still, no one likes to lose money, and most people prefer to avoid risk if they can.

Why would anyone invest in risky assets? For the simple reason that risk and return generally go hand in hand. To the extent that markets are efficient, investors are compensated for volatility with higher returns. This proposition generally holds true even at the most conservative end of the investment spectrum. Investors who can accept a modest degree of risk in their cash investments will typically be rewarded with a higher yield. (Risk in this context can mean credit risk, price risk, reinvestment rate risk, or certain forms of structural risk such as call risk.)

Tax Status

The last of the major decision factors is the investor's tax status. The higher one's marginal tax rate, the greater are the benefits to investing cash in some sort of tax-preferred vehicle. Money market funds that invest in short-term municipal obligations, for example, are generally exempt from federal taxation (though some are subject to the federal alternative minimum tax). Some funds are designed to be exempt from both federal and state income tax, and residents of high-tax states are well advised to consider this alternative.

Tax laws seem to change nearly every year and are amazingly complex, so a complete understanding of one's personal tax status is necessary to make optimal investment choices. Still, a good rule of thumb is to take a tax-exempt yield and divide it by the difference between your marginal tax rate and 1. Example: If you are paying a marginal federal tax rate of 28% (0.28), your taxable equivalent of a tax-exempt 3.5% yield is 4.86% (3.5% divided by 0.72 = 4.86%). This calculation yields the fully taxable equivalent for a given tax-exempt yield, allowing easy comparison. If you are subject to alternative minimum tax the comparisons become more complicated, and a tax adviser's help may be useful. Certain non–income-based state taxes may also influence the choice of cash investment vehicle.

Magnitude of Assets

Magnitude of assets to be invested can be a factor in the decision process. A person with $1,000 to invest will have fewer attractive choices than one with $100,000, for example, due to the minimum initial investment required by certain mutual funds. Certificate of deposit buyers with greater sums to invest typically get more attractive rates. Buying individual debt securities requires a certain level of assets in order to make diversification economically feasible. Certain short-term debt securities must be bought in minimum lots of $250,000, for example, and some may not be sold directly to individual investors at all. Very large investors have fewer constraints, but must be mindful of such size-dependent considerations as deposit insurance limits.

Legal Constraints

Legal constraints affect every investment decision. If the assets in question are constrained to certain specific types of investment, then the cash or cash-like alternatives selected for the portfolio must conform to those limits.

Interested Parties

One other factor that may influence the cash investment decision is the presence of other interested parties. These may be beneficiaries of a trust, secondary beneficiaries of a retirement plan, or ordinary heirs of an estate. To the extent that the owner of the assets wishes to consider the future positions of beneficiaries, the risk tolerances, time horizons, tax statuses, and so forth of those persons may be relevant.

Available Investment Options

Having considered the factors involved in assessing investment alternatives, we now turn to the choices available in the marketplace for the investment of cash. We have already discussed bank offerings. Checking, savings, and money market accounts and CDs are all standard bank products whose particular characteristics may vary from institution to institution and from market to market. The key benefits offered by bank products are federal deposit insurance and (in the case of checking accounts) complete liquidity.

Beyond the bank lobby we will find a host of competing investments, typically securities of one form or another, and mutual funds that are professionally managed pools of such securities. (Unlike traditional bank products, most mutual funds are not FDIC-insured and do not receive a fixed rate of return.) Among the securities generally considered suitable choices for cash investment are Treasury bills and other short-term obligations of the U.S. government and its agencies, short-term corporate debt, and short-term municipal securities. Mutual funds specializing in each of these three categories are widely available.

Treasury Bills

Treasury bills are direct obligations of the United States Treasury and carry the full faith and credit of the U.S. government. They are issued with terms to maturity of one year or less. Treasury bills (T-bills, in the trade) are sold as discounted instruments, meaning that the investor earns a return by buying the T-bill at less than face value and receiving full face value at maturity.

The Treasury issues longer-maturity securities as well. They are described as notes or bonds and may have initial maturities of up to 30 years. When these longer securities age sufficiently, such as a five-year note that has been outstanding for four years, they fall into the sphere of cash investment.

Agencies

Agencies of the federal government may also issue short-term debt in either discounted or coupon-bearing form. The Federal National Mortgage Association (Fannie Mae), the Federal Home Loan Mortgage Corporation (Freddie Mac), the Student Loan Marketing Association (Sallie Mae), and a host of other agencies fall into this category. Generally speaking, debt issued by these entities is *not* backed by the full faith and credit of the U.S. Treasury, but is supported by borrowing rights or some other form of preferential government mechanism. Agency debt securities are generally rated in the highest category for credit quality by the various independent rating agencies. Minimum investment levels vary, but are seldom lower than $1,000.

Short-Term Corporate Debt

Short-term corporate debt includes commercial paper, which is unsecured borrowing for general corporate purposes, typically sold on a discounted basis; medium-term notes, which are similarly unsecured, but pay coupons and are typically sold at par rather than at a discount; and floating-rate notes, which may have two years, five years, or even longer to final maturity, but which periodically adjust the interest coupon they pay to accord with prevailing market rates. The period between adjustments may be a week, a month, a quarter, or longer. Some floating-rate notes are tied to specific target rates such as the 90-day T-bill rate or the prime rate. A typical floating-rate note might adjust monthly to the one-month T-bill rate and pay a yield premium or spread of an extra 0.5% to compensate the investor for the credit risk inherent in corporate debt. Floating-rate notes come in all shapes and sizes, with practically infinite combinations of reset frequency, reference rate, and spread available.

Short-Term Municipal Securities

Short-term municipal securities are debt issued by states, local governments, and various agencies and authorities associated with them. The two types of security most likely to be of interest for cash investment are short-term notes (i.e., those with a year or so to maturity), and longer-term instruments with "puts" or demand features that allow the holder to redeem the security for cash prior to scheduled maturity. These demand features might be exercisable with notice of a month, a week, or even as little as one day. Longer-duration puts are also common.

Most of these securities, whether government, corporate, or municipal, are available to individual investors, though some may require large minimum investments. Some debt from these categories is issued in accordance with specific securities regulations that prevent investment by all but the largest and most sophisticated investors, typically institutions such as mutual funds, pension funds or insurance companies. All the securities discussed may be purchased in commingled fashion via the conduit known as a mutual fund.

Mutual Funds

For many investors, the mutual fund vehicle may be the most efficient, convenient, and rewarding way to invest cash, whether for transactional, reserve, or core investment purposes. The structure of a mutual fund is described elsewhere in this volume (Chapter 11), and the options available for cash investment are no different structurally in an equity or bond mutual fund. The difference is in the type of security held.

There are two broad categories of mutual funds relevant for the cash investment function. The first is *money market funds*, which are designed to have a stable net asset value (NAV) of $1. An investment in money market funds is not insured or guaranteed by the Federal Deposit Insurance Corporation or any other government agency. Although money market funds seek to preserve the value of your investment at $1 per share, it is possible to lose money by investing in the fund. The second category, *variable NAV funds*, consists of short-term debt funds that hold securities with longer maturities and in some cases lower quality than money market funds, and do not attempt to keep their NAVs completely stable.

Money market funds are arguably the most successful investment product of modern times, holding over $1 trillion of assets spread among hundreds of funds. The popularity of money market funds is easily explained: They provide competitive yield, a very high degree of liquidity, convenience, and stability of principal. Money market funds differ from all other mutual funds in one crucial respect: They are managed to minimize the chance of a change in NAV. Money market funds are offered to the public at $1 per share, and when an investor redeems shares he or she will receive $1 per share. Interest is accrued outside of the NAV and is typically posted monthly. Given the stable $1 NAV, investors can buy and sell shares of a money fund without creating taxable gains and losses.

Most money market funds allow investors to withdraw cash on one day's notice (or even the same day, in some cases) and permit free check writing and wire transfers. Money market rates float up and down as market rates move, an advantage in a rising rate environment, but a drawback when rates are falling. Money market funds are highly regulated, with only a narrow range of permitted investments with respect to both maturity and credit quality. Money market funds are not insured by the federal government in the way that bank deposits are, but money fund investors draw comfort from the fact that high credit standards, short maturity, and broad diversification substantially mitigate the risk of principal loss.

There are subdivisions within the money market fund universe. Some funds invest primarily in corporate obligations, the income on which is taxable. These funds are usually identified as *general-purpose money market funds*.

Other funds specialize in the short-term obligations of municipalities, and these funds are typically exempt from federal taxation. These funds are usually described as *tax-exempt* or *municipal money market funds*. Some tax-exempt money market funds concentrate their holdings in particular states, providing income that is free from both federal and state income tax. The absolute yields on these funds tend to be lower than their non–state-specific peers, and each individual investor must consider his or her own tax situation to determine which type of fund will provide the highest after-tax yield.

Some money market funds purchase only obligations of the U.S. government and its agencies. These are known as *government money market funds*, and their yields are typically lower than those of general-purpose funds. A subset of the government money market fund is the *Treasury money market fund*, holding only securities of the U.S. Treasury such as T-bills and T-notes. These funds yield even less than the slightly less restrictive government funds and are at the most conservative end of the mutual fund risk spectrum.

Other than by type of security held, money market mutual funds are classified according to certain structural features. Foremost among these is the division between *retail-oriented funds* and *institutional funds*. Retail-oriented funds typically offer check writing, fund exchange privileges, and other service features. Minimal initial balances are generally in the $1,000 to $2,500 range. Institutional funds, in contrast, seldom offer check writing, may not permit exchanges, and require minimum balances of anywhere from $100,000 to $1 million, or even higher. Institutional funds typically offer same-day liquidity to their customers, who tend to be corporations, foundations, endowments, or other large professionally managed asset pools.

In between pure retail money market funds and those that cater to institutions are the *high minimum funds*, which have one foot in each camp. These funds generally offer some retail features, but demand minimum account balances of $20,000 or higher. The target market for this hybrid category is the high-net-worth individual who carries a significant cash balance.

Some mutual fund families market discrete products to each of the market segments, while others use a "class of shares" approach. In a class of shares scheme there is one pool of assets that is distributed via different share classes, each of which has a different level of service and associated fees and expenses. Generally, classes that offer more features and require lower balances also entail higher expense ratios, while high-balance classes with fewer features charge lower expense ratios, and consequently deliver higher net yield to the investor. Deciding which class of shares is appropriate for you requires identification of the convenience features you require as well as the dollar amount you're willing to invest.

Selecting a Money Market Fund

We have seen that money market funds are stratified by tax status, type of security purchased, and minimum required balance. In addition to analyzing these considerations, the prospective investor should also compare funds with respect to performance and certain nonperformance features.

Performance-Related Factors

Money market fund performance can be measured in a multitude of ways. Funds typically quote their yields on a *seven-day simple yield* basis, which is simply the average daily yield of the fund over the prior seven calendar days, excluding reinvestment of interest. A *seven-day effective yield* is the same calculation expanded to include reinvestment of interest; this figure is sometimes called a seven-day compound yield. The seven-day yield is a standard convention. The yield of a money market fund changes every day as new securities are purchased into the portfolio and existing holdings mature. Sometimes yields on a given day may change sharply due to Federal Reserve activity, certain calendar effects, or other technical factors. The seven-day yield attempts to smooth out some of this variability.

Money market funds also quote a *30-day yield*, which is like the seven-day yield but averaged over a longer time frame. In all cases the yield is retrospective (i.e., a 30-day yield represents an arithmetic average of the fund's yield over the prior 30 calendar days). No claim is made as to prospective performance.

For money market funds, yield and total return are almost identical concepts. Money funds seldom trade out of securities for significant gains or losses. When they do, these gains and losses are treated as adjustments to income, and flow through the fund's yield rather than affecting its NAV. For practical purposes, then, to know the history of a fund's yield is to know its total return. Yields quoted by money market funds are net yields, meaning that the fund's expense ratio has already been deducted.

Money market funds are tracked and ranked by two statistical services, Lipper, Inc. and iMoneyNet, Inc. iMoneyNet publishes a weekly report on money fund yields, and ranks the top 10 in each category. The report is widely disseminated via the popular press. Lipper produces a monthly report on money fund performance, ranking the competitors by total return over one-month, three-month, one-year, and longer time frames. The two statistical services draw upon slightly different universes of funds, so rankings are not always identical.

It is a good idea to look at the performance of a fund over the long haul as well as in a shorter-term time frame. Some funds temporarily boost the net yield to investors by reducing or waiving management fees and expenses. These temporary waivers are generally a good deal while they last. Still, some investors may not relish the idea of hopping from fund to fund, chasing the latest promotional fee waiver, and would prefer to go with a fund with a long-term track record of good performance. The two are not mutually exclusive, of course. Some funds have a long history of partial fee waivers and consistently attractive yields.

Non–Performance-Related Factors

Non–performance-related factors should also be considered when choosing a money market fund. In addition to yield, a money market fund will also disclose the average maturity of its investments. According to Securities and Exchange Commission (SEC) regulations, a money market fund cannot purchase a security with a final maturity longer than 13 months (with a few very technically oriented exceptions that need not concern us here). Despite this ability to buy slightly longer than one-year obligations, the dollar-weighted average maturity of all the securities in the fund may not exceed 90 days. This restriction prevents excessive interest rate sensitivity, and shields a money market fund's NAV from all but the most extreme interest rate changes.

A fund's maturity posture can have an effect on its yield, however. A fund running an average maturity of 30 days, for example, will reflect the results of a change in prevailing market rates quicker than a fund with a 70-day average maturity, all other things being equal. This is a benefit in a rising rate environment, and a liability when rates are falling. If you have a conviction that short-term interest rates are headed lower, then you might want to consider a money fund that maintains a longer average maturity posture. Conversely, if you believe rates are headed up, you will benefit from that rise more quickly if you select a fund with a shorter average maturity. Many money market fund portfolio managers attempt to predict the direction of short-term rates and will extend or shorten their funds appropriately in an attempt to add value. Some are more successful at this than others.

Other important non–performance-related factors are customer service, the range of choices available within a fund family, and the convenience with which an investor can access and manipulate his or her account. A fund family with knowledgeable phone representatives, a useful web site, a stable of competitive stock and bond funds, and an overall commitment to top-notch customer service should get the nod over a sponsor that cannot offer these benefits, all other considerations being equal. In fact, for some investors it's worth giving up a little yield in order to have superior customer service. The ideal fund would offer both a consistently competitive yield and great service.

After you have analyzed the decision factors relevant to your financial situation and selected an appropriate fund, the process of evaluation should be ongoing. Monitor your fund's yield with respect to its peer group, read the annual and semiannual reports to understand the fund manager's strategy, keep tabs on the average maturity of your fund, and be on the lookout for events that may indicate a change in the character of the fund. These might include a change in portfolio manager, a shift in the expense structure, or even the sale or merger of the sponsoring fund complex. Your money market fund may require less ongoing scrutiny than the bond or stock funds in your portfolio, but don't forget to review it on occasion, if only to confirm that it meets your objectives with respect to tax status, convenience, and accessibility.

Beyond Money Market Funds

Money market funds are a solid choice for the investment of both transactional cash and reserve cash. For some people they are also a logical choice for core cash. There are, however, alternatives to the traditional money market fund that may be worthy of consideration for core cash balances that are more amenable to a modest degree of risk exposure.

There is a "bright line" between the money market fund category and every other type of mutual fund, in that money market funds are supposed to maintain a stable $1 NAV while non–money market funds can and do experience share price fluctuation. There is no such bright line between near-cash alternatives and the rest of the universe of income-oriented mutual funds, so picking the fund types to consider for core cash balances is something of a judgment call. Of the commonly recognized fund categories, the two best candidates for inclusion in the "beyond money fund" field are *short-term bond funds* and *ultrashort-term bond funds*. The distinction between the two is that while short-term bond funds may typically run an average maturity as long as three years, an ultrashort-term fund is generally limited to a one-year maximum average maturity. I will make the semiarbitrary assertion that anything longer than a short-term bond fund is simply too volatile to serve as a cash equivalent, but others might argue that even an intermediate-term bond fund could be acceptable for the generalized portfolio risk-reduction function.

Within the short- and ultra short-term bond realm there are categories and subcategories that vary with respect to risk profile and return potential. There are short-term bond funds that invest in international securities, for example, and those that specialize in high-yield bonds with short maturities. At the other end of the risk/return spectrum are the short-term government bond funds, which hold the majority of their assets in Treasury or agency securities. There are also tax-exempt short-term bond funds and tax-exempt short-term high-yield funds.

What all these fund categories have in common is the potential for both higher return and higher risk than their plain-Jane cousins, the money market funds. The incremental risk might be in the form of credit exposure, interest rate sensitivity, foreign currency exposure, or some combination of all three. The added return potential will vary according to market conditions. Sometimes investors receive significant extra yield as a reward for taking on more credit risk, for example, while at other times the yield pickup will be modest.

Historically, short-term bond funds have provided a higher level of total return than have money market funds. Investors have earned a modest premium for holding assets with slightly longer maturities. However, the premium is a compensation for the risk of loss of share value. According to Vanguard, Inc., during the 10 years ended December 31, 1999, short-term bond funds provided an average annual total return of 7.49%, versus 5.05% for money market returns. The magnitude of this difference partly reflects the fall in interest rates over the period (which increases bond fund returns). Going forward, the relative difference in performance is likely to narrow.

Selecting a Bond Mutual Fund

The process of selecting a mutual market fund other than a money fund to be the investment vehicle for a portion of your cash is similar to the routine described earlier for choosing a money fund. Tax considerations, historical performance, and fund family service capability are at least as important considerations, and certain additional factors must be considered. While money market funds are generally constrained to very similar portfolio objectives and allowable securities, ultrashort- and short-term bond funds vary widely by type of permitted investment and portfolio management approach. A fund's investment guidelines will be described in detail in the prospectus and statement of additional information. These documents should be studied closely to identify the types of risk taken by a particular fund in pursuit of its objectives.

Fund expenses also matter. All other things being equal, a fund with lower expenses has an advantage over a fund with higher expenses. Of course, all other things are *not* equal. I would rather pay a larger expense ratio and receive superior returns, risk management, and customer service than pay a lower expense ratio for an inferior product. Since the impact of fund expenses is already reflected in the returns reported to the public, investors can readily compare performance on an after-fee basis.

Though the additional effort of sifting through the many non–money market fund choices available in the marketplace may be onerous, the prospect of earning a meaningfully higher return on one's core cash balances should be a powerful inducement. If an investor can earn 1% or even 0.5% higher return on cash balances that he or she intends to hold over a multiyear time frame, the extra work will be justified.

Effect of Changes in Interest Rates on Bond Funds

When interest rates rise, the value of a share of a bond fund will decline. This is discussed in more detail in Chapter 19 on debt instruments. To put it simply, the bonds owned by the bond fund decline in worth because they are paying lower rates of interest than newly issued bonds are paying. In general, the longer the maturity of a bond, the more sensitive its price to changes in interest rates. Therefore, a fund with a longer average bond maturity will be affected more by changes in interest rates than a fund with shorter average bond maturities; for example, the share values of ultrashort-term bond funds will be affected less by changes in interest rates than the share values of short-term bond funds.

A more precise measure of how changing interest rates affect the share price of a bond fund is *average duration*. To determine what percentage change you could expect with a change in interest rates, simply multiply the change in interest rates by the bond fund's average duration (in years). For example, for a bond fund with an average duration of two years, a rise in interest rates of 1% will cause the value of the fund shares to decline by 2%. Counteracting the decline in share value is your ability to reinvest the interest payments you receive at higher rates.

It should be noted that the relationship between duration and interest rate sensitivity is not constant. Bonds are subject to shifts in the shape of the yield curve, as well as the general trend in rates. For example, if short-term rates rise significantly, but intermediate rates remain stable, a two-year bond may suffer greater price erosion than a five-year bond, even though the five-year bond has a greater duration. Similarly, sometimes Treasury rates fall while yields on corporate bonds actually rise (the sort of behavior we've seen in early 2000!). In this situation the performance of a bond is driven more by its credit characteristics than by duration.

Strategies

If you need cash in three months or a year, a money market fund is a great parking place. You can typically get your cash out simply by writing a check. In the interim you're earning a competitive rate of interest. I think that this is the right answer regardless of whether rates are rising or falling, due to convenience and flexibility considerations. Whether a money market fund's return will outperform the returns of alternatives such as T-bills or CDs depends on whether the future course of short-term rates is accurately reflected in the term structure (yields for given maturity dates). Sometimes it is, and sometimes it isn't.

Besides convenience, the two big advantages of mutual funds are instant diversification and the value added by fund management. The mutual fund structure allows an investor to own a diversified basket of securities in a cost-efficient way. Hopefully, the investor is also receiving the benefit of the manager's wisdom and experience in selecting securities. The manager's job is to add incremental return while managing overall risk more astutely than the average investor.

If you are buying T-bills, T-notes, or T-bonds, it makes sense to match their maturity to the dates that you anticipate needing the cash for expenses. For bonds that make regular interest payments or bond funds, match duration to the time of future expenses. It turns out that your total return is least affected by changes in interest rates if you match the duration to the time that you will need the cash.

A Comprehensive Cash Investment Strategy

In this chapter I have suggested that investors implement a cohesive, unified approach to cash investment. Such an approach ought to begin with an inventory of current cash and cash-like holdings, take consideration of the various buckets into which cash might fall among transactional, reserve, and core characterizations, and evaluate one's own situation with regard to tax status, risk tolerance, and a host of other relevant considerations. We have considered the various cash investment options among bank products, direct securities holdings, and the mutual fund marketplace, giving special consideration to the money market mutual fund and the somewhat more adventurous non–money fund alternatives.

By moving through the process described, the individual who carries significant cash balances ought to end up with a mosaic of cash investments that fit his or her needs with respect to liquidity, safety, and yield. Some investors may conclude that a single vehicle serves all their cash needs adequately, but many will likely determine that a mix of cash alternatives best achieves their overall objectives.

Cash management is probably the least glamorous aspect of managing one's personal wealth, but with a moderate level of effort, the satisfaction of a well-tailored cash investment strategy will be realized.

Fundamental Stock Analysis

Robert Arffa

A stock share is a share of a business. The most appropriate means of determining the value of a share of the stock is to determine the value of the business. If the share is determined to be worth more than the current price, its purchase is expected, over time, to result in higher than average returns. Fundamental analysis of stock values is the major tool in the search for undervalued stocks and avoidance of overvalued stocks.

People have been estimating the purchase price of a business since commerce began. Over the past 60 years, modern finance has emerged as an academic discipline that has endeavored to create a scientific basis for such determinations. The development of finance has largely paralleled the development of statistics as a branch of modern mathematics. Just as Newton, 400 years ago, developed laws to explain the movements of ordinary physical objects, finance has applied statistical formulas to the behavior of markets and to the values of stocks and other assets. I will try to explain logically the application

George Vahanian, Merrill Lynch, Pittsburgh, Pennsylvania, assisted in preparation of this chapter.

of these finance principles to the valuation of stocks, without overwhelming you with formulas.

Valuing a stock is essentially no different from trying to value any other asset in a personal financial situation or business environment. The same principles underlie each problem. Here are three simple examples:

1. A dentist, Dr. Floss, is thinking about an office expansion.

2. Ms. Candue, a patient of Dr. Floss and an executive of a publicly traded bottling company, is contemplating an investment on behalf of her company.

3. This same Dr. Floss is trying to decide whether to buy stock in Ms. Candue's bottling company.

I hope that as we go through these three problems we will develop a framework of ideas for valuing businesses and stocks.

Three Little Examples of Asset Valuation

Dr. Floss's Expansion

Dr. Floss is a successful dentist. He currently works in a two-lane (chair) office; he regularly treats patients in one lane, while his hygienist, the personable Ms. Perky, treats patients in the other lane. Ms. Perky's schedule is full, and there's a two-month wait for an appointment. The situation may even worsen, because a local HMO that is rapidly gaining in market share is a champion of preventive care and pays 100% of the cost of annual exams and cleanings. Dr. Floss wonders whether he should invest in another dental lane and hire a second hygienist. He has determined that the expansion will cost him approximately $100,000.

The money for the expansion is not a problem. The doctor has accumulated $200,000, half of which is kept in a money market account earning 5% annual interest. The remaining half is invested in a stock index fund that has averaged an annual return of 12%. Since the success of the expansion is not a sure thing, it would certainly be riskier than keeping the money in the money market account. Given the competitive nature of dentistry today, Dr. Floss's expansion is probably as risky as or riskier than investing in the stock index fund. Also, since he will withdraw money from the stock fund to finance his expansion, he will be losing the 12% return he would have received otherwise. Therefore, he figures that he should invest in expansion only if he expects to earn a return of more than 12% per year on his investment.

Dr. Floss estimates that the practice will earn an additional $15,000 a year from the additional lane and hygienist after paying all expenses, including salary. Therefore, he calculates that he will be getting a 15% return on his $100,000 investment, which he feels is worth the risk.

Of course, in the real world, the decision would be much more complicated. He would have to consider other factors, including how much additional dental work he could generate from the hygienists' examinations, tax deductions obtained from depreciation of his business investment, and leasing versus purchasing the equipment.

Ms. Candue's Business Investment

Ms. Candue runs a bottling company. She is considering purchasing a new capping machine, which can speed up the whole operation. The machine will cost $1 million, but this will be offset by additional profits generated from the greater volume of bottles filled and capped. By coincidence, Ms. Candue's company earned $1 million in profits last year. It is a publicly traded company, with 800,000 outstanding shares, each valued at $10. Should she give the money to her shareholders (as dividends), invest it in bonds so it is available for future needs, or purchase the equipment? If the bonds could earn 7% and the new machine could increase profits by $150,000 (15%), the decision is clear: She should purchase the machine. The profits, and the return on their investment in the business, although not paid to the stockholders, should increase the value of their shares.

But what if the machine would increase profits by only $100,000, or 10%? This is more than she could get by investing in bonds, but less than the investors could get by investing in an index fund (remember Dr. Floss was getting 12%), and less than the investors are currently earning on Ms. Candue's business ($1,000,000 profit divided by 800,000 shares = $1.25 profit, divided by $10 share = 12.5%). Therefore, in this case the investors would prefer receiving the money in dividends, so they could invest it more productively elsewhere.

Dr. Floss's Stock Investment

After administering nitrous anesthesia, Dr. Floss questions Ms. Candue about investing in the bottling company. She tells him that the company currently has a return on investment (return on equity or ROE) of 12.5%. However, this should increase, because she has decided to purchase the new capping machine that will increase profits by 15%, and she may be able to land a new contract with a popular beverage company. Moreover, this information is not yet publicly known.

Should Dr. Floss invest in Ms. Candue's company? It sounds as though it probably will provide greater return than his stock index fund that is returning 12%. However, he estimates a 15% return from his investment in his own business, and he has more confidence in this return, partly because he has more control over it. Therefore, he decides to expand his practice instead of investing in Ms. Candue's company.

Now I'd like to go through some of the mathematical methods for determining stock values, mainly to illustrate the concepts. Don't worry about these complex formulas. If you're really interested, some sources are given at the end of the chapter.

Discounted Cash Flow Valuation

There are two general approaches to valuation, *discounted cash flow valuation* and *relative valuation*. While the first tries to determine value based solely on the profitability characteristics of the company being analyzed, relative valuation estimates the value by looking at the pricing of comparable companies. The process is called determination of intrinsic value through fundamental analysis. Such intrinsic value is then compared with the current market price to determine whether the market has undervalued or overvalued the stock.

The type of investment analysis we've performed regarding Dr. Floss and Ms. Candue is called discounted cash flow valuation. The basic concept is to relate the value of an asset to the present value of expected future cash flows. In other words, if someone were to give you a note that entitles you to receive $115,000 one year from now, what would it be worth today? Account must be taken of the fact that you could earn a return on your money elsewhere. Therefore, you must *discount* the future cash by at least what you could safely earn elsewhere to see if it would be worth it for you to purchase the note. The present value of the future cash is determined as follows:

$$\text{Present value (PV)} = \frac{\text{Future value (FV)}}{(1 + r)}$$

where r = comparable return earned elsewhere (called the discount rate).

The discount rate used in the formula varies, depending on the returns available from other investments, and the riskiness of the future cash flow. Therefore, the value of r will be different for each stock, and possibly for each investor as well, depending on his or her risk tolerance and investment options.[1]

For example, Dr. Floss has decided not to invest in a stock unless he can exceed the return (r) that he will get from investment in his practice, 15% (0.15—which he uses as the discount rate in the present value formula). For Dr. Floss, the present value of the note is $100,000.

$$PV= \frac{\$115,000}{(1 + 0.15)} = \$100,000$$

With most public companies the cash flow is not returned directly to share-holders as dividends, but largely reinvested in the company. If reinvested successfully, the company's earnings increase over time and the value of a share of company increases commensurately.[2] If the growth of cash flow is assumed to be constant, the following formula for discounted cash flow can be applied:

$$PV = \frac{CF_t}{k_e - g}$$

where CF_t = expected cash flow next year
   k_e = cost of equity of the firm
   g = growth rate in cash flow for the firm forever

Before you give up and skip to the next chapter, take another look at this formula. The cost of equity (k_e) is similar to r, the return we used in the first formula. It is the rate of return that investors require in order to make an investment in the company. It differs for each company, and varies over the life of the company.[3] This formula is generally used in order to determine whether a stock is fairly valued or under- or overvalued. However, it can also be used to calculate your average rate of return, if you purchased shares at the current price. If you can estimate the growth rate of the firm, and substitute current price for PV:

$$K_e (r) = \frac{CF_t}{PV} + g$$

Warren Buffett finds companies with stable, predictable growth, and purchases them if he can obtain them at a price that results in a rate of return of at least 15% (see Chapter 8).

In general, companies (and products) follow a long-term pattern, from introduction to rapid growth, slow-mature growth, and gradual decline. An extended prediction usually entails different growth rates over periods of varying length. Both two-stage and three-stage growth models have been designed in order to take this into account.

Predicting Future Cash Flow

Past cash flow can be readily determined from the company's financial reports. However, estimation of future cash flow is necessary for these calculations. Analysts can arrive at their estimates in several ways: They can base

For Ms. Candue's company:

Next year's cash flow per share = $1,150,000/800,000 shares = $1.4375

Current price = $10 per share

If we assume the company's earnings will continue to grow at 15% per year
(g = 0.15):

$$r = \frac{1.4375}{10} + 0.15 = 29.375\%$$

Therefore, if the growth estimate is accurate, and you can purchase the stock for
$10 per share, you could obtain a return of over 29% per year.

FIGURE 5.1 Projecting Return on Investment for Ms. Candue's Company

them on past growth in earnings and cash flow, they can use earnings estimates made by other analysts who follow the firm, or they can make their own
determinations based on the company fundamentals and prediction of the market for their products. Often the final result is a blend of these approaches.

Unfortunately, past growth rate has little predictive value in forecasting future growth rate. One study compared company growth rates in two consecu-
tive five-year periods, from 1981 to 1985 and from 1986 to 1990, and found
that the correlation was not significantly different from 0.[4] Past growth rate
may be more useful for companies with steady past growth in cash flow, with
little change in size, in noncyclical industries, and without significant expected changes in business operations.

Analysts' earnings estimates are of more value, but only from one to three
quarters ahead.[5] Long-term forecasts, over three to five years, are better than
historically oriented measures, but still poor predictors.[6]

Use of company fundamentals entails a lot more research and analysis.
There is no end to the level of detail that can be utilized. In addition to the
company's fundamentals, analysts try to take into account previous behavior
of companies in the same industry, future competition, effect on the company's industry by other industries, and expectations for the entire economy.
The simplest of these measures, one that we touched on in our discussion of
Ms. Candue's bottling firm, is based on the relationship between retained
earnings and the return on equity.

- Total earnings = dividends plus retained earnings
- Payout ratio = dividends divided by total earnings

- Retention ratio = retained earnings divided by total earnings
- Return on equity = net income divided by book value of equity
- Expected growth = retention ratio multiplied by return on equity

The company invests a portion of its earnings in future business, and is expected to have earnings from this investment similar to those it has obtained from previous investments. If the company invests in projects with attractive profit opportunities, those where the return is greater than the current return expected by investors (k_e), the company will increase in value. Also, to justify plowing earnings back into the firm, the projects must have prospective returns that exceed those shareholders can find elsewhere. In Ms. Candue's case, the new capping machine will return 15%, which is greater than either the company's current 12.5% ROE or the 12% return on a stock index fund, so the company should increase in value.

Relative Valuation

Although discounted cash flow methods are theoretically the most accurate means of determining intrinsic stock value, in reality they are often quite difficult to utilize. Arriving at the correct future growth rate and cost of equity of the firm (k_e) is difficult or impossible.

Relative valuation methods employ a different means of valuing stocks, which is less dependent on these inputs. In relative valuation, the correctness of a company's stock price is estimated by comparison of the company to comparable companies. This technique also examines the financial characteristics of the company, but rather than deriving a value solely from those, it determines whether the company's stock should be higher or lower than the stock of other companies. For example, if you are valuing a pharmaceutical manufacturer, you would determine the price/earnings (P/E) ratio of a group of pharmaceutical manufacturers. You would then assess the financial prospects of each company to determine how your company is likely to fare compared to the others. If it has more promising drugs coming out, if sales of current products have been steadily increasing, then its P/E should be higher than average.

Price/sales, price/book value, price/cash flow, price/dividends, and company market value/replacement value are the ratios commonly used in relative valuation.

Most Wall Street analysts rely on relative valuation. It is easier to perform and easier for average investors to understand. However, relative values are also easy to misuse and manipulate. The definition of comparable firms is subjective, and a biased analyst can choose a group of comparable firms that confirms his or her impressions of the company's value. Relative valuation also relies on the efficiency of the market. It will not detect overvaluation of an entire industry, or the market as a whole.

Usually companies from the same industry are selected for comparison; however, it may be more appropriate to select companies with the same growth rate, risk, and cash flow characteristics. Stock databases can be searched for these characteristics to identify the companies. Statistically, formulas can be derived using growth rate, beta, and cash flow to predict a company's multiple. Such linear regressions have moderate accuracy, showing correlations of 0.4 to 0.6 with the major relative value multiples.

Price/Earnings Ratio

The price/earnings ratio is the most widely used multiple. It is available in most stock listings, and is simple to comprehend. Ultimately, the expected growth and riskiness of the company determine the P/E. The price investors are willing to pay for a given amount of current earnings is affected by their expectations about future earnings. This can be mathematically demonstrated by relating the P/E to the fundamentals used in discounted cash flow models. I will not review the derivation, but include the formula to illustrate the relationship:

$$P/E = \frac{\text{Payout ratio}(1 + g_n)}{r - g_n}$$

where g_n = growth rate (forever)

You can see that the P/E is directly proportional to the payout ratio, the ratio of dividends to total earnings. For companies that pay significantly less in dividends than they can afford, like many high-growth companies, the ratio of cash flow to total earnings can be substituted for the payout ratio. The price/earnings ratio is also directly proportional to the expected growth rate. Since the discount rate (r) is directly proportional to the perceived riskiness of the company, the P/E is lower as riskiness increases.

Many analysts compare the expected growth rate to the P/E. Companies whose P/E is less than their expected growth rate are viewed as undervalued. The Motley Fool (David and Tom Gardner) champions this approach. One research study[7] supported this contention. The author studied the period from January 1982 to June 1989 and found that the lowest P/E: growth rate stocks outperformed the market in 26 of the 30 quarters, for a total compounded return of 1,536% versus 356% for the S&P 500 index.

However, the relationship is not so simple. At least three other factors must be taken into account: interest rates, the expected duration of high growth, and the riskiness of the company. The higher the interest rates, the shorter the expected period of high growth, and the greater the risk, the lower the P/E. Also, as mentioned, the higher the payout ratio, the higher the P/E.

It has been repeatedly demonstrated that low-P/E stocks have outperformed the overall market, and high-P/E stocks have underperformed the market, on a risk-adjusted basis.[8] Stocks with low P/Es relative to other companies in the same industry tend to outperform.[9] It appears that investors tend to overvalue growth companies and undervalue more stable firms.

Price/Book Value Ratio

The relationship between stock price and company book value per share has frequently been used by investors to identify undervalued stocks. Benjamin Graham and David L. Dodd in their 1934 landmark book on security analysis[10] recommended purchasing stocks whose price was less than two-thirds of book value per share. Although it is rarely possible to obtain good companies at this valuation today, the ratio is still useful in fundamental stock analysis.

Price/book value (P/BV) ratio is a relatively stable and simple measure of value. Since accounting standards are fairly consistent among firms, P/BV ratios can be more readily compared than other measures. Also, unlike P/E, even companies with negative earnings can be valued using P/BV.

It is important to understand that book value is an accounting term, and may be quite different from the actual market value of the company. Book value does not necessarily reflect the value of each company asset, or its earning potential. The book value of an asset is calculated from its original cost, depreciated as allowed by Internal Revenue Service and accounting conventions.

Theoretically, the most important determinant of the P/BV ratio is the return on equity. The higher the payout ratio, the higher the rate of growth of earnings, and the lower the perceived risk, the higher the P/BV ratio.[11]

Studies have consistently shown the value of the P/BV ratio in stock selection. Stocks of companies with lower ratios outperform those of companies with higher ratios.[12] However, low P/BV may indicate increased risk—that the company is in financial trouble, with the possibility of bankruptcy. Since P/BV is most related to ROE, the company is truly undervalued only if a relatively low P/BV is associated with a relatively high ROE. Damodaran selected the stocks of companies in the bottom quartile of P/BV and the top quartile of ROE between 1981 and 1990, and looked at their returns the following year.[13] The average return was 25.60% for this group versus 17.49% for the S&P 500 index and 10.61% for companies with P/BV in the top quartile and ROE in the bottom quartile.

Price/Sales Ratio

The price/sales ratio has been increasingly used in determining stock value. It has several advantages:

- Unlike P/E and P/BV, price/sales ratio never becomes negative, and can therefore be applied to even the most financially troubled companies.

- Sales revenue is a straightforward amount, less subject to manipulation than earnings and book value.

- Price/sales (P/S) is less volatile than P/E.

The stability of P/S can also be a disadvantage, because it will not reflect other company financial problems. For example, if the costs of operations are rising dramatically, but sales are increasing, the P/S will not reflect the precipitous drop in earnings and the true lowered value of the company.

The key determinant of P/S is the profit margin. The price/sales ratio is also proportional to the payout ratio and growth rate, and inversely proportional to perceived risk.[14] There is some evidence that low-P/S portfolios outperform the overall market, but the effect is relatively small.[15] Theoretically, undervalued companies are those with a low P/S and a high profit margin. As described for P/BV and ROE, if each year from 1981 to 1990 you selected companies that were in the bottom quartile in P/S and in the top quartile in profit margin, their return the following year would average 23.76% versus 17.49% for the S&P 500 index.[16]

Overview

Valuation of companies is constantly changing. Several different mathematical models are available to estimate company value. There are two basic types of models, discounted cash flow and relative valuation. Which model is most appropriate depends on the characteristics of the company; there is no single best model for all situations. Although the models are quantitative, the inputs are subjectively derived. Therefore, the numbers obtained are only as good as the inputs used. The application of these models is both a science and an art.

Discounted cash flow models are a theoretically superior method of independently determining value, but arriving at the correct inputs is quite challenging. Accurate predictions of growth rate and the cost of equity of the firm are necessary in order for the company valuation to be accurate. Even small errors in growth rate result in large changes in present value.

Discounted cash flow valuation is most appropriately used for companies with a consistent pattern of cash flow in the past (steady or rising), where future performance appears to be predictable, and where risk can be estimated in order to determine the appropriate discount rate. Firms with negative earnings, with cyclical patterns of cash flow, or undergoing restructuring, mergers, acquisitions, initial public offerings, or other major changes are less amenable to discounted cash flow valuation.

Stock analysts most commonly use relative valuation methods. They can be applied to any company and are simpler to comprehend, but do not indicate whether entire sectors or the market as a whole are incorrectly valued. Which multiple is used as the basis of evaluation, and arrival at the appropriate multiple value for the company are the major choices. The appropriate multiple value can be determined by fundamental analysis, comparable firms, or a cross-sectional regression of a stock database.

Price/earning ratio is the most widely used multiple. It is meaningless when earnings are negative or distorted by temporary conditions, such as restructuring or accounting write-offs. Price/book value or price/sales ratios may be more appropriate in these situations. Finding comparable firms is usually the key step in valuation. Theoretically, they should have a similar business mix, growth rate, and risk profile. The more difficult it is to find companies that fit this description, the less appropriate the technique. In such cases statistical regression of stock databases or fundamental derivation of company multiples may be superior.

In reviewing relative valuation multiples, we have identified some that have been predictive of higher investment returns:

- Low price/earnings ratio

- Low ratio of P/E to growth rate

- Low price/book value ratio

- Low ratio of P/BV to return on equity

- Low price/sales ratio

- Low ratio of P/S to profit margin

Conclusion

After we've gone through all of this, I feel that I should discuss the nonbelievers' claims. Most finance professors doubt that anyone can consistently find undervalued stocks in our active, efficient capital markets. Having seen the rules of the game, do you think that you could?

If others are using only subjective pricing of stocks, you might eke out a little greater profit using this approach. I say "eke out" because if there were a way to make a real killing, it wouldn't take long for people to find out about it, and the advantage would disappear. Quantitative stock analysis has grown tremendously in recent years. It has been estimated that about $500 billion is now invested based on this approach. Therefore, even if there were a clear advantage to it, the advantage would be smaller than in the past.

What about all the company research reports produced by professional analysts at brokerages, banks, investment services, mutual fund companies, and other organizations? We'll hear from some examples in later chapters of this book. Maybe you can find analysts with superior skills and use their reports to aid your search for undervalued stocks. However, the vast majority of reports result in purchase recommendations, while only a handful recommend selling. This is quite suspect—how could they all be finding most stocks undervalued? We know that the situation should be the reverse.

What about those top-ranked analysts? A lot of the time the basis of their rankings is not their ability to correctly value stocks, but the reliability of their factual company information. Those who have recommended winning stocks are often just lucky or are choosing riskier investments that are expected to have a higher return.

So, should you just choose stocks at random, and ignore all I've told you? First, the exercise is worthwhile in gaining a better understanding of how the market values stocks. I also think that you can use fundamental analysis to avoid some overvalued stocks, and probably to find a few undervalued ones. We've also learned that you can obtain better than average returns by selecting groups of stocks with certain fundamental characteristics, such as a low P/E and a low ratio of P/E to growth rate.

Suggested Reading

Damodaran, A. *Investment Valuation: Tools and Techniques for Determining the Value of Any Asset*. New York: John Wiley & Sons, 1996.

Bodie, Z., A. Kane and A. J. Marcus, eds. *Investments, (Third Edition)*. Chicago: Irwin Press, 1996, p. 521–559.

Notes

1. To calculate the value of cash payments over multiple years the formula becomes:

$$PV = \frac{CF_1}{(1+r)} + \frac{CF_2}{(1+r)^2} + \frac{CF_3}{(1+r)^3} \cdots \frac{CF_n}{(1+r)^n}$$

2. For our purposes, cash flow is income after meeting all expenses, including capital expenditures, working capital needs, tax obligations, and interest and principal payments

on debt (also called free cash flow to equity or FCFE). All extraordinary gains or losses should be removed from the calculations. This may be different from the net income reported on the company's balance sheet.

3. The cost of equity can be estimated using risk and return models (such as the capital asset pricing model or the arbitrage pricing model).

4. A. Damodaran, *Investment Valuation: Tools and Techniques for Determining the Value of Any Asset* New York: John Wiley & Sons, 1996, p. 126–127.

5. O'Brien, P. 1988 Analysts' forecasts as earnings expectation. *Journal of Accounting and Economics* 10:53-83.

6. J. H. Vander Weide and W. T. Carleton. 1988. Investor growth expectations: Analysts vs. history. *Journal of Portfolio Management* 14:78-83.

7. D. J. Peters. Valuing a Growth Stock. *Journal of Portfolio Management* (1991) 17:49–51.

8. S. Basu, "The Investment Performance of Common Stocks in Relation to Their Price-Earnings: A Test of the Efficient Market Hypothesis," *Journal of Finance* (1977) 32:663–682; H. Levy and Z. Lerman, "Testing P/E Ratio Filters with Stochastic Dominance," *Journal of Portfolio Management* 11:31–40.

9. D. A. Goodman and J. W. Peavy III, "Industry Relative Price-Earnings Ratios as Indicators of Investment Returns," *Financial Analysts Journal* (1983) 39:60–66.

10. B. Graham, D. L. Dodd and S. Cottle, *Security Analysis, (Fourth Edition)*. New York: McGraw-Hill, 1962.

11. The discounted cashflow formula can be transformed to: P/BV = (ROE – gn) / r – g_n

12. E. F. Fama and K. R. French, "The Cross-Section of Expected Returns," *Journal of Finance* (1992) 47:427–466; B. Rosenberg, K. Reid and R. Lanstein, "Persuasive Evidence of Market Inefficiency," *Journal of Portfolio Management* (1985) 11:9–17.

13. Damodaran, p. 334.

14. The discounted cash flow formula can be transformed to: P/S = (profit margin × payout ratio)/r – g_n where profit margin = earnings per share/sales per share

15. B. I. Jacobs and K. N. Levy, "Disentangling Equity Return Irregularities: New Insights and Investment Opportunities." *Financial Analysis Journal* (1988) 44:18–44; A. J. Senchack Jr. and J. D. Martin, "The Relative Performance of the PSR and PER Investment Strategies," *Financial Analysts Journal* (1987) 43:46–56.

16. Damodaran, p. 352.

CHAPTER 6

Growth Investing

Richard Driehaus

Growth Investing—An Overview

Growth investing is one of several investment styles or methodologies used to determine which stocks offer investors the potential for the best performance (as measured by an increase in value) over a given time period. Other noteworthy investment styles include value investing, GARP (or growth-at-a-reasonable-price) investing, and private enterprise value investing. The key distinction of the growth style of investing is that it assumes the best stocks are those of companies (or industries) that are growing rather than "staying the course" or in decline. Growth can be defined in many ways. From a fundamental perspective, growth companies have or are projected to have increases in revenues, earnings per share, and cash flow, with a rate of increase greater than that of the average company within their industry. In addition, growth companies usually pay a low dividend relative to their share price, or no dividend at all, because earnings are plowed back into the company to provide capital to grow the business, rather than paid out to shareholders through dividends.

Looking for Growth: Bottom-Up and Middle Down

A useful place to start looking for a growth company is at the individual company level, from the bottom up. From this perspective a company is analyzed on a stand-alone basis—economic, market, and industry considerations are not as relevant as the company itself. This assumes that a good growth company will continue to prosper, regardless of the state of the economy as a whole, general market conditions, or the outlook for its industry.

Another way to find a solid growth company is to determine which industries are rapidly growing, and select the best companies within these industries. This is a "middle down" approach. A thriving industry can contribute to the success of all companies that operate within the industry—a rising tide lifts all boats—and an investor can prosper by selecting the best stocks of companies in an industry, because they should do better than their competitors.

The "middle down" approach does not necessarily apply specifically to industry analysis; it can also be used within the context of trend spotting or thematic investing. For example, when one looks (from the top) at everything going on within a society (the economy, the culture, the political environment, etc.) one may be able to spot certain trends that are emerging. Once an investor has spotted a trend, he or she may try to find companies that will benefit from it, expecting that such companies will enjoy above-average growth in the future because of the trend.

The Life Cycle

Growth can also be defined as a phase in the normal development of a company. Companies and industries typically go through a life cycle that is broken down into five stages: conceptual, early development, rapid expansion, mature growth, and stabilization or decline. Companies in the *conceptual stage* or the *early development stage* are typically funded by venture capital or other private sources and have not yet become publicly held companies. Their business plan may be based on a novel idea or technology that is still in its infancy. Companies and industries in this phase are just emerging, and are probably not familiar to the average person. Examples are the biotechnology industry in the early 1980s (Biogen, Genentech) and the Internet sector in the early to mid-1990s (America Online, Yahoo!). In fact, some of the most successful companies were not initially understood at the time of their initial public offering. Examples of companies that were not easily understood in their early development include retailers such as Home Depot and Wal-Mart, technology companies such as Microsoft and Sun Microsystems, and medical companies such as Medtronic and Alza.

Companies in the *rapid expansion stage* are better established and have started to experience rapidly growing revenues and earnings, increasing market share, higher production levels, and so on. Industries in this phase are attracting interest, and although competition between companies is virtually nonexistent, there is an abundance of start-up business entering the field. The *mature growth stage* is represented by companies that are well-established, widely recognized businesses that continue to have increasing revenues and earnings. Mature industries may still be growing, but have become more competitive. Companies in the *stabilization stage* or *decline stage* have stopped growing and may be losing market share, have products that have become obsolete, or be facing a highly competitive climate. Declining industries are those that have been replaced by new technology or have become so competitive that every participant must lower price to survive.

Growth investors are looking for companies in the first four stages of development: conceptual, early development, rapid expansion, and mature growth.

More on the Fundamentals

The most common metric used to ascertain and analyze a company's growth is its earnings per share, because it indicates how profitable the company has been over a given period of time (the earnings numerator) and how the profitability is translated into shareholder value (the per share denominator). However, other basic accounting measures are also used to analyze growth, such as revenues and cash flow.

Each quarter's results should be compared with those from the same quarter of the prior year. This takes out the seasonality bias, which can be high for some companies such as retailers, where the bulk of revenues or earnings are produced in only one or two quarters in each year. H&R Block, the income tax preparation company, and Toys 'Я' Us, the children's toy and clothing retailer, are examples of seasonal business models, while companies involved in home building, basic materials, or semiconductors tend to be cyclical. For companies whose business is not seasonal or cyclical, it is also helpful to look at the pattern of revenue and earnings growth on a *sequential* quarterly basis (one quarter to the next). Growth investors want to see a trend where these fundamental measures increase in sequential quarterly reports.

While these accounting measures are helpful, it is important to remember that the as-reported numbers tell the investor what the company has done in the past, and not necessarily what it will do in the future. However, in most cases it is reasonable to assume that a company showing above-average historic growth in any of these measures should continue to do so in the future.

One must also determine that the quality of the earnings report is high—that there are no nonrecurring factors that may have made earnings artificially higher, due to accounting methods or one-time events that occurred during the period in question. If nonrecurring items are included, they should be factored out of the analysis to give a more accurate assessment of the company's intrinsic growth.

Investors are mainly concerned with future growth, because that is what will determine future share price and their investment return over time. Thus, it is important to assess growth from a forward-looking perspective. Growth investors should ask themselves these questions: What are the company's projected earning per share and revenues for this year? For next year? What revenue level or earnings per share are projected for the current quarter? For the next quarter? What is the company's annualized projected earnings growth rate for the next three or five years? Analysts review a great deal of information to arrive at the earnings and revenue projections, incorporating many factors, including the industry growth rate (historic and projected), the company's products and their market shares, their pipeline of potential new products, the abilities and strategies of the company's management, and the general outlook for the economy and for the sector that a company operates in. Investors can use these projections to determine which companies have the best potential as growth stocks.

In addition, growth can be measured by a company's operating statistics. For example, in the retailing industry, same-store sales (revenues produced by the same unit base, measured year-over-year) is an important gauge of growth. In manufacturing companies, such as semiconductor manufacturers, backlog (anticipated production needed to fulfill orders) may be analyzed. In mining and mineral companies, the buildup of reserves is important. In airlines, the load factor and revenue per passenger mile are growth indicators. The key is to determine, for a given industry, which operating statistics are most useful in predicting future growth.

Corporate vision is also important and is not as easy to assess as some of these other measures. An investor should try to ascertain whether a company's leaders can grasp the big picture and look beyond what is happening internally at the company they manage. It has been noted that it may not matter how well you execute if you lack corporate vision. Corporate vision allows a company to not only keep up with the changing environment but hopefully stay ahead of it.

The sustainability of future growth must be estimated. Questions to consider include: Will the company remain an industry leader? Will competition cut its market share? Will the industry as a whole continue to grow? How will new products or technology affect the industry and this company in particular? A lot of knowledge and research is helpful, but this is where the art of investing has a great role.

Tools of the Trade

The most important tool of the trade is a company's earnings report. All public companies must make unaudited quarterly financial reports available to the public within 45 days of the last day of the quarter, and they must disclose audited annual financial results within 90 days of the close of their fiscal year. The standard formats for these disclosures are the 10-K (annual) and 10-Q (quarterly) reports that are filed with the Securities and Exchange Commission, which are available over the Internet. Most companies also provide shareholders and other interested parties with annual reports and quarterly reports. These tend to be more promotional in nature, but contain essentially the same information as government filings.

However, neither of these reports tends to be as timely as the earnings press releases. These go out to the wire services when a company files the more formal reports. The press releases provide a brief summary of the important financial data that the company is reporting, along with commentary from management about the quarter that has closed, and possibly information about the outlook for the company. Growth stock portfolio managers and analysts usually review the press release as a first step to gauge the company's progress, and may use the other reports for more information. In addition, management may sponsor a conference call to review the quarter and discuss the future for the company. However, these calls are typically open to only Wall Street investment analysts and the institutional investment community, not individual shareholders.

Growth stock investors should also pay attention to forecasts of earnings per share and revenues made by the "sell-side" or (Wall) Street analysts, and may also make their own projections. Sell-side or Street analysts work for investment banks and broker-dealers that bring companies public and trade issues for institutional and retail investors. Database providers, such as the First Call, Zacks Investment Research, and I/B/E/S International, Inc., gather earnings estimate data and calculate consensus forecasts. Because growth stock investing is future-oriented, these estimates are very important. In addition, published estimates may not be the same as "whisper" estimates. Sometimes, a Street analyst will publish a projection, but "whisper" what he or she really thinks a company will report to his or her best institutional ("buy-side") clients. Street analysts also have a tendency to underestimate earnings, increasing the likelihood of a positive surprise, so analysis of forecasts should be done with this caveat.

Another source of information is direct contact with company management. Many companies have a designated person whose sole responsibility is to handle investor relations. This person is usually the initial point of contact to get information on the company. However, the best source of information is usually top management—the chief executive officer, the chief financial officer, and the heads of important operating divisions. Institutional investment professionals and Wall Street analysts are generally able to develop a dialog with top management because they may hold a meaningful position in the company's stock or are in a position to advise those who do. However, it is much more difficult for individual investors to gain such access.

In addition, sell-side investment firms may hold industry conferences or company meetings designed to facilitate information flow between management and the institutional investment community, and these conferences are a good way to "visit" a lot of companies in a short period of time. Again, individual shareholders are usually not invited to these meetings.

Investors can also find stock ideas from reading newspapers (especially the *Wall Street Journal* and *Investor's Business Daily*), business magazines, trade journals, Internet sites, and so on. They can also discover good growth stocks by talking to people outside the investment business. People at the grassroots level of a company are more likely to give a forthright account of what is really going on within their company or industry, sometimes before the Street, the business press, or other investors have caught on to the story. Valuable information can also be obtained from customers and employees of competing companies.

Gathering and analyzing earnings reports and reading relevant publications can take a lot of time, especially if an investor is looking for ideas across all industries. This is one reason why investment management firms may employ several analysts, each devoted to a specific industry or sector, so that they can be focused and selective in their research.

Thoughts on Valuation

It should probably be no surprise that growth companies come with higher price tags, as measured by the P/E ratio. While a value investor would not typically buy a high-P/E stock, it comes with the territory for a growth investor. We believe that high P/Es are justified for growth stocks. If you are buying stock in a company that is expected to exhibit higher than average revenue and earnings growth, you should expect to pay more for it. We don't emphasize valuation constraints in our research process, because we are basically optimists—what may be a high-priced stock now could go higher in the future.

Some growth stock investors, who accept that high-P/E stocks are a fact of life, will still choose to put a limit on how much they may be willing to pay for a stock. This is particularly true of GARP or growth-at-a-reasonable-price investors. If a valuation parameter must be used, it may be relevant to compare the P/E ratio to the company's earnings growth rate, and focus on stocks where the P/E ratio is less than the company's forecasted earnings growth rate.

Performance Measurement for Growth Investors

Performance of a stock or a portfolio of stocks should always be assessed in an appropriate context. Returns should not be measured solely on an absolute basis (for any style of investing) because absolute measurement does not really tell you very much. Most professional investors agree that performance should be measured on a relative basis—by comparison to the performance of a relevant benchmark or index over the same period of time.

Relevant benchmarks should reflect only growth stocks and include companies of similar size to those held in the portfolio. This is because styles and market cap segments tend to be in favor or out of favor over time, and the use of an inappropriate benchmark may lead to an erroneous comparison. The key for growth stock investors is to determine the relevant benchmark. See Chapter 12 for further discussion of benchmarking.

Growth Investing: Make or Buy?

This chapter has focused on a methodology for selecting growth stocks for one's investment portfolio. For individual investors, growth stock investing can be a rewarding and enjoyable experience—it is satisfying to research and select what you think will be the next Wal-Mart, the next Microsoft, or the next America Online, and it is even more enjoyable to see it actually happen. We encourage people to get involved in researching and investing in a handful of growth companies on their own.

However, growth investing can take a lot of resources—time, money, and personal commitment. It is time-consuming to sift through all of the public companies to find a good growth stock, and it can be costly—research information can be expensive. Furthermore, one must be personally committed to an investment philosophy, and shouldn't waiver. Therefore, if an investor wishes to make a meaningful asset allocation to growth stocks, we recommend that a professional investment manager manage the majority of the portfolio, either through the purchase of a mutual fund or on an institutionally managed account basis.

There are several reasons why we advocate professional management. An investment management firm offers a staff of portfolio managers and analysts who are dedicated to finding the best investments for a given product—it's their full-time job, not simply a hobby. They have access to a lot of information the individual investor typically does not have—direct contact with company management and Wall Street analysts, special research information services, trade journals, and so on. An investment management firm also offers an individual investor years of experience that the investor may not have. The individual investor can also enjoy the benefits of diversification by buying a mutual fund or hiring an investment manager, because the investment manager is usually managing a large portfolio and can buy many more stocks to diversify the portfolio. Therefore, the manager reduces what is called the specific risk—the portfolio's risk compared to the overall market.

Selecting a Growth Manager

There are three things to consider in the manager selection process. First, one should consider the level of the manager's (or mutual fund's) style purity—examine how closely they stick to their stated philosophy. Some managers try to change what they do based on whatever they assess the current investment climate to be. They may buy growth stocks one day and value stocks the next, or large-cap stocks and then smaller stocks, or they may buy technology stocks and then health-care stocks. Therefore, the investors may not be getting the type of manager they thought they were, and it is difficult for managers to succeed over time if they are constantly changing the way they invest.

Given that you are confident that the manager you have selected is a true growth-style manager, you should nevertheless look at the manager's track record. It is one thing to be something; it is quite a different thing to succeed at it. Choose a manager who has been able to produce above-average returns relative to other growth managers.

Finally, a successful track record should be built over a long time period. There are a lot of "one-shot wonders" who have excellent performance over a relatively short time period, but fail to succeed consistently over longer periods. It is important to look at a manager's or fund's longer-term track record, at least over a full market cycle, in order to determine if the manager or fund can consistently come through with above-average performance.

Monitoring the Manager

Once an appropriate manager has been selected, monitoring the performance is up to the investor. It is important for the investor to do this with the understanding of two important caveats. The general market environment won't be in your favor all of the time, nor will the growth style of investing. The road will be bumpy along the way. Therefore, we believe you should not try to "time" the market—you should accept the rough spots and have the patience to weather any adversity that arises. Furthermore, market timing strategies rarely produce above-average returns, and dramatic market moves are likely to take place over short time periods, increasing the possibility that you end up on the wrong side of the market at the wrong time.

There will also be time periods when a growth investor will look like a wallflower at the high school dance—everyone's dancing to the value style and no one cares about growth stocks. Fortunately, there will also be times when the growth investors are voted "most popular." It is important to realize that styles and market conditions ebb and flow. For this reason, performance monitoring and evaluation should be done, when possible, on both an apples-to-apples basis and over a full market cycle.

The Driehaus Philosophy

Our investment philosophy falls within the growth style of investing. However, we tend to look for the most rapidly growing companies within the growth stock universe and, as such, there are several nuances that should be mentioned. But first, I'll start with some background on our philosophy.

History

I began developing the firm's investment philosophy when I was still a teenager in the 1950s. I read the popular financial columnists in the newspaper, such as Sylvia Porter and Sam Seholsky, in order to learn about investing and find out what stocks they recommended. I made two investments, based on outside recommendations—an aggressive stock, Sperry Rand, and a conservative stock, Union Tank Car Company. Unfortunately, Sperry Rand dropped by a third and Union Tank Car didn't move, so I decided to do my own research. I began by going to the Chicago Public Library to read magazines, newspaper articles, and investment advisory letters, and I also subscribed to various investment advisory services.

One service that I found particularly interesting was John Herold's "America's Fastest Growing Companies," which introduced me to the world of growth stock investing. He highlighted growth stocks such as Avon and Baxter Laboratories, which as I recall had experienced remarkable earnings growth and had appreciated roughly 2,000–3,000% from 1949 to the mid- to late 1950s, when earnings growth began to slow to 8–12% per year. Because the stocks had already made a large move and earnings had slowed, I decided it might be better to find stocks of younger companies that were still in their high-growth phase, yet hadn't advanced so much in price.

Coincidentally, a major change in the economy was starting to take place—the emergence of technology. With this as a backdrop, I began to develop my own investment philosophy, based on the concept that earnings growth is the principal factor in determining common stock prices over the long term. Only through sustained earnings growth can cash flow be expanded, dividends raised, and book values increased. After an early career working as an analyst and portfolio manager for several investment firms, I founded my own firm in 1980. Today, our firm is still focused on applying my core investment philosophy, offering both managed accounts focused on small and mid-cap-sized domestic companies, as well as hedge funds and a family of international equity mutual funds.

Implementation—How We Look for Growth

Earnings growth is paramount to our investment philosophy. We assess growth using the more traditional barometers mentioned earlier. However, we tend to take things a step further—we are a bit more selective. Not only do we want to invest in those companies with above-average growth rates, we also raise the bar, selecting companies that have the highest growth rates within the market or within their respective industries.

We also look for companies that have accelerating earnings and revenue growth rates, or earnings momentum; characterized by revenues or earnings that not only are increasing, but are increasing at a higher rate each successive quarter. One of our favorite mottos is: If growth is good, acceleration is even better. In addition, we buy companies that report positive earnings surprises. Earnings surprises are a measure of how a company's actual reported results differ from what the investment community had expected. A positive surprise signals that a given company was able to succeed better in a given quarter than anyone had expected, and may be a clue that the underlying business is growing faster than anticipated. Companies that exceed expectations are generally assumed to be able to continue to do so in future reporting periods. We also look for companies that have upward estimate revisions. Based on better-than-expected business factors, analysts will increase their estimates for future revenue and earnings potential. In general, the greater the upward revision, the more attractive the stock may be for investment. In addition, we expect growth to be sustainable, as estimates are increasing and as companies exceed expectations. Finally, qualitative analysis of the earnings is also considered. We assess whether the earnings are of high quality: Have conservative accounting principles been used? Have nonrecurring items been eliminated? Have comparable tax rate adjustments been made?

We also focus on the relevant operating statistics in assessing growth. For example, we may look at the monthly same-store sales pattern for a retailer. If the same-store sales are increasing each successive month over a period of time, the company is more likely to be an attractive investment. We may follow the backlog trend for a semiconductor manufacturer; if it increases each sequential quarter, this would be viewed positively.

Valuation considerations are *not* an important aspect of our stock selection and portfolio management process. We do not adhere to any rule that requires selling a stock if a P/E ratio is too high, nor do we place emphasis on buying stocks because the P/E ratio is low. In fact, we typically buy stocks with relatively high P/E ratios because they tend to have the highest earnings and revenue growth.

We assess the market timeliness of a stock under consideration. We look at the technical pattern of a stock to determine whether it would be an attractive investment. We generally want to see an increasing price trend and increasing trading volume, on both an absolute and a relative strength basis, rather than a declining technical pattern. It is better to buy a stock that is already rising in price and take the risk that it could fall than to buy a stock that is trading at lows with the hope that it will turn around. Relative strength is a measure of a company's stock price relative to its industry group or the market as a whole. Increasing relative strength is preferred.

We also use more subjective criteria in our investment process. For example, we identify emerging socioeconomic trends, and may seek companies that will benefit from them. We may also look at established trends or high-growth industries and try to determine what other companies will benefit, beyond those that are obvious. For example, in late 1998 and early 1999 the Internet service providers and browsers were the hot area in technology investing. Companies such as America Online and Yahoo! were in the spotlight. We chose to look beyond these companies and invest in the Internet infrastructure—in companies such as QLogic and Emulex that were not at the forefront of the Internet revolution, but were in the background, providing products and services that would enhance the usage of the Internet. On a company-specific basis we try to select stocks of companies that are "best of breed"—the companies that have the best product or service relative to the competition, or that may be rapidly gaining market share.

Our analytical approach heavily emphasizes individual stock selection. Stock selection is very important because we believe that you need to hit a couple of home runs (stocks that perform dramatically better than their peers or the market as a whole) rather than a series of singles or doubles to win the investment ball game.

Our Sell Discipline

Much of this discussion has focused on how we *buy* growth stocks. We also follow a sell discipline that is an equally important aspect of our investment process. Some investors advocate "buy and hold"; we favor "buy and hold until conditions change, then be ready to sell quickly." Our sell discipline is basically the reverse of the growth parameters we look at when selecting new stocks. We may sell a stock because of a slowdown in earnings or revenue growth, an earnings disappointment, downward estimate revisions, and so on. We may also sell a stock simply because another one is more attractive to own at that time.

Close monitoring of all of our positions is important, because things can change rapidly. We are constantly vigilant so that we can, when necessary, move out a stock that is no longer attractive. We believe in cutting losses quickly while letting our winners run. In fact, one of the key advantages of professional investment management is that dedicated managers learn of news very quickly, and have the capacity to respond to news rapidly. While this may result in higher-than-average portfolio turnover, we view this as a defense mechanism that protects us from further downside.

Growth Means Change

One of the key attributes of how we invest is our open attitude toward growth investing. One of our favorite quotations is, "Minds are like parachutes—they work best when open" by Lord Thomas Dewar.

Some investors tend to be very rigid in applying their philosophy, yet we are very flexible. We believe that growth, by its very nature, is related to change. As such, we must be ready to change our process as needed, developing new ways to assess growth. We also strive to be quick to recognize change among the companies and industries that we invest in, and capitalize on the opportunities that change presents to us. We embrace change and adapt to it.

Growth Investing in the New Millennium

The growth style of investing has proven to be a successful strategy over the past 50 years, and this has coincided with an era of dramatic economic growth as well as rapid technological innovation. The three trends are interrelated: Technological innovation has fostered dramatic economic growth, which in turn has created a favorable environment for growth-style investing. While economic forecasts are not my area of expertise, I feel it is safe to say that the growth style of investing should continue to reward investors who are committed to implementing the philosophy and who have the patience to stick with it through a full market cycle. While implementation may change as new industries and businesses emerge, the fundamental tenet of the philosophy, that earnings growth is the principal factor in determining common stock prices over the long term, should remain the cornerstone on which growth investing is built.

Value Investing: A Philosophy for Life

David Winters

alue investing is the purchase of a dollar of assets for as little as possible. The value investing approach was originally formulated by Benjamin Graham (1894–1976), who coauthored *Security Analysis* in 1934 and *The Intelligent Investor* in 1950. Both of these books are revered by devotees as presentations of the core guiding principles of their profitable, low-risk strategy of investing. *Security Analysis* is widely considered to be the bible for true value investors. Although Ben Graham was a professor at Columbia Business School, he was not an ivory tower academic, but rather a practitioner whose real-life experiences shaped his conclusions. The cataclysmic declines of security prices during the 1929 crash and the Great Depression that followed helped mold the principles and mathematical formulas Ben Graham developed.

Security Analysis emphasized the fundamental analysis of financial statements and the methodical valuation of businesses. Securities were to be purchased only when their "intrinsic value" exceeded by a substantial margin the current market price. Numerous ratios, formulas, and rules were prescribed to determine a stock's and/or bond's underlying value. The student of Graham would apply these principles to provide stock market profits based on knowledge, not speculation. *The Intelligent Investor* is a book written for a wider audience; the subtitle is *A Book of Practical Counsel*. The two chapters that distill *The Intelligent Investor* are 8 and 20. Chapter 8 describes the inevitable fluctuations in stock prices that should be used to accumulate securities when prices are low and to sell when prices are high. Ben Graham compares the behavior of the stock market to a manic-depressive individual whose wild mood swings fluctuate from ebullience to deep depression. Mr. Market is a manic fellow whose swings are to be taken advantage of, not heeded. Ben Graham's message was to be rational and unemotional. The true value investor's mission was to use Mr. Market's love/hate relationship with security prices to the investor's advantage. If the lemmings are all running over the cliff, the value investor could profit from their collective behavior by acquiring securities at depressed prices.

Chapter 20 of *The Intellegent Investor*, "Margin of Safety: the Central Concept," presents the key insight that acquiring a security at a price far below its underlying value provides a substantial cushion against future loss. With such a margin of safety, the investor is less likely to suffer permanent loss of capital, even if the market declines.

Graham advises operating investment activities in a businesslike manner. The most basic of Graham's principles is to determine the net-net current value of a company using the following formula: Take the sum of cash and marketable securities at market, receivables, and inventory (possibly at a discount); subtract all liabilities; and divide by shares outstanding. The inventory should be of sufficient quality that over a reasonably short period of time it could be converted to cash with minimal loss of value. Otherwise an appropriate discount should be applied. This definition of net-net would yield the simple liquidation value of an enterprise. Today, Graham might also check the funding status of the pension plan, and environmental or product liabilities to determine whether any additional balance should be deducted from the net-net valuation. If the stock price is two-thirds or less of net-net current asset value, the likelihood of permanent loss would be minimal. A portfolio of such lowly valued securities should produce an adequate return over time with minimal risk.

Other techniques espoused by Graham include: arbitrage, the purchase of a security at a discount to an announced deal, and acquiring bargain-priced senior securities such as bonds.

In 1956 Ben Graham wound up his investment partnership. His passion for investing had diminished and he moved on to the next phase of his life. However, several of Ben Graham's best students who had worked with him at Graham-Newman Corporation later had extremely successful careers on their own, including Walter Schloss, Irving Kahn, and Warren Buffett.

Spectrum of Value Investors

For these and other practitioners of value investing, Benjamin Graham provided the road map for a successful career in investing. The ways the individuals have interpreted, applied, or expanded the basic principles have determined their paths. Value investors as a group are fanatical believers in their chosen approach; the philosophy often becomes intertwined in their daily lives. Rarely will a true believer willingly pay retail for any item. Sales and bargain purchases are the modus operandi. Following the crowd is anathema to them. Over time, value investors' approaches have gravitated toward several groups or camps.

Strict Practitioner: Peter Cundill

Peter Cundill of Peter Cundill and Associates is one of the members in the strict practitioner camp. Peter's long-term record is excellent. (See Table 7.1 and 7.2.) He focuses on balance sheet strength and the net-net current asset value of a security according to the tenets of Benjamin Graham. He is a chartered accountant and a true forensic digger into company reports and accounts. From his base in Vancouver, British Columbia, Cundill has searched the world over for companies trading at a discount to net-net. As U.S. and Canadian markets' valuations have escalated, Peter has found numerous candidates in Japan.

Collectors

As we gravitate along the spectrum of value investors, the next stop may be described as collectors.

Tweedy Browne

Tweedy Browne and Company has its roots in the 1920s as a brokerage firm and the operator of a partnership (Tweedy, Browne & Knapp or TBK Partners) that invested in obscure, extremely undervalued securities. Benjamin Graham bought securities from Tweedy. The firm identified many securities that it was willing to purchase at the right price. An analogy that has been

TABLE 7.1 Performance of Value-Oriented Mutual Funds

	Performance through December 15, 2000			
	1 year	3 years	5 years	10 years
Franklin Mutual Advisers				
Mutual Beacon	13.76	10.29	14.77	16.68
Mutual Discovery	15.05	11.44	16.26	n/a
Mutual European	19.91	20.36	n/a	n/a
Mutual Qualified	12.79	8.62	13.94	16.73
Mutual Shares	12.74	8.66	14.19	16.62
Mutual Financial Services	23.66	11.60	n/a	n/a
Templeton Growth Fund (A)	2.81	6.74	11.90	14.32
Legg Mason Value Trust	−5.20	21.56	28.30	n/a
Tweedy Browne Global Value	11.85	15.79	18.06	n/a
Tweedy Browne American Value	11.08	7.76	16.18	n/a
Cundill Value (Canadian Dollars)[1]	22.30	11.10	10.90	12.70
S&P 500	−6.07	12.32	18.18	17.71
Morningstar Domestic Stock Average[2]	3.43	7.17	8.95	n/a
Morningstar World Stock Fund Average[3]	−6.30	10.22	10.80	n/a
Morningstar Foreign Stock Fund Average[4]	3.03	7.34	8.55	n/a

[1]Performance through 11/30/2000, Canadian Dollars.
[2]Morningstar Domestic Stock Fund Average: Average returns of funds in the Morningstar universe that invest in companies with market capitalizations greater than or equal to $1 billion but less than or equal to $5 billion.
[3]Morningstar World Stock Fund Average: Average results of all mutual funds in the Morningstar universe that invest throughout the world while maintaining a percentage of assets (normally 25%–50%) in the United States.
[4]Morningstar Foreign Stock Fund Average: Average returns of all mutual funds in the Morningstar universe that have 90% or more of their assets invested in non-U.S. stocks.

TABLE 7.2 Annual Performance of Value-Oriented Mutual Funds

	1999	1998	1997	1996
Franklin Mutual Advisers				
Mutual Beacon	16.80	2.37	23.03	21.15
Mutual Discovery	26.80	−1.90	22.94	24.93
Mutual European	46.81	4.74	23.16	n/a
Mutual Qualified	13.64	0.50	24.88	21.22
Mutual Shares	15.00	0.45	26.38	20.76
Mutual Financial Services	4.70	6.06	n/a	n/a
Templeton Growth Fund (A)	30.44	−2.48	16.18	20.55
Legg Mason Value Trust	26.10	48.04	37.05	38.43
Tweedy Browne Global Value	25.28	10.99	22.96	20.23
Tweedy Browne American Value	2.00	9.59	38.87	22.45
Cundill Value (Canadian Dollars)	33.30	−10.70	3.50	10.80
Dow Jones Industrial Average	25.50	18.40	25.00	29.10
S&P 500	21.04	28.58	33.36	22.96
Russell 3000 Value	6.65	13.50	34.83	21.60
Morningstar World Stock Fund Avg[1]	38.06	12.47	11.90	16.23
Morningstar Foreign Stock Fund Avg[2]	44.21	12.64	5.42	12.09

[1]Morningstar World Stock Fund Average: Average results of all mutual funds in the Morningstar universe that invest throughout the world while maintaining a percentage of assets (normally 25%–50%) in the United States.

[2]Morningstar Foreign Stock Fund Average: Average returns of all mutual funds in the Morningstar universe that have 90% or more of their assets invested in non-U.S. stocks.

1995	1994	1993	1992	1991	1990
25.93	5.61	22.94	22.82	17.71	−8.22
28.63	3.62	35.85	n/a	n/a	n/a
n/a	n/a	n/a	n/a	n/a	n/a
26.55	5.77	22.66	22.75	21.06	−10.12
29.11	4.55	20.99	21.32	20.99	−9.82
n/a	n/a	n/a	n/a	n/a	n/a
19.83	0.82	32.70	4.21	31.33	−9.06
40.76	1.89	11.26	11.44	34.73	−16.98
10.70	4.36	n/a	n/a	n/a	n/a
36.21	−0.56	n/a	n/a	n/a	n/a
8.20	15.40	43.10	7.20	5.40	−9.50
36.90	5.00	17.10	7.30	24.20	−0.40
37.58	1.32	10.08	7.62	30.47	−3.10
37.03	−1.95	18.65	14.90	25.41	−8.85
16.77	−1.64	16.46	−4.70	19.00	−18.50
9.71	−0.63	16.51			

used is of a fisherman with many lines out in a large and often murky pond. On any given day, it was unclear which, if any, fish would bite on Tweedy's proffered hooks. The long-term results of his firm's approach have been excellent.

As the firm's capital and reputation have grown, fishing for small stocks in out-of-the-way places has become a less and less significant part of the business. Tweedy Browne manages two mutual funds, one focused on U.S. securities and the other a global fund (Tables 7.1 and 7.2). Tweedy has expanded beyond the original definitions of cheapness but still searches for companies whose shares trade at a significant discount to their intrinsic value. Tweedy purchases stocks in many different industries and waits for the usually inevitable realization of true underlying value.

Sir John Templeton

One of the original global value investors was a gentleman who started looking for bargains overseas earlier than most. Sir John Templeton is by all accounts an exceptional individual, a great investor and generous philanthropist. In 1940 he acquired an investment counseling firm, and in 1954 Templeton Growth Fund was launched. (See Table 7.3.) In the 1960s Sir John was a buyer of Japanese stocks at prices of three and four times earnings. Very few foreign investors understood the scope of the opportunity. By the 1980s, when Japanese security prices reached astronomical and ultimately unsustainable levels, Templeton was long gone.

He advocated searching for the best bargains wherever in the world they existed, and selling the most richly valued securities. Sir John was often attracted to markets that had been under extreme selling pressure. Sir John Templeton laid the groundwork for many investors who followed his financial trailblazing.

The Workout Specialists

A workout is a security that's future worth will be determined by a negotiation or a series of restructurings or asset sales. Workout specialists therefore focus on investments that require active involvement by management and/or the investors to surface value.

Max Heine

Max Heine traded in extremely undervalued securities, as did Benjamin Graham. Max's expertise was as a buyer of liquidations, bonds of companies in bankruptcy, and work-out situations. Bankruptcy, which to many was a taboo

TABLE 7.3 Performance Chart—Templeton Growth
Fund—Class A (Annual Returns at Net Asset Value)

1955	7.04%	1978	19.21%
1956	4.64%	1979	26.84%
1957	−16.91%	1980	25.89%
1958	48.81%	1981	−0.24%
1959	14.00%	1982	10.81%
1960	13.84%	1983	32.91%
1961	18.29%	1984	2.17%
1962	−13.52%	1985	27.79%
1963	5.14%	1986	21.24%
1964	28.85%	1987	3.11%
1965	22.14%	1988	23.60%
1966	−5.30%	1989	22.56%
1967	13.74%	1990	−9.06%
1968	37.76%	1991	31.33%
1969	19.66%	1992	4.21%
1970	−6.44%	1993	32.70%
1971	21.92%	1994	0.82%
1972	68.56%	1995	10.83%
1973	−9.92%	1996	20.55%
1974	−12.07%	1997	16.18%
1975	37.60%	1998	−2.48%
1976	46.74%	1999	30.44%
1977	20.38%	YTD 2000	−4.41
		as of 9/30	

area, was for Max a consistent source of profits. By buying the defaulted senior securities of an issuer at a big discount to liquidation value, the investor had very little risk and the potential for sizable returns. As Max got more comfortable with the defaulted credit, he would acquire more junior claims, such as subordinated or unsecured bonds.

Max also acquired the reorganized and newly minted equity of companies emerging from bankruptcy. These securities often traded very cheaply, since Wall Street tends to ignore the stock of a formally bankrupt entity. The financial community considered this stock tainted by the previous financial failure. In addition, the bankruptcy process is complicated and usually contentious and time-consuming. These factors created many opportunities over the years. Even when companies never successfully reorganized and their remaining assets liquidated, profits could be made.

Max was also interested in common stocks of companies that would be attractive takeover prospects. Often the spread between the takeover price and the market price provided an arbitrage profit. Once a deal was announced and there was a positive spread, Max would take advantage of the opportunity to invest profitably.

Michael F. Price

Into this intellectually fertile environment arrived Michael F. Price, who started working for Max Heine in the mid 1970s, while he was in his early twenties. Michael's timing was superb. The devastating 1973–1974 bear market that ravaged Wall Street was over and there were huge numbers of undervalued securities, many railroad bankruptcies, and numerous arbitrage opportunities from an active merger and acquisition environment. Together, Max Heine and Michael Price used this three-pronged approach in their Mutual Shares Fund: (See Table 7.4.)

1. *Undervalued stocks.* Mutual purchased shares of companies trading at a substantial discount to intrinsic value. Analysis determined a catalyst for unlocking of true value. At times Mutual was willing to be the catalyst through shareholder activism.

2. *Arbitrage.* Mutual participated in announced tender offers and takeover bids and spin-offs. Arbitrage is a profitable way to invest cash and make the managers smarter about what businesses are truly worth, helping the process of evaluating undervalued securities.

3. *Bankruptcies.*

Michael had several insights that expanded on Max's proven methods. In the 1970s, Michael realized that buying bank claims was another way to

TABLE 7.4 Performance Chart—Mutual Shares Fund—Class A

1950	N/A	1976	52.73%
1951	N/A	1977	17.83%
1952	N/A	1978	14.76%
1953	N/A	1979	40.48%
1954	N/A	1980	15.03%
1955	N/A	1981	11.83%
1956	N/A	1982	15.45%
1957	N/A	1983	35.50%
1958	N/A	1984	13.84%
1959	N/A	1985	28.65%
1960	N/A	1986	16.29%
1961	N/A	1987	16.41%
1962	N/A	1988	30.69%
1963	N/A	1989	14.93%
1964	N/A	1990	–9.82%
1965	N/A	1991	20.99%
1966	N/A	1992	21.32%
1967	32.21%	1993	20.99%
1968	39.88%	1994	4.55%
1969	–19.24%	1995	29.11%
1970	–8.72%	1996	20.76%
1971	22.28%	1997	26.38%
1972	–1.15%	1998	0.45%
1973	–7.47%	1999	15.00%
1974	9.25%	YTD 2000	8.36%
1975	26.81%	as of 9/30	

participate in the bankruptcy arena. As these claims were not liquid and the market for trading claims was embryonic, a wonderfully inefficient pricing environment existed. Like Max, by buying senior and then, as comfort and research dictated, more junior claims, Michael was able to accumulate sizable positions in securities at huge discounts to intrinsic and ultimately realizable value. Mutual Shares was one of the few public mutual funds where investors could participate in this arcane and specialized area.

Michael's second insight was that it was possible for investors to assert control over companies in bankruptcy. This maneuver was achieved several times with favorable results. Having learned to exert influence through the bankruptcy process, Michael had his third and probably most well-known insight: He could influence the decisions of management of nonbankrupt companies.

By accumulating over 5% of the equity of a corporation and filing a document called a 13D with the Securities and Exchange Commission, he could legally help shape events. Although many other investors have been activists, Michael took the process to the level of an art form. In the 13D, Michael would suggest how management could surface value. After the filing and the usual media attention, Michael would keep up the pressure on management to perform. Often these tactics were quite successful.

A Share of a Great Business

Warren Buffett

Warren Buffett was one of Ben Graham's best students, and Graham invited him to work at his investment company, Graham Newman. When Graham closed this company in 1956, Buffett returned home to Omaha and founded a partnership that utilized his mentor's investment principles. The outstanding record Buffett assembled in the next 13 years established him as one of the investment greats.

During those years, Buffett Partnership acquired control of a bargain-priced security called Berkshire Hathaway, a New England–based textile firm. The shares were selling at a statistically cheap price. Buffett redeployed capital from the textile business into more profitable ventures.

In 1967, Buffett's company acquired National Indemnity, a Nebraska-based property and casualty insurer. Most insurance companies lose money in their basic insurance business, but earn profits from investing the policy premiums in a portfolio of bonds. Buffett's insight was that if the insurance company had disciplined underwriting standards that produced a profit in the insurance business, a steady flow of investment capital could be acquired at effectively zero cost. By making more astute investments, substantial profits could be made. This model was superior to typical investment companies, where cash tends to flow in when security prices are rising and flow out when prices decline. Value investors seek just the opposite—increasing investment purchases as prices decline. Thus, Buffett designed a cash flow engine to help drive Berkshire Hathaway.

Charlie Munger, Buffett's friend and later partner, influenced the development of the second great insight. Munger realized that investing in a small number of businesses with excellent fundamental economics would produce superior long-term results. Holding these select stocks over the long term would enable their investments to compound tax free. Munger helped Buffett gravitate toward these better businesses. It was worth paying more for a business enterprise if the long-term economics were so favorable that the shares would never need to be sold.*

Looking Ahead

Bill Miller

Bill Miller has produced one of the best investment records of the 1990s. Miller is an innovative thinker who has expanded the definition of bargain purchases. He has developed a thought process called a complex adaptive system, which attempts to dissect the various agents that contribute to a market. This method analyzes multiple factors, including the underlying economics of the business and the behavioral characteristics of the players, in order to test the viability of the business model and calculate its value. Miller can use this method to identify large inefficiencies in security pricing. Unlike many value investors, Miller has been able to identify fabulous technology opportunities.

Summary

All of the investors described were/are firmly rooted in the value investing approach, each having found a path to fit his personality. Benjamin Graham is revered for his teachings, writings, and investment results. The philosophy of value investing has the flexibility to accommodate a spectrum of interpretations. There are many paths to investment nirvana, and value investing provides many important tools to navigate the securities markets.

---

*Editor's note: Buffett's investment technique is discussed in more detail in the next chapter.

This brief description does not pretend to be a comprehensive overview but rather a summary along an evolving road of achievement. Most value investors have elements of each of the camps described. Also consistent is the notion that cheapness is a virtue. For most individuals, acquiring securities or other material items would not necessarily be dictated by purchase at the lowest price. For value investors bargain purchases are the passion. One can picture several value investors talking about who has identified the most undervalued security. For value investors their hallmark is low risk and high returns over time. It is also key to the principles of margin of safety and doing thorough work. Geoffrey Scott, a Canadian value investor, likes to quote the old maximum "Well bought is half sold."

My Philosophy

Having grown up at Mutual Series Fund, Inc., and been a part of the success of the organization over the years, I am a true believer in the approach that Max Heine and Michael Price developed. Their lessons have been ingrained in my investment approach. I carefully examine the underlying economics of the company. Often a winning long-term strategy has been to pay slightly more for a better-quality business (i.e., a company that has favorable economic fundamentals.) Companies with good business characteristics, such as the ability over time to increase business values, are more likely to be rewarding than are companies whose securities are merely cheap. The accretion of asset value also provides greater downside protection when markets or overall conditions hit a rough patch.

The other major lesson I have learned is to pay careful attention to the management—their motivations, integrity, and level of commitment to all shareholders. Essentially, when investing in a company, you are handing your wallet to that particular management team. The possible outcomes are (1) your wallet never comes back (very bad); (2) your wallet comes back with little difference in the cash in the billfold (not good, and the time value of money works against you); or (3) your wallet comes back with *much* more cash: the *best* outcome. Ultimately, management does matter a lot, and how managers behave will largely determine the outcome for investors.

Purchasing securities in a good business that is trading at a material discount to intrinsic value and has an honest, motivated management team is a solid way to make money in the long run. I have also described this approach as acquiring quality at a discount. Over time, the relationship with management usually becomes strong. Mutual has had the ability to make suggestions to improve operations or corporate structure, which often results in higher valuations for all holders. Many companies have come to view us as productive and positive investors who think as owners and act in a responsible manner to surface values for all shareholders.

Other Stock Selection Strategies

Robert Arffa

Introduction

In this section I would like to review some specific investment strategies. We will start with two of the most successful investors of recent times, Warren Buffett and Peter Lynch. Their styles differ, but I think that in each case we can learn from that perspective. Then we will proceed to some other stock selection methods that have been used with good results.

A key caution: Do not take these descriptions as endorsements of the techniques. Although they have worked in the past, as applied by specific investors, there is no guarantee that they will work in the future.

Warren Buffett: Investing from a Business Perspective

Warren Buffett is one of the most successful investors in the United States. He is director and largest stockholder in Berkshire Hathaway, Inc. Buffett owns

42% of the company. Since Buffett took control of Berkshire in 1965, the value of the corporation has grown from $22 million to over $20 billion. Between 1965 and 1997 the annual compound return of his investments was 23.8%. Warren Buffett is the only billionaire who has made his money solely by investing in the stock market.

Berkshire Hathaway is a holding company. It owns insurance companies, newspapers (including the *Washington Post*), Borsheim's Jewelry Company, Dexter Shoes, a large share of Coca-Cola, and many other companies.

Unfortunately, Warren Buffett has never written a book describing his investment style. However, he has made his philosophy clear, and various authors have tried to summarize his investment approach so that other investors can attempt to emulate it. For example, Robert G. Hagstrom Jr. has been writing about Warren Buffett since 1984; in 1994 he wrote *The Warren Buffett Way: Investment Strategies of the World's Greatest Investor.*[1] Former daughter-in-law Mary Buffett and David Clark wrote *Buffettology: The Previously Unexplained Techniques That Have Made Warren Buffett the World's Most Famous Investor.*[2]

There were two main influences on Buffett's investment style, Benjamin Graham and Philip Fisher. Graham ran an investment firm and taught at Columbia University in New York. With another professor at Columbia, David Dodd, he wrote two of the classic texts on investing, *Security Analysis* and *The Intelligent Investor.* He championed a relatively conservative value investment style that emphasized purchasing companies with promising earnings for less than their net asset value. This would provide a margin of safety against loss due to unforeseen events. He based his decisions on quantitative analysis of the financial statements, material that could be obtained by any investor.

Graham stressed the difference between investment and speculation. Investments, after thorough analysis, promise relative safety of principal and a satisfactory return. Any operation not meeting these requirements would be speculation. The speculator tries to anticipate and profit from price changes rather than seeking to acquire good companies at reasonable prices.

Philip Fisher emphasized a company's ability to grow sales and profits. He looked for companies with above-average growth potential, capable management, commitment to research and development, a capable sales organization, and a high profit margin. Unlike Graham, he used these more qualitative analyses and would conduct extensive interviews with the company and its competitors. Also, while Graham saw security in diversification, Fisher preferred to concentrate on only a few well-understood stocks.

In 1969 Buffett said, "I'm 15 percent Fisher and 85 percent Benjamin Graham."[3] He combines Graham's quantitative analysis of a company's finances with Fisher's qualitative understanding of the company's management and prospects. Like Graham, he tries to purchase shares of a company when they are at a significant discount to the value of the underlying business. Like Fisher, he investigates all aspects of the company and its competitors. He gets to know the management, and uses an extensive network of contacts to learn about the business and its competitors. Also like Fisher, he does not stress diversification. According to Mary Buffett and David Clark, other influences include: Lawrence Bloomberg, John Burr Williams, John Maynard Keynes, Edgar Smaith, and Charlie Munger (Warren Buffett's partner).

The main principle of Warren Buffett's investment style is to purchase good companies at reasonable prices. He does not attempt to predict the direction of the stock market or to anticipate the movement of a company's share price. He buys businesses, not pieces of paper. Buffett says that Graham's statement "Investing is most intelligent when it is most businesslike" represents the "nine most important words ever written about investing." No one would buy a business without analyzing the books. Those who buy a stock without understanding the company's operations are speculating, not investing.

If Buffett purchases a good company at a discount, the underlying business will continue to grow, probably at a rate greater than average, and sooner or later other investors will come to realize the true value of the company's shares. He has said, "As far as I'm concerned, the stock market doesn't exist. It is there only as a reference to see if anybody is offering to do anything foolish."[4] The stock market exists merely to serve you in buying and selling your interests. Think of the economics of ownership of the companies, not the movement of the price of shares. He follows the operations of the companies in which he owns stock very closely, but pays little heed to the current stock prices. In the short run prices fluctuate widely above and below a company's par value, but in the long run the price of a stock should approximate the value of the business.

How to Select a Business

Buffett first discovers what businesses he would like to buy, then he waits for them to be available at the right price. The business should be simple and understandable. If you don't understand the properties of its products, the market for them, and its competition, you can't intelligently assess its prospects.

You should understand all aspects of the business, including:

- Sources of revenue, including products and services
- Costs of producing these products and services (e.g., raw materials)
- Cash flow
- Competition

■ Pricing flexibility

■ Inventories

■ Receivables

■ Working capital needs

■ Research and development spending

■ Debt

■ Future capital needs

The company should have a history of successful operations. It has to demonstrate the ability to earn significant profits over an extended period. An interruption in this pattern is not a reason to ignore the company, but may instead be an opportunity to purchase a good business at a bargain price. However, avoid purchasing companies that are solving difficult business problems or making fundamental changes. These increase the risk of major mistakes.

Optimally, you want to choose a business that sells a product or service that is needed and is unique or consumable (including provision of repetitive services). This type of company (called a consumer monopoly) can better withstand economic and competitive pressures. It is free to raise prices and generally earns a high rate of return on invested capital. Buffett has a test to identify a consumer monopoly. He asks himself whether, if he had access to billions of dollars and the best managers, he could start a business and successfully compete with the business in question. Financially, these companies are characterized by strong increasing earnings, low debt, high return on equity (ROE), retention of earnings (rather than paying them as dividends), and a low cost of maintaining current operations (replacement of plant and equipment, research and development of new products).

By contrast, a commodity business is one whose products or services are indistinguishable from those of its competitors. Examples are producers of raw foodstuffs, lumber, steel, paper, and textiles. Commodity businesses earn above-average returns only if their price is lower or their service better than that of their competitors. They are much more susceptible to problems such as errors in management or below-cost selling by competitors. Financially these companies are characterized by low profit margins, low ROE, and erratic profits. There is an absence of brand-name loyalty, and there are multiple producers of the product(s) and substantial excess production capacity in the industry. Profits depend on management's ability to efficiently use tangible assets.

Businesses lie on a continuum between these two extremes, with a small percentage of them being true franchises. However, even a weak franchise has more favorable long-term prospects than a strong commodity business.

Management

Evaluating the ability of management is difficult, and largely subjective. The most important decision made by management is how to allocate its capital: What does the management do with its excess cash earnings? Good managers invest cash in projects that produce earnings at rates higher than the cost of capital. If the management reinvests cash in the company, the profits on this investment should at least equal those it could get by investing elsewhere, such as in government bonds.

Another option for managers is to buy a business, in either the same or a different industry. You should be skeptical of such a purchase. Often the price paid is too high, and management is more likely to make mistakes operating a new business, particularly if is not in the same industry. "Management should view its function as increasing shareholder wealth, not fiefdom building."[5]

If they cannot find a good internal opportunity to reinvest their cash, they should buy back shares of stock, or, less desirably, return it to shareholders as dividends. Buffett prefers to own non–dividend-paying stocks to reduce tax payments and maximize total return—profits reinvested in the business grow tax-deferred.

Good managers are candid with their shareholders. They provide ample, understandable information about all aspects of their businesses. They should admit their failures and describe corrective actions as well as how they will avoid making the same mistake in the future. Managers who mislead shareholders or are overly optimistic in their reports do shareholders a disservice.

On the other hand, no matter how good management is, it cannot turn around a business that is fundamentally unsound. That leads us to the next section on assessing the financial prospects of a business.

Finances

The best quantitative measures of company performance and managerial expertise are return on equity, operating margins, and cash flow. Cash flow generated in profits is the most important determinant of the value of a business. Cash flows are not all valued equally—businesses that require a lot of fixed assets in order to operate will require a larger portion of their earnings to reinvest in upgrading those assets in order to stay competitive. Thus less of the earnings in high-fixed-asset businesses is available for growth investment or to return to shareholders.

Earnings figures should be corrected to more accurately reflect the business's cash-generating ability. Buffett calls these corrected figures "owner earnings" and calculates them as follows: To net income add depreciation, depletion, and amortization charges; then subtract the capital expenditures needed to maintain the company's economic position and unit volume.

Another way that earnings per share can be misleading is if the equity base is changing. Many companies retain a portion of the previous year's earnings in order to increase their equity base. If earnings are increasing, but equity is increasing at the same rate, the company is not performing better. This is part of the reason why Buffett emphasizes ROE over earnings per share. You will recall that ROE is the ratio of operating earnings to shareholders' equity. In the case just mentioned, while earnings per share increase, the rate of ROE remains the same.

In order to properly calculate ROE, the value of securities should be what it was at the beginning of the year, excluding all capital gains and losses and excluding all extraordinary items. The company should be able to achieve a good ROE without increasing its debt-to-equity ratio. The debt-to-equity ratio should be comparable to those of other companies in the same business.

Another important financial measure of a business is the profit margin. A company must be able to convert sales into profits. High profit margins indicate that the managers are running a tight ship and controlling spending, and that they are able to demand a good price for their products or services.

"It is our job to select a business with economic characteristics allowing each dollar of retained earnings to be translated eventually into at least a dollar of market value."[6] The market may not reward the company in the short term, but over time, if a company has been able to achieve above-average return on equity, it will be reflected in increased stock price.

Determining the Value of a Business

Irrespective of whether a business grows or doesn't, displays volatility or smoothness in earnings, or carries a high price or low in relation to its current earnings and book value, the investment shown by the discounted-flows-of-cash calculation to be the cheapest is the one that the investor should purchase."[7]

The value of a business is determined by the current value of the expected net cash flow over the life of the business. In order to perform this calculation you must be able to make a reasonable projection of the future cash flow of the business. Buffett will not purchase a company unless he is able to project future cash flow with confidence. This requires the business to be one that is relatively simple and understandable, and the company must have a consistent history and a fairly predictable future. For Buffett, this excludes many industries, such as high technology.

The price you pay for a company also determines your annual rate of return. With the use of a financial calculator and accounting formulas, you can calculate the present value of the future cash flow. You must select an appropriate interest rate to determine the current value of future cash flow. Buffett uses the rate of the long-term U.S. government bond.

If a company consistently earns 15% on equity, its shares will appreciate more than those of a company that earns 10% on equity. In addition, Buffett purchases the business only when its price is significantly less than its value. This creates the margin of safety that protects him from unforeseen changes in cash flow. If the value of the business is as predicted, Buffett will earn an extra bonus when the market corrects share price to more accurately reflect the price of the business.

Portfolio

A business owner does not need to be highly diversified; you do not need to include businesses from each of the major industries. You only need to select the best businesses available. Owning portions of 5 to 10 businesses should be sufficient. You do not sell businesses just to make a profit; you sell them only if their long-term earnings prospects deteriorate or you find a company with better earnings potential.

Buffett measures the progress of his businesses by calculating the total earnings: For each company multiply earnings per share by the number of shares you own. His goal is to create the portfolio of companies that will produce the highest level of total earnings over time.

Summary

Can the average investor emulate Buffett's style? Probably not. As simple as this sounds, it is very difficult to do. You must be independent and confident enough to be convinced that the majority of investors are wrong about a company. You must be able to ignore short-term concerns about the economy, interest rates, or the particular business sector. You must also spend the time to learn how a company operates, to study the financial reports, and to determine the prospects and value of a company. You must do this for many companies, until you find a few that you can purchase at an attractive price.

Peter Lynch: Beating the Street

Peter Lynch was called the nation's #1 money manager by *Time* magazine. He managed Fidelity's Magellan Fund from 1977 to 1990. During his tenure an investment of $10,000 grew to $280,000, and the Magellan Fund grew from

$18 million to $14 billion in assets, the largest fund in the country. Mr. Lynch described his investment philosophy in two books he coauthored with John Rothchild, *One Up on Wall Street* and *Beating the Street*. He also writes a regular column for *Worth* magazine.

Finding Potential Winners

Mr. Lynch believes strongly that individual investors not only can do as well as professional managers, they can do better. The average investor has an edge over the professionals. While most professionals live in isolation on Wall Street and have no business experience other than in the investment world, we have personal knowledge of companies in our neighborhoods and workplaces. Through our work, purchases, families, and friends we are constantly exposed to companies and their products. This occurs in every industry and in every region of the country. Lynch estimates that the average person comes across a likely investment prospect two or three times a year. Individuals can learn of new companies and products months or even years before the general public or Wall Street.

Potential investment leads include: new products selling well, a new medicine, change in business at an old store (chain), and learning of a company's hidden or undervalued assets. For example, an alert shopper would have noticed the success of discount clubs such as Costco, Wholesale Club, and Pace in the early 1980s, and an investment would have grown two- to threefold before the Wall Street analysts even started following these companies. Lynch discovered Hanes because his wife was crazy about L'eggs; his daughter Mary led him (literally) to the Body Shop, to buy banana bath oil.

"If you like the store, chances are you'll love the stock."[9]

Lynch never had a system or overall strategy.

My stockpicking was entirely empirical, and I went sniffing from one case to another like a bloodhound that's trained to follow a scent. I cared much more about the details of a particular story—for instance, why a company that owned TV stations was going to earn more money this year than last—than about whether my fund was under-weighted or over-weighted in broadcasting. What could happen is that I would meet with one broadcaster who would tell me that business was improving, and then he'd give me the name of his strongest competitor, and I'd check out the details, and often end up buying the second broadcaster's stock. I followed scents in every direction."[10]

Lynch constantly searched for better opportunities. If he found a company that was more undervalued than one he already owned, he'd make the switch.

Professional investors tend to act with a herd mentality. They are reluctant to stick their necks out by investing in relatively unknown companies or companies out of favor with the crowd. Some are even restricted to large, well-known companies by their directors. Therefore, if you can be an independent thinker, you can beat the market. Avoid the hot stocks in hot industries. Rather, find great companies in cold, nongrowth industries.

Focus on the companies, not the stocks. The key to making money is to own successful companies. It's even better if you can purchase the company's stock when it is relatively underpriced. Often there is no correlation between the success of a company's operations and the price of its stock over the short term—a few months or even a few years. However, over the long term there is a very high degree of correlation between the success of the company and the rise of its stock. The converse is that you should sell a stock when the company's fundamentals deteriorate, no matter what the market or economy is doing.

Selecting the Winners

Getting the lead is just the beginning. You then have to analyze the company, its market, and its competitors in order to determine whether it's a good investment. You also have to decide what effect your discovered product or asset will have on the company's bottom line. For example, a huge jump in sales of a new product will have little effect on the value of a giant company like Procter & Gamble. You have much more growth potential with new products of smaller companies.

Early in his evaluation Peter Lynch places the company into one of six general categories:

- *Slow growers*: large, aging companies, which tend to grow at 2% to 4% a year.

- *Stalwarts (medium growers)*: large companies exhibiting 10% to 12% annual growth.

- *Fast growers*: small, aggressive new enterprises that typically grow at 20% to 25% per year.

- *Cyclicals*: large companies whose sales and profits rise and fall at regular intervals.

- *Asset plays*: companies with assets that Wall Street hasn't noticed.

- *Turnarounds:* failing companies, possibly in bankruptcy; may turn around or disappear.

The companies in each category should be judged differently. The only point in purchasing a slow grower is for the dividends. Therefore, you should make sure that the dividends have been paid consistently in the past. Also, the lower the percentage of earnings that the dividends represent, the more likely that the company can maintain the dividend payments.

You can make a decent profit (30% to 50%) in a stalwart if you can buy it at the right price. They also offer some protection during down markets. Money can be made in cyclicals, but you have to be able to detect upswings and downswings early. You might have an edge if you work in a profession that's related to one of these industries, such as automobiles or aluminum. Also keep an eye on inventories and other indicators of the relationship between supply and demand. Earnings tend to peak and the P/E multiple tends to shrink as a company reaches the end of its cycle.

Asset plays are companies with assets that other analysts either are not aware of or underestimate their value.

Turnarounds can be very productive, but successful investing requires a very careful analysis of the company's finances and business prospects. You must make sure that the company will have enough cash on hand and cash flow to pay off its creditors and meet its long-term debt obligations. How is the company going to turn around its earnings (e.g., rid itself of unprofitable divisions, increase sales, cut costs)?

Fast growers have the most potential for high returns, but also entail significant risks, including bankruptcy. The company should already be profitable. Ideal growth companies have annual increases in earnings in the 20% to 25% range. Peter Lynch is wary of companies that seem to be growing faster than 25%.

Fast-growing companies do not have to be in a fast-growing industry—in fact, it's probably better if the company is in a nongrowth industry. Such companies should have a new product or service and room to expand within the industry. Make sure that the company has already demonstrated that it can be successful in more than one city, to prove that expansion can work, and that there are ample markets to expand into. Expansion should be accelerating rather than decelerating.

FINANCIAL CHARACTERISTICS OF GOOD COMPANIES

- P/E ≤ growth rate.

- Consistent growth in earnings.

- Increasing cash (cash plus marketable securities).

- Cash > long-term debt.

- Buying back shares (number of shares outstanding decreasing year to year).

- <10% debt/equity.

- High profit margin for a long-term holding; low profit margin for a turnaround.
- Financial strength rating of at least "B" by Value Line.

OTHER FAVORABLE ATTRIBUTES

- The company has a lack of competition; a niche.
- The business is simple to understand.
- The business is dull or disagreeable.
- The company has a dull or odd name.
- It is a spin-off of a large parent company.
- It is relatively unknown: low institutional ownership, not followed by analysts.
- Its products are considered essentials, bought in good times and bad.
- It uses and benefits from advancements in technology.
- Insiders are buying stock.
- Management has significant personal investment.

REASONS TO AVOID STOCKS

- It is a hot stock in hot industry.
- It has an exciting name.
- It's "the next _____" (e.g., the next IBM).
- The company is acquiring companies in unrelated industries.
- It's a "whisper" stock—a long shot related to you in a low voice at a cocktail party.
- The company is a middleman or supplier dependent on a few large corporate customers.

Lynch would review all the financial statements; talk with analysts, other fund managers, and investor relations representatives; visit the corporate headquarters and speak with directors; talk to competitors; and visit sites of retail operations. Although the average investor does not have the resources and access that Peter Lynch has, it is possible to obtain most of the same information.

You must make sure that the company is in good financial condition. If you aren't able to understand the balance sheets, read an expert evaluation, such as in Value Line or Standard & Poor's. You can call the company to obtain specific information. You can visit the headquarters, particularly if it's in the neighborhood. The shabbier it looks, the better. Check out the company's product: Visit the store or restaurant; purchase the product; take their cars for a test-drive.

A Few Pointers

There is no quicker way to tell if a large growth stock is overvalued, undervalued, or fairly priced than by looking at a chart book. Buy shares when the stock price is at or below the earnings line, and not when the price line diverges into the danger zone, way above the earnings line."[11]

For a retail company or a restaurant chain, the earnings growth that propels the stock price comes mainly from expansion. Make sure that there is plenty of room for expansion, same-store sales are on the increase, the company is not crippled by excessive debt, and it is following its expansion plans as described to shareholders.

"If you're prepared to invest in a company, then you ought to be able to explain why in simple language that a fifth grader could understand, and quickly enough so the fifth grader won't get bored."[12] You have to develop a mental story about the company that explains why someone should buy the stock. Your story should include what will make the company succeed, and what pitfalls it will have to overcome along the way.

"Searching for companies is like looking for grubs under rocks: if you turn over 10 rocks you'll likely find one grub; if you turn over 20 rocks you'll find two. [Between 1986 and 1990] I had to turn over thousands of rocks a year to find enough new grubs to add to Magellan's outsize collection."[13]

There tend to be more buying opportunities between October and December.

Following the Company

You should reevaluate the company story every few months. Read the quarterly reports and/or read the evaluation by Standard & Poor's. Ignore doomsayers, brokers, and so-called experts. Convince yourself that a price drop in a good stock is a buying opportunity, not a time to sell.

Sell when the story changes or when you find a better opportunity. If the reasons you bought the company no longer apply, sell. As discussed earlier, the reasons for purchasing stocks vary with the category the stock falls into, so the reasons for selling will vary as well.

For example, consider selling a fast grower if:

- Everyone's touting the stock and institutions own a large portion of shares.

- The P/E is growing to an absurd level.

- The room for expansion is rapidly shrinking.

■ Same-store and new-store sales are down.

Consider selling a stalwart if:

■ New products have had mixed results, and there do not appear to be good new products coming out in the next year.

■ The company's P/E is 25% higher than those of similar-quality companies in the same industry.

■ No officers or directors have bought shares in the past year.

■ Sales have been slowing, even if profits have been maintained by cutting costs.

Portfolio

The part-time stock picker doesn't need to find 50 or 100 winning stocks. He or she probably has time to follow eight to 12 companies, buying and selling shares as conditions warrant. You don't have to own more than five companies at any one time. It takes only a couple of big winners in a decade to make the effort worthwhile.

Dogs of the Dow (and Variations)

This technique has gained recent popularity, partially because it is very easy to follow, and the historical results have been excellent. It has been championed by Michael O'Higgins, a money manager who described the technique in his book *Beating the Dow*,[15] and Tom and David Gardner, better known as the Motley Fool.

The major tenets of this theory are that:

■ The 30 Dow industrial stocks are so large and financially strong that, no matter what bad news befalls them, they will survive and eventually recover.

■ The investing public typically overreacts to unfavorable developments and undervalues securities, even these giant blue chips.

■ By investing in bargain-priced, out-of-favor Dow stocks, your returns can greatly exceed those of the Dow Jones Industrial Average (DJIA).

■ You can identify the out-of-favor Dow stocks by their higher yield and lower price. Generally the dividend remains stable, but the price has been reduced, so that the ratio of dividend to price (yield) is increased. Overall, the lower-priced Dow stocks have exhibited greater percentage price appreciation than higher-priced Dow stocks.

Stock Selection

The basic technique is very simple. You find the prices and yields of the 30 Dow industrial stocks. These can be obtained from the *Wall Street Journal*, the *New York Times*, *Investor's Business Daily*, or any other paper with a comprehensive financial section. You can also obtain a listing from Dow Jones & Co. (http://averages.dowjones.com/home.html).

Find the 10 highest-yielding stocks. If there is a tie, take the stock with the lower price. Of these 10 stocks, select the five with the lowest prices. Buy equal dollar amounts of the five stocks. After one year, repeat the calculations and change your portfolio accordingly. Sell any stocks no longer on the list, and use the funds to purchase the new "dogs."

Results

Between January 1973 and June 1991 the DJIA rose 559.31%. Over the same period investing in the five lowest-priced/highest-yield stocks, as described, returned 2,819.41%, excluding commissions and taxes. This portfolio outperformed the DJIA in 14 of the 18 years. (See Table 8.1.)

Variations

You can purchase all 10 of the highest-yielding Dow stocks. Although the average annual return was lower (Table 8.1), the returns were generally better than the five lowest-priced/highest-yield stocks in years the DJIA decreased.

The lowest-priced of the 10 highest-yield Dow stocks tends to perform poorly. It tends to be a company with more significant financial problems. The next-to-lowest-priced stock, however, tends to be the best performer. Between January 1973 and June 1991, annual investments in these stocks returned 6,245% compared to the DJIA's 559.31%. Therefore, if you are not afraid of putting all your eggs in one basket, you could invest the entire amount in only this stock.

Another variation, based on this finding, is to omit the lowest-priced of the five lowest-priced/highest-yield stocks, and to double the amount invested in the next-to-lowest-priced stock. This method was publicized by the Motley Fool web site.

You could use a more traditional measure of value, the price-to-book value ratio. If you had selected the 10 stocks with the lowest price-to-book value ratios each year, the return would have been 1,283.39%.

Comments

This strategy is certainly easy to follow. You don't even have to do the calculations yourself. The Motley Fool lists 10 highest-yielding Dow stocks and

TABLE 8.1 Performance History of Dogs of the
Dow Strategy, 1961–1999

	Dogs of the Dow	DJIA
1961	27.13%	22.74%
1962	– 2.13%	– 7.25%
1963	18.34%	22.98%
1964	26.66%	17.94%
1965	16.38%	17.31%
1966	–18.46%	–15.08%
1967	34.18%	21.80%
1968	10.52%	10.06%
1969	– 8.25%	– 9.27%
1970	– 8.93%	5.06%
1971	11.41%	9.06%
1972	22.18%	16.72%
1973	318.98%	–10.86%
1974	– 3.37%	–15.64%
1975	63.09%	44.24%
1976	38.54%	29.37%
1977	2.21%	–12.56%
1978	4.11%	2.50%
1979	14.75%	11.34%
1980	45.39%	25.30%
1981	– 1.26%	– 3.26%
1982	26.96%	19.53%
1983	36.77%	35.58%
1984	11.00%	– 0.12%
1985	39.71%	30.98%
1986	24.06%	21.87%
1987	11.08%	15.74%
1988	14.48%	13.70%

TABLE 8.1 Continued		
	Dogs of the Dow	DJIA
1989	12.33%	31.95%
1990	−17.34%	− 9.14%
1991	59.14%	30.36%
1992	20.19%	11.04%
1993	30.49%	17.91%
1994	6.10%	3.70%
1995	30.13%	36.69%
1996	26.62%	24.32%
1997	17.70%	22.33%
1998	12.49%	15.95%
1999	− 7.60%	20.57%
Worst:	−18.46%	−27.57%
39-Year Performance Measures (1961–1999)		
Average Return[1]	15.61%	12.39%
Standard Deviation[2]	0.1876	0.1553
Sharpe Ratio[3]	0.5830	0.4690
25-Year Performance Measures (1975–1999)		
Average Return[1]	19.36%	16.68%
Standard Deviation[2]	0.1943	0.1463
Sharpe Ratio[3]	0.7160	0.7167

Note: Returns are based on stocks chosen the first trading day of the year and sold the first trading day of the following year. Returns include dividends, and are adjusted for splits, spin-offs, and so on to reflect as closely as possible the returns an investor would have received from following the strategy at that time.

[1]The average return quoted here is *not* the arithmetic average (mean). It is the compound average growth rate (CAGR).

[2]The higher the standard deviation, the more volatile the strategy.

[3]The Sharpe ratio combines the average return with the standard deviation. A higher Sharpe ratio means the strategy has provided better risk-adjusted returns.

their prices daily. You can also purchase mutual funds that invest according to this strategy.

Historically, the returns were excellent, but more recently they have been disappointing. Since the prices of the Dow stocks vary daily, so will their yield and price rankings. Different stocks will be included in the portfolio depending on which day you invest, and the difference in returns can be substantial. In addition, since you are selling most of the stocks annually, taxable accounts will incur capital gains taxes annually.

Private Information

The most certain way of gaining advantage over the market is by having information not available to the public. That is why such information, in many cases, is illegal to use. For example, if you are involved in a merger or acquisition, either as an employee of one of the parties involved or acting as an agent for one of them, it is illegal for you to profit from your knowledge or to give information to others so that they may profit.

However, under many circumstances you may gain knowledge about a company or product that the investing community either is not aware of or does not understand the implications of. As a physician, I am aware of research on new products, not only in my field, but also through colleagues in other disciplines. I can appreciate, better than other investors, the potential for these products, and the odds that new developments will come to fruition. For new products that are released I may better perceive the market prospects.

Similar advantages accrue to anyone with expertise in a discipline or a segment of the marketplace. A clerk in a department store can see which products are selling.

As discussed in the section on Peter Lynch, this information is usually not sufficient. You must also investigate the company. How much will this new product affect its bottom line? What other products does the company sell? What is the financial condition of the company now?

After your investigation, you can estimate the risks and potential benefits of your investment, and then you can decide what portion of your portfolio you are willing to risk.

Notes

1. John Wiley & Sons, New York.
2. Rawson Associates, New York, 1997.
3. *Forbes*, November 1, 1969, p. 82.

4. Quoted in Peter Lynch, *One Up on Wall Street*, New York: Simon & Schuster, 1989, p. 78.
5. *Buffettology*, p. 137
6. Warren Buffett, "Berkshire Hathaway Letters to Shareholders, 1977–1983," p. 53.
7. Berkshire Hathaway annual report, 1992, p. 14.
8. Simon & Schuster, New York, 1981 and 1993.
9. *Beating the Street.*
10. Ibid., p. 87.
11. *Beating the Street*, p. 147
12. Ibid.
13. Ibid., p. 141
14. McGraw-Hill, New York.
15. Michael O'Higgins and John Downes, *Beating the Dow*, New York: HarperCollins, 1991.

The Efficient Markets Hypothesis

Jonathan Clarke, Tomas Jandik, and Gershon Mandelker

The efficient markets hypothesis (EMH), popularly known as the random walk theory, is the proposition that current stock prices fully reflect available information about the value of the firm, and there is no way to earn excess profits (more than the market overall) by using this information. It deals with one of the most fundamental and exciting issues in finance—why prices change in security markets and how those changes take place. It has very important implications for investors as well as for financial managers. The first use of the term "efficient market" was in a 1965 paper by E. F. Fama, who said that in an efficient market, on the average, competition will cause the full effects of new information on intrinsic values to be reflected "instantaneously" in actual prices.

Many investors try to identify securities that are undervalued and are expected to increase in value in the future, and particularly those that will increase more than others. For example, investment managers believe that they *can* select securities that will outperform the market. They use a variety of forecasting and valuation techniques to aid them in their investment decisions. Obviously, any edge that an investor possesses can be translated into substantial profits. If a manager of a mutual fund with $10 billion in assets can increase the fund's return, after transaction costs, by one-tenth of 1%, this would result in a $10 million gain. The EMH asserts that none of these techniques are effective (i.e., the advantage gained does not exceed the transaction and research costs incurred), and therefore no one can predictably outperform the market.

Arguably, no other theory in economics or finance generates more passionate discussion between its challengers and proponents. For example, noted Harvard financial economist Michael Jensen writes, "There is no other proposition in economics which has more solid empirical evidence supporting it than the efficient market hypothesis,"[1] while investment maven Peter Lynch claims, "Efficient markets? That's a bunch of junk, crazy stuff" (*Fortune*, April 1995).

The efficient markets hypothesis (EMH) suggests that profiting from predicting price movements is very difficult and unlikely. The main engine behind price changes is the arrival of new information. A market is said to be "efficient" if prices adjust quickly and, on average, without bias to new information. As a result, the current prices of securities reflect all available information at any given point in time. Consequently, there is no reason to believe that prices are too high or too low. Security prices adjust before an investor has time to trade on and profit from a new a piece of information.

The key reason for the existence of an efficient market is the intense competition among investors to profit from any new information. The ability to identify over- and underpriced stocks is very valuable (it would allow investors to buy some stocks for less than their "true" value and sell others for more than they were worth). Consequently, many people spend a significant amount of time and resources in an effort to detect mispriced stocks. Naturally, as more and more analysts compete against each other in their effort to take advantage of over- and undervalued securities, the likelihood of being able to find and exploit such mispriced securities becomes smaller and smaller. In equilibrium, only a relatively small number of analysts will be able to profit from the detection of mispriced securities, mostly by chance. For the vast majority of investors, the information analysis payoff is not likely to outweigh the transaction costs.

The most crucial implication of the EMH can be put in the form of a slogan: *Trust market prices!* At any point in time, prices of securities in efficient markets reflect all known information available to investors. There is no room for fooling investors, and as a result, all investments in efficient markets are fairly priced; that is, on average investors get exactly what they pay for. Fair pricing of all securities does not mean that they will all perform similarly, or that even the likelihood of rising or falling in price is the same for all securities. According to capital markets theory, the expected return from a security is primarily a function of its risk. The price of the security reflects the present value of its expected future cash flows, which incorporates many factors such as volatility, liquidity, and risk of bankruptcy.

However, while prices are rationally based, changes in prices are expected to be random and unpredictable, because new information, by its very nature, is unpredictable. Therefore stock prices are said to follow a *random walk*.[2]

Three Versions of the Efficient Markets Hypothesis

The efficient markets hypothesis predicts that market prices should incorporate all available information at any point in time. There are, however, different *kinds* of information that influence security values. Consequently, financial researchers distinguish among three versions of the efficient markets hypothesis, depending on what is meant by the phrase "all available information."

Weak-Form Efficiency

The weak form of the efficient markets hypothesis asserts that the current price fully incorporates information contained in the *past history of prices*. That is, nobody can expect to be able to detect mispriced securities and beat the market by analyzing past prices. The weak form of the hypothesis got its name for a reason—security prices are arguably the most public as well as the most easily available pieces of information. Thus, one should not be able to profit from using something that "everybody else knows." On the other hand, many financial analysts attempt to generate profits by studying exactly what this hypothesis asserts is of no value—past stock price series and trading volume data. This technique is called technical analysis.

The empirical evidence for this form of market efficiency, and therefore against the value of technical analysis, is pretty strong and quite consistent. After taking into account transaction costs of analyzing and trading securities, it is very difficult to make money on publicly available information such as the past sequence of stock prices.

Semistrong-Form Efficiency

The semistrong form of the market efficiency hypothesis suggests that the current price fully incorporates *all publicly available* information. Public information includes not only past prices, but also data reported in a company's financial statements (annual reports, income statements, filings for the Securities and Exchange Commission, etc.); earnings and dividend announcements;

announced merger plans; the financial situation of the company's competitors; expectations regarding macroeconomic factors (such as inflation, unemployment); and so forth. In fact, the public information does not even have to be of a strictly financial nature. For example, for the analysis of pharmaceutical companies, the relevant public information may include the current (published) state of research in pain-relieving drugs.[3]

The assertion behind semistrong market efficiency is still that one should not be able to profit using something that "everybody else knows" (the information *is* public). Nevertheless, this assumption is far stronger than that of weak-form efficiency. Semistrong efficiency of markets requires the existence of market analysts who are not only financial economists able to comprehend implications of vast financial information, but also macroeconomists, experts adept at understanding processes in product and input markets. Acquisition of such skills must take a lot of time and effort. In addition, the public information may be relatively difficult to gather and costly to process. It may not be sufficient to gain the information from, say, major newspapers and company-produced publications. One may have to follow wire reports, professional publications and databases, local papers, research journals, and so on in order to gather all information necessary to effectively analyze securities.

As we will see later, financial researchers have found empirical evidence that is overwhelmingly consistent with the semistrong form of the EMH.

Strong-Form Efficiency

The strong form of the market efficiency hypothesis states that the current price fully incorporates *all* existing information, both public and private (sometimes called inside information). The main difference between the semistrong and strong efficiency hypotheses is that in the latter case, nobody should be able to systematically generate profits even if trading on information *not* publicly known at the time. In other words, the strong form of EMH states that a company's management (insiders) would not be able to systematically gain from inside information by buying the company's shares 10 minutes after they decided (but did not publicly announce) to pursue what they perceive to be a very profitable acquisition. Similarly, the members of the company's research department are not able to profit from the information about the new revolutionary discovery they completed half an hour ago. The rationale for strong-form market efficiency is that the market anticipates, in an unbiased manner, future developments and therefore the stock price incorporates all information and evaluates it in a much more objective and informative way than the insiders. Not surprisingly, though, empirical research in finance has found evidence that is inconsistent with the strong form of the EMH.

Common Misconceptions about the EMH

As was suggested in the introduction to this chapter, EMH has received a lot of attention since its inception. Despite its relative simplicity, this hypothesis has also generated a lot of controversy. After all, the EMH questions the ability of investors to consistently detect mispriced securities. Not surprisingly, this implication does not sit very well with many financial analysts and active portfolio managers.

It can be argued that in liquid markets with many participants, such as stock markets, prices should adjust quickly to new information in an unbiased manner. (Less liquid markets, like art and real estate, may indeed not be as efficient.) However, much of the criticism leveled at the EMH is based on numerous misconceptions, incorrect interpretations, and myths about the theory of efficient markets.

Myth 1: The efficient markets hypothesis claims that investors cannot outperform the market. Yet we can see that some of the successful analysts (such as George Soros, Warren Buffett, and Peter Lynch) are able to do exactly that. Therefore, EMH must be incorrect.

The efficient markets hypothesis does not imply that investors are unable to outperform the market. We know that the constant arrival of information makes prices fluctuate. It is possible for an investor to make a killing if newly released information causes the price of the security the investor owns to increase substantially. What EMH does claim, though, is that one should not be expected to outperform the market predictably or consistently.

It should be noted, though, that *some* investors could outperform the market for a very long time by chance alone, even if markets are efficient. Imagine, for the sake of simplicity, that an investor who picks stocks randomly has a 50% chance of beating the market. For such an investor, the chance of outperforming the market in each and every one of the next 10 years is then $(0.5)^{10}$, or about one-tenth of 1%. However, the chance that there will be *at least one investor* outperforming the market in each of the next 10 years sharply increases as the number of investors trying to do exactly that rises.

In a group of 1,000 investors, the probability of finding one ultimate winner with a perfect 10-year record is 63%. With a group of 10,000 investors, the chance of seeing at least one who outperforms the market in every one of the next 10 years is 99.99%, a virtual certainty. Each individual investor may have dismal odds of beating the market for the next 10 years. Yet the likelihood of, after the 10 years, finding one very successful investor—even if he or she is investing purely randomly—is very high if there is a sufficiently large number of investors. This is the case with the state lottery, in which the probability of a given individual winning is virtually zero, but the probability that *someone* will win is very high.

The existence of a handful of successful investors such as Soros, Buffett, and Lynch is an expected outcome in a completely random distribution of investors.[4] The theory would be threatened only if you could identify who those successful investors would be *prior to* their performance, rather than after the fact.

Myth 2: The efficient markets hypothesis claims that financial analysis is pointless and investors who attempt to research security prices are wasting their time. "Throwing darts at the financial page will produce a portfolio that can be expected to do as well as any managed by professional security analysts."[5] Yet we tend to see that financial analysts are not driven out of market, which means that their services are valuable. Therefore, EMH must be incorrect.

There are two principal counterarguments against the equivalency of dart throwing and professional analysis strategies. First, investors generally have different tastes—some may, for example, prefer to put their money in high-risk high-tech portfolios, while others may like less risky investment strategies. Optimal portfolios should provide the investor with the combination of return and risk that the investor finds desirable. A randomly chosen portfolio may not accomplish this goal. Second, and more importantly, financial analysis is far from pointless in efficient capital markets. The competition among investors who actively seek and analyze new information with the goal to identify and take advantage of mispriced stocks is truly essential for the existence of efficient capital markets. In fact, one can say that financial analysis is actually the engine that enables incoming information to get quickly reflected into security prices.

So why don't all investors find it optimal to search for profits by performing financial analysis? The answer is simple—financial research is very costly. As we have already discussed, financial analysts have to be able to gather, process, and evaluate vast amounts of information about firms, industries, scientific achievements, the economy, and so on. They have to invest a lot of time and effort in sophisticated analysis, as well as putting many resources into data gathering, purchases of computers, software, and so on.[6] In addition, analysts who frequently trade securities incur various transaction costs, including brokerage costs, bid-ask spread, and market impact costs (see Chapter 18).

Therefore, any profits achieved by the analysts while trading on mispriced securities must be reduced by the *costs of financial analysis*, as well as the *transaction costs* involved. For mutual funds and private investment managers, these costs are passed on to investors as fees, loads, and reduced returns. There is some evidence that some professional investment managers are able to improve performance through their analyses. However, this may be by pure chance. In general, the advantage gained is not sufficient to outweigh the cost of their advice.

In equilibrium, there will be only as many financial analysts in the market as optimal to ensure that, on average, the incurred costs are covered by the achieved gross trading profits.[7] For the majority of other investors, the chasing of mispriced stocks would indeed be pointless, and they should stick with passive investments, such as index mutual funds.[8]

Myth 3: The efficient markets hypothesis claims that new information is always fully reflected in market prices. Yet one can observe prices fluctuating (sometimes very dramatically) every day, hour, and minute. Therefore, EMH must be incorrect.

The constant fluctuation of market prices can be viewed as an indication that markets *are* efficient. New information affecting the value of securities arrives constantly, causing continuous adjustment of prices to information updates. In fact, observing that prices did *not* change would be inconsistent with market efficiency, since we know that relevant information is arriving almost continuously.

Myth 4: The efficient markets hypothesis presumes that all investors have to be informed, skilled, and able to constantly analyze the flow of new information. Still, the majority of common investors are not trained financial experts. Therefore, EMH must be incorrect.

This is an incorrect statement of the underlying assumptions needed for markets to be efficient. Not all investors have to be informed. In fact, market efficiency can be achieved even if only a relatively small core of informed and skilled investors trade in the market, while the majority of investors never follow the securities they trade.

Evidence in Favor of the Efficient Markets Hypothesis

Since its introduction into the financial economics literature over 35 years ago, the efficient markets hypothesis has been examined extensively in numerous studies. The vast majority of this research indicates that stock markets are indeed efficient. In this section, we briefly discuss the evidence regarding the weak-form, semistrong-form, and strong-form versions of the efficient markets hypothesis.

Weak Form of Market Efficiency

The random walk hypothesis implies that successive price movements should be independent. A number of studies have attempted to test this hypothesis by examining the correlation between the current return on a security and the return on the same security over a previous period. A positive serial correlation indicates that higher-than-average returns are likely to be followed by higher-than-average returns (i.e., a tendency for continuation), while a negative serial correlation indicates that higher-than-average returns are followed, on average, by lower-than-average returns (i.e., a tendency toward reversal). If the random walk hypothesis were true, we would expect zero correlation. Consistent with this theory, Fama in 1965 found that the serial correlation coefficients for a sample of 30 Dow Jones Industrial stocks, even though statistically significant, were too small to cover transaction costs of trading.[9] Subsequent studies have mostly found similar results, across other time periods and other countries.

Another strand of literature tests the weak form of market efficiency by examining the gains from technical analysis. While many early studies found technical analysis to be useless, recent ones offers evidence to the contrary. In 1992 Brock, Lakonishok, and LeBaron[10] found that relatively simple technical trading rules would have been successful in predicting changes in the Dow Jones Industrial Average. However, subsequent research has found that the gains from these strategies are insufficient to cover their transaction costs. Consequently, the findings are consistent with weak-form market efficiency.

Semistrong Form of Market Efficiency

The semistrong form of the EMH is perhaps the most controversial, and thus has attracted the most attention. If a market is semistrong-form efficient, all publicly available information is reflected in the stock price. It implies that investors should not be able to profit consistently by trading on publicly available information.

Investment Managers

Many people suggest that mutual fund managers are skilled investors who are able to beat the market consistently. Unfortunately, the empirical evidence does not support this view. In one of the first studies of its kind, Michael Jensen found that over the period 1955 to 1964 mutual funds achieved a risk-adjusted performance of approximately 0% per year.[11] In other words, mutual fund managers exhibited no special stock-picking ability. Furthermore, this return fell to –0.9% per year after taking into consideration commissions and expenses. More recently Burton Malkiel compared the performance of managed general portfolio funds to the performance of the S&P 500 Index. During 1984–1994, the S&P 500 gained 281.65%, while the equity funds on average appreciated by only 214.80%.

Multiple studies have demonstrated that mutual funds, on average, do not exceed the return of the market index. This has been demonstrated in both large markets and smaller, supposedly less efficient markets. Equally important to investors is whether they can identify some managers or mutual funds that can consistently beat the index. The findings show that a mutual fund's performance over the past 1, 3, 5, or 10 years has not been predictive of its future performance.

There are some perverse findings. In July 1999, the *Wall Street Journal* reported on a study comparing the performance of managed equity funds based on the fees they charge shareholders.[12] One would expect that the higher fees would be charged by funds performing more substantial market research. The results showed that, when taking the fees into consideration, on average the low-fee funds tended to slightly outperform the high-fee funds. William Sharpe states: "The key issue is that past performance is a thin reed for how to predict future performance. Expense ratios and turnover are generally better predictors."

Event Studies

If markets are efficient and security prices reflect all currently available information, new information should rapidly be converted into price changes. Let's look at a hypothetical example. Assume that the research department of CJM Products, an agricultural research corporation, developed a new, revolutionary type of corn that can be grown in the desert. The selling of such a durable crop is potentially a very profitable activity. Assume that on Monday, the price of one share of CJM's stock is $100, and that the estimated present value of the corn development project is $50 per share. What will happen on Tuesday morning when CJM announces the discovery of the new corn type?

If the market is efficient, the stock price would quickly adjust to this new information. The price would jump instantaneously to $150 to fully reflect the effect of the new project announced by the company. The efficient capital market theory implies that market participants will react *immediately and in an unbiased manner*. That is, one can expect that the stock price should not underreact and trade below $150 nor overreact to the announcement and trade above $150 in a predictable manner. This situation is illustrated in Figure 9.1. That way, no investor buying or selling shares after the announcement is made (say, on Tuesday morning) could be expected to make money based on the

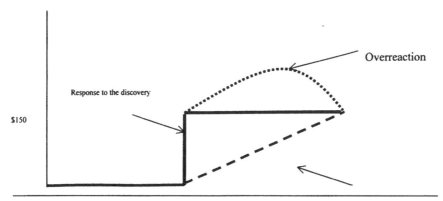

FIGURE 9.1 Possible Price Reactions to the Announcement of CJM's Discovery of a New Type of Corn

company's announcement—the CJM stock price would have already fully incorporated the impact of this information!

Many research studies have examined announcements similar to this example, to determine whether the market reacts as predicted. Many types of events have been studied, including mergers and acquisitions, seasoned equity offerings, spin-offs, dividend announcements, and so on. The evidence generally indicates that the market reacts quickly to these various corporate announcements—often in a matter of minutes. Thus, investors cannot expect to earn superior returns by trading on the announcement date.

In a widely cited study, Eugene Fama, Lawrence Fisher, Michael Jensen, and Richard Roll (hereafter FFJR) examined the stock price reaction around stock splits.[13] Conventional wisdom had long held that stock splits were good news for investors, because they were generally followed by dividend increases. FFJR found that stock splits were preceded, on average, by periods of strong performance, most likely because firms tend to split in good times. However, following the split, they observed no evidence of abnormal stock price performance. That is, investors would not be able to profit by purchasing the stock on the split date. This evidence is consistent with the efficient markets hypothesis.

There is overwhelming evidence in the financial literature suggesting that targets of takeover attempts gain significantly upon an announcement of the acquisition plan by the bidder. Figure 9.2 provides an example of average changes in stock prices of target companies around the announcement of takeover attempts. Interestingly, there is a small upward drift in price prior to

Cumulative abnormal return

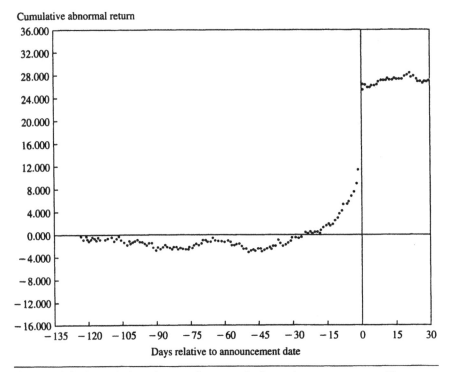

Days relative to announcement date

FIGURE 9.2 Cumulative abnormal returns before takeover attempts: Target companies
Source: Arthur Keown and John Pinkerton, "Merger Announcements and Insider Trading Activity," *Journal of Finance* 36 (September 1981).

the announcement, indicating that some information leaked out. However, notice that after the announcement the stock price changes are, on average, close to zero (without any visible trend). This finding is consistent with the efficient markets hypothesis, since it suggests that the full effect of the information (about the announcement of the takeover attempt and the potential implication of the takeover for the target's value) is incorporated immediately.

Strong Form of Market Efficiency

Empirical tests of the strong-form version of the efficient markets hypothesis have typically focused on the profitability of insider trading. If the strong-form efficiency hypothesis is correct, then insiders should not be able to profit by trading on their private information. Jaffe (1974) finds considerable evidence that insider trades are profitable.[14] A more recent paper by Rozeff and Zaman (1988) finds that insider profits, after deducting an assumed 2% transactions cost, are 3% per year.[15] Thus, it does not appear to be consistent with the strong form of the EMH.

Evidence Against the Efficient Markets Hypothesis

Although most empirical evidence supports the weak form and semistrong form of the EMH, they have not received uniform acceptance. Many investment professionals still meet the EMH with a great deal of skepticism. For example, legendary portfolio manager Michael Price does not leave anybody guessing which side he is on: "Markets are not perfectly efficient. The academics are all wrong. 100% wrong. It's black and white."[16] We will discuss some of the recent evidence against efficient markets.

Overreaction and Underreaction

The efficient markets hypothesis implies that investors react quickly and in an unbiased manner to new information. In two widely publicized studies, DeBondt and Thaler present contradictory evidence.[17] They find that stocks with low long-term past returns tend to have higher future returns, and vice versa—stocks with high long-term past returns tend to have lower future returns (long-term reversals).

These findings received significant publicity in the popular press, which ran numerous headlines touting the benefits of these so-called contrarian strategies.[18] The results appear to be inconsistent with the EMH. However, they have not survived the test of time. Although the issues are complex, recent research indicates that the findings might be the result of methodological problems arising from the measurement of risk.[19] Once risk is measured correctly, the findings tend to disappear.

One of the most enduring anomalies documented in the finance literature is the empirical observation that stock prices appear to respond to earnings for about a year after they are announced. Prices of companies experiencing positive earnings surprises tend to drift upward, while prices of stocks experiencing negative earnings surprises tend to drift downward. This "post-earnings-announcement drift" was first noted by Ball and Brown in 1968[20] and has since been replicated by numerous studies over different time periods and in different countries.[21] After more than 30 years of research, this anomaly has yet to be explained.

Another study reported that stocks with high returns over the prior year tended to have high returns over the following three to six months (short-term momentum in stock prices).[22] This momentum effect is a fairly new anomaly, and consequently significantly more research is needed on the topic. However, the effect is present in other countries and has persisted for a long time.

A variety of other anomalies has been reported. Some indicate market overreaction to information, and others underreaction. Some of these findings are simply related to chance: If you analyze the data enough, you will find some patterns. Dredging for anomalies is a rewarding occupation. Some apparent anomalies, such as the long-term reversals of DeBondt and Thaler, may be a by-product of rational (efficient) pricing.

Value versus Growth

A number of investment professionals and academics argue that so-called value strategies are able to outperform the market consistently. Typically, value strategies involve buying stocks that have low prices relative to their accounting book values, dividends, or historical prices. In a provocative study, Lakonishok, Schleifer, and Vishny find evidence that the difference in average returns between stocks with low price-to-book ratios (value stocks) and stocks with high price-to-book ratios (glamour stocks) was as high as 10% per year.[23] Surprisingly, this return differential cannot be attributed to higher risk (as measured by volatility)—value stocks are typically no riskier than glamour stocks. Rather, the authors argue, market participants consistently overestimate the future growth rates of glamour stocks relative to value stocks. Consequently, these results may represent strong evidence against the EMH. It was also interesting that nearly the entire advantage of the value stocks occurred in January each year. However, current research indicates that the anomalous returns may be caused by a selection bias in a popular commercial database used by financial economists,[24] or by inappropriate adjustments for risk.

Small Firm Effect

Rolf Banz uncovered another puzzling anomaly in 1981.[25] He found that average returns on small stocks were too large to be justified by the Capital Asset Pricing Model, while the average returns on large stocks were too low. Subsequent research indicated that most of the difference in returns between small and large stocks occurred in the month of January. The results were particularly suprising because for years financial economists had accepted that systematic risk or beta was the single variable for predicting returns. Current research indicates that this finding is not evidence of market inefficiency, but rather indicates a failure of the Capital Asset Pricing Model.[26]

Implications of Market Efficiency for Investors

Much of the existing evidence indicates that the stock market is highly efficient, and consequently, investors are unlikely to gain from active management strategies. Such attempts to beat the market are not only fruitless, but they can actually reduce returns due to the costs incurred (management, transaction, tax, etc.).

Investors should follow a passive investment strategy, which makes no attempt to beat the market. This does not mean that there is no role for portfolio management. Investments can be optimized through diversification and asset allocation, and by minimization of transaction costs and taxes. In addition, the portfolio manager must choose a portfolio that is geared toward the time horizon and risk profile of the investor. The appropriate mixture of securities may vary according to the age, goals, tax bracket, employment, and risk aversion of the investor.

Conclusions

The goal of all investors is to achieve the highest returns possible. Indeed, each year investment professionals publish numerous books touting ways to beat the market and earn millions of dollars in the process. Unfortunately for these so-called investment gurus, these investment strategies fail to perform as predicted. The intense competition between investors creates an efficient market in which prices adjust rapidly to new information. Consequently, on average, investors receive a return that compensates them for the time value of money and the risks that they bear—nothing more and nothing less. In other words, after taking risk and transaction costs into account, active security management is a losing proposition.

Although no theory is perfect, the overwhelming majority of empirical evidence supports the efficient markets hypothesis. The vast majority of students of the market agree that the markets are highly efficient. The argument really centers on *how* efficient they are. The opponents of the efficient markets hypothesis point to some recent evidence suggesting that there is under- and overreaction in security markets. However, it's important to note that these studies are controversial and generally have not survived the test of time. Ultimately, the efficient markets hypothesis continues to be the best description of price movements in securities markets.

Suggested Reading

Ball, Ray, "The Theory of Stock Market Efficiency: Accomplishments and Limitations," *Journal of Corporate Finance* (May 1995).

Banz, R. F., "The Relationship Between Return and Market Value of Common Stocks," *Journal of Financial Economics* (April 1981).

Fama, E F., "Efficient Capital Markets: A Review of Theory and Empirical Work," *Journal of Finance* (May 1970).

Fama, E.F., "Efficient Capital Markets: II," Journal of Finance (December 1991).

Fama, E.F, "Market Efficiency, Long-term Returns, and Behavioral Finance," *Journal of Financial Economics* (September 1998).

Malkiel, B., *A Random Walk Down Wall Street, 7th ed.*, W.W. Norton & Co., New York, NY, 1999.

Tanous, P., *Investment Gurus*, New York Institute of Finance, Englewood Cliffs, NJ, 1997.

Notes

1. Michael Jensen, "Some Anomalous Evidence Regarding Market Efficiency," *Journal of Financial Economics* (June/September 1978).
2. Interestingly, in his book *A Random Walk Down Wall Street*, Burton Malkiel notes: "On Wall Street, the term 'random walk' is an obscenity. It is an epithet coined by the academic world and hurled insultingly at the professional soothsayers."
3. One should not be surprised that investment companies analyzing many of the high-tech industries have started employing experts from nonfinancial areas (such as medical doctors, pharmacists, biochemists, etc.) in order to be able to assess viability of projects undertaken by high-tech companies.
4. There may be other reasons why some investors can appear to be long-term winners. Noted University of Chicago professor Merton Miller claims in the book *Investment Gurus* by Peter Tanous (1997): "In practice, it often comes down to not suffering a loss as big as the huge gain you made a while ago. Thus, a fellow like George Soros may be skating on thin ice. You see, he made a big killing and if he would now just do modest investments, he would never lose it. He'd be a winner on balance over any time horizon. But if he insists on plunging again, he is just as likely to take a bigger loss. He may wind up giving it all back."
5. Burton Malkiel, *A Random Walk Down Wall Street*.
6. It should be noted that human capital is not cheap. The *Wall Street Journal* frequently reports that the salaries of star financial analysts reach multimillion-dollar values per year.
7. More precisely, one would expect that if the market for financial analysts is also efficient, the achieved profits should not only cover the incurred research and transaction costs, but also provide a fair (as opposed to abnormal) return on those costs. Indeed, in that case, the profits achieved by star analysts such as George Soros or Peter Lynch can be considered a fair return on their substantial investment into their human capital.
8. One more aspect of the impact of financial analysis on profits of investors should be mentioned here. Some investors (including star investors such as Warren Buffett) not only target the mispriced securities, but also get actively involved in improvement of

companies they own (for example, by firing incompetent managers). Since such investors actively create value, there is no need to assume that they should not generate any abnormal returns.

9. E. F. Fama, "The Behavior of Stock-Market Prices," *Journal of Business* (January 1965).

10. W. Brock, J. Lakonishok, and B. LeBaron, "Simple Technical Trading Rules and the Stochastic Properties of Stock Returns," *Journal of Finance* (December 1992).

11. Michael Jensen, "Risks, the Pricing of Capital Assets and the Evaluation of Investment Portfolios," *Journal of Business* (April 1969).

12. Pui-Wing Tam, "Fund Managers Get Raises for So-so Showings," *Wall Street Journal*, July 20, 1999.

13. E. F. Fama, L. Fisher, M. Jensen, and R. Roll, "The Adjustment of Stock Prices to New Information," *International Economics Review* (February 1969).

14. J. Jaffe, "Special Information and Insider Trading," *Journal of Business* (July 1974).

15. M. Rozeff and M. Zaman, "Market Efficiency and Insider Trading: New Evidence," *Journal of Business* (January, 1988).

16. Taken from *Investment Gurus* by Peter Tanous.

17. W. DeBondt and R. Thaler, "Do Security Analysts Overreact," *American Economic Review* 80(2): 52–57, 1990; W. DeBondt and R. Thaler, "Further Evidence on Investor Overreaction and Stock Market Seasonality," *Journal of Finance* (1987).

18. For example, see B. Donelly, "Investors' Overreactions May Yield Opportunities in the Stock Market," *Wall Street Journal* (January 7, 1988).

19. See E. F. Fama and K. French, "Multifactor Explanations of Asset Pricing Anomalies," *Journal of Finance* 51:55–84 (March 1996).

20. Ball, R. and P. Brown, 1968, "An empirical evaluation of accounting income numbers." *Accounting Research*, 159–178.

21. V. Bernard and J.Thomas, "Evidence That Stock Prices Do Not Fully Reflect the Implications of Current Earnings for Future Earnings," *Journal of Accounting and Economics* 13, 305 (1990).

22. N. Jegadeesh and S. Titman, "Returns to Buying Winners and Selling Losers: Implications for Stock Market Efficiency," *Journal of Finance* 48:65–91 (1993).

23. J. Lakonishok, A. Shleifer, and R. Vishny, "Contrarian Investment, Extrapolation, and Risk," *Journal of Finance* (December 1994).

24. See, for example, S. P. Kothari, J. Shanken, and R. G. Sloan, "Another Look at the Cross-Section of Expected Stock Returns," *Journal of Finance* (March 1995).

25. R. W. Banz, "The Relationship Between Return and Market Value of Common Stocks," *Journal of Financial Economics* (April 1981).

26. See E. F. Fama and K. French, "The Cross-Section of Expected Stock Returns," *Journal of Finance* (June 1992).

Stock Mutual Funds

Robert Arffa

In stock mutual funds, investors' dollars are pooled to purchase a portfolio of stocks under the supervision of professional management. Each investor shares in the mutual fund's income, expenses, profits, and losses in proportion to the number of shares owned. The officers and directors of a fund company choose a professional investment adviser to make all the stock purchase and sale decisions. Most commonly, a separate company employs this adviser. The individual manager may change, but almost always the investment adviser company remains the same throughout the fund's life.

Mutual Funds versus Stocks

The primary reason to invest in a mutual fund is to receive professional management of your stock investments at a relatively low cost. Hiring a professional manager on your own usually requires a minimum investment of $500,000. However, cost is not the only factor. Many people with total investments in excess of $1 million are still better served by mutual funds.

Table 10.1 lists some pros and cons regarding mutual funds. The past performance records of mutual funds and fund managers are readily available, both from the fund and from independent sources. In contrast, there is usually no way to obtain objective performance results on a stockbroker or a brokerage firm. Since past performance records are the main means of comparing investment managers, standardized data are indispensable. Other data, including risk measurements such as beta and standard deviation of return, costs, funds under management, and financial status of the management company are also readily available.

Diversification is necessary to optimize the ratio of risk to reward. Diversification can readily be achieved with even small amounts of money through use of a mutual fund. In addition, optimum asset allocation often involves investment in a

TABLE 10.1 Advantages and Disadvantages of Mutual Funds Compared to Private Stock Ownership

Advantages	Disadvantages
Professional management Diversification	In spite of professional management, fund returns often do not surpass those of passive indexes
Past performance records readily available	Can be overdiversified
Easy to invest and withdraw funds	Tendency to avoid smallest companies
Reduced transaction costs	No control over tax consequences (capital gains and dividends)
Facilitates automatic (regular) investment	Total costs may be higher than private investment manager or investing independently
Easy to switch from one fund to another within a fund family	
Automatic reinvestment of dividends and capital gains	Limited exposure to certain stocks because of fund limits on investment
Access to otherwise difficult or inaccessible markets	No personal relationship with manager
Funds must disclose unfavorable facts, such as being sued	

broad variety of stocks—large, small, growth, value, and international. Individual investors or even professional managers cannot have expertise in all categories. Particularly for foreign investing, mutual funds are a much simpler means of obtaining access. Therefore, even if you decide to select stocks yourself, you may choose to purchase mutual funds for some sectors of your asset allocation.

On the other hand, mutual funds have some disadvantages relative to owning your own stocks. Probably the biggest potential disadvantage is that you have little control over the tax consequences of your investment. Typically, the manager buys and sells stocks in order to maximize *pretax* annual return. Every time a trade is made, capital gains (or losses) are generated and the tax consequences are passed on to you. It is also of no consequence to the manager whether the stock produces dividends rather than growth in value, as long as the total return is maximized. However, your net return after taxes can be significantly different, depending on the choices made. (This is discussed in detail in Chapter 18.)

A mutual fund company's income is determined by the size of the assets under its management. Investors generally pick mutual funds based on the most recent annual return(s), even though this may not be the best strategy. Therefore, short-term returns may be overly emphasized. Also, in some cases stocks are bought or sold just prior to the semiannual reporting of stock holdings to shareholders, in order to eliminate poorly performing stocks from the portfolio, or to make it look like profitable stocks had been held all along. This trading may not be in the investors' best interest.

Mutual funds are limited by law to investing no more than 5% of their assets in any one company. Also, the law limits the percentage of a company's stock that a mutual fund can own. This makes mutual funds unlikely to invest in very small companies. They can't own enough of the company to make the investment (dollars and research) worthwhile. This also limits the proportions of a fund's assets that can be invested in the companies it feels are most likely to perform well. A large fund, like Fidelity Magellan, has to expand into companies that are not as attractive, and dilute its investment in the companies it likes best, in order to invest all its funds under management.

Overdiversification and inappropriate asset allocation can occur with a mixture of mutual funds. For example, owning several funds that invest in large-cap stocks can result in a portfolio that provides no advantage in return over an S&P 500 index fund, but the total expenses are much higher. Mutual funds do not always invest in the types of companies you expect them to. For instance, a "global" fund may have 80% of its money invested in U.S. stocks, a fund may keep a lot of its assets in cash if the manager feels that the market is going to decline, or the mixture of small versus large or growth versus value companies may not be what is advertised.

The costs of owning mutual funds can be greater than those you would incur by investing yourself. In 1992 the average annual expenses charged by an equity mutual fund was 1.5%.[1] If you own 10 or 15 stocks and hold on to each of them for 5 to 10 years, your expenses (as well as the tax consequences) can be much lower than this. Also, once your total portfolio becomes very large, say in excess of $1 million, you can hire a professional manager who will charge you less. (See Chapter 17.)

Now, after going through all these disadvantages, I should reassure you that it is possible to avoid most of them through careful mutual fund selection. For example, there are now funds that are specifically designed to minimize their tax consequences. There are funds with low turnover, long-term perspective, and low expense ratios. The important thing is to be aware of these potential problems when selecting your mutual funds.

Fees and Loads

Sales Load (Commission)

A "load" fund is one in which a percentage of the money you invest is diverted to the mutual fund company instead of buying shares of its assets. The maximum percentage by law is 8.5%, and the average load is 4% to 5%. This is called a *sales charge*, or *front-end load*, and may be paid as a commission to your broker, kept by the fund company, or paid to other shareholders. It is paid every time you invest money in the fund, even years after the broker made the recommendation.

Historically, other than the effect of the sales load, there has been no difference in the average performance of load and no-load funds. Whether or not a mutual fund carries a sales load is primarily a marketing decision. The fund company has to decide whether it can attract more investment assets by marketing and selling directly to investors without paying commission, or by paying salespeople (brokers) to promote their funds. Some fund companies use a mixture of techniques: no-loads, low-loads marketed directly to investors, front-end loads sold by salespeople, and others.

For example, Fidelity has selectively added front-end loads to its best-performing mutual funds. It has found that investors have been willing to pay these loads with the hope of obtaining superior future performance.

12b-1 Fees

Section 12b-1 was part of the Investment Company Act of 1940 that enabled fund companies to pass their marketing and distribution fees on to the fund investors. The management fee charged to the fund had previously covered these expenses. Although used initially to cover advertising and other promotional costs, it also became a means of providing sales incentives to brokers. Instead of charging a sales commission up front, the 12b-1 fee is paid to fund management at regular intervals out of the fund's net assets, just like the management fees. Therefore these fees are essentially invisible, and often go unrecognized unless the purchaser carefully reads the fund prospectus. It is often just a more discreet way of compensating the salespeople.

The National Association of Securities Dealers has capped a fund's total 12b-1 fees. They are limited to 7.25% of new gross sales if there is no continuing 0.25% service fee, and at 6.25% of new gross sales if there is a service fee. The effect of this limit on the 12b-1 fee charged to the investor is variable, depending on how fast the fund's assets are growing.

Back-End Load

This is also called a *contingent deferred sales charge* (*CDSC*). Originally some funds charged *redemption fees*, typically 1% to 2%, that were used to deter frequent trading. They would be incurred only if the purchased shares were sold within a relatively short period, such as two months to one year. Some firms have expanded this to make sure that they recoup sales commissions on no-load or low-load funds. Initially the fund charges the investor a low load, or no load at all, but still pays the salesperson a commission. It recoups the commission from earning management fees on the fund. However, it takes several years for the fund to recoup the commission from fees, so the investor is charged proportionately if the shares are sold before that point. For example, deferred sales charges will be as much as 6% for shareholders redeeming within the first year, 5% the second year, and continuing to decline by 1% per year until the charge disappears. However, CDSCs are frequently combined with an annual 12b-1 fee that does not disappear with time. The total effect of this is displayed in Table 10.2. This technique is primarily used by brokerage firms to compensate their salespeople.

Menu of Loads

An increasing number of fund companies are allowing the investor to choose from a menu of load options. The same fund can be offered with three "classes" or "series" of shares: Class A with a front-end load, Class B funds with a 12b-1 fee coupled with a CDSC equaling the front-end load (as in Table 10.2), and Class C with a level load such as 1% a year.

Operating Expenses

The operating expenses include all the costs of running and promoting the mutual fund. The chief administrative expenses are incurred in record keep-

TABLE 10.2 Contingent Deferred Sales Load—Total Expense

Year	CDSC Exit Fee	Annual 12b-1 Fee	Cumulative Load Paid If Sold
1	5%	1%	6%
2	4%	1%	6%
3	3%	1%	6%
4	2%	1%	6%
5	1%	1%	6%
6	0%	1%	6%
7	0%	1%	7%*
8	0%	1%	8%*
9	0%	1%	9%*
10	0%	1%	10%*

*In some funds the maximum load is limited to 6%.

ing and providing transaction services to shareholders. This typically amounts to 0.2% to 0.4% of fund assets. Also included in operating expenses is the *management fee* (or *investment advisory fee*), which is the amount that the mutual fund pays to the investment adviser for its services. The management fee generally ranges from 0.5% to 1% of the fund's assets per year. Other operating expenses included state and local taxes, legal and accounting expenses, custodial fees, and the director's fees. These average 0.1% to 0.3% of fund assets.

The total operating expense expressed as a percentage of assets is called the *expense ratio*. The expense ratio ranges from 0.15% to over 2% of assets, and averages about 1.4%. Surprisingly, this ratio has more than doubled over the past 35 years, in spite of significant cost savings from economies of scale resulting from growth in average fund size. A study by Sheldon Jacobs demonstrated that expense ratios are higher in load funds and negatively related to fund size. No-load international funds had a median expense ratio of 1.5%.[2]

Mutual fund families vary widely in their average expense ratios. In one survey[3] the families with the lowest average ratios were Vanguard (0.36%), Dimensional Fund Advisors (0.65%), SEI (0.69%), GE (0.71%), and American (0.72%); those with the highest were Ivy (2%), Alliance (1.94%), Morgan Stanley Dean Witter (1.93%), Merrill Lynch (1.85%), and Lexington (1.81%).

Other Fees

Some fund groups charge a *sales load on reinvested dividends* or capital gains. This is also deceptively called *dividend reinvestment at offering price*. This can have a significant effect on total returns, particularly for equity-income or bond funds.

A few funds, primarily index funds, try to minimize operating expenses by charging fees to investors who cause the fund to incur expenses. The fees are paid to the other investors. They generally amount to a front load of 0.5% to 1% of the amount invested and a small redemption fee. They primarily cover the administrative and transaction costs the fund incurs when investors buy and sell shares. These fees are also used to discourage short-term investing and market timing. Vanguard and Dimensional Fund Advisors (DFA) index funds, which have the lowest expense ratios, apply these types of fees. These should not be considered loads, but rather a beneficial way of equitably attributing costs to investors.

Effects of Loads and Other Costs on Investment Results

Independent research has not demonstrated any average difference in performance between funds that charge sales loads, back-end loads, or 12b-1 fees and those that do not.[4] These fees are primarily marketing costs, designed to compensate your investment adviser or to cover promotional expenses of the mutual fund company. Charging a load does not improve performance or lower other costs commensurately. Therefore, the only reason to invest in a fund with a load is if you cannot find a comparable no-load fund that you expect to produce similar returns.

If a fund charges a 5% up-front sales load, in order to match the returns of a no-load fund its return will have to be over 5% greater than the no-load fund over the period that you hold it. If the total returns of a 5% load and a no-load fund are equal, the value of the investment in the load fund will always be 5% lower.

Table 10.3 shows that if the annual return of the load fund is 1% greater than the return of the no-load fund (9% versus 8%) it takes until the sixth year before the value of the investment catches up with the investment in the no-load fund.

The situation with back-end (CDSC) loads is similar, except that the load diminishes over time. If you hold on to the fund long enough you will not be charged a load. Therefore, you should invest in these funds if you either (1) expect the return to exceed the no-load fund by the amount of the load over the period of your investment or (2) plan to hold on to the fund beyond the

TABLE 10.3 Effect of 5% Sales Load on Total Return of
$100 Invested—Higher Load Fund Return

	Fund A (5% Load)		Fund B (No-Load)	
Year	Annual Return	Value of $100 Invested	Annual Return	Value of $100 Invested
Initial		$95.00 (after load)		$100.00
1	9%	$103.55	8%	$108.00
2	9%	$112.87	8%	$116.64
3	9%	$123.03	8%	$125.97
4	9%	$134.10	8%	$136.05
5	9%	$146.17	8%	$146.93
6	9%	$159.32	8%	$158.68

time that the load is charged. Keep in mind that this applies to the time after the *last* investment. If you continue to invest regularly (including reinvesting dividends and capital gains if the load is applied to these as well), you will continually be paying loads.

Operating costs and 12b-1 fees are a continuing drag on returns. All things being equal, it is better to buy a fund that does not charge a 12b-1 fee and has low operating costs. The average return of the stock market has been approximately 10% per year. If your total annual expenses are 2.2%, they will consume 22% of the return; if they are 0.3% they will consume only 3% of the return.

Efficient market adherents believe not only that very few managers will beat the index over an extended period, but also that it is impossible to predict who those managers will be. Therefore, the most important predictor of mutual fund return is the fund expense ratio. A study performed by Sheldon Jacobs[5] helps illustrate this. He compiled the total five-year returns of funds with expense ratios of 2% or more. Only 126 out of 1,360 funds had five-year histories and expense ratios of 2% or more in 1997. Table 10.4 compares the five-year returns of these funds with those of all stock funds.

You can see that these high-expense funds did not perform as well as funds with lower expenses. Only 24% ranked in the top 40% of all funds and 61%

TABLE 10.4 Rankings of Stock Funds with Expense Ratios of 2% or More Compared to All Funds (Five Years Ending June 1997)

Quintile Ranking (All Stock Funds)	Number of Funds	Percentage of Funds
1 (Best)	14	11%
2	17	13%
3	19	15%
4	31	25%
5 (Worst)	45	36%
Total	126	100%

Data Source: Morningstar.

ranked in the bottom 40%. The high-expense funds were more than twice as likely to exhibit below-average performance than above-average.

It is important to realize that loads are almost totally ignored in the reports of mutual fund performance in the press. Therefore, it is up to you to determine all the loads and subtract them from the fund returns. (Operating expenses and transaction costs *are* taken into account in the figures reported.) The effects of taxes must also be considered for taxable accounts.

Effect of Turnover

Transaction Costs

Transaction costs are the expenses the fund incurs in buying and selling stocks. Included are not only brokerage commissions but also bid-ask spreads and the effect of buying or selling large blocks of shares on the share price. (These are discussed in Chapter 18.) These costs are reflected in the mutual fund share price and performance, but are nearly impossible to obtain. Clearly, they are proportional to the rate of turnover (purchase or sale) of the stocks in a fund and are inversely proportional to the size of the fund. You can estimate the total transaction costs by multiplying the reported turnover rate by 1.2% (or .012).[6] By this estimate, a fund with a turnover of 100% per year will have transaction costs of about 1.2%. This is a significant drag on returns. It should be added to the total loads, fees, and operating expenses when predicting investment returns.

Ways to Lessen the Load

If you decide to purchase a load mutual fund, you can sometimes save a portion of the load: purchase one fund in a family of funds, where the family allows free switching between funds. After one month switch to a similar fund in the same family. You then record a short-term capital loss (usually about the size of the load) that is tax deductible. For example, if you invest $10,000 in a fund with a 5% load, the initial value of your fund holding is $9,500. If one month later the share price is the same, you sell it for $9,500, and record a $500 capital loss, which is tax deductible or can be used to offset capital gains.

You may also be able to save on commissions by switching into another fund from the same family with a higher load, without incurring additional charges. For example, you invest $10,000 in a fund with a 3% load, and one month later switch the money into a fund that normally charges a 5% load. If there is not a large change in share price, you pay $300 in commission rather than $500. You may also be able to use the short-term loss for tax advantages, as in the first example.

Tax Efficiency

A fund with a high turnover rate not only incurs significant transaction costs, but it also incurs more taxable capital gains. Mutual fund returns are received in four forms: dividends, short-term capital gains, long-term capital gains, and unrealized gains. *Dividends* are payments in cash by the companies in which stock is held by the fund. *Short-term capital gains* are the profits on stocks bought by the fund and sold after less than one year. *Long-term capital gains* are the profits on stocks bought by the fund and sold after holding them for more than one year. *Unrealized gains* are increases in value of stocks still held by the fund.

Under current tax law (1999) dividends and short-term capital gains are taxed at your current income tax rate. The highest marginal income tax rate is 39.6%. The maximum tax rate on long-term capital gains is 20%.

Whenever a mutual fund sells stock, the capital gains or losses are passed on to you. If a fund sells all of its stocks at least once a year, all returns will be short-term capital gains and dividends, and therefore subject to income tax rates. The returns of a fund that rarely sells stock, such as an S&P 500 index fund, will be nearly all in unrealized gains, with a small portion in dividends and long-term capital gains. When you sell your shares in this fund you will pay a maximum of 20% tax on the profits. Therefore, in the first case most of your profits are taxed at 39.6%, and in the second at 20%. This can make a tremendous difference in your after-tax return.

Descriptive Measures of Stock Funds

Risk versus Reward

In general, the riskier an investment, the greater the expected average return. In practical terms, risk is how likely you are to lose money, and how much money you could lose. Statistically, the best way to measure this is the variability in the price of a fund over time.

Now, I am about to go into some simple statistics, but please don't skip this section. I promise to keep it in English as much as possible, and with only the simplest of equations. If you understand what these terms mean and how they apply to stocks and mutual funds, you will be a better investor.

Variability in price can be described as either beta or standard deviation. Beta is a measure of the fund's volatility relative to other funds. It is the average percentage change in the value of the fund accompanying a 1% increase or decrease in the value of the S&P 500 index. For example, a fund that has a beta of 1.5 will go up about 50% more than the index when the market goes up, and will decrease in value about 50% more than the index when the market goes down. An S&P index fund, by definition, has a beta of 1.0. (See Table 10.5.)

The standard deviation of the fund is a measurement of the spread in the fund share price over time. Standard deviation is the most widely used statistical measure of spread. It can be used as a measure of the average daily deviation of share price from the annual mean, or the year-to-year variation in total return.[7]

In contrast to beta, standard deviation describes only the fund in question, not how it compares to the index or to other funds. The standard deviation of the annual returns of the S&P 500 index over the past 50 years is 16.5 (versus 10.6 for 20-year government bonds, and 3.1 for Treasury bills). Therefore, funds with standard deviations of their annual returns greater than 16.5 are more volatile than average.

Volatility is only one type of risk. Other risks not measured by beta and standard deviation, include bankruptcy, illiquidity, and consistent poor performance. Unfortunately, there is no way to quantitatively measure these risks.

R-squared

R-squared is another useful statistical measure. R-squared (r^2) is a statistical measure of the relationship between two variables. It tells you how much of the variation in one score is determined by the variation in the other. R-

TABLE 10.5 Historical Betas of Different Fund Types,
15 Years Ending December 31, 1992

Fund Type	Beta	Average Annual Total Return
Aggressive growth	1.19	13.9
Small company	1.16	16.1
Growth	1.01	15.6
Value	0.87	13.7
Equity income	0.76	14.0
International	0.65	
Standard & Poor's 500 index	1.00	14.6

Data Source: John C. Bogle, *Bogle on Mutual Funds*, New York: Irwin, 1994, p. 84.

squared is the square of the correlation (r) between two variables. R-squared ranges from 0, where there is no relationship, to 1, where there is a perfect relationship, and knowing the score on one scale will tell you the exact score on the other. For example, the correlation between intelligence and how far you advance in education is 0.57.[8] However, the relationship between intelligence and how well you do in your career is only 0.2.[9] This means that 32% (r^2) of the reason we get higher degrees relates to our intelligence. However, only 4% of our success on the job can be explained by intelligence.

In analyzing mutual funds, r^2 is used to determine the extent to which a fund's return is explained by movement of the market as a whole. For most growth funds the appropriate comparison is the S&P 500 index. For a small-company growth fund the Russell 2000 index is most often used. For a typical equity fund, comparison with the S&P 500 index gives an r^2 of 0.8 to .09. This means that from 80% to 90% of its return is explained by the performance of the overall stock market. The remaining 10% to 20% of return is explained either by the types of stocks being different from those of the index or by the skill (or lack of it) of the portfolio manager. If a manager is keeping a lot of money in cash or buying many smaller-company stocks, the funds' correlation with the S&P 500 index will decline. If the r^2 of a fund is 0.95, the return of the fund is almost entirely explained by the movement of the market itself, and you may be better off investing in the index instead.

Types of Stock Funds

The number and types of stock mutual funds grew tremendously in just 25 years, from 463 in 1972 to 1,432 in 1997. This growth is a reflection of the increased popularity of this investment and the large profits that can be made by fund companies and advisers. You can find a fund that specializes in nearly any class of stock, investment style, industry, or country in which you would want to invest. This creates lots of investment opportunities but can make the selection of funds a daunting challenge.

There are many ways of classifying stock mutual funds. In this chapter I will give the traditional categorization (Table 10.6). In Chapter 12 Eugene Fama Jr. and Weston Wellington of Dimensional Fund Advisors will go through some of the newer methods of analyzing funds, based on economic theory.

Growth Funds

The traditional description of a growth fund is one that seeks return through an increase in stock price (capital appreciation), with dividend income of relatively little importance. Most seek appreciation in stock price over a period of years.

Aggressive Growth Funds

Aggressive growth funds try to increase returns through riskier investments. They may also be called maximum capital gains or maximum capital appreciation funds. Manager of aggressive growth funds buy stocks they think have the greatest potential for a rapid increase in price. These are often smaller companies in popular industries, such as technology, with highly volatile stock prices. These companies often have recently exhibited the most rapid growth, and are predicted to grow the most in the near future. The funds might also gamble on the possibility of a company receiving a takeover offer, or turning around from bankruptcy. They occasionally use riskier investing techniques, such as margined portfolios, options, and short selling.

Aggressive growth funds are the most volatile. They tend to be the funds that go up the most in bull markets and decline the most in bear markets. In the third quarter of 1990, when the average growth fund lost 13.8%, the average aggressive growth fund lost 21.9%. Aggressive growth funds also tend to be the most inconsistent in performance. On average, they have the highest betas and standard deviations, and the lowest r^2 scores.

The good news is that, on average, aggressive growth funds have outperformed the average growth fund. If you want to make a killing in a bull market, choose an aggressive growth fund, but you've got to be lucky enough to pick

TABLE 10.6 Classification of Equity Mutual Funds

I.   Domestic broad stock funds

    A. Growth

        1. Aggressive growth

        2. Large company versus small company

        3. Growth versus value

    B. Growth and income (equity income)

II.   International funds

    A. European

    B. Pacific

    C. Emerging markets

    D. Specific country

    E. Growth

    F. Value

III. Sector Funds

    A. Industry

        1. Utilities

IV.   Socially conscious

V.   Balanced

VI.   Asset management

VII. Closed-end funds

VIII. Hedge funds

the right fund and to get out before the market turns around. You also have to be able to tolerate the significant loss that can occur if you guess wrong.

Growth Funds versus Value Funds

Regular growth funds tend to have longer-term goals than aggressive growth funds have. They buy stocks whose predicted growth is slightly less rapid. They tend to own larger, better-known companies, with a long history of increasing earnings. They tend not to utilize riskier investment techniques, such as buying on margin, short sales, options, or purchasing restricted securities or commodities. On average they are less volatile than aggressive growth funds, and therefore have lower betas, lower standard deviations of return, and higher r^2 values. Over long periods their returns have been slightly lower than those of aggressive growth funds.

Growth funds may be specialized according to the size of the companies in which they invest, or into growth or value investing styles. Companies can be ranked according to size by *market capitalization* (cap), the total value of their outstanding stock (number of shares existing times price per share). *Large-cap* or *large-company* stock funds invest predominantly in companies in the upper half of the spectrum, while *small-cap* or *small-company* funds favor stocks in the lower half. Keep in mind that with companies growing and stock prices rising, the median capitalization of companies on the New York Stock Exchange is over $1 billion. Therefore, a "small company" for a small-cap fund can be up to $1 billion in market cap. Funds that hold stocks from only the bottom 20% of the size spectrum are called *micro-cap* funds.

Stocks can also be rated along a spectrum between "growth" and "value." Growth companies are those that are highly rated by the market. Their earnings are increasing; they have relatively low dividend yields, higher price-to-book (lower book-to-market) ratios, and higher price-to-earnings ratios. Growth funds choose them because they think these stocks will continue to grow and their stock price will continue to rise, even though they're not cheap now. *Value* funds look for companies that are bargains at their current prices. They are undervalued by the market, and once the market figures this out their stock price will rise. They tend to have lower price-to-earnings and price-to-book value ratios and higher dividend yields.

Growth and Income Funds

Growth and income funds, also known as *equity income* funds, seek to provide a major portion of their total return through dividend income. Therefore, they own companies that have historically paid proportionally higher dividends (greater dividend yield). The dividends are usually paid consistently, even when the stock value or market as a whole goes down. This reduces volatility and the downside risk (so beta and standard deviation tend to be lower). Growth and income funds emphasize larger, established companies with a long history of dividend payments. Since much of their total return depends on income (average 44% for the period 1977–1992), they tend to be more affected by changes in interest rate. Also, more of the total return of the fund is taxed at the income tax rate rather than the lower capital gains rate.

International Funds

International or *foreign* stock funds are those that hold stocks of corporations based outside the United States. It is important to distinguish between *global* and *international* funds. *Global* funds invest in companies both in the United States and abroad; usually the fund manager determines the percentage of domestic and foreign stocks. An international fund invests exclusively overseas. It can be generalized or specialized. Broader geographic categorizations include *European, Pacific, emerging markets*, and *Latin American.* Emerging markets are all of those other than the United States, Canada, Japan, Australia, New Zealand, and Western Europe as far east as Scandinavia. Other funds available include those dedicated to companies of a specific country, such as Japan, Canada, or Mexico, and those specializing in large, small, growth, or value companies. International investing is covered in Chapter 15.

Sector Funds

Sector funds are those which buy stocks of companies in just one industry, such as automotive, banking, biotechnology, computers, or telecommunications. (Funds that invest in one sector of the economy, such as small growth companies, or one style of investing, such as value of contrarian, may also be considered sector funds.)

Fidelity, Vanguard, and Invesco offer large selections of sector funds. Sector funds are, by definition, less diversified than general funds, and are therefore more volatile. The returns can be spectacular or dismal. For example, on August 8, 1988, the one-year total return of Fidelity Select sector funds ranged from +38.9% for telecommunications to –42.5% for gold, while the median return for large-cap funds was 13.6%.

John C. Bogle, founder of the Vanguard Group, wrote the following advice about sector funds:

> Sector funds, designed for trading back and forth in the securities of a particular industry (such as automobiles, oils, or chemicals), were a mainstay of mutual fund industry during the 1930s and 1940s. The idea

was for investors to jump from one industry to the next as each danced through its inevitable market cycle of leadership and followership. But investors insisted on buying the industries whose stock prices had recently risen the most. Thus, investments were often made at the peak of the industry's performance, only to be liquidated in the subsequent valley. So the concept failed to serve investors well, and it was given a decent and well-deserved burial in the late 1950s. Sector funds returned in 1981, and the same pattern has predictably re-emerged: investment near the peak, liquidation near the trough. . . . Mutual fund investors should own sector funds only for a specific purpose and only for a small portion of their equity assets. Mutual fund speculators should enjoy them to their hearts' content, providing that they do not mind the burden of sale charges, high expense ratios, and the transaction costs engendered both by surging cash inflows and outflows and by truly awesome rates of portfolio turnover (200% per year is not uncommon)."[10]

I would add that if you are going to invest in sector funds you are more likely to be successful if you buy on weakness rather than strength. In other words, buy an industry that has been underperforming the market and the industry's historic average, not one that has been leading the pack. The leading exponent of this type of analysis is Abby Joseph Cohen of Goldman Sachs, and it is possible to obtain her predictions from the brokerage.

Utility funds are atypical of sector funds. They buy shares in electric, gas, telephone, and water utility companies. Until recently, nearly all of these companies were monopolies closely regulated by local, state, and federal governments. They typically had slow, steady earnings and paid high dividends (higher that those of equity income funds). Therefore, their performance was strongly tied to interest rates and they behaved like bond funds: Their prices rose when inflation was low and interest rates were stable or falling. However, deregulation is changing utilities and making them more like other industries. Their future performance will be less predictable.

Balanced Funds

Balanced funds, also called *domestic hybrid* or *asset allocation* funds, are mixtures of assets. Typically they consist of a stock component, a bond component, and a money market component. The intent is to provide a complete investment program in a single portfolio. The allocation of assets among stocks, bonds, and cash may be fixed or adjustable, according to the manager's recommendations.

Funds in which the manager can vary the asset allocation are usually called asset allocation or asset manager funds. The funds may purchase individual stocks and bonds, or shares of stock or bond funds offered by the same fund family. The stock portfolios tend to be value oriented and the bond portfolios relatively high quality.

Fixed-allocation balanced funds vary in risk level, growth versus income, and recommended investment horizon. For example, the Vanguard Life Strategy funds are divided into income, conservative growth, moderate growth, and growth portfolios. The asset mixtures are shown in Table 10.7.

Another type of balanced fund is a *life-cycle* fund. These adjust their asset mix over the years, gradually becoming more conservative as their investors age. These are usually named after the target maturity (retirement) age. The Fidelity Freedom funds are examples of this type of fund, with portfolios targeted for the years 2000, 2010, or 2020. The funds' investments become more conservative as they near their targets, and after reaching the target year continue on with low-risk, income-producing investment.

These types of funds can be good options if you can find one with the asset mixture you desire. Putting all of your assets in one balanced fund is not necessarily riskier than owning a selection of funds. It can be the same as hiring a private investment manager to handle all your investments. Balanced funds are particularly useful for people with small sums to invest, because they provide instant diversification.

Multifunds

These are funds that invest in a selection of other funds. Usually the other funds are from the same fund family. The Vanguard Life Strategy funds in

TABLE 10.7 Composition of Vanguard Life Strategy Portfolios

Vanguard Fund	Income Portfolio	Conservative Growth Portfolio	Moderate Growth Portfolio	Growth Portfolio
Total Stock Market Portfolio	5%	20%	35%	50%
Total International Portfolio	—	5%	10%	15%
Total Bond Market Portfolio	50%	30%	30%	10%
Short-Term Corporate Portfolio	20%	20%	—	—
Asset Allocation Fund*	25%	25%	25%	25%

*The Vanguard Asset Allocation Fund shifts its assets among stocks, bonds, and cash to seek the most favorable returns, based on the predictions of the fund managers.

Table 10.7, Vanguard Star, T. Rowe Price Spectrum (growth and income port-folios), Eric Kobren's Insight Management funds (moderate growth and growth), and FundTrust (aggressive growth, growth, growth and income, and income) are examples. It is important to determine the total loads and expenses of the fund and the funds in which it invests, because the impact on returns can be substantial.

Special Types of Funds

Social conscience or *socially responsible* funds invest in companies that meet standards of ethics as well as financial success. They may choose companies with clean environmental records and promotion of female and minority employees, and avoid those that manufacture weapons, mistreat animals, sell tobacco or liquor, or operate casinos or nuclear power facilities. Examples of this type of fund are Pax World, Parnassus, Calver-Ariel Appreciation, and Dreyfus Third Century. Restricting the fund manager's options in this way does tend to reduce return. The average risk-adjusted return of social conscience funds is about one percentage point less than the returns of comparable less politically correct funds.[11]

U.S. *regional* funds invest in companies located in one part of the United States. *Tax-efficient* funds are those designed to maximize after-tax return. They try to maximize long-term capital gains and minimize dividends and turnover (short-term capital gains). It can pay to look at these funds for taxable accounts. Examples are Vanguard Tax-Managed Funds (balanced, capital appreciation, and growth and income). T. Rowe Price Tax-Efficient Balanced Fund, and J. P. Morgan Tax-Aware (disciplined equity and U.S. equity). The advantage of this type of fund is discussed in Chapter 18.

Closed-End Funds

Closed-end mutual funds issue a fixed number of shares at an initial public offering. Afterward the shares trade in the marketplace at either a premium or a discount to their net asset value. The initial offering price includes a sales commission, so the price of the shares is always greater than the value of the assets purchased. Thereafter shares in equity closed-end funds usually trade at a discount to their net asset value (the discount averages about 10%). The reason they may be discounted might be because there is little incentive for brokers to sell them, there is little promotion of the fund, investors may undervalue shares because of a history of poor performance, the market is reduced generally or for the fund's specialty, or it may contain illiquid stocks.

The value of your investment is determined not only by the value of the stocks owned, but also by the level of the discount. You should only consider purchasing an established equity closed-end fund at a discount, and preferably at a greater discount than its historic average.

Hedge Funds

Hedge funds are a diverse group of investment organizations. Today the term is typically applied to any investment limited partnership. Originally, the term was used only for partnerships that use *hedging* as part of their investment technique.

Hedging is employing a method of protecting against market uncertainties. Usually this involves holding both long and short positions. Long positions involve the traditional buying and then selling of securities, while short positions are the selling of securities you borrow, with the expectation of replacing them at lower prices in the future. Many hedge funds use leveraging (taking out loans to buy stocks or bonds) and derivatives (such as futures and options) to increase returns.

Probably the best description of hedge funds is that they are private mutual funds, with a limited number of wealthy investors. They usually are set up as limited partnerships, with up to 100 limited partners. These partnerships are not controlled by securities law, and are exempt from most of the regulations that govern mutual funds. They are not required to publicly disclose information, such as their holdings, past return, or investment strategy. Therefore, a group of firms has arisen that specialize in following and recommending hedge funds for investors.

Investing in a hedge fund has some status appeal, since they are only for the rich, are fairly secretive, are run by high-profile managers, and use sophisticated investment techniques. However, they charge high fees (generally 1% of assets plus 20% of profits annually) and are relatively illiquid (typically investors can redeem only once a year). Some aim to be less risky than the average mutual fund, but others are quite speculative, highly leveraged, and subject to tremendous losses. Hedge funds are discussed in Chapter 16.

Choosing Mutual Fund Types

With this large selection of mutual fund types to choose from, how do you decide? The first step is to determine your asset allocation. This tells you what percentages of your investments go into stocks, bonds, cash, real estate, and other investment vehicles. You also have to determine how aggressive you want to be within each category—how much risk you will tolerate for the possibility of higher returns. Your asset allocation is based on your goals, investment period, risk tolerance, and possibly expectations of market performance. Asset allocation is discussed in Chapter 22.

Once you have determined the portion of your assets you wish to invest in domestic stocks, you have to decide how much you will invest in mutual funds, use to purchase stocks on your own or with a broker, or give to a private investment manager to purchase stocks for you. Determining how much you will place in unmanaged index funds and how much you'll invest with selected managers will be discussed in the following chapters.

Notes

1. John C. Bogle, *Bogle on Mutual Funds: New Perspectives for the Intelligent Investor*, NY: Irwin Professional Publishing, 1994.
2. Sheldon Jacobs, *Guide to Successful No-Load Fund Investing, Second Edition*, Irvington-on-Hudson, NY: No-Load Fund Investor, Inc., 1998, p. 163. Institutional funds were excluded.
3. *Mutual Fund Forecaster*, October 1998.
4. Computer Directions Advisors, Inc., 1979 (now CDA/Wiesenberger); *Consumer Reports* (March 2000).
5. Jacobs, p. 162.
6. Reported turnover rate is the lesser of purchases or sales of stocks as a percentage of average total fund assets. Therefore, the total of executed purchases and sales is approximately double the turnover rate. Transaction costs run approximately 0.6% of total executed trades.
7. Standard deviation equals the square root of the variance. To determine the variance of N number of scores, you: (1) determine the deviation of each score from the mean of all scores (= x); (2) find the sum of x^2 for all scores; (3) divide the sum by (N − 1). Determine the standard deviation by finding the square root of this quotient.
8. R.S. Ball, "The Predictability of Occupational Level from Intelligence," *Journal of Consulting Psychology*, 2 (1938), 184–186.
9. E. E. Ghiselli, *The Validity of Occupational Aptitude Tests*, New York: Wiley, 1966.
10. From *Bogle on Mutual Funds: New Perspectives for the Intelligent Investor*, New York: Irwin Professional Publishing, 1994, p. 77.
11. Samuel A. Mueller, University of Akron, 1988; cited in Jacobs, p. 134.

CHAPTER 11

Index Funds and Managed Funds: Echoes of Archilochus

John C. Bogle

The Greek philosopher Archilochus observed that "The fox knows many things, but the hedgehog knows one *great* thing." This ancient saying, dated to 670 B.C., has been interpreted to describe the *philosophical* contrast between the human pursuit of many different, even contradictory, goals related by no central principle and the search for a single overarching universal condition of human existence.[1] In the modern mutual fund industry, this contrast is manifest in two competing approaches to the investment markets: indexing and active management. The fox, that artful, sly, astute animal of the fields and the woods, finds its counterpart in the active manager who survives by knowing many things about complex markets and sophisticated investment strategies. The hedgehog, that durable nocturnal animal that survives by curling into a ball, its sharp spines giving it almost impregnable armor, is represented by the index fund manager, a financial institution that knows only one great thing: that in the long term, investment success is based on simplicity.

Since 1975, when I created the first index mutual fund, the philosophical clash between the fox and the hedgehog has been recast as a real-world drama, played out daily in the mutual fund arena. In theory, both the fox and the hedgehog can marshal persuasive arguments for the superiority of their respective investment approaches. Considered in the cold, hard light of fact, however, the debate resolves itself in favor of the hedgehog. In this chapter, I explore the differences between the active investment strategies of the fox and the simple indexed strategies of the hedgehog; I review the records of each camp; I explain why a hedgehog strategy ultimately proves the most productive approach for the long-term investor; and I attempt to puncture some of the myths that have arisen about the shortcomings of a hedgehog approach to long-term investing.

The Foxes—Truly a Skulk

In the mutual fund business today, indeed in our global financial system, the foxes hold sway. The skulk—a large crowd of fund foxes—holds to the idea that investing is complicated and complex, so much so that to achieve investment success individual investors have no choice but to employ professional portfolio managers. Only these experts, or so it is said, can possibly steer them through a hyperactive system that constitutes the complex maze of the global financial markets. In seeking to invest your money successfully, the industry's managers present powerful credentials, including excellent education, years of experience, cunning, and even investment legerdemain; they hover over their portfolios by the hour, constantly monitoring and changing holdings, often with astonishing frequency, not only as a company's products and prospects change, but as its market price waxes and wanes.

Their methodology is complex. Fund managers evaluate individual stocks; they try to determine the extent to which a company's stock price may discount its future prospects; they sift through the financial tea leaves for intimations of the market's direction. Further, some among this skulk expect slyly to sell stocks when the market is high, and buy them back when the market falls. In all, the managers add extra opportunity and accept the extra risk required in the search for superior returns. Alas, however, to the limited extent that these strategies have proven to work effectively—and for a relative handful of funds at that (of course, it would be absurd to imagine they could work for all funds as a group)—the very costs incurred by the fund managers have almost always been so high as to consume any value added, even by the most cunning of the portfolio manager-foxes. Fund shareholders have been left with annual returns that are generally less than 85% of the returns realized in the stock market.

Table 11.1 displays the annual returns provided by the market and the re-

TABLE 11.1 Average Annual Returns

Period Ended 3/31/99	U.S. Stock Market[1]	Average Equity Fund[2]	Fund as % of Market
5 Years	23.6%	18.0%	76.3%
10 Years	17.7%	14.8%	83.6%
15 Years	17.3%	14.3%	82.7%
20 Years	16.9%	14.4%	85.2%

[1]Wilshire 5000 Index.
[2]General Equity Fund, Lipper, Inc.

turns earned by mutual fund shareholders. In the past five years, the average equity fund earned only 76% of the stock market's 23.6% annual return. The 20-year comparison is more favorable to the fund managers, but still disappointing. Since 1979, the average fund has provided 85% of the stock market's annual return. The reason for this shortfall is largely fund costs. The *all-in* costs of the fund foxes now approach 3% per year on average: 1.5% from management fees and expenses, often 1% or more from the costs of churning the portfolio, plus another 0.5%-plus annually for investors who pay sales commissions. Now, let's think long-term instead of short-term.

Assume annual stock market returns of 10%. Let's be conservative and set the total croupier's take—the amount gathered by the managers, dealers, and brokers—at 2.5% per year. The *positive* impact of compound interest that magnifies long-term returns, unfortunately also magnifies the *negative* impact of costs, so that an assumed 2.5% annual cost consumes 33% of the investor's capital in a decade. As time goes on, costs consume 48% of capital in a quarter century, and—believe it or not—almost 70% of your capital (i.e., what capital you would have otherwise had) in 50 years. *The investor, who puts up 100% of the initial capital, receives but 30% of the long-term pretax return.* The remaining 70% has been consumed by the financial foxes.

These numbers are more than mere mathematical abstractions. Figure 11.1 shows that since the greatest bull market in history began in 1982, a $10,000 investment in the average equity mutual fund would have increased to $113,000; the same investment in the stock market (the Wilshire 5000 Index) would have grown to $175,000—a staggering $62,000 increment simply for *not* being a fox.

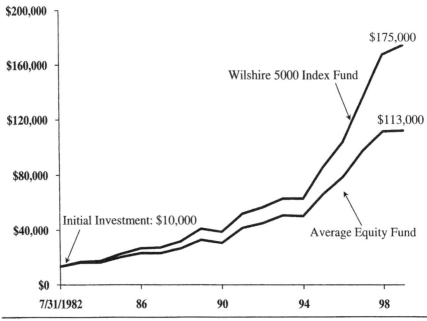

FIGURE 11.1 Wilshire 5000 Index Fund versus Average Equity Fund, July 1982–March 1999
Source: Lipper, Wilshire Associates

When Mr. Market Speaks, Funds Listen

To the extent that another investment approach can avoid, or at least minimize, the inherent pitfalls that are built into the traditional mutual fund system, that approach will hold the winning hand. Where might that approach begin? By investing for the long term. The ultimate example of long-term investing is simply buying and holding the stocks of U.S. businesses. Short-term speculation, its polar opposite, is buying shares—pieces of paper, if you will—of hundreds of stocks listed on the nation's stock exchanges, and then feverishly trading them in the market casino. The strategy of America's most successful investor is the paradigm of long-term investing. Warren Buffett purchases the shares of a few businesses and holds them, ignoring the noise created by someone he calls "Mr. Market," who comes by and offers him a different price for the businesses in his portfolio each day. The foxy managers of the fund industry, however, do precisely the opposite, trading the pieces of paper in their portfolios at turnover rates of 50% to 200% annually. Mr. Buffett's hedgehog-like buy-and-hold strategy is the essence of simplicity, the direct opposite of the complexity that is at the heart of the strategy of the foxes. Heed his words:

> The art of investing in public companies is . . . simply to acquire, at a sensible price, a business with excellent economics and able, honest management. Thereafter, you need only monitor whether these qualities are being preserved. Most investors, both institutional and individual, will find that the best way to own common stocks is through an index fund that charges minimal fees. Those following this path are sure to beat the net results (after fees and expenses) delivered by the great majority of investment professionals. Seriously, costs matter. For example, equity mutual funds incur corporate expenses—largely payments to the funds' managers—that average about 100 basis points, a levy likely to cut the returns their investors earn by 10 percent or more over time."[2]

Enter the Hedgehog

Successful long-term investors like Warren Buffett are almost impossible to identify in advance, but Mr. Buffett nominates an unconventional adversary to take on the foxes: the index fund. The one great thing the hedgehog knows is an utterly simple, self-evident, overarching mathematical truth: The returns of all investors must equal the returns of the stock market as a whole. A return of 10% per year in the market clearly can't be parlayed into a return of 11% for the average investor. Equally obvious conclusion: Investor returns, less the costs of investing, must fall short of market returns by the amount of investment expenses.

That early insight, such as it may be, first surfaced in my Princeton University thesis about the mutual fund industry. Studying the record, almost 50 years ago, I had concluded that "mutual funds can make no claim to superiority to the market averages." My readings in the academic journals around the time Vanguard was formed gave powerful theoretical reinforcement to that conclusion, and my careful study of mutual fund returns in the 1945—1975 period added powerful pragmatic evidence that confirmed the inability of fund managers to add value to their investors' assets. Vanguard's very first strategic decision, made in 1975 only months after we began, was obvious: to form the first market index mutual fund in history—an unmanaged portfolio of the 500 stocks in the Standard & Poor's 500 index. Derided for years as "Bogle's folly," it took, unimaginably, another full decade until a single competitor had the guts—or wisdom—to follow. In the words of the *Wall Street Journal*, the Vanguard 500 Index Fund has become, heaven forbid, "the industry darling."

With $80 billion of assets, our pioneering index fund is now the second-largest mutual fund in the world. The decisions that followed over the years took the same direction. Following that first S&P 500 index fund, we formed index funds covering our entire stock market, a wide variety of U.S. stock market sectors, international equity markets, and the bond market. Index funds hold every stock in a particular index, weighted according to its representation in the index. They operate without the putative benefit of a skilled, experienced, highly compensated professional portfolio manager. Index funds simply capitalize on the immutable mathematics of the investment markets:

$MR - C = IR$: Market return minus cost equals investors' return.

We have no power to control the market's returns. Instead, index funds attack that element of net return that *is* within our power to control: cost. A sensibly designed index fund holds costs to minimal levels, providing investors with the greatest possible share of the returns earned by whichever market they choose to track.

The Ultimate Hedgehog

The most fully realized example of the indexing concept is an all-market index fund, modeled on the Wilshire 5000 Equity Index. It is the essence of simplicity, investing in the entire stock market; diversified across almost every publicly held corporation in the United States; essentially untouched by human hands; nearly bereft of costly portfolio turnover; remarkably cost-efficient; and extraordinarily tax-effective. Mr. Buffett says his favorite holding period for a stock is "forever." I say that owning an all-market index fund is owning every publicly held business in America forever. No wonder Mr. Buffett repeatedly endorses the index fund: "By investing in an index fund, the know-nothing investor can actually outperform the professionals." There is a sharp difference—both in cost and in investment philosophy—between a conventionally managed mutual fund and an index fund, and therein lies a difference, not merely in *degree*, but in *kind*. It is the difference between the fox and the hedgehog. In my bolder moments, I believe that the index fund will, by its crystal-clear example of the causal link between cost and return, finally prove to be the vehicle that will change not only the focus of the mutual fund industry, but its very structure.

An index fund based on the Wilshire 5000 Equity Index represents 100% of the market, so, in an environment of, say, 12% returns, such a fund, carrying an annual cost of 0.2%, will provide a return of 11.8%, or 98% plus. Another reasonable choice is an S&P 500 index fund, which is based on an index that includes 75% of the value of all U.S. stocks. Because of the powerful surge of the large-cap stocks in the S&P 500, the 500 index fund is the popular favorite of the day, but I do not believe that large caps, important as they may be in the market's mix, are destined for permanent ascendancy. So some caution is called for in projecting the S&P 500 index's recently huge margin of superiority over active managers into the future. Small- and mid-cap stocks, the dogs of recent years, will have their day. In the long run, large- and small-cap stocks are apt to provide similar returns, so either fund should work out just fine. But over the short run, a total stock market index fund will obviously provide a closer tracking of the total market—the quintessential rationale for the theory of indexing.

Figure 11.2 displays the annual spread between the return of the average equity fund and the Wilshire 5000 index, reduced by the 0.2% expense ratio that is incurred by the industry's largest total stock market index fund; it also shows the cumulative returns of investments in both portfolios. Despite occasional stretches of superior performance, actively managed funds have tended to lag the annual performance of a total stock market index fund. This shortfall results primarily from mutual fund operating expenses and management fees—the expense ratio—and from the costs of buying and selling securities for the portfolio—transaction costs. To a lesser extent, the performance differ-

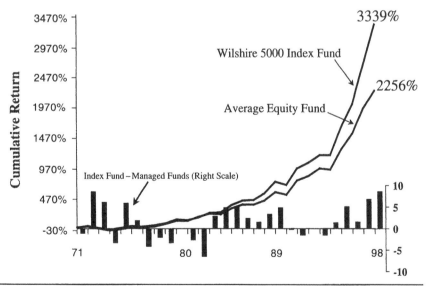

FIGURE 11.2 Wilshire 5000 Index Fund versus Average Equity Fund, 1971–1998

ence between actively managed funds and the index fund can be attributed to the level of cash reserves held in the actively managed portfolios, to active managers' security selections, and to the performances of the market's different investment styles. Because a large number of actively managed funds invest in smaller stocks than those that dominate the major indexes, their relative performance improves when smaller stocks are in favor.

During the 1970s, the index fund held a relatively small margin of advantage of 0.98% per year over actively managed funds. Before an average expense ratio of 1.03% and portfolio transaction costs of perhaps 0.25%, the average equity fund outperformed the index fund by about 30 basis points per year. (One basis point equals $1/_{100}$ of a percentage point.) As a basis for faith in the powers of active management, this minor triumph is less than it seems. First, the performance data are survivor-biased. The record includes only the performance of those funds that operated in the 1970s and have survived to the present day. It should go without saying that those funds that didn't survive were invariably the worst performers. The result is an upward bias in the industry's performance record of 1 to 4 percentage points annually, which would suggest that the average fund actually lagged the index fund before costs.[3] Second, the industry's average expense ratio was lower during the 1970s. The mutual fund industry might conceivably have been able to squeeze past the index when it traveled with a light expense burden, but today the average fund labors under heavy expense freight.

Indeed, during the 1980s, as the industry's expense ratios rose, the average managed fund lagged further behind the index fund. Its average shortfall increased by 67%, to 1.64 percentage points. An average expense ratio of 1.18% accounted for 72% of the managed funds' lag. Portfolio transaction activity accelerated, too, penalizing fund shareholders with trading costs that rose to perhaps 0.35% to 0.4% annually. During the 1990s, the shortfall continued to increase, rising by 38% to an annual average of 2.26 percentage points. Fully 65% of the lag can be attributed to the fund industry's average expense ratio of 1.46%. With average portfolio turnover of 86% annually, suggesting that each stock is held for little more than a year, the average managed fund now incurs transaction costs of 0.5% to 1% annually, accounting for at least 25% of its shortfall to the index fund. We can chalk up the remaining 25% to undistinguished stock selection and the average fund's modest investment in cash reserves during history's most bountiful bull market.

At the end of this 28-year period, these seemingly modest differences in annual return resulted in a more than 1,000 percentage point difference in cumulative return: 3,339% for the index fund, 2,256% for the average managed fund. A $10,000 investment in the index fund grew to $344,000. Those who cast their lot with the foxy fund managers amassed just $236,000. They paid a

$108,000 penalty for their decision to follow a complex approach to investing in the stock market.

Identifying the Winning Foxes

Were there fund managers who succeeded in outpacing the all-market index fund? Yes. Of the 186 managers who survived the period, 57 funds outperformed the index. The most successful fund trounced the index fund by 6.8 percentage points annually. (Because this comparison excludes the sales charges paid as the price of admission to about two-thirds of all equity mutual funds, it significantly understates the advantage of a low-cost index fund purchased without a sales charge.) Was it possible to have identified these superior performers in advance? It appears not. At the start of the period, those 57 funds with the brightest futures managed an aggregate $7.5 billion of assets, just 17% of the $45 billion total invested in equity funds. In retrospect, it's clear that some foxes were sufficiently cunning (or lucky) to outwit the hedgehog, but it's equally clear that their promise went largely unrecognized by the investing public.

And once the superior long-term performers have been identified, the outstanding mutual funds with outstanding records may already be colliding with an immutable principle of the financial markets: reversion to the mean. The one thing that appears certain about the future relative performance of successful funds is this: *Performance superiority will not be sustained.*

During the 1980s, for example, the top quartile of funds beat the market by nearly 3 percentage points annually, only to lag the market by more than 1 percentage point during the 1990s—a reversion of 4.2 percentage points. Of these 40 top-quartile funds from the 1980s, fully 39 funds had their margins over the market reduced in the 1990s, including 30 funds that provided returns below those of the market.

This is not a statistical aberration. The reversion to the mean among the top-quartile funds from the 1970s, for example, was –4.8% during the 1980s, virtually identical to the reversion of –4.2% for the top quartile funds in the 1980s to the 1990s. Reversion to the mean, a sort of law of gravity, seems almost preordained in fund performance, frustrating the dreams of so many investors who invest on the basis of past returns.

Taxes and Strategy

These comparisons, like almost all performance comparisons, are based on the pretax returns earned by mutual funds. But for the 40 to 50 million shareholders who own mutual funds in taxable accounts, the pretax returns are an economic fiction. What matter are not the pre-tax returns reported in the financial press and in mutual fund annual reports, but the after-tax returns earned by the investor. For the most part, neither the hedgehog nor the fox deliberately practices tax-management techniques, but their diametrically opposite strategies hold important implications for the taxable investor. The rapid portfolio turnover that so hobbles the fox on a pretax basis does even greater damage on an after-tax basis. By contrast, the buy-and-hold strategy of the hedgehog, which proves so productive on a pretax basis, is even more rewarding after taxes.

Holding stocks forever, deferring the realization of capital gains indefinitely, is a marvelous strategy for the taxable investor. By deferring the realization of gains, and thus the tax due on those gains, the investor effectively secures an interest-free loan from the U.S. Treasury. The tax will be due someday, of course, but in the meantime the loan is put to work in the stock market, shrinking the value of your future obligation to the U.S. government. A dollar in taxes deferred for 25 years, and invested at an annual return of 8%, has a present value of just 15 cents. The many foxes who realize sizable gains in the present must reckon with the tax collector today, forsaking the 85-cent bonus earned by the buy-and-hold investor.

The after-tax records of indexed and managed funds make this difference clear. Index funds have produced some 92% of the pretax market return during the past decade. Managed funds have earned less than 70% of the market's pretax return. Because of rapid portfolio turnover, the managed funds realize high levels of capital gains, with some one-third of these gains realized after holding periods of less than 12 months. These short-term gains are taxable at ordinary income rates, which can be twice as high as the long-term capital gains rate.

Figure 11.3 displays the pretax and after-tax returns for the average mutual fund and for the longest-operating index fund from April 1989 to April 1999. On an after-tax basis, the index fund's impressive 4.1% pretax margin of advantage over the managed funds rises to 5.4 percentage points annually. (Although this comparison is based on a large-cap–dominated S&P 500 index fund, the only index fund with a 10-year record, an all-market index fund would most likely have enjoyed a 2.9 percentage point margin of advantage before taxes, and 4.2 percentage points after taxes.)

Just like expense ratios and portfolio turnover, taxes, as it turns out, are just one more cost—and a huge one—that separates the returns earned by investors in the managed equity funds from the returns earned by a market index fund. The argument that *tax-deferred* investors should own foxy funds is quite tenuous enough; the argument that *taxable* investors should own them nearly collapses beneath the weight of evidence to the contrary. The hedgehog has either won a good fight or crushed the foxes in a landslide.

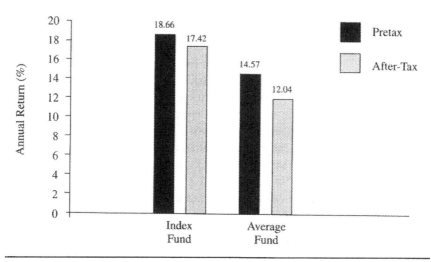

FIGURE 11.3 Pretax and After-Tax Returns, 10 Years Ended April 30, 1998

The Foxes Respond

In the quest for investment success, the simple strategy of the hedgehog has trumped the complex machinations of the fox. The foxes cannot dispute these conclusions. Instead, they ignore them or derogate the hedgehog with criticisms—some of which may even be valid.

But they go too far. Their most vociferous charge is that index funds are riskier than managed funds, and that actively managed funds will outpace passively managed indexes during periods of market decline. This myth has taken hold among investors and the financial media alike, though, mercifully, it may have finally been erased by the brief bear market in the summer of 1998. The myth was that, since indexes are at all times 100% invested in stocks, the cash reserves held by active managers would lessen the shock of the decline in their portfolios. What is more, so the myth went, smart managers, recognizing that a market decline was in prospect, would raise even more cash in advance, and gain considerable downside protection during the ensuing market storm.

First, the fact is that, at the traditional levels of equity fund cash reserves, cash is the tail and not the dog. Simple logic compels the conclusion that a 5% to 10% tail of cash cannot possibly wag the dog represented by a 90% to 95% equity position. And mutual funds hold equity portfolios that have proven to be somewhat riskier than the portfolios of the major indexes, which are dominated by higher-quality, larger-cap stocks. As a result, the indexes have traditionally provided not less, but more, downside protection than actively managed funds during market declines.

Taking into account both the cash position and the more volatile portfolio of the average mutual fund, the record confirms that index funds based on the Standard & Poor's 500 index and the Wilshire 5000 index are somewhat *less* risky. *Morningstar Mutual Funds* calculates a risk factor for each fund based on returns in the months in which it underperformed the risk-free U.S. Treasury bill. The data show that, over the past decade, the S&P 500 index was some 15% less risky than the average mutual fund, and the Wilshire 5000 index was 18% less risky. (Morningstar risk ratings: average fund, 1.00; S&P 500 index, 0.85; Wilshire 5000 index, 0.81.)

Looked at in a different way, over the past decade the standard deviation of return of the S&P 500 has been 3% lower than that of the average equity fund, and the Wilshire 5000 has been 5% lower. Given this record, it should not have been surprising that in 1998's brief bear market, funds again fell more than the averages—8% more than the Wilshire 5000 (off 20.7%) and 15% more than the S&P 500 (off 19%). The average equity fund fell by 22.2%.

What happened to the vaunted ability of fund managers to raise cash before market drops (and to reinvest that cash after the drop is over)? It simply wasn't there. Quite to the contrary: Managers have been terrible market timers. Funds have consistently tended to hold large amounts of cash at market lows and small amounts at market highs. For example, cash equaled only 4% of assets immediately *before* the 1973–74 market crash, but increased to about 12% at the ensuing low; at the beginning of the bull market in 1982, equity funds held cash equal to 12% of assets. In mid-1998, just before the stock market's steep decline, cash reserves stood at less than 5% of equity fund assets. Managers, in short, have been bearish when they should have been bullish, and bullish when they should have been bearish. It is not a formula for success.

Wily Reasoning, Wrong Conclusion

The foxes level a second charge at the hedgehog, but it, too, proves a canard: "Indexing works only in efficient markets," such as those represented by the actively traded, very liquid large-capitalization stocks that dominate the S&P 500 index, and not to other presumably less efficient markets.

Plausible as that argument may sound, it is specious. For the success of indexing is based not on some notion of market efficiency, but simply on the inability of all investors in any discrete market or market segment to outpace the universe of investments in which they operate. Efficiency relates to a market price structure that generally values all securities properly at any one time, which means that good managers and bad alike will have difficulty in differentiating themselves *either way*. In inefficient markets, to be sure, good managers may have greater opportunities to outpace their universe, but the excess returns earned by good managers must inevitably be offset by inferior returns of the exact same dimension by bad managers. (Here again, there are good stock pickers and bad stock pickers.)

However, costs of mutual funds operating in so-called inefficient markets are higher than funds operating in efficient markets. For example, expense ratios and transaction costs of small-cap funds are systematically higher than those of large-cap funds. It also turns out that, once account is taken for the relatively higher risks that they assume, mid-cap and small-cap mutual funds have actually realized slightly *larger* shortfalls to the indexes in their market sectors than their large-cap cousins have realized. A study of mine that was published in the *Journal of Portfolio Management*[4] showed that the advantage in risk-adjusted return—which was 3.5% per year for large-cap funds—was 4.2% for mid-cap funds and 4.4% for small-cap funds (Figure 11.4). Note particularly the progressively widening difference in risk as cap size falls—large-cap funds are 1.6 percentage points riskier than the large-cap index, 2.6 percentage points for

	Return	Risk	Risk-Adjusted Return
Large Cap			
Funds	13.0%	10.6%	1.04
Index	15.0	9.0	1.28
Index Adjusted*	16.5%	10.6%	1.28
Index Advantage	3.5%		
Mid Cap			
Funds	13.8%	12.3%	0.95
Index	15.1	9.7	1.22
Index Adjusted	18.0%	12.3%	1.22
Index Advantage	4.2%		
Small Cap			
Funds	15.1%	14.7%	0.92
Index	15.4	11.1	1.12
Index Adjusted	19.5%	14.7%	1.12
Index Advantage	4.4%		

*Index return adjusted to equalize index risk and fund risk. Data: 12/31/1991–12/31/1996.

FIGURE **11.4** Fund Categories versus Comparable Indexes

mid-cap relative to the mid-cap index, and 3.6 percentage points for small-cap funds versus the small-cap index.

Costs of international funds are higher still, not only because of higher expense ratios but because of much higher custodial expenses, taxes, commissions, and market impact costs. As a result, not only do the exact same principles of indexing apply in international markets, but an even larger margin of superiority for the passively managed international index should probably be expected.

The past results (as shown in Figure 11.5) are erratic, based on a small sample of funds and indexes with pronounced country biases. (The MSCI EAFE—Morgan Stanley Capital International Europe, Australasia, Far East—and Pacific indexes, for example, carry a far larger weighting in the Japanese stock market than the average international and Pacific managed fund.) But over the past 20 years, the positive margin for the international index over the average international fund was 0.4% annually, while Vanguard's European and emerging markets index funds have outpaced their actively managed peers by 3.4% and 3.2% annually since their inceptions. Indexing, it turns out, works—as it must—with high effectiveness in all the far-flung corners of the world of equity investing.

Inefficient markets, to be sure, may provide managers with more opportunities to do well. But the added returns of those who do well must inevitably be offset by the return shortfalls of those who do not. Given the higher costs of owning funds that operate in less efficient markets, it proves to be a bad trade-off. For ex-

	1978–1988	1988–1998	1978–1998
MSCI EAFE Index	22.2%	5.9%	13.8%
International Funds	17.6	8.6	13.4

			7/90–12/98
European Index Fund			14.0%
European Managed Funds			10.6

			7/90–12/98
Pacific Index Fund			−1.71%
Pacific Managed Funds			1.04

			6/94–12/98
Emerging Markets Index Fund			−5.1%
Emerging Markets Managed Funds			−8.3

FIGURE 11.5 International Indexes versus International Funds

ample (Figure 11.6), assume that: the top 10% of managers can outpace an efficient market by 3% per year over time, but in an inefficient market by 5%; the bottom 10% of managers do the reverse; and total fund costs are 1.5% per year in efficient markets at 2.5% in inefficient markets. Results: 1) the top managers provide excess returns of 1.5% in efficient markets and 2.5% in inefficient markets; but 2) the bottom 10% provide returns of –4.5% and –7.5%, respectively.

Clearly, the symmetrical pattern of precost returns quickly becomes asymmetrical after the deduction of costs. Put another way, the onus of costs erodes the superiority of the top equity managers, even as it magnifies the deficiency of the bottom-tier managers. But it does so by larger amounts—in both cases—in inefficient stock markets. Thus, ironically enough, equity indexing may well prove to work more productively in inefficient markets than in efficient markets.

The Conflict Continues

After a half-century observing this industry, I may have become too much the philosopher, maybe even too much the cynic. But it occurs to me that most mutual fund managers are barking up the wrong tree. I just can't imagine that any of those foxes in the mutual fund industry don't understand the simple arithmetic that gives the index fund its powerful advantage, let alone the extra boost added by its extraordinary tax-efficiency.

The reality, unfortunately, is that it is not the *investment* success of the *client* that dictates mutual fund strategy. It is the *business* success of the *fund manager*. The survival of this industry, as we know it today, depends on the maintenance of the status quo by the foxes. Financial success for the mutual fund manager is represented far less by earning even a market return on the investor's capital than by earning a staggering return on the manager's capital. (If you don't believe that, merely compare the returns that the managers have earned on their own capital to the returns they have earned on the funds they supervise.)

	Before Costs		After Costs	
	Top 10%	**Bottom 10%**	**Top 10%**	**Bottom 10%**
Efficient Markets	+3%	–3%	+1.5%	–4.5%
Inefficient Markets	+5	–5	+2.5	–7.5

*Assumed fund costs: 1.5% in efficient markets, 2.5% in inefficient markets.

FIGURE 11.6 Manager Returns Relative to Market Averages (Hypothetical)

Were this not so, managers would not seek huge asset size for their actively managed funds, which clearly impedes the achievement of superior returns, nor spend billions on marketing shares to new investors, the cost of which is borne by existing shareholders who receive no benefit in return—except perhaps the pleasure of seeing their former portfolio manager perform on television with Don Rickles and Lily Tomlin. Marketing functions have superseded those of management, and the interest of the managers has superseded the interest of the fund shareholders.

That I am virtually the industry's sole apostle of indexing makes the hedgehog thesis easy to ignore. But even when Warren Buffett, with his unchallenged credentials, speaks—"Most investors . . . will find that the best way to own common stocks is through an index fund that charges minimal fees . . . [They] are sure to beat the net results . . . delivered by the great majority of investment professionals"—this industry fails to listen. Except, that is, for the former chairman of one giant fund complex who defends his firm against the clear truth that underlies the superiority of the index with these words: "Investors ought to recognize that mutual funds can *never* [his word] beat the index." Despite industry recalcitrance, investors are slowly beginning to respond to the example of the hedgehog. Index funds still account for a very modest share of industry assets, but they have claimed almost half of every dollar invested in equity funds over the past year. Compelled by the demands of clients, more fund firms are beginning to offer index funds, too, albeit with a marked lack of enthusiasm.

I doubt that we will soon become a nation of hedgehog investors. The opposing forces are simply too great, the ranks of the foxes too strong. But perhaps the increasing attention to index funds marks the beginning of a very gradual acceptance of the hedgehog's simple principles for long-term investment success. The index fund is not merely another kind of mutual fund. It approaches investing not as a matter of trading pieces of paper for advantage, but as a matter of owning businesses and watching them grow. *Through an all-market index fund, investors own the shares of virtually every publicly held business in the United States, and hold them forever.* This overarching principle—the one great thing that the fund hedgehog knows—is not merely a good strategy for the long-term investor. It is a winning strategy.

Notes

1. I give special note to the extraordinary British philosopher Sir Isaiah Berlin, whose 1953 essay "The Fox and the Hedgehog" was the source of my inspiration to use this theme.

2. In 1996 letter to shareholder.
3. In one of the most comprehensive studies of its kind, Princeton professor Burton Malkiel found that, from 1982 to 1991, survivor bias enhanced reported returns by 1.4 percentage points annually. From 1976 to 1991, survivor bias enhanced returns by 4.2 percentage points annually.
4. John C. Bogle, "The Implications of Style Analysis for Mutual Fund Performance Evaluation," *Journal of Portfolio Management* (Summer 1998), pp. 34–42.

CHAPTER

12

Evaluating Mutual Fund Performance

Eugene Fama Jr. and Weston Wellington

How do you tell whether a mutual fund you own is performing as well as it should? In assessing the merits of dishwashers or TV sets, the notion of grading performance by comparison to alternative products is straightforward. But the investment industry has created a vast number of products, and developing a proper basis for comparison is more challenging. In the absence of thoughtful analysis, investors can easily be persuaded that a fund with high returns relative to some alternative investments is performing well when, in fact, the reverse may be true.

The purpose of analysis is an effort to answer the question, "Am I better off investing in this fund than if I had invested in a simple index fund that reliably captured market rates of return?" Prior to the introduction of index funds, this question was of interest only to economists developing finance theory. With low-cost index funds for a multitude of asset classes easily available to investors, this becomes a key issue. Index funds make no effort to seek out "attractive" stocks or avoid "unattractive" ones. They simply buy and hold all appropriate securities in an index (hundreds, perhaps thousands), keeping investment costs to a minimum. Since their development in the mid-1970s as an outgrowth of academic research on stock market behavior, index funds have grown significantly and continue to do so, with assets in various indexed strategies exceeding $2 trillion worldwide. Index funds have succeeded because they represent a reliable, low-cost way to capture market rates of return. Conventional actively-managed funds, which attempt to outperform an indexed approach through stock picking or market timing, are burdened with higher costs for research and trading compared to indexed vehicles—frequently three to five times higher. Since higher investment costs directly reduce investment returns, fund analysis seeks to determine if the additional costs of active management are in fact recovered through higher returns. Many studies of money manager performance over the past 30 years reveal that the majority of funds over time fail to recoup these costs.

If comparing funds to indexes or index funds is useful, which index should one use?—the Dow Jones Industrial Average (30 stocks), the S&P 500 Composite index (500 stocks), the Russell 2000 index (2000 small-company stocks), the Wilshire 5000 index (7,000+ stocks), or all of these?

The broadest measure of U.S. market performance among popular indexes is the Wilshire 5000 index, since it incorporates the vast majority of all publicly traded firms in the United States. Mutual funds such as Vanguard Total Stock Market allow investors to capture the returns of this benchmark easily and inexpensively. Many investors assume that outperforming such an index is relatively simple, since all one has to do is overweight the winning companies and weed out the obvious losers. In a market that sets prices for all stocks through competitive bidding, however, these distinctions are quickly reflected in prices, and outperforming the index turns out to be quite a challenge. For the 10-year period ending December 1999, for example, only 28% of U.S. equity fund managers in the Micropal database outperformed the Wilshire 5000 index.

If the Wilshire 5000 represents the universe of all U.S. stock market opportunity, should one use this index as a basis of comparison and call it a day? It's certainly useful as a "first cut" analysis, particularly over periods of five years or more, and the simplicity of the approach is appealing. But many mutual funds do not fish from the entire universe of U.S. stocks in making security selections, and using a single broad-based index can be misleading. Some mutual funds intentionally focus on particular types of stocks, such as small-company stocks or distressed value stocks, and these types of stocks can behave very differently from a broad market index, especially over shorter time periods such as one quarter or one year.

Total return for the Wilshire 5000 index in 1998, for example, was 23.45%, but large-company stocks as measured by the S&P 500 returned 26.58% while small companies as measured by the Russell 2000 index returned –2.56%. In analyzing investment skill, a small-company fund manager who delivered 12% in 1998 gets much higher grades than a large-company manager who returned 24%. Absolute returns for the small cap manager were lower, but the large-company manager failed to improve upon market returns that were there for the taking, while the small-company manager outperformed his or her sector by a large margin.

Returns-Based Style Analysis

The next level of analysis, therefore, is to identify what the manager's typical investment universe consists of (through close reading of the prospectus, annual report, etc.) and compare results to an index more closely reflecting the investment style. The most thorough approach, however, relies upon returns-based style analysis to determine a manager's true investment style with more precision, and blending various index-like factors to develop a customized benchmark to grade against. In other words, rather than limit the comparison to several popular indexes, consider an entire universe of possible benchmarks, each of which reflects a blending of various factors. This is the fairest way to judge a manager, since results are compared to a theoretical benchmark that reflects the manager's factor exposure. For example, if a fund on average had 75% of assets in large stocks and 25% in small stocks, an appropriate benchmark would be constructed by weighting a large- and small-company index in the same proportion and comparing results.

Returns-based analysis looks at the actual pattern of historical returns in determining the fund's investment category or style. Rather than rely on portfolio holdings information that is often outdated or unobtainable, the analysis focuses strictly on results. The theory is: If a fund looks like a duck, walks like a duck, and quacks like a duck, it probably is a duck. If a fund goes up sharply when small-cap stocks rise and goes down sharply when small-cap stocks plummet, it should be categorized as a small-cap fund even if the fund holdings include large-company stocks. Software for returns-based-style analysis is commercially available. However, there is an art to the analysis, particularly to the selection of benchmark indexes, and to the interpretation of the findings and their use in implementation of an investment plan. It is probably best to find an investment adviser with experience applying the technique.

This is beginning to sound complicated. Won't this approach get muddled by dozens of possible investment styles or factors? It turns out not to be the case. Research by Eugene Fama of the University of Chicago and Kenneth French of

MIT concludes that the behavior of diversified equity portfolios such as mutual funds is determined principally by exposure to three simple risk factors. This is good news for consumers of investment products, since it means that the analysis is fairly straightforward. The factors themselves are not intuitively obvious, however, and we will now examine them in greater detail.

Fama-French Three-Factor Model

In a landmark study issued in 1992, Fama and French studied the entire universe of U.S. stocks starting in 1963. They sought to find if there were differences in average returns among stocks, and if there were common factors that could explain those differences. Subsequent research extended the inquiry back to the 1920s. After examining many possible factors that might explain returns (earnings, dividends, leverage, company size, etc.) Fama and French determined that two fundamental characteristics, company size and book-to-market ratio, account for more of the variations in returns than all the other characteristics combined. The third factor in their model is called the market factor, the difference in returns attributable to being invested in stocks rather than risk-free fixed-income securities such as Treasury bills.

Their findings suggest that, over time, performance relative to the entire market or to other investors depends almost entirely on (1) the amount of stocks in general, (2) the proportion of small-cap stocks versus large-cap stocks, and (3) the proportion of high book-to-market (BtM) stocks versus low book-to-market stocks. High BtM stocks have relatively high book values (what the accountants say a company is worth) relative to market value (what investors say the company is worth). The way to get a high BtM ratio is to have a low stock price. This usually reflects investor uncertainty or disappointment with the future earnings prospects for the company. Stocks falling into this category are often called "value" stocks, but perhaps a more accurate description would be "distressed."

Low BtM stocks are the mirror image: They are growth companies with rosy earnings prospects, and the stock price, reflecting this investor confidence, is high relative to its book value (price-to-book is just the inverse of book-to-market, so a low BtM firm has a high market price relative to its book value.) Fama and French found that, on average, small-company stocks and high-BtM or value stocks had higher returns than large-company or growth stocks. An important observation was that these higher returns were not a free lunch but represented extra return as reward for bearing greater risk.

How you structure your stock portfolio along these measures, rather than specific stock selection, is the most crucial investment decision. Together these three factors specify what the market rewards with higher returns. Designing portfolios that target these factors allows us to capture the returns associated with them. We call this "engineering" portfolios for better returns.

Why Do Company Size and Book-to-Market Determine Returns?

A fundamental principle of economics is that risk and return are joined at the hip. Systematic differences in returns must relate to differences in risk. Investors expect markets to compensate them for increased uncertainty and an increased chance of loss, and prices reflect this expectation. It's difficult to imagine the world working any other way. Who would invest in risky stocks if the expected return were lower than risk-free Treasury bills?

Most people agree that the stock market is riskier than T-bills and that small stocks are riskier than large stocks. The notion that high book-to-market stocks are riskier and have greater returns than low BtM stocks is tougher to accept. What's so special about BtM? It's just a fundamental measure. On the surface, there's no economic reason BtM should relate to differences in returns.

There *isn't* anything special about BtM. It does not describe risk. However, sorting stocks by BtM also seems to sort them by their true underlying source of risk, the level of their distress relative to healthier growth firms. The key to book/market lies in the denominator, market price. High book/market stocks are lower-priced stocks. This is usually because the stock is a poor earner, which makes it riskier. *Riskier means higher expected returns.* The connection between BtM and returns makes sense when we focus on the denominator, the market price.

Cost of Capital

The Nobel prize awarded to Merton Miller in 1990 recognized his pioneering research into the cost of capital. When markets work, the cost of capital to a company equals the expected return on its stock. This is a simple but profound notion. Companies seeking capital come to the marketplace with earnings prospects. Investors supplying capital want the highest return with the least risk. Prices for new stock or bond issues represent the clearing price satisfying each party. Prices change in the secondary market in response to new developments, but no matter how far removed from the initial offering, they always reflect the risk of the underlying capital venture.

The cost of debt capital is easy to measure: A bond issue priced to yield 7% to the investor represents a 7% cost of debt capital to the issuer. No such precision is available for computing the cost of equity capital, so economists use asset-pricing models to develop reasonable estimates.

Suppose Microsoft and Apple Computer each go to the bank for a loan. Which company will have to pay the higher interest rate? Apple will; its future is uncertain and the bank will demand extra compensation for bearing the additional risk. Apple therefore incurs a higher cost for its capital.

The stock market works the same way. The market expects a higher return for Apple stock than for Microsoft stock. This induces investors to purchase Apple even though Microsoft seems to have better earnings prospects (it seems safer). Put differently, if the two companies had the same expected return, no one would buy Apple. This doesn't mean Apple stock will always outperform Microsoft (remember, if we know *for sure* what will happen, it isn't risk). We have to conclude the market will set Apple's price at a discount, so the *expected* return is higher. Otherwise we'd be assuming Microsoft were riskier. This is an example, in any case. In practice, we always want to hold broadly diversified portfolios to capture the true factors in returns and minimize the "noise" in individual stock returns.

Using the Model in Practice

Because the Fama-French model is an asset-pricing model, it can perform a number of useful functions:

■ Calculate expected returns based on factor exposure.

■ Analyze proposed portfolios and reallocations.

■ Analyze manager style and success.

■ Analyze contributions of additional asset classes.

We focus here on the first two.

Expected Returns Based on Factor Exposure

The model allows us to calculate the way portfolios take different types of risk and calculate their expected returns based on these risks. The portfolio's exposure to these factors is used to predict its expected return. Figure 12.1 shows how we plot portfolios for their factor exposures. The crosshair has two dimensions, size along the vertical axis and BtM along the horizontal axis. The axes represent exposures to the two factors. Portfolios that take a lot of size risk plot higher along the size axis and portfolios that take a lot of BtM risk plot farther right along the BtM axis.

Notice that the market portfolio is midway between growth and value (by definition), but lies much closer to the large end of the size spectrum. This is because the market portfolio is capitalization weighted. Because all equity

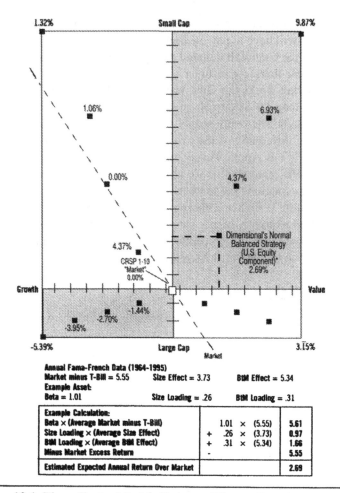

FIGURE 12.1 Three-Factor Model: Estimated Return Premiums over Market

portfolios take similar market risk, we don't need a third axis for beta. The market sits at the crosshairs. All portfolios are plotted relative to the market.

Analyzing Portfolios

The crosshair "map" is a universe of opportunities. Portfolios can and do land anywhere on the plot. From its location, the portfolio's expected return over time can readily be calculated. The amount by which an actively managed portfolio historically outperformed or underperformed this expectation constitutes their "alpha."

The model compares a manager to an indexing of his (or her) precise factor exposures, rather than to one or more benchmark indexes that may or may not reflect what the manager invested in. A small-cap manager, for instance, may overweight value stocks relative to his benchmark, the Russell 2000 small-cap index. As a result, he outperforms it. Judged against the benchmark, he had a premium return that he uses to justify a premium fee. But, since the manager invested heavily in value-type stocks within the small-cap universe, he would be expected to generate higher returns, according to the model. The extra return was simply compensation for taking additional systematic (value) risk. Why should the manager get credit? The job of an active manager is to provide additional returns that can't be achieved through indexing.

In this example, the model would place the manager somewhere to the right of the Russell 2000 along the value spectrum. We should insist the manager outperform that benchmark before crediting him with a premium return. Active manager fees are supposed to pay for smart stock selection, not additional returns that are compensation for taking additional risk.

Is Alpha Everything?

Structure, the way you position your portfolio on the crosshair map, will largely determine your return. Over time, the amount of return due to the manager's skill in stock selection or timing (alpha) is nearly always negligible. Some managers beat the market every year, but it tends to be different ones each year. Yet active managers typically focus on alpha and are less concerned with how consistently and strongly they expose their portfolios to the risk factors. They fail to provide reliable exposure to the predictive factors *and* they typically fail to provide reliable alphas.

Painting the Right Picture

Investors should not abdicate the decision on the appropriate degree of risk in their portfolios. When you hire an equity manager, it's because you want the risk—and the expected rewards—associated with owning stocks. Similarly, if you hire a small-cap or value stock manager, you do so to ensure these risk/return dimensions are included in your investment strategy. Your degree of exposure to these risks is a matter of preference and investment horizon. If you hire a small-cap manager who changes to a large-cap manager, he's usurping the biggest part of your responsibility. Structuring an investment portfolio is like making a painting: You combine different factors to create an overall picture. Managers are most useful for the vivid, consistent way they deliver the

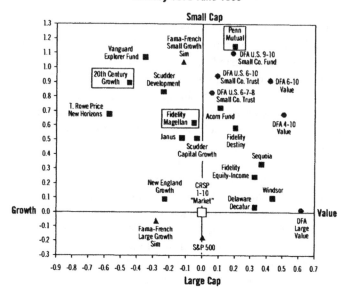

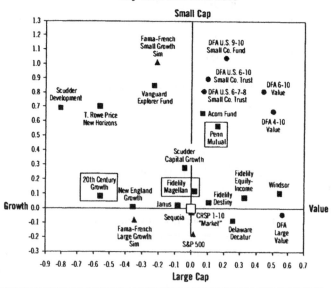

FIGURE 12.2 Three-Factor Model: Manager Profiles

factors. If one day you squeeze the cadmium red tube and green comes out, how can you paint the picture you want?

Figure 12.2 shows regression results for several popular active managers from the Morningstar database. Their returns for the period 1976–1995 were run through the model, with no outside information about their market caps or BtM ratios. The plots show the managers' average factor exposures during the first and second halves of the total period.

The positions shifted significantly over time. Twentieth Century Growth spent the first half of the period, on average, as a growth fund with a small-cap (Russell 2000–like) size. In the second half it was still a growth fund, but the size increased to that of the market average. Pennsylvania Mutual used to be a micro-cap in size, but moved to a mid-cap size in the latter half of the period.

As evidenced by these examples, funds tend to migrate toward the market. We can speculate why. The market is still the general benchmark they're compared to (often incorrectly), and they don't want to be too different. Also, as funds get more popular they often increase the market cap of their holdings to accommodate new investment dollars. When funds move like this they subvert your asset allocation decision.

A Powerful Tool for Investors

The real advantage of the model is that it gives the investor a framework for investment strategy. It identifies the sources of risk that compensate investors with returns. Investment decisions are simplified and less stressful. In the absence of such a model, investors are often confronted with a confusing array of asset classes and money managers. Vehicles and asset classes are interchangeable when the central problem is managing three simple factors.

In a world where most investors are guessing which managers or asset classes will have excess returns, the model leads investors to structure and monitor portfolios in a straightforward, unemotional manner. Questions and problems are answered using a consistent philosophy. Simplifying the process encourages discipline, the key element for long-term investment success.

When to Sell Your Fund

Robert Arffa

Emotionally, it's much more difficult to withdraw your money from a mutual fund than it is to invest in one. Yet, knowing when to sell a fund is, if anything, more important than knowing when to buy one. Unfortunately, while everyone gives fund selection advice, almost no one offers sell advice.

The decision to sell tends to be more difficult to make than a decision to purchase because of both the number of factors involved and the emotional import. The ability to sell appropriately distinguishes professional managers from amateurs. Professionals are more likely to deal with mistakes quickly, while amateurs are inclined to wait, nurturing the often unrealistic hope that their poorly performing funds will surge again.

The simple answer is to sell when performance has been subpar and you don't think it's going to turn around. What is subpar performance? You have to compare the fund to those with a similar investment style, for example, large-cap, value, balanced, or aggressive growth. Compare the fund both with the appropriate index and with the average performance of funds of the same type. These measures and some other more precise analyses are discussed in Chapter 12. Your fund should not consistently be in the bottom 25% to 40%.

Over what period should you tolerate below-average performance? There is no simple answer. It depends on the reason for the underperformance. Look first in the most recent fund report. Responsible fund groups will compare their fund with the appropriate index and candidly explain any underperformance. In some cases the reason is appropriate. For example, the fund's investment style, small-cap growth companies, may not be associated with good returns for the period. A change in the market is usually not a good reason to sell your fund. The market moves in cycles that are often unpredictable. Sooner or later your fund's style of investing will be favored, and if the management is good, the fund will again do well.

In other cases, the fund admits that it made a mistake, and then it takes corrective measures, so that future returns should be better. For example, the previously superior Strong funds turned in awful performances in 1989. In a February 1990 report to shareholders, the managers explained that the primary problem had been heavy investments in junk bonds. While junk bonds had been winners for several years, they were big losers in 1989. Strong management decided that henceforth they would limit junk bond holdings to 5% of a fund's assets. The funds have performed relatively well since.

If you feel that the explanation is satisfactory and that an appropriate response has been made, hold on to the fund. If the fund's reports do not give a satisfactory explanation, check for these possibilities:

- There has been a change in portfolio manager.

- Investment style has changed (e.g., from small company to midsize or large, or from growth to value).

- The fund has grown too large; for example, a small-company fund has grown to over $200 million dollars in assets, or a value-oriented fund has to lower its criteria to find companies in which to invest (you will see increases in price-to-earnings and price-to-book value ratios).

- A new concept in investing isn't working out (e.g., global short-term income funds, funds investing in adjustable-rate mortgages); the concept initially looked promising, but turned sour.

Other Reasons to Consider Selling

Consider selling if your fund has a high cash position, particularly if you think the market is going to rise. If you have determined your appropriate asset allocations and invested accordingly, a fund can disturb this by switching into cash or by changing its investment style.

If the fund is in net redemptions (more money is flowing out than in), there may be a serious problem. Other investors may have information that you do not possess. Therefore, you should investigate. Even if there aren't serious management problems, a mass exodus can create significant problems by itself. The managers have to sell a lot of holdings to obtain cash for redemptions, and this means that they have to sell good investments and generate capital gains.

Other reasons to consider selling:

■ The fund has been tax-inefficient.

■ You need to realize a tax loss.

■ You need to simplify your portfolio and consolidate holdings by merging some similar funds or small holdings that are less than 1% of assets.

■ You are concerned that a bear market is coming, so you'd like to switch from aggressive to more conservative investments—or vice versa, if you expect a bull market.

Other Situations

Notification That the Fund Manager Will Change

Some will advise you to sell whenever there is a change in management. You have no track record for the new manager. However, for large fund companies this frequently does not apply. For example, manager changes at Fidelity appear to have little impact on performance. This is probably because there is a large advisory organization that supports the manager, and there is a pool of trained managers from which to choose the new one. Therefore, if the fund group is large, you can almost always wait to see how the new manager performs. However, if the organization is small and the fund's success has been attributed to one or two adept managers, if they leave, so should you.

Load Fund Underperformance

Perhaps your fund isn't performing well, but there's a contingent deferred sales charge (CDSC) or other back-end load. If you would otherwise sell the fund, you shouldn't let the load deter you. It's better to take the loss and move on to a better fund. The same applies to front-end load funds. However, if you own a load fund that is performing well, don't sell.

Merger Announcement

If you receive a proxy statement announcing that the fund's management wishes to merge your fund into another fund, usually this is a good sign: The general rule is that losers are merged into winners. Therefore, the fund that is acquiring yours probably is a better one. However, you should evaluate the new fund the same way you would a new investment.

Cash for a Charitable Gift

If you have a large unrealized capital gain in a fund, don't sell it in order to make a donation. Donate the shares instead. Another thing you can do is to set up an account at the Fidelity Charitable Gift Fund. This is considered a tax-exempt charity, and donations are deductible (and irrevocable). The fund invests in Fidelity funds, and you can distribute cash to the nonprofit organizations of your choice at any time in the future.

Guidance Gleaned from the Gurus

Peter Tanous

For my book *Investment Gurus* (Prentice Hall, 1997) I interviewed some of today's greatest investment minds. I was amazed by what I learned, even with 30 years' experience in the financial services industry. Sitting down and talking to these gurus led to discoveries that no one person is likely to have uncovered otherwise. At least my 30 years' experience helped me ask the right questions. In this chapter I will try to pass along the benefit of their expertise. For the text of the interviews and my approach to developing an investment plan, please consult my book.

The Gurus

There are about 20,000 registered investment advisers in the United States. My firm, Lynx Investment Advisory, Inc., is hired by individuals and institutions to select the best managers from this large pool and to monitor their performance. So I have a lot of experience in seeking out and evaluating investment advisers. For this project I chose the best of both equity investment (money) managers and academics. The money managers were chosen on the basis of the following criteria:

- An investment approach that sounds reasonable

- A history of outstanding investment performance

- High Sharpe ratio (return relative to risk; see glossary)

I also tried to select an assortment of managers who use different investment styles—value, growth, momentum, small-company, and large-company. I chose both mutual fund managers and private investment managers. Finally, I relied on my impressions from years of experience in the investment industry. The gurus I interviewed were:

Michael Price formerly ran Mutual Shares mutual funds (now part of Franklin/Templeton Funds). He is one of the best known and most successful value investors.

Richard H. Driehaus runs Driehaus Capital Management, Inc. He is a private investment manager who specializes in small-cap stocks and uses a momentum investing style.

Mario Gabelli runs Gabelli Funds, Inc., which manages mutual funds and institutional and private investments. He is primarily a value-style investor.

William F. Sharpe Professor of finance, Stanford University Graduate School of Business, is a Nobel laureate.

Peter Lynch, retired manager, Fidelity Magellan Fund, is probably the most legendary mutual fund manager in history.

Laura J. Sloate runs Sloate, Weisman, Murray & Company, a private investment management company. She uses a value approach.

Scott Sterling Johnston, founder of Sterling Johnston Capital Management, a private investment management adviser, describes his investment style as small-cap growth.

Eugene Fama is professor of finance at the University of Chicago Graduate School of Business.

Bruce Sherman runs Private Capital Management, Inc., a private investment management company. He uses a value investment approach.

Eric Ryback runs Lindner Funds, a mutual fund company. He is best known for the Lindner Dividend Fund, which emphasizes higher-yielding stocks.

Merton Miller, professor emeritus of finance, University of Chicago Graduate School of Business, is a Nobel laureate.

Foster Friess manages the Brandywine Fund, a mutual fund that uses a growth, bottom-up style of stock selection.

Van Schreiber, of Deutsche Morgan Grenfell, is a private investment manager who uses a growth investment style.

Rex Sinquefield, chairman, Dimensional Fund Advisors, Inc., uses exclusively index funds.

John Ballen is manager of MFS Emerging Growth Fund, a small-cap growth fund.

Roger F. Murray, late S. Sloan Colt Professor Emeritus of Banking and Finance, Columbia University Graduate School of Business, taught value-style investing and originated the concept of IRAs.

Robert B. Gillam, of McKinley Capital Management, Inc., a private investment manager, uses quantitative analysis and a momentum style.

David E. Shaw runs D. E. Shaw & Company, a private management firm. He uses high-tech quantitative techniques to exploit market inefficiencies.

The Questions

When I set out upon my interviews I had six basic questions in mind:

1. Is investing in stocks the most intelligent path to wealth for most of us?

2. If so, is it possible to beat the market consistently?

3. Which style of investing is best?

4. What are the key characteristics of investment geniuses?

5. What did we learn from the gurus that we can use in our own investment program?

6. How can we replicate the gurus' success either when investing ourselves or by finding gurus to manage our money?

The Answers

I will go through the questions one by one. I will not review all the background material, since this is presented in other chapters. The first question is the simplest to answer: There is no doubt in my mind that investing in stocks is the most intelligent path to wealth for most of us.

Is it Possible to Beat the Market Consistently?

This is the question that strikes at the very heart of the efficient market debate (discussed in Chapter 9). I interviewed proponents of both sides, the academics who feel that you can't consistently beat the market, and the investment managers who strive to do it every day. First, let's review the arguments briefly.

Efficient Market Theory

The efficient market theorists believe that everything that the public knows about a stock is accurately reflected in its price. When new information comes along, the stock price changes rapidly in response. There is no such thing as an undervalued stock, and you can not reliably pick stocks that are going to outperform others. Therefore, without private information, no investor can know more than the rest and outperform the market. Research, forecasts of earnings, newsletters full of advice, and all the rest of stock-picking paraphernalia are a waste of time. Rex Sinquefield called it "investment pornography."

Over time, stocks provide more return than Treasury bills or bonds because stocks are riskier, so you are more likely to lose money investing in them. The return from any investment is proportional to the risk you take. Even among the spectrum of stocks, some types provide greater returns than others, on average, because they are riskier. Historically, value stocks have outperformed growth stocks, and small-capitalization stocks have outperformed large. So, if you want higher returns than the market as a whole, buy more small stocks or value stocks for your portfolio. If you want less risk and are willing to tolerate lower returns, tilt your portfolio toward large growth stocks.

The Market Is Inefficient, and Good Managers Can Exploit This

Active managers believe that a good investment manager can beat the market. There are undervalued securities in the market to be discovered. With hard work, good research, and a talent for investing, you can have an edge over the competition. Of course, not all the managers can beat the market, since all of them together constitute the market. However, in every field there will always be some exceptional performers who excel. Do you doubt this? They point to their records—"I've beaten the market consistently over the past (so many) years." That's proof, isn't it?

Not really, say the efficient market theorists. It's just luck. If you have 2,000 managers invest for 10 years, what are the odds that one of them will beat the market all 10 years? Well, if you flip a coin, what are the odds of getting heads 10 times in a row? One in 1,024. Therefore, just by luck, two of the 2,000 managers will beat the market for 10 years and will be hailed as the new gurus. The keys are persistence and predictability. Will these "outliers" still be at the top in the next 5 or 10 years? All the studies suggest that the great managers of today are the has-beens of tomorrow. What good is great performance if you can't predict it in advance?

Conclusions

There it is, my friends: the great debate in finance. Before I tell you my conclusions, let me tell you that my firm recommends both passive and active investment strategies, based on the requirements of the client, so I have no turf to protect. As I traveled across the country researching this question, I tried to keep an open mind, and I found both arguments very compelling. However, in the end I think that our active management gurus proved their point. There were simply too many examples of stocks that were discovered by a great manager before anyone else knew what was going on. A vivid example was one given by Michael Price:

One of his investment techniques is to look at every merger announcement. It tells you what businesspeople are willing to pay for a business, the best indication of value. In 1976 a company called Crane Co., which made plumbing supplies and was run by Thomas Mellon Evans, made an offer for a company called Fansteel. Price had to determine why Thomas Mellon Evans wanted to buy all of Fansteel. Fansteel made refractory metals, which add strength and conductivity in alloys. He researched each of these metals, but couldn't find anything on one that Fansteel handled, tantalum. Then, he looked in the Yellow Pages and found a local company called Tantalum Corporation of America. He called and was connected to a guy named Larry. It turned out that Larry was a metals broker who dealt in tantalum. He said two significant things: Evans must be interested because of all the Thai slag (where tantalum comes from) in Fansteel's warehouses. This was a very valuable asset not disclosed on Fansteel's balance sheet. The second thing was that Price ought to look at Kawecki Berylco.

I'll let Michael Price tell the rest of the story (from my interview):

So, not only did I start buying Fansteel right away because I discovered a hidden asset, and we made some money on that, but I found in Kawecki Berylco a $9 stock with a $15 book value per share and a very clean balance sheet. It was controlled by Molycorp.

And then I looked at Molycorp and found a company that controlled it, called International Mining. So I looked at International Mining, and found that they owned a bunch of companies including Kawecki, Molycorp, and others. So I laid it all out on a chart and started buying stock in every one of the companies, because, at the time, metals prices were taking off. There were shortages in the government stockpiles of some of these special metals. I figured out that if you bought stock in Molycorp you got all of them. Then I bought all the others and they all got taken over. Every single one of them.

Price picked Kawecki Berylco, Molycorp, and International Mining because he did his homework. He discovered hidden value in these companies via thorough research. Our gurus recalled many other good stock picks discovered by painstaking research.*

The market is not inefficient; it just takes time for efficiency to be achieved. The market is constantly in the process of becoming efficient. New information is not instantaneously reflected in stock prices, or prices may be temporarily inaccurate. For example, Richard Driehaus combines skill with uncanny investment ability to take advantage of positive earnings surprises. He can identify winning companies and purchase their stock before the full value of their earnings increase is reflected in the stock price.† Also, through painstaking research and seasoned judgment the gurus can uncover information that is not generally known and reflected in the stock price. In time, the information becomes more generally known and the stock price moves up or down toward its new true value.

What about the "persistence" issue? I think that it is possible to find Gurus who outperform over extended periods, at least three, four, or five years. If you put in the time and the work it is possible to beat the market, but I don't want to delude you into thinking that it is easy. It is very difficult.

Which Style of Investing is Best?

Over the past 70 years value stocks have outperformed growth stocks, and small-cap stocks have outperformed large-cap stocks. The economists tell us that these stocks are riskier, and the market rewards risk with increased return.

Editor's Note: Michael Price's former associate, David Winters, wrote Chapter 7.
†*Editor's Note:* Richard Driehaus describes this technique in Chapter 6.

So, if you want to play the odds, invest in small-cap value stocks. However, we cannot be certain that the market will continue to favor these styles. Also, in the past the pattern tended to cycle between favoring one style and another. There were even extended periods when growth stocks outperformed value stocks and large caps outperformed small caps. And, as Peter Lynch told us about style, if value funds are out of favor, even Mario Gabelli and Michael Price can't be expected to perform as well as the average growth fund, if growth is in favor.

The right answer, in my opinion, is to diversify your portfolio among the different styles. Although in the long run the return might be slightly lower, the return will be more consistent, and you'll sleep better.

What Are the Key Characteristics of Investment Geniuses?

- *Discipline.* Every one of them was consistent in investment approach despite the times, the current state of the market, or the fad of the moment.

- *Intelligence.* They are a very intelligent group. You have to be very smart to succeed in this competitive business.

- *Hard work.* I saw countless examples of the amount of work these people put in to identify companies that are worth buying. As in so many of life's endeavors, you get out of it what you put in.

The Great Intangible

Some of the gurus have something extra that is hard to put a finger on. They seem to have a sixth sense, an intuition that tells them, looking at the same numbers that everyone else is looking at, to sell or buy against the crowd. If there is such a thing, how much does it contribute to performance? Can you be a guru without it? I think that you can. Even if that something extra does exist, I suspect it is not the main determinant of great investment success. We saw too many other criteria that make for success.

What Did We Learn from the Gurus That We Can Use?

Finding Stocks to Buy

Here are some of the ideas that stood out in my mind. A lot of you have read Peter Lynch's books, but his advice is worth repeating. In order to find great companies you start by observing—what companies are doing well in your own backyard, what products are being talked about. Then you get information about these companies and see if you can make a case for buying them early.

What kind of research should you do before buying a company? The late

Professor Roger Murray spelled out his recommendations: pick an industry, analyze the companies in it, do spreadsheets, do ratio analysis, narrow your field to two to six companies, and start all over again. Yes, by now you should be convinced that finding great investments involves work.

I learned something from the momentum investors, such as Richard Driehaus and Bob Gillam. They demonstrate that you can make a lot of money buying companies that are hitting new highs. You shouldn't be afraid of jumping in, or think that you already missed the boat. These managers look for accelerating earnings trends, positive earnings surprises, and stocks headed in only one direction. However, this approach is not for the fainthearted or buy-and-hold investor. If something changes, these stocks can plummet, and you may have to get out just as fast as you got in. It's probably best to leave this approach to the pros.

How about value investing? I spoke to a number of value managers, including Michael Price, Mario Gabelli, and Laura Sloate. This approach makes sense for some industrious investors, because you might be able to find the undervalued stocks, those jewels in the rough that have not been discovered by the market or that have unrecognized assets. You might have special insight because of your personal expertise or experience that gives you an advantage over the crowd. We're coming around again to Peter Lynch's approach.

There's another strategy that intrigued me. Bill Sharpe, who is a Nobel laureate and ordinarily is not a proponent of active management, described his favorite active management strategy. This is sometimes called a "market neutral" strategy, and is employed mainly by some hedge fund managers. Sharpe asks a great manager to buy (long) the 10 stocks he thinks are most likely to go up, and to sell (short) the 10 stocks he thinks are most likely to go down. This technique reduces the effect of the market as a whole going up or down. Even if the market goes down, the long stocks should go down less than the market and the shorted stocks go down more, and vice versa if the market goes up. The returns more purely reflect the manager's ability to pick the best and worst stocks, not the unpredictable direction of the market.

When Do I Sell?

Deciding when to sell a stock is much harder than deciding when to buy it. For that reason many of our gurus use formulas that force them to be disciplined. For example, certain small-cap managers sell when a company becomes too big to still be considered small. Other managers set specific profit objectives (e.g., an increase of 30%). Conversely, if the price of a stock drops by a certain percentage they automatically sell. You can't go broke this way, but you will sell some stocks when you could have made a lot of money by holding on to them.

I like to use a less mechanical approach. The main question is: Has the picture changed? I apply the same criteria I used when I bought the stock, and if I can no longer find good reason to buy the stock at its present (higher) price, maybe it's time to sell. Have the fundamentals of the company deteriorated? Is the price of the stock no longer reasonable? Is the business still growing? Has the competition caught up to my company?

I use the same criteria when a stock declines. Has the picture changed, or is the price just going down because the market is declining? If new factors have made the company less attractive, and I would not buy the stock at its current price, I sell it. You must be willing to take a loss. Don't take it personally. It's probably not because you made a mistake, but because something happened that you couldn't foresee. The message is: Whether you have made a profit or a loss should be immaterial to your investment sell decision.

An important corollary to this is: Don't try to time the market. No one, not even one of our gurus, has come up with a reliable way to predict the market's movement. Yes, some prognosticators have been lucky and called a major downturn in the market, but how many have been able to do that two or three times? Or, have told you when to get back in? No one.

Can You Do This Yourself?

Maybe yes and maybe no. First, remember what it takes: discipline, time, hard work, experience, and a consistent style. Are you able and willing to allot the time to do the research and to track the stocks you purchase, the industries, and the market as a whole? Does one investment style make sense to you, and are you willing to commit to it? Does it fit your personality and talents?

If the answers to these are yes, should you give it a try? First, I think that it's best to own a style-diversified portfolio, one with growth, value, small-cap, and large-cap components, to help ride out the ups and downs of the market. You cannot possibly become an expert in all the different styles, never mind international stocks and real estate. So, pick the style you're most likely to excel with and turn to outside help for balance and diversification.

Let's assume you are a bright, disciplined, hardworking person. If you weren't you wouldn't have become a professional. Suppose you and your friend, who's just as smart and hardworking as you, decide to become jet pilots. Your friend decides to keep his job as a nuclear physicist, but you retire from heart surgery and devote all of your time to learning to fly. You take every course, follow every training program, and fly eight hours a day and most weekends. Your friend does the required course work, flies whenever he has the time, and manages to meet the minimum criteria to obtain his license. Who are you going to be more comfortable taking your family flying with?

Now let's bring the analogy home. You're an ophthalmologist, and you like to follow the markets. You read some books on investing, and you do some research on companies, although admittedly it's pretty basic research. From time to time you decide to buy a stock, because you uncovered it yourself, someone in the surgeons' lounge touted it, or you read a great story about it in a newsletter. Do you believe that your likelihood of investment success is going to be as good as someone who is just as smart as you (or dare I say smarter?) who spends all of his or her time managing money?

Forgive me, but I don't think so. It's hard enough to be good at investing. There are tens of thousands of professional investors working at it full-time who can't match the results of our gurus. Are you more likely to achieve returns on a par with the top professionals, or to be able to identify an investment manager or mutual fund that winds up in the top tier? Stick with the odds, don't take up part-time jet piloting, and don't manage the bulk of your assets yourself. Let the professionals do the job for you.

You still want to invest for yourself? Go ahead and try it. But do it right, and do it with only a small percentage of your total assets. You will succeed only if you are serious about putting in the time and effort. Remember that it's about work, not luck.

International Investing

Robert Arffa

Why Should You Consider Investing Internationally?

Foreign stocks account for approximately 55% of the world's stock-market value. According to modern portfolio theory, not taking advantage of these investment opportunities means investors will be taking unnecessary risks. Since U.S. stock and bond markets typically move differently than the markets in other countries, diversifying around the world will lower the volatility of your portfolio. For example, when U.S. stocks prices are declining, international stocks may rise in value. Over the long run, the addition of international investments to your portfolio will lower its volatility (risk) without significantly affecting the total return.

Very few investors select only companies in one industry. However, diversifying across countries but staying within a single industry reduces volatility far more than diversifying across industries within a single country. Let's say that you select a diversified portfolio of 40 to 50 U.S. stocks. Then you select another portfolio of 40 to 50 different U.S. stocks. On average, the correlation between the portfolios is greater than 0.9. You gain little benefit by owning a greater number of stocks. In contrast, the correlations between the movements of the U.S. portfolio and portfolios of stocks in other large industrialized countries are typically less than 0.5. Therefore, the international portfolio is much more likely to be going up when the U.S. portfolio is going down, so the combination has less volatility than either portfolio alone. The incorporation of international stocks mutes the effect of U.S. business cycles on your investment portfolio.

While the U.S. stock market has performed exceptionally well in recent years, over longer periods non-U.S. stocks have performed as well as U.S. stocks. For the period December 31, 1969, to June 30, 1997, the average annual return of U.S. stocks was 12.6%, and the standard deviation of these returns was 17.5%.[1] The average annual return of non-U.S. stocks was 12.4%, with a standard deviation of 17.6%.

Comparisons of U.S. and foreign stock returns vary considerably depending on the period analyzed (Table 15.1). In some comparisons foreign stocks are more volatile, and in others U.S. stocks have more volatility. However, the most consistent finding is that the markets do not move in unison. It is this

TABLE 15.1 Returns of U.S. and International Stocks

Year	U.S. Stocks (S&P 500)	International Stocks (MSCI EAFE) Index)	Emerging Markets (MSCI Select Emerging Markets Free Index)
1988	16.6%	28.6%	40.4%
1989	31.7%	10.8%	65.0%
1990	–3.1%	–23.2%	–10.6%
1991	30.55	12.55	59.95
1992	7.65	–11.8%	11.4%
1993	10.1%	32.9%	74.8%
1994	1.3%	8.1%	–7.3%
1995	37.6%	11.6%	–5.25
1996	23.0%	6.4%	6.0%
1997	33.4%	2.1%	–11.6%

lack of correlation of foreign and domestic economic cycles that provides the greatest benefit to U.S. investors.

Research shows that for any two assets that do not move in unison, there are combinations of investments in the assets that result in a lower risk (volatility) than either asset alone.

Some investment advisers have suggested that the markets all over the world will become progressively more synchronous: Global trade is uniting most countries into a single economic entity so all of these markets will react to a significant event in any one of them. However, the evidence does not support this. Gary Brinson analyzed the correlations during overlapping two-year intervals (based on quarterly log excess returns) between 1972 and 1998, and found no evident trend over the period.[2] Bruno Solnik, a professor of finance, agreed in a recent article in *Investment Policy*: "Contrary to some media statements, this international correlation has not increased markedly over the past 25 years."[3]

Other Reasons

Investors who search worldwide often find more bargains than do those who limit their search to the United States. Some of the best companies and some of the best stock values in the world are found outside this country. These include household names such as Toyota, Honda, Sony, Nestlé, and Canon. Even some companies that people believe are American, such as Burger King, are actually based overseas (United Kingdom). There is no reason to exclude these companies from consideration just because they are not based in the United States. If you believe that cellular phone producers are a great investment, you wouldn't limit yourself to Motorola. You would also consider Nokia of Finland or Ericsson of Sweden. If you think that telecommunications providers will experience tremendous growth in the next decade, why not consider countries where the industry is in its infancy, rather than just those with well-established providers? Seven of the world's 10 largest automobile companies are based outside the United States. All 10 of the world's largest construction companies and all 10 of the world's largest real estate companies are based outside the United States.

Another approach, championed by John Templeton, is simply to extend your style of investing to companies around the world. Templeton was a value investor; he considered the country where a company is headquartered to be far less important than its current valuation and potential for growth. However, by searching throughout the world for the best investment values you can create a globally diversified portfolio of stocks. The relationship between the value of a share of a company and its stock price varies over time, according to the country's economy and the vicissitudes of the marketplace. Holding a group of stocks in different countries and markets reduces the effect of local market fluctuations on the total value of your portfolio. Some markets will be putting a higher price on a company's earnings, and other countries will be putting a relatively low price.

This type of global diversification has the same advantages as those described in portfolio theory. The difference is that the diversification is a result of the process of the global search for value, rather than the allocation of a fixed percentage of assets for international investment. When a market is highly priced, good stock values will be harder to find; more bargains will be discovered when the market is depressed. Therefore, the constant search for value will lead to regular redistribution of assets from high-priced to underpriced markets.

There is reason to believe that less developed countries have greater growth potential than the most advanced economies. As these countries become more involved in the global economy they can experience tremendous expansion. For example, during the 10 years ending December 31, 1997, the average annual stock market return in the United States was 18.42%. During the same period the average annual return in Argentina was 36.16%, Mexico 32.23%, and Brazil 29.81%.[4]

What Percentage of Your Portfolio Should Be in International Equity?

There is no simple answer to this question. The answer depends on your risk profile, investment term, and other portions of your asset allocation. Statistically, the recommendations are very dependent on the periods used to derive the past return and correlation inputs. However, in general experts report that making international holdings 15% to 30% of your total equity allocation increases the risk/reward profile of your portfolio. About 10% to 15% of the total international portion should be allocated to emerging markets.

How Does International Equity Investing Differ from U.S. Equity Investing?

The normal market risk of stock ownership is similar for most international investments. Market volatility in developed countries is similar to that of U.S. equity markets, but tends to be higher in emerging markets. However, international investing entails some special risks:

- Currency risk
- Political risk
- Information risk
- Risk due to reduced liquidity

Currency Risk

When you purchase and sell stocks in a foreign country, the trades are made in the local currency. Therefore, when you sell your stock (or receive dividends) the funds received must be converted into dollars. If the exchange rate between the local currency and dollars has changed since you purchased the stock, your total return is affected. If the foreign currency has increased in value relative to the dollar, your total return will be increased—your foreign earnings translate into more dollars. On the other hand, if the foreign currency weakens relative to the dollar, your return will be proportionately reduced.

For example, the return of the MSCI EAFE index during 1997 was 13.82% in local currencies. However, this converted to a gain of only 2.06% in U.S. dollars.[5] The opposite effect is also observed: In 1994 the return in local currencies was −1.78%, but in U.S. dollars there was a gain of 8.06%.

Political Risk

Political risk is a term used for the effect of government activity on investment value. Even in the United States the actions of the president and Congress can have significant effects on the worth of a business or industry. In less developed countries there may additionally be risks of assassinations, coups, war, radical insurgency, or government takeover of businesses or assets. More commonly, the government's trade and monetary policy and the security regulations are less predictable. Exchange controls, currency devaluations, and foreign ownership limitations may be imposed. These risks must be taken into account when investing in any country. However, in general it appears that total political risk is declining as democracy and free markets become more prevalent.

Information Risk

It is hard to keep track of what is happening in a single foreign country, and harder to monitor multiple countries. Information about the government, political climate, economy, industry, and specific company are more difficult to acquire and analyze. Many foreign companies do not provide investors with the same type of information as required of U.S. public companies. Even the information they provide is not as assured of being accurate, since accounting practices are not as standardized.

The other side of this issue is that there may be greater investment opportunities abroad because information is harder to come by. American markets are thought to be more efficient because nearly all public information about a stock is rapidly disseminated and acted upon. It may be more possible for investment managers to get an edge by uncovering information unknown to competitors.

Reduced Liquidity

Some foreign markets have lower trading volumes and fewer listed companies. More thinly traded companies have greater trading costs. The bid-ask spread is greater, the market impact of purchases and sales is greater, and you may have difficulty finding a buyer when you want to sell. In addition, some countries restrict the amount or type of stocks that foreign investors can purchase.

Other Risks

Foreign markets have different investment methods and regulations. For example, in the United States you often let your broker hold your shares (usually in an electronic ledger). In emerging countries, the transfer and safekeeping of shares aren't as predictable. There is the potential for mistakes, significant lags in transfer of ownership, or difficulty in maintaining control of shares held by a custodian that goes bankrupt. If you have a problem with your investment, you may not be able to sue the company in the United States. Even if you can sue in this country, you may not be able to collect on a U.S. judgment against a foreign company.

Hedging Currency Risk

Scary as all of these risks sound, most are not common occurrences unless you venture into emerging markets with political or economic instability. Currency risk, however, is significant. However, in many cases currency risk is avoidable through a technique called *hedging*. Currency forwards, futures, options, or swaps are purchased in amounts equal to the equity investment. If the currency declines relative to the dollar, the return on the currency investment will offset the loss in dollar value of the equity investment.

However, there is a price to hedging. Purchasing futures or options entails some cost, and the total investment return will be reduced by this cost. Also, hedging is possible only in countries with a practical forward currency exchange market. Without specifying the details, think of currency hedging as equivalent to purchasing currency insurance. The insurance will cover any currency losses, but incurs a cost whether the currency goes up or down.

Should you choose a fund that hedges? In a recent survey, about 13% of all foreign stock funds reported that they actively hedge currency exposure; 57% said they occasionally hedge, and 30% said they never hedge.[6] Long-term investors should not hedge, because over long periods currency moves tend to cancel themselves out, leaving you with a lower total return due to the cost of hedging. Even within widely diversified international portfolios currency moves tend to cancel out. If a fund is exposed to 20 to 30 different currencies, some will fall relative to the dollar, and others will rise. Hedging also may decrease the diversification value of your international investment, by increasing the correlation of its returns with the returns of U.S. equities.

Another strategy to reduce currency risk is buying shares of companies that benefit from currency devaluation. These are principally companies that export, so exports increase with devaluation and their foreign currency revenue offsets local currency costs.

Take note that hedging is not the same as betting on currency moves. Be wary of any manager who makes large currency bets. No one can predict currency moves, and the risks can be great. (Consider the recent downfall of Long-Term Capital Management LP.)

How to Invest Internationally

ADRs

Shares of many large foreign companies can be purchased in the United States via American depositary receipts (ADRs) issued by U.S. banks.[7] Each ADR corresponds to a fixed number of company shares, anywhere from a fraction of one share to a high multiple of shares. You can handle all transactions, including dividends, in dollars.

The bank purchases and holds the corresponding number of shares in the country of origin, and converts the currency for you. Essentially, it is the same as owning a foreign stock; the return reflects both the return of the stock in its own country and the relative value of the local currency and the dollar. The depositary banks charge for their services, automatically deducting their fees and expenses from your dividends and trades.

When a corporation *sponsors* its ADRs in conjunction with a U.S. bank, it agrees to provide English-language versions of its corporate shareholder documents, and the ADR holder typically has voting rights. *Unsponsored* ADRs are set up by U.S. banks without the direct cooperation of the corporation. They usually do not confer voting rights. Only sponsored ADRs can be traded on the major U.S. stock exchanges.

U.S.-Traded Foreign Stocks

Some foreign stocks trade here in the same form as in their local market, rather than as ADRs. Canadian stocks, for example, often trade this way.

Purchasing Stocks on Foreign Markets

If a company trades only on a foreign stock market, you may be able to purchase it through a broker. These companies do not file reports with the Securities and Exchange Commission, so researching them may be more difficult.

U.S. Multinationals

Could you just buy shares of U.S. companies with global operations? No. Even though their business activity reflects the international markets, their stock performance is more closely tied to the U.S. market. U.S. multinationals tend to be owned by U.S. investors, who respond to the ups and downs of the U.S. market.

WEBS

Recently investors have been offered a new option in international investing, WEBS (World Equity Benchmark Shares). These are country-specific market indexes that trade on the American Stock Exchange and are managed by Barclays Global Fund Advisors. Barclays constructs the portfolios to track the performance of the country's Morgan Stanley Capital International (MSCI) index. Each represents about 60% of the country's market capitalization.

WEBS are like other index funds. They are traded just like any stock, are bought and sold in U.S. dollars, do not require a large investment, and are relatively tax efficient because of low portfolio turnover. Their expense ratios are typically around 1%.

Mutual Funds

If you have personal knowledge of a foreign corporation, such as through business dealings, it may be worthwhile for you to purchase its shares through ADRs. It is rare that any individual can judiciously manage a diversified portfolio of foreign companies through ADRs. To obtain optimum diversification you should invest in a variety of industries in regions around the world in order to achieve your goal.

WEBS are like sector funds in that you are concentrating rather than diversifying your investment. Predicting which market is going to have the greatest return over the next year or decade is not possible.

Mutual funds are a better choice for most investors. Global diversification can be achieved with a small amount of money and effort. A wide variety of index funds and professionally managed funds are available. They can be classified according to style and geography. The geographically broadest funds can invest anywhere in the world, including the United States, and the narrowest ones invest only in companies of a single foreign country. The style classification has two dimensions, large versus small company size and growth versus value stocks.

Global

Global mutual funds invest in a combination of U.S. and foreign stocks. The proportion of each can vary widely, even for a single fund over time. Usually they follow a particular investment style, looking for companies meeting similar criteria, wherever they are based. Most commonly they emphasize long-term growth. Global funds can make asset allocation more difficult, because the proportion of foreign stocks can vary and the funds' holdings can duplicate those of investors with diversified U.S. equity portfolios.

International Stock Funds

Funds labeled "international" can invest anywhere outside the United States. Their investment strategies vary considerably. The most widely held international funds invest in the stocks of more developed countries, such as the United Kingdom, France, Germany, Australia, Japan, and Hong Kong. Most emphasize large-cap companies and long-term growth. They may take into consideration their predictions for the country's or region's economy or currency, or simply purchase the most promising companies regardless of the country in which they operate.

Regional Funds

Regional international funds limit their international investments to a particular geographic region, such as the Pacific, Europe, or Latin America.

Emerging Market Funds

Countries that are less economically developed, such as those evolving from an agricultural to an industrial economy, or countries switching from a socialist or communist market to a free market, are considered *emerging markets*. Argentina, Turkey, Indonesia, India, Thailand, Brazil, South Africa, and Poland are examples. The markets in emerging countries offer the potential for more rapid growth than more mature markets do. However, they also entail greater risk. The markets and governments tend to be less stable, currency fluctuations can be dramatic, and liquidity is reduced.

Single Country Funds

These funds invest only in companies based in a single country. They offer the potential for high returns, but they are considered highly risky because of their narrow focus.

Managed versus Index Funds

Funds that track a variety of international indexes are available. Their main drawback is that the indexes are usually made up of the stocks of large, well-known companies. Very few small-company stocks will be represented. Index funds do not have the ability to shift assets away from a country experiencing a prolonged market decline. For example, many managed Pacific regional funds outperformed the index in 1998, because they reduced their exposure to Japanese stocks relative to the index.

However, overall the advantages of active management are not clear. The cost of index funds tends to be much lower than those of managed funds. For example, the Vanguard Total International fund has an expense ratio of 0.34%, whereas the average managed international stock fund has an expense ratio of approximately 1.65%; the Vanguard Emerging Markets Index has an expense ratio of 0.58%, versus 2.11% for managed funds.

Active managers have argued that their superior stock selection ability will be more evident in less efficient markets. Emerging markets is commonly the asset class for which this argument is most strongly applied. However, there is little evidence that skilled managers can consistently outperform the index. In 1998 the Vanguard Emerging Markets Index fund declined by 18.2%. The average return of the 164 actively managed emerging markets funds tracked by Morningstar Inc. was –26.9%.[8] Of 16 actively managed emerging markets funds with a five-year track record, only one beat the return of the passively managed Dimensional Fund Advisors (DFA) fund over the same period.

Closed-End Funds

Many international mutual funds are offered as closed-end investments. In closed-end funds the number of shares is fixed at the beginning. Once the original shares are sold, no more are available to new investors. However, the existing shares are traded in the marketplace. Since the number of shares does not change, the fund does not have to buy and sell stocks in response to purchases and redemptions. No cash needs to be available to handle redemptions. The fund manager can remain fully invested, and follow his or her strategy without regard to the panic or exuberance of fund shareholders. This can be a great asset to investors. However, this reduced liquidity can also be a disadvantage in that if you need to sell, your shares may sell at a discount to their net asset value. Read the fund prospectus carefully, because some are able to use leverage, purchase of private companies, and other riskier strategies.

About 25% of all U.S. closed-end funds are devoted to international stocks. Most of these are focused in some way: on emerging markets, or by region, industry, or company size. Thus, most closed-end funds are a concentrated and therefore more risky bet.

Value versus Growth

The long-term past advantage of U.S. value stocks over U.S. growth stocks has been clearly demonstrated (see Chapters 7 and 9). In international markets, value investing has shown similar advantages. However, value investing overseas is more difficult than at home. Selecting value stocks requires accurate estimates of the true worth of the company. This is more challenging abroad, because the financial data is harder to come by. Even for large companies in developed countries, such as Germany, good information is not easy to obtain. For smaller companies in emerging markets, it may not be possible.

Benchmarks

The most commonly available international indexes are constructed and maintained by Morgan Stanley Capital International (MSCI). They measure the performances of 45 stock markets around the world. From these MSCI constructs country and regional indexes, global industry indexes, and economic sector indexes. Indexes are called "free" if they include only securities that are available to foreign investors.

The most frequently cited index in international investing is Morgan Stanley Capital International's Europe, Australasia, Far East index (EAFE, pronounced EE-feh). This is designed to measure the investment returns of the developed countries outside of North America. It currently includes approximately 1,700 stocks from 22 countries. Stocks are selected in a complex process designed to represent all industries. This index can be used to evaluate the performance of broad international stock funds.

Growth and value portfolio indexes covering developed, emerging, and individual country markets are also available from MSCI. These indexes use price-to-book-value ratios to classify all the companies in the standard indexes as growth or value. Small company indexes are also available.

MSCI produces a total emerging markets (EM) index as well as regional EM indexes. The International Finance Corporation (IFC) provides data on 50 emerging markets. Unmanaged funds from Dimensional Fund Advisors (DFA) are available in multiple international categories, including small capitalization and value, and can be used as benchmarks.

Costs

International investing is costlier than domestic investing. Both operating expenses and transaction costs are higher. In 1998 the average expense ratio for international stock funds was 1.66% and the average for emerging market stock funds was 2.11%, compared to 1.42% for U.S. stock funds.[9]

Other costs, which are not reported to investors, are also higher. Brokerage costs, exchange fees, taxes, custodial fees, and so forth have been estimated to be as high as 2% of assets per year, compared to 1% for U.S. funds. International funds are more likely to charge a sales or redemption load. More than half of all international funds assess a load, typically ranging from 2% to 6%.

Conclusion

International investing does present greater risks and expenses than does domestic investing. However, for most investors, the benefits make international investing worthwhile. Few investors will be able to create and monitor a portfolio of international stocks on their own. Emerging markets, which can be a very profitable investment arena, are even more difficult for the individual investor. Professional management through mutual funds still remains the most sensible strategy for most investors.

Notes

1. Standard deviations are annualized on the basis of continuously compounded quarterly rates of return. Returns are annual geometric averages. Data from G. P. Brinson, "Global Management and Asset Allocation," in *Investment Management*, P. L. Bernstein and A. Damodaran, eds., New York: John Wiley & Sons.
2. Brinson, "Global Management and Asset Allocation."
3. *Investment Policy*, Vol. 1 (4) (May/June 1998), p. 9.
4. Morgan Stanley Capital International indexes as reported by Lipper Analytical Services, Inc.
5. Data from Morgan Stanley Capital International.
6. J. A. Prestbo and D. R. Sease, *The Wall Street Journal Book of International Investing*, New York: Hyperion, 1997, p. 61.
7. A directory of ADRs can be obtained from the Bank of New York, ADR Division, 101 Barclay Street, 22 Floor, West Building, New York, NY 10286. Or phone (212) 815-2175.
8. Larry Swedroe, "Those Really 'Inefficient' Emerging Markets," Brill's Mutual Funds Interactive (www.brill.com/expert/expls0199.html), 1999.
9. Vanguard Funds, *Vanguard Plain Talk: International Investing 1999*.

Hedge Funds 101

E. Lee Hennessee and Charles Gradante

Hedge funds are a diverse group of private investment partnerships. The investment managers are not registered with or regulated by the Securities and Exchange Commission, so they have greater investment latitude. The strategies employed by managers vary widely, and range from very conservative to very aggressive.

Investment in hedge funds has been growing tremendously over the past decade, but they still remain a relatively unknown and underutilized asset class. Compared to traditional equity portfolios, such as the Standard & Poor's 500, hedge funds offer higher returns at lower risk. Hedge funds tend to have lower volatility, with some protection of assets during down markets.

In addition, the performances of some types of hedge funds exhibit relatively low correlation with the U.S. equity and fixed-income markets, providing the potential to improve portfolio diversification. Unlike traditionally managed portfolios, hedge funds are both an offensive and a defensive investment approach. When added to a traditionally managed portfolio, hedge funds can lower volatility (standard deviation) and enhance overall returns. Therefore, hedge funds are not just for the wealthy, aggressive few—nearly everyone could benefit from the addition of hedge funds to their portfolios.

History and Evolution of Hedge Funds

The term "hedge" in the United States has its origins in the agriculture industry. Farmers were the first hedgers, selling crops or cattle yet to be raised or harvested at a price for future delivery. In doing so, they locked in a price today and were not exposed to future market fluctuations. In essence, they hedged their long market exposure. Even today, farmers cannot get loans from their local banks without hedging some of their crop.

The hedge fund concept has been in practice since 1950, and has grown to an industry of approximately $324 billion at the turn of the millennium. A. W. Jones put the original idea of hedge funds into practice. A great stock picker, A. W. Jones was comfortable with his long-only portfolio of selected stocks, but was dismayed by the impact of general market fluctuations on his portfolio. In an effort to mitigate the effects of random market fluctuations, he decided to incorporate a portfolio of stocks sold short. The stocks sold short were thought to be fundamentally overvalued and likely to correct in a down market. This hedging strategy was predicated on the long portfolio outperforming in a bull market, while the short portfolio would not create a drag on performance; it might possibly even add to the portfolio's returns, since there are always stocks that lose value, even in a bull market. During periods of market decline, the short portfolio would outperform the long portfolio or at least lessen (hedge) the decline in the long portfolio's value.

By placing a modest percentage of his funds in short positions, A. W. Jones would be able to produce respectable gains in rising markets and mitigate losses associated with down markets. Through this portfolio structure, Jones could emphasize his alpha (his ability to select stocks that outperform the broad market) and minimize his beta (the amount by which his portfolio would react in step with general market movements).

Hedge Fund Characteristics 1987–2000

During the past decade the hedge fund industry has grown over 1,000% due to the ability of hedge funds to capitalize on market inefficiencies, provide less volatility than the broad equity markets, and outperform the equity market (see Figures 16.1 and 16.2).

Hedge funds performed better than mutual funds or the S&P 500 in average and down markets. Average markets are defined as those where the S&P 500 index increased by 4% to 20%, within one standard deviation (8%) of the historic average annual return of 12%. (For example, this occurred in 1988, 1992,

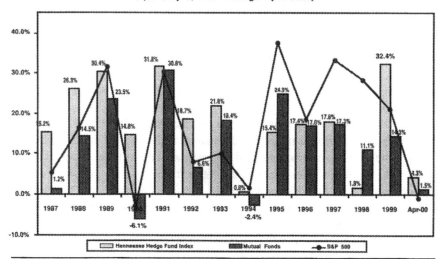

FIGURE 16.1 Hennessee Hedge Fund Index, Mutual Funds, and S&P 500,
Annual Performance 1987–April 2000
Source: Hennessee Group LLC.

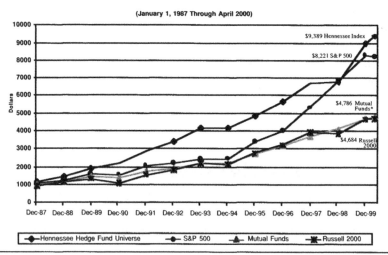

FIGURE 16.2 Hennessee Hedge Fund Index, Mutual Funds, and S&P 500,
Cumulative Growth of $1,000
Source: Hennessee Group LLC.

1993, and 1999.) Hedge funds underperformed in markets characterized by excessive valuation, speculative trading, and momentum trading (for example, 1995, 1996, 1997, and 1998).

Hedge fund portfolios are a necessary asset allocation to any sophisticated portfolio of investments. Additionally, the growth of the industry is supported by the creation of new hedge fund strategies whereby hedge fund managers are providing access to markets traditionally not available to most investors, with less risk exposure.

Growth of the Hedge Fund Industry

The growth of the hedge fund industry has been influenced by many factors, including: the growth and globalization of world markets; refinement of hedge fund money managers' expertise; advancement of technology (e.g, trading systems, prime brokers); maturity of stock loan functions; and, of course, strong markets. With the expansion of the global markets and the development of new securities types and strategies, there is increasing opportunity for the growth of nontraditional asset classes. Traditionally, investors had limited access to overseas markets and strategies due to poor market conditions, political instability, and lack of resources. As capital markets within underdeveloped countries strive to increase their accessibility to global investors, market inefficiencies arise that attract hedge fund managers. As hedge fund managers profit from these inefficiencies, the capital markets become more efficient. Also, with the development of the Internet, new and improved investment instruments and technologies are becoming available to hedge fund managers.

Finally, the growth of the hedge fund industry has been profoundly affected by the great bull market of the 1990s, accompanied by the highest levels of volatility in the market's history. Employing modern risk management tools (options, swaps, short sales, etc.), hedge funds have caught the eye of investors who want reduced volatility and greater downside risk management without sacrificing much of the upside.

With the increase in wealth nationwide, and the desire of these people to preserve capital, hedge fund managers have found it easier to find sources of capital. The demand for hedge funds has also allowed managers to spin off, from either traditional money management firms or other hedge fund companies, to open their own hedge funds. As Figure 16.3 indicates, the hedge fund industry will likely continue to flourish in the future.

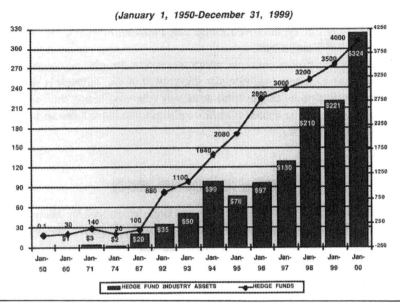

FIGURE 16.3 Hedge Funds Assets and Hedge Fund Managers
Source: Hennessee Group LLC.

What Is a Hedge Fund?

A hedge fund is a private pool of capital sold through a private placement. The *offering memorandum* details the domicile (onshore or offshore), the number of investors, the type of investor, compensation of the manager, and the rights of those investing. The entity additionally defines the market in which the investments are being made, the instruments and security types being used, and the potential risk and return profiles.

The *general partner*, who in most cases is also the hedge fund manager, often invests a large percentage of his or her own liquid net worth in the fund. The *limited partners* (those without control over the fund's investments) provide the remainder of the capital. Although a hedge fund is a private placement, the hedge fund manager must comply with Securities and Exchange Commission (SEC) guidelines, establishing that all limited partners are accredited investors. As defined by the Securities Act of 1933, Rule 215, an accredited investor is any natural person whose individual net worth, or joint net worth with that person's spouse, at the time of his or her purchase exceeds $1 million; any natural person who had an individual income in excess of $200,000 in each of the two most recent years or joint income with that person's spouse in excess of $300,000 in each of those years and has a reasonable expectation of reaching the same income level in the current year. A super-accredited investor has a net worth of $5 million in liquid assets. Privatization also limits the number of investors allowed, either 99 slots for a 3(c)7 fund for accredited investors or 499 slots for a 3(c)1 fund for super-accredited investors. Investments usually require minimums ranging between $100,000 to $5 million.

Since mutual funds are well-known investments, a comparison to hedge funds will enhance an understanding of hedge funds. A distinguishing factor between hedge funds and traditional money managers is the incentive-based fees. Most mutual funds charge an ongoing percentage fee based on the amount of assets invested. However, a majority of hedge funds couple an asset-based fee, also known as a management fee, with an incentive fee. The typical annual management fee is 1% of assets, charged monthly or quarterly. The incentive fee is a percentage of the annual profits earned by the fund paid to the manager, normally 20%. Furthermore, hedge funds are private pools of capital, are unregistered and are not traded in public markets, while mutual funds are public pools of capital and are traded on equity exchanges.

Another distinctive feature is that mutual funds offer daily liquidity, while generally hedge funds are less liquid. Many hedge funds require a lockup period of up to one year with monthly or quarterly redemptions allowed thereafter. Withdrawal provisions are an essential component of a particular hedge fund manager's strategy and are typically long-term in nature.

Lastly, hedge funds differ from mutual funds by the frequency of valuation. Most mutual funds offer investors a daily published net asset value (NAV), but most U.S. hedge funds provide a monthly estimate of percentage gain or loss. This is audited annually for U.S.-domiciled funds. However, monthly audits are performed for offshore domiciled funds because they normally offer monthly liquidity to the investor. Although mutual funds offer portfolio disclosure, hedge funds are not required to do so. Nonetheless, hedge fund managers are disclosing more information about their funds than ever before, understanding that more transparency, not less, will attract new capital and new investors to hedge funds.

Similar to mutual funds, hedge funds utilize specific strategies involving an investment method, a buy/sell process, market and instrument focus, and risk management. Although each hedge fund manager employs his or her own specific money management style, most managers' fund strategies can be one of several style categories. According to the Hennessee Hedge Fund Advisory Group of New York (an international hedge fund investment advisory firm, which advises individuals and institutions on over $1 billion in hedge fund assets), the hedge fund universe is made up of 22 specific hedge fund strategies. Each strategy is established to take advantage of specific hedging techniques and to generate profit in positive or negative market conditions. The strategies described in Table 16.1 vary by the investment tools used and the desired returns targeted. Each strategy has different risk/reward characteristics, and therefore it is important to research each money management strategy in depth before investing. It is advisable to use a consultant, preferably a registered investment adviser, to assist in navigating through the wide range of portfolio style weightings, manager selection, and manager monitoring.

Hedge Fund Industry Demographics

The hedge fund industry saw an enormous amount of growth during 1999. According to the 2000 Hennessee Group Manager Survey, managers saw an increase in new capital of 15% (Figure 16.4). The Hennessee Group believes that as of the turn of the year the hedge fund industry had approximately $324 billion and approximately 4,000 hedge funds (Figure 16.5).

The typical hedge fund investor is a sophisticated, high-net-worth individual. Such individuals make up just over 50% of a manager's capital on average. However, each year the percentage of inflow from individuals decreases as pensions, endowments, foundations, family offices, and institutions become increasingly aware of the benefits of hedge funds in their portfolios (Figure 16.6).

Hedge fund investors, particularly institutions, are demanding increased transparency on the part of the funds—they want more information about their investment activities and performance. Confirming this sentiment, 91% of the Hennessee Group's Year 2000 Investor Survey participants stated that transparency is "important or mandatory." In response, the hedge fund community has opened itself up to providing investors with more information on their investment strategies. According to the Manager Survey, 55% of the participating managers will provide complete disclosure to their clients. Although institutional investors make up a smaller percentage of capital, managers are becoming aware of the large amounts of assets and allocations these institutions bring to the funds, and are trying to meet their needs.

Fees, Hurdle Rates, and Taxes

As stated before, hedge funds charge a management fee, typically 1%, and an incentive fee, usually 20%. The management fee is based on a percentage of assets within the fund each year, usually prorated on a monthly or quarterly

TABLE 16.1 Hedge Fund Money Management Styles

Style	Definition	Typical Holding Period of Manager's Positions	Expected Volatility
Convertible Arbitrage	This type of arbitrage involves the simultaneous purchase of a convertible bond and the short sale of shares of the underlying stock. Interest rate risk may or may not be hedged.	Medium term	Low
Distressed	Primary investment focus involves securities of companies that have declared bankruptcy and may be undergoing reorganization. Investment holdings range from senior secured debt (uppermost tier of a company's capital structure) to the common stock of the company (lower tier of the capital structure).	Medium/long term	Moderate
Emerging markets	This strategy focuses on investing in lesser-developed, non-G7 countries whose financial markets provide exploitable pricing inefficiencies. Popular geographic regions include Latin America, Eastern Europe, the Pacific Rim, and Africa. Asset classes range from equities and bonds to local currencies.	Short/medium term	High
Europe	Style predominately entails investing in and shorting of European equities that may include peripheral eastern and central regions.	Medium term	High
Event driven	This strategy combines merger arbitrage, distressed, and high yield investing, in addition to value-driven special-situations equity investing. Usually dependent on an event as the catalyst to release the position's intrinsic value.	Medium term	Moderate

(Continued)

223

TABLE 16.1 Continued

Style	Definition	Typical Holding Period of Manager's Positions	Expected Volatility
Financial	Style predominately entails investing in and shorting of bank stocks equities and stocks of other financial institutions.	Long term	Moderate
Fixed income	Strategy employs a variety of fixed income-related strategies ranging from relative value-based trades (basis, TEDs, yield curve, etc.) to directional bets on interest rate shifts. Style also includes credit-related arbitrage, which typically entails the purchasing (or selling) of corporate issues and the simultaneous selling (or purchasing) of government issues.	Short/medium term	High
Growth	Style predominately entails investing in and shorting stocks of companies that exhibit an acceleration (or deceleration) of earnings growth, revenues, and market share.	Medium term	Moderate
Health care/ Biotech	Style predominately entails investing in and shorting of medical-related stocks, which include, but are not limited to, biotechnology, pharmaceuticals, HMOs, and medical information.	Medium term	High
High yield	Style predominately entails investing in and shorting of non-investment-grade corporate bonds, which offer attractive coupon yields. Interest rate risk may or may not be hedged.	Medium term	Moderate
International	Participants of this style tend to be bottom-up stock pickers within global regions that are undergoing economic changes. Conversely, international managers will short global equities whose underlying company fundamentals remain poor against a backdrop of poor economic conditions.	Medium term	Moderate

Latin America	Style predominately entails investing in and shorting of equity and/or debt within the various Latin American regions.	Medium term	High
Macro	Dominant investment theme is to capitalize on changes in the global macroeconomic environment through participation in the various capital markets. A top-down methodology allows managers of this strategy to utilize all asset classes (equities, bonds, currencies, derivatives) available in the global capital markets.	Medium term	High
Market neutral	Strategy entails long and short equity exposure with nearly no dollar net exposure. In theory, systemic market risk is greatly reduced by being dollar, beta, sector, and market cap neutral. Strategies within this style range from quantitative modeling ("black box" or statistical arbitrage) to fundamental pairs trading.	Short/medium term	Low
Merger arbitrage	Style typically involves the simultaneous purchase of stock in a company being acquired and the sale of stock in its acquirer. Many merger arbitrage managers attempt to mitigate deal risk by engaging in strategic takeovers only after they are announced.	Medium term	Moderate
Multiple arbitrage	Category includes hedge funds that employ more than one arbitrage strategy. Portfolio manager opportunistically allocates capital among the various strategies in order to create the best risk/reward profile for the overall fund. Common strategies include merger arbitrage, convertible arbitrage, fixed-income arbitrage, long/short equities pairs trading, and volatility arbitrage.	Medium term	Moderate
Opportunistic	Style involves long/short equities managers who maintain a flexible net exposure to reflect the changing dynamics of the market on a minute-to-minute or daily day-trading basis. Managers typically utilize technical and/or fundamental analysis. Portfolio turnover can be high as managers implement trading disciplines such as tight stop losses and defined exit target prices.	Short term	Low/moderate

(Continued)

TABLE 16.1 Continued

Style	Definition	Typical Holding Period of Manager's Positions	Expected Volatility
Pacific Rim	Style predominately entails investing in and shorting of Japanese and other Asian equities. Many managers also include Australia and New Zealand as regional investment choices.	Medium term	High
Regulation D	The investments are fully hedged in the form of convertible securities, which are convertible into common stock of the issuers at floating prices set at a discount to the historical price of the stock. The investment is typically held until the registration of the underlying common stock is declared effective by the SEC (normally 75 to 90 days), at which time the manager can sell the registered shares in the public markets and realize the hedged spread between the market price and the discount conversion price of the stock.	Short term	Low/moderate
Short bias	The entire portfolio consists of short sales, usually fundamental, technical, or event driven. This style can be used as a hedge for long-only portfolios and by those who feel the market is approaching a bearish cycle.	Medium term	High
Technology	Manager invests at least 50% of partnership capital in the technology sector.	Medium term	Moderate
Value	Style predominately entails investing in undervalued equities, which trade below intrinsic, or net asset value. Undervalued securities may be defined as, but not limited to, equities with low P/E ratios or low price-to-book-value ratios. Managers also focus on companies that generate substantial free cash flow and pay special attention to the use of the cash to retire debt, share repurchase programs, and other methods to realize shareholder value.	Long term	Low/moderate

(January 1, 1995-December 31, 1999)

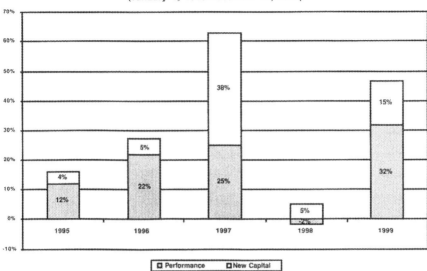

FIGURE 16.4 Annual Performance and New Capital
Source: Hennessee Group LLC.

basis, and is deducted directly from the investor's account. The incentive fee is the manager's share of the profits based on performance. Although the fee may be calculated monthly or quarterly, the incentive fee is typically paid annually. A *hurdle rate* and a *high-water mark* are two provisions that an investor must review when discussing fees. A hurdle rate is the return, most often the Treasury bill rate, that must be earned before the manager starts collecting an incentive fee. A high-water mark occurs after a negative year and requires the manager to generate profits exceeding the previous year's loss before being able to collect the incentive fee. For example, if the hedge fund is down 10% in one year, the fund must return 11.11% the next year before the manager is able to collect the incentive fee. The specifics on fees and expenses are described in the offering memorandum.

The tax implications of hedge funds vary from style to style, but some general points can be made. Most U.S. hedge funds are organized as limited partnerships and the investor bears the tax consequences incurred by the manager. Long-/short-term profits or losses and UBTI (unrelated business taxable income) are figured into each investor's tax calculation. Many hedge funds are managed for principal protection, not tax efficiency. Offshore funds are not

(January 1, 1950–December 31, 1999)

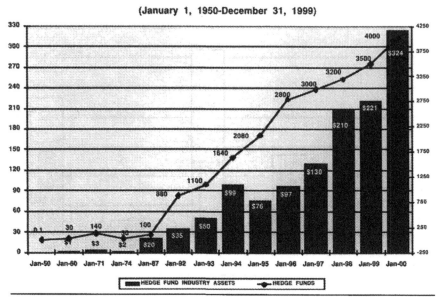

FIGURE 16.5 Hedge Fund Assets (Billions of Dollars) and Number of Hedge Fund Managers
Source: Hennessee Group LLC.

subject to U.S. tax laws for their U.S. investors. It is important to refer to the manager's offering documentation to uncover the tax provisions of the fund.

Hedge Fund Investor Profile

At the start of 2000, the Hennessee Group LLC sent out an investor survey to over 2,500 known hedge fund investors with $5 million or more invested, including high-net-worth individuals, pensions, foundations, endowments, family offices, and corporations, both U.S. and non-U.S. The findings contradicted the typical media portrayal of hedge fund investors as risk-taking high rollers. Hedge fund investors are some of the most sophisticated investors in the world. The survey uncovered that investors have over 33% of their investable assets in hedge funds. Moreover, the Hennessee Group found that over 80% of hedge fund investors are more than satisfied with their hedge fund investments and plan to increase their hedge fund allocations in the future. The average hedge fund investor began investing in hedge funds nearly 10 years ago. As their hedge fund experiences increase, their confidence in and allocation of assets to hedge funds also increase.

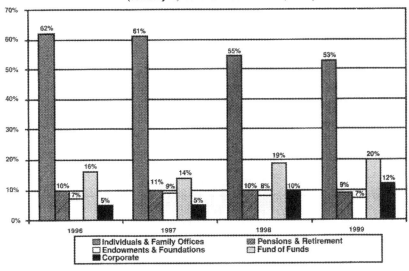

FIGURE 16.6 Sources of Capital
Source: Hennessee Group LLC.

The survey concluded that most investors initially invested with three hedge fund managers, and as of January 2000 those investors had increased the number of managers to 13 on average. When choosing a manager, the investors would evaluate the manager on a variety of issues. Performance was the most important, followed by downside risk protection and diversification, with tax efficiency being the least important. Additionally, the Hennessee Group found that 91% of the investors cite transparency, defined as the viewing of certain portfolio attributes, as an important factor when evaluating a hedge fund manager.

Why Invest in Hedge Funds?

Investing in hedge funds allows investors to diversify their overall investment portfolios and protect capital from the downside risk inherent in the equity markets. The investment style provides the exposure to protect against risks innate in traditional portfolios, while also realizing absolute return. The attractiveness of hedge funds is that they can lower return volatility (standard deviation) while enhancing return (see Figure 16.7).

Another attraction to hedge funds is that hedge fund managers invest their

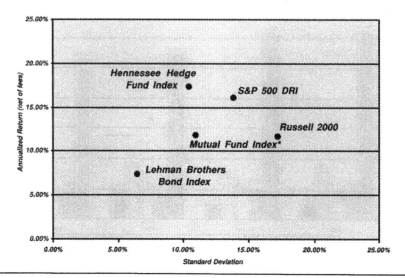

(January 1987-April 2000)

FIGURE 16.7 Hedge Funds and Mutual Funds versus S&P 500 Comparative Risk/Return Analysis
Source: Hennessee Group LLC.

own capital into their funds. Investors find it comforting that hedge fund managers are investing their money alongside that of investors. Investors also know, as mentioned earlier, that managers are paid an incentive fee, typically 20%, based on their performance. Investors understand that if the manager does not perform, the manager will not get the incentive fee. The fee is just that: an incentive for the manager to perform. Recently, the industry has begun to see more use of hurdle rates before a performance fee is earned.

Perhaps the most convincing reason for investing in hedge funds is the downside risk protection. Although the 1990s saw the longest-running bull market in history, during the rare down months managers found that shorting stock protected their returns and added to the effect that compounding has on returns (Figure 16.8). One example of short protection was in 1999 when the S&P 500 was down in February, May, July, August, and September and total hedge fund return, as represented by the Hennessee Hedge Fund Long/Short Equity Index, was up for the same period (see Table 16.2).

Table 16.2 points out that shorting can enhance a portfolio's risk/return profile. Note that despite the fact that hedge funds *did not* beat the S&P in every positive month (only four out of seven), hedge funds way outperformed the

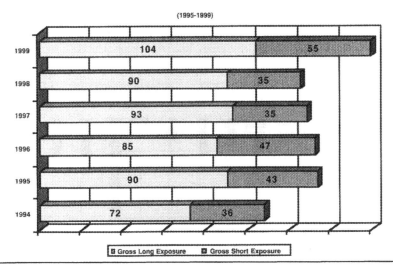

FIGURE 16.8 Five-Year Long/Short Exposure
Source: Hennessee Group LLC.

TABLE 16.2 Hennessee Hedge Fund Long/Short Equity Index versus S&P 500, 1999

	YTD	Jan.	Feb.	March	April	May
Hennessee Long/Short	41.88%	4.66%	–2.70%	3.55%	5.50%	1.66%
S&P 500 w/dividends	21.03%	4.18%	–3.11%	4.00%	3.87%	–2.36%

	June	July	Aug.	Sept.	Oct.	Nov.	Dec.
Hennessee Long/Short	4.70%	1.04%	–0.46%	0.41%	2.00%	5.84%	9.90%
S&P 500 w/dividends	5.55%	–3.12%	–0.50%	–2.74%	6.33%	2.03%	5.89%

S&P 500 year-to-date (41.88% versus 21.03%). You don't have to beat the S&P in all up months to outperform it; just beat it in all (or most all) down months while achieving 80% of the upside in positive months.

In short, hedge fund investors have learned that hedge funds live up to the first principle of sound investing—capital preservation. If you avoid the down months, you will compound out at a higher rate than the S&P even if you do

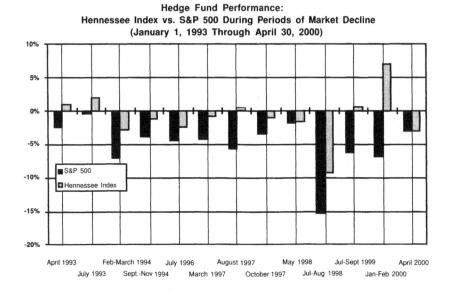

FIGURE 16.9 Down Market Analysis
Source: Hennessee Group LLC.

not beat the S&P in up months (on average). It is clearly demonstrated by down market analysis (Figure 16.9) that hedge funds outperform the S&P 500, on average, in down months. Table 16.3 displays the numbers behind the down market analysis and presents the substantial differentials between the S&P 500 and hedge funds during periods of market decline.

The final chart (Figure 16.10) is a comparative market analysis that demonstrates how hedge funds compare with the S&P 500 during (1) all months, (2) S&P up months, and (3) S&P down months. It is evident that the average hedge fund provides better performance during all months and slightly less performance during S&P 500 up months; but, most importantly, hedge funds offer superior performance during S&P 500 down months (a differential of 3.13%), thus protecting investor's capital.

Creating a Hedge Fund Portfolio

When making any investment, it is important to research all of the viable options available in order to make an intelligent decision. It is important to construct a portfolio that meets the needs and goals of the investor, while looking

TABLE **16.3** Differential Table

Month	Year	S&P 500	Hennessee Hedge Fund Index	Differential
April	1993	–2.31%	1.04%	3.35%
July	1993	–0.30%	2.10%	2.40%
Feb.–March	1994	–6.96%	–2.69%	4.27%
Sept.–Nov.	1994	–3.89%	–1.11%	2.77%
July	1996	–4.42%	–2.43%	1.99%
March	1997	–4.11%	–0.80%	3.31%
August	1997	–5.60%	0.34%	5.94%
October	1997	–3.34%	–0.91%	2.43%
May	1998	–1.72%	–1.63%	0.09%
July–Aug.	1998	-15.37%	–9.25%	6.12%
July–Sept.	1999	–6.25%	0.71%	6.96%
Jan.–Feb.	2000	–6.82%	7.05%	13.87%
April	2000	–3.01%	–3.00%	0.01%
Total		–64.08%	–10.58%	53.51%

at performance and downside risk protection. The first step is to define the investment objectives. Each of the investor's portfolios may have a different objective, being either that of performance, capital preservation, or volatility of returns. The first stage also provides an opportunity for the investor to define the parameters of the portfolio, the structure, and possible strategies to be used. The structure and strategy should be aligned with the overall investment goals of the portfolio. When the investor has implemented the parameters of the portfolio, the most appropriate structure and strategies will be uncovered logically. Next, each individual hedge fund should also satisfy the overall goals, objectives, parameters, and strategies of the portfolio. To make this determination, the investor must have a broad understanding of the available funds and services.

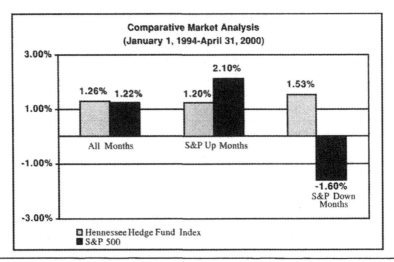

FIGURE 16.10 Comparative Market Analysis
Source: Hennessee Group LLC.

However, finding and evaluating hedge funds is difficult, and even practiced professional financial consultants are unlikely to have much experience with them. Hedge fund managers are legally prevented from advertising, and public information is limited. The number of hedge funds has grown tremendously over the past few years. Adding complexity is the tendency for some hedge fund managers to drift to other strategies without notifying investors. There are only a few private organizations that accumulate information on hedge funds. For these reasons, it is helpful for investors to bring in a hedge fund consultant.

Like any other consultant, hedge fund consultants are experienced professionals in the industry who are aware of the available products and services for investors. Consultants will help investors understand the industry while setting realistic goals, parameters, and structures. Consultants also provide assistance with selection of appropriate hedge fund strategies, risk/reward expectations, leverage limitations, liquidity provisions, market exposures, and other essential consideration. The investor and consultant will also define the parameters of risk control, regulatory issues, investment limitations, and performance controls.

Next, the consultant will establish, with the investor, the number of funds that would be appropriate to meet the investment goals and objectives. Diversification is key with any investment, so as to decrease overall portfolio risk. Diversification will also allow a portfolio to perform efficiently within different market environments while each manager pursues his or her particular strategy. Due to investment minimums, some funds may not be appropriate for some portfolios. As already noted, there are many strategies to choose from, and investors must choose the strategy or strategies most appropriate for their particular needs.

After selecting a hedge fund strategy, you should analyze managers within that category. There are many qualifications that an investor must look at when choosing hedge fund managers. The first, and probably most important, phase is the evaluation of the specific investment strategy and methodology of the manager. Does the manager meet the goals and objectives of the investor? Does the manager's core strategy and investment process, including downside risk protection, leverage, liquidity, diversification, concentrations, portfolio turnover, research, shorting, hedging, risks, and transparency complement the portfolio? Has the manager's strategy been consistent over time?

Second, the investor must look at the performance record of the fund. Analyzing hedge fund performance is a difficult process requiring a concerted effort and an understanding of the issues involved. In general, it is fairly easy to screen out the poor performers, but identifying the best among the good is much more difficult. The investor must remember to look at the performance in terms of the market conditions at that time. The longer the track record, the more likely it is that the manager has experienced a variety of market conditions and situations.

If the manager ran a hedge fund prior to his or her current fund, ask for the performance track record from the previous establishment. An investor should also look at the manager's asset size over time. Has the manager had large amounts of redemptions or additions? Has the manager handled the influx of money efficiently?

Lastly, the investor should look at the personal background of the manager. Not only is the educational background important, but also one must look at the past experiences of the manager. How much of the manager's own money is in the fund? Have there been any SEC violations? What is the manager's past work experience in trading, research, and portfolio management? When possible, ask for references from other investors and do a background check.

Because of the complexity of this process, consultants play a vital role in hedge fund selection and the determination of the portfolio strategy.

After the Investment

After the initial investment has been made, it is important not to walk away, as one does with mutual funds, and hope that the investment does well. With hedge funds, the investor (or consultant) must actively monitor the manager's performance. Hedge funds should undergo continuous review (as should all investments) so as to maintain the integrity of the original investment goals, objectives, and risk. The monitoring process is the time to continue the portfolio transparency process and be assured that the investor is getting the best risk/reward results originally planned for the portfolio. The manager's performance should be compared to your established goals, benchmark indexes, and performances of other managers utilizing similar strategies.

Unfortunately, the general partner must provide all information about the invested portfolio voluntarily. Your consultant can assist in obtaining the desired information, and may have greater leverage than you would on your own. Always be suspicious of someone who tells you nothing, even if performance has been good. Also, remember that as a limited partner you have no authority to intervene in the fund management. You can only decide whether to stay invested.

Choosing a Consultant

Choosing a consultant is just as important as choosing an investment. As noted, consultants provide an expertise and depth to hedge fund investing that most investors cannot provide alone. Like anything else, when choosing a consultant the investor must do some research before committing him- or herself. Investors should look for a consultant who will work with them on their investment goals and objectives. The investor must also discuss with the consultant the process of researching, monitoring, and investing in hedge fund managers.

After choosing the manager(s), how does the consultant go about ongoing due diligence? What kind of ongoing services does the consultant offer? How does the consultant go about making recommendations? What is the background of the staff? How many clients are there, and how much money is under management? Again, choosing a consultant is very similar to choosing a hedge fund manager and requires a disciplined due diligence process. Most importantly, make sure the consultant is not representing the manager as marketing agent. Understand how the consultant is compensated and if there is any conflict of interest. An investment advisory agreement is standard and appropriately defines the relationship between the investor and the consultant. Finally, choose a consultant who is a registered investment adviser.

Private Investment Management

Lisa Blonkvist

nvestment management for individual investors, often referred to as "managed money," is assumed by most to be a recent development, since most investment management firms have developed within the past 25 years. It traces its roots, however, to the bull market of the 1920s when a number of very wealthy individuals, such as the Carnegies, the Mellons, and the Rockefellers, decided to create their own banks. With the establishment of these banks came trust departments that were very active in managing the investments of their wealthy elite clients.

After World War II, there was a trend within both the public and private sectors to establish pension funds for employees. As a result, the need for money management grew, generating an industry of advisory firms specializing in portfolio management. The growth of the managed money industry led to the development of investment management firms that not only managed large corporate pension and thrift plans, but also began to take on individual clients who had a high net worth. As the number of these firms grew, the minimum account sizes that individual investors were required to place with firms were reduced. Today, there are over 24,000 investment advisers registered with the Securities and Exchange Commission (SEC) or with the appropriate state regulatory agency.

With so many investment managers available to choose from, there are many factors to consider when deciding whether to invest with a professional money manager. This chapter seeks to address four basic questions:

1. Why should I use a private investment manager?
2. How do I select a manager or team of managers who are right for me?
3. How should I evaluate my manager's performance?
4. When should I consider replacing my current manager?

Why Should I Select a Private Investment Manager?

Why should individual investors consider entrusting their hard-earned money to an investment manager, rather than purchasing stocks and bonds on their own or taking advantage of the professional management provided by a mutual fund? Use of private investment managers allows financial consultants and individuals to build a team of specialists custom-tailored to potentially meet their specific objectives in terms of risk, return, investment style, asset class, tax management, liquidity, and time horizon. Each investment manager has a defined style with a complete track record, which can be evaluated qualitatively and quantitatively prior to investing.

Once the money is given to the managers, your portfolio is built based on the manager's current buy list. This contrasts with buying shares of a mutual fund, where you buy what is already held in the mutual fund and inherit all the tax implications of the existing portfolio. Since each portfolio is custom-built and independently managed, not commingled with holdings of other investors, you know what is owned at all times and control cash flows in and out of the portfolio. You are able to monitor the account's progress closely, since you are given daily confirmations, monthly statements outlining all the activity, and quarterly evaluations comparing your portfolio's performance to appropriate benchmarks.

First, compared with private investors, professional managers have the benefit of a formal financial education and practical training in their field. This provides investment managers with greater insight into the past, present, and future economic and political climate both domestically and abroad. Investment managers also have better access to information and the ability to interpret that information. Investment managers not only keep daily watch for breaking news, corporate news, earnings reports, and the latest economic indicators, but they have the ability to perceive underlying trends and to place developments in perspective. Investment managers have access to information that is not widely reported. They are constantly in communication with the management of various corporations to evaluate the current business climate, management structure, and future earnings prospects of each firm. This access to information is a valuable resource that an individual investor cannot hope to obtain. In addition to their experience, perspective, and focus, investment managers are usually supported by a team of people that have significant knowledge of financial markets and investment experience themselves, creating a team approach to all their services. Finally, investment managers are more focused on making decisions based on facts and personal knowledge of the companies, and less susceptible to the emotions that often sway do-it-yourself investors.

Of all the advantages that an investment manager has over most private investors, perhaps the most important is time. Investment managers are paid to continually track the investments of their clients, and to make decisions in a timely manner. Most private investors simply do not have the time to monitor their investments, assess the prevailing market conditions, and foresee the future trends to aid their decisions. As a result, an individual investor may not be able to maximize the performance of his or her portfolio. This is supported by studies of professional investment managers. The Consulting Group division of Salomon Smith Barney found that for the period June 30, 1980, to June 30, 1990, professional equity advisers had an average annualized return of 20.07%, compared with an annualized return of 16.89% for the S&P 500 index.[1] Additionally, the study found that equity managers provided the most value added during down cycles in the market. During three periods when the S&P 500 dropped in value (December 1980 to December 1981, June 1983 to June 1984, and September 1987 to December 1987), the equity managers surveyed outperformed the S&P 500 in each period: 7.0% to –4.9%, –3.9% to –4.7%, and –17.16% to –22.6%, respectively.

Professional Money Managers versus Mutual Funds

Compared with do-it-yourself investing, mutual funds provide advantages that are similar to those gained by using an investment manager. Both mutual funds and investment managers use professional money managers to decide which securities to buy and sell and at what time they should be traded. In using professional money managers to oversee their portfolios, the investors gain the advantages of using a professional manager to make investment decisions. In addition, both mutual funds and investment managers typically adhere to a particular investment strategy or discipline. However, there are significant differences between mutual funds and private investment managers that investors should be aware of. These differences can be placed into four categories: structural, cash management, tax, and cost differences.

The structural differences between mutual funds and private investment managers revolve around one fundamental distinction: A mutual fund investor purchases shares in the fund that invests the collective funds of the group as a whole, while a managed account investor has a segregated, separately managed account that can be customized (Figure 17.1). To expand on this distinction, take a mutual fund investor who purchases shares in a particular fund. The money is commingled with that of other shareholders, and the investor inherits the properties of each of the fund's investments, including unrealized gains or losses. When the mutual fund manager sells a position, all current shareholders participate in the gain or loss based on the original purchase of the investment regardless of their points of entry. Further, as long as the investor owns shares in the mutual fund, he or she has an unrealized gain or loss, depending on whether the fund's share price has appreciated. At the point that the investor sells his or her shares, additional gains or losses will be realized.

By contrast, a managed account investor establishes an account with an investment manager, giving the money manager discretion to execute trades based on the manager's stated discipline. The managed account investor owns all of the securities that are held in their portfolio, and will realize any gains or losses when the manager sells the individual securities. There is no past history of the holdings, since they were bought exclusively for the individual investor. Further, the investor can request that the money manager harvest gains or losses at any time, to help in managing their overall tax situation in a highly customized manner.

Mutual funds hold a distinct advantage over privately managed accounts when it comes to the minimum investment required. Most mutual funds require a minimum investment of $1,000, while most private investment managers typically require a minimum account size of $100,000 or greater.

As a result of the structural differences between separately managed accounts and mutual funds, there are cash management differences that investors should be aware of. Mutual funds must keep some of the commingled funds of their investors in cash, in order to provide proceeds to those investors who choose to liquidate their positions in the fund. Generally, mutual funds have a good idea how much of the total portfolio to keep in cash. However, during certain periods, investors in the mutual fund may become skittish for one reason or another and many may select to sell their shares. The mutual fund may be forced, in turn, to sell some of its positions that the fund otherwise would continue to hold, in order to provide enough cash for investor redemptions.

During market downturns, a mutual fund may be prevented from fully taking advantage of what it sees as a buying opportunity because it must use its cash reserve to reimburse investors. By contrast, a separately managed ac-

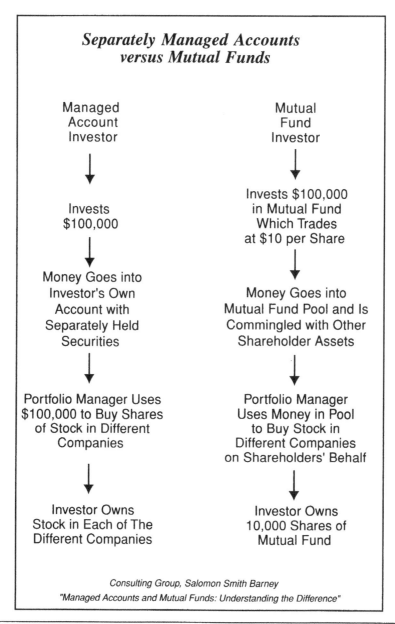

Separately Managed Accounts versus Mutual Funds

Managed Account Investor	Mutual Fund Investor
↓	↓
Invests $100,000	Invests $100,000 in Mutual Fund Which Trades at $10 per Share
↓	↓
Money Goes into Investor's Own Account with Separately Held Securities	Money Goes into Mutual Fund Pool and Is Commingled with Other Shareholder Assets
↓	↓
Portfolio Manager Uses $100,000 to Buy Shares of Stock in Different Companies	Portfolio Manager Uses Money in Pool to Buy Stock in Different Companies on Shareholders' Behalf
↓	↓
Investor Owns Stock in Each of The Different Companies	Investor Owns 10,000 Shares of Mutual Fund

Consulting Group, Salomon Smith Barney
"Managed Accounts and Mutual Funds: Understanding the Difference"

FIGURE 17.1 Separately Managed Accounts versus Mutual Funds
Source: Consulting Group, Salomon Smith Barney.

count does not have such limitations. An investor may choose to be fully invested in the market, and during periods of down market activity the investment manager may be able to take advantage of buying opportunities that a mutual fund manager cannot. Further, an investor can communicate specific cash flow needs to the investment manager and/or consultant, and the investment manager can inform you of unusual buying opportunities. This individualized communication, strategies, planning, and performance are only possible when an investor's account is segregated.

The structural differences between mutual funds and private investment managers also can significantly affect tax consequences of investments. Mutual funds are required by law to distribute any capital gains earned during the course of the year to each shareholder based on the number of shares owned. They tend to ignore the tax consequences of their actions since they are geared more toward tax-deferred investors, and performance ratings are nearly always based on pretax gains. Turnover tends to be high (the average domestic equity fund's turnover is 88% annually[2]), resulting in both short- and long-term taxable gains. As a result, after-tax returns are often significantly lower than the fund's reported pretax earnings. In a separately managed account, on the other hand, an investment manager can strategically sell securities that are below purchase price to help offset the tax liability that may be incurred on other securities sold at a profit. Unlike mutual fund shareholders, investors who place their money in managed accounts are able to establish their own cost basis for each of the securities owned in the portfolio. This can also significantly reduce the amount of taxes that are owed. In short, the flexibility provided by having a separately managed account allows the investment manager to employ a number of tax-efficient strategies that are not possible when investing in a mutual fund.

Finally, there are significant cost differences between mutual funds and separately managed accounts (Figure 17.2). While some managed accounts charge trading commissions in addition to a fixed management fee that is expressed as a percentage of assets in an account, most managed accounts employ what is known as a wrap fee. A wrap fee is a set fee expressed as a percentage of the assets invested with the private manager, usually between 1% to 3%. This fee includes the investment manager's management fee, custody of the assets, transaction costs, confirmation, statements, quarterly monitoring, due diligence, and consulting services. The consulting services of a financial consultant include helping an investor define one's financial objectives, designing an asset allocation strategy based on those objectives, searching for the appropriate manager to help achieve those objectives, and, finally, monitoring the progress both qualitatively and quantitatively. The advantage

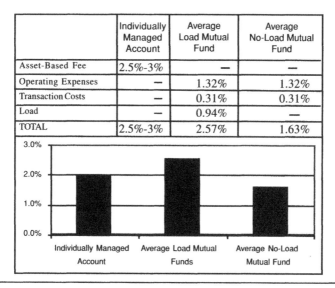

	Individually Managed Account	Average Load Mutual Fund	Average No-Load Mutual Fund
Asset-Based Fee	2.5%-3%	—	—
Operating Expenses	—	1.32%	1.32%
Transaction Costs	—	0.31%	0.31%
Load	—	0.94%	—
TOTAL	2.5%-3%	2.57%	1.63%

FIGURE 17.2 A Cost Comparison
Source: Eagle Asset Management Individually Managed Accounts and Mutual Funds, December 1993.

of the wrap fee is that it makes estimating the costs of investing a simple task for the investor and often results in more services at a lower effective rate.

Unlike privately managed accounts, mutual funds can have a number of hidden costs that are difficult to estimate for the investor. Mutual funds, like investment managers, charge a management fee that is generally expressed as an expense ratio. The expense ratio for a mutual fund can be found in the fund's prospectus. Typically, a mutual fund's expense ratio is between 1% and 2%. While a fund's expense ratio is easy to determine, its transaction costs can be difficult to estimate. Commissions on mutual fund trades are simply reflected in the adjusted cost basis and sale price of each security. Thus, the more actively the fund trades, the more commissions an investor will have to pay. The investor, however, never expressly pays out these commissions; instead, they simply result in a lower return realized by the investor. In addition, if the services of a financial consultant are employed to help determine an investor's financial objectives and select the appropriate mutual fund, then the fee paid to the financial consultant will raise the cost of investing even higher. In short, while the initial cost of investing in mutual funds may appear much lower than the cost of hiring a private investment manager, the true costs of investing in mutual funds may be much closer to the costs of a separately managed account without the benefits of customization.

Finally, for professionals who have complex financial needs and the ability to diversify and meet the higher minimum investments, a professional investment manager can provide significant added value to a portfolio.

How Do I Select a Private Investment Manager?

Once you've decided that investing in a separately managed account with a private investment manager is the appropriate alternative for you, the next step is determining which manager (or team of managers) is best for you. Over the years, a variety of vendors have emerged that track money managers' performances by style and provide this database to individuals, consultants, and financial planners for a fee. Among the best known are Effron Enterprises' Plan Sponsor Network (PSN), Mobius Group's M-Search Investment Database System, and Nelson Information's MarketPlace. Most of the larger consulting organizations access a variety of sources along with their own proprietary databases such as Polaris, Salomon Smith Barney's Consulting Group database, to provide the most comprehensive resources to their clients. While a number of investors will embark on this search process alone, others find that hiring an investment management consultant, as the first step, is the key to finding the appropriate manager.

The Role of the Investment Management Consultant

How can an investment management consultant help you find a private investment manager? First, investment management consultants work for a third-party organization and can provide an independent opinion of managers. Further, they are consistently monitoring the universe of money managers to help identify the best in each discipline both using qualitative and quantitative measures.

Investment management consultants initially help prospective investors define their financial objectives and concerns. Based on the financial objectives that are established, the consultant can work with the investor to develop an appropriate asset allocation to help maximize the likelihood of achieving those objectives.

Next, the consultant will identify the mix of investment styles within the asset allocation and identify the appropriate benchmarks to screen for the manager candidates. Investment management consultants can use their databases to filter through the thousands of managers and identify the most appropriate candidates for their particular investor's objectives. This database also allows the consultant to further screen the managers based on a number of qualitative and quantitative characteristics.

Once a manager has been selected, an investment management consultant can facilitate communication between the manager and the investor. Finally, investment management consultants monitor important market developments and changes within investment management firms that may not be apparent to the investor. A consultant is able to monitor investment managers and determine whether they are following their stated discipline and meeting the financial objectives of the investor.

Finding the Right Investment Management Consultant

Finding the right investment management consultant can be as challenging as finding the appropriate investment manager. There are four general guidelines to follow when evaluating an investment management consultant. First, evaluate the consultant's level of education, certifications, and the years and level of experience in investment management consulting. Second, evaluate the services that are provided; do they add value and do they meet your needs? Third, evaluate the ability of the consultant to communicate effectively. A good consultant must be able to communicate well not only with the investment managers he or she is evaluating, but also with the investor. Fourth, evaluate the level of dedication the consultant has to servicing your particular investment needs. A financial consultant is someone with whom investors have an ongoing relationship; they are not used simply to identify the investment manager, but also to monitor the manager and ensure that the investor's goals are being met.

The first step in the investment manager search process is to determine your financial objectives. This is generally done through a risk/return questionnaire administrated by an investment management consultant. While there are many different risk/return questionnaires used for this purpose, each one is trying to provide insight into the investor's tolerance for portfolio volatility as well as identify return expectations. The major determinant of an investor's expected returns is the amount of risk that investor is willing to undertake. An investor's risk tolerance, generally measured as the amount of volatility in a portfolio, depends on several factors. What are the ultimate objectives of investing? To build a retirement nest egg? To pay for a child's education? To preserve wealth or increase it? Or all of the above? What is the time horizon for investing? What is the individual's investment history? What planning or structure is in place to transfer the assets to the next generation? Is the purpose of investing to earn a stream of income from dividends, interest, and capital gains? Or is the purpose to build wealth? By sitting down with an investment management consultant and answering these questions, you can provide the basis on which a set of financial objectives will be developed and be ready for implementation.

The second step in the search process is to determine the appropriate asset allocation. The importance of designing an appropriate asset allocation should not be underestimated. A study published in the early 1990s found that 91.5% of portfolio performance was a result of asset allocation, easily outdistancing security selection and market timing (Figure 17.3).[3] To find the ideal asset allocation, investment management consultants use an investor's financial objectives and risk tolerance to plot a point on a risk-return graph. Next, a graph known as the efficient frontier is plotted on the risk-return graph.

The most appropriate mix of asset classes/investment styles for the investor is identified, and then a search is conducted to find the manager (or team of managers) best suited for that investor. There are five common equity investment management styles: value, contrarian, growth, aggressive growth, and tactical asset allocation. Within each investment style, the manager's investment disciplines can be further segmented by capitalization—small, midsize, and large companies or some defined combination.

It should be noted that the categories of manager styles are simply broad characterizations of investment disciplines. For instance, there are "core" managers, who include a combination of value and growth companies. Other

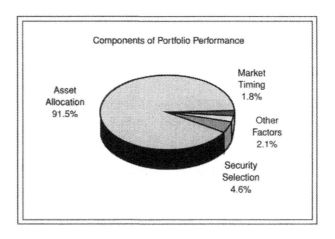

FIGURE 17.3 Components of Portfolio Performance
Source: "Determinants of Portfolio Performance II: An Update," by Gary P. Brinson, Brian D. Singer, and Gilbert L. Beebower, *Financial Analysts Journal*, May–June 1991.

investment styles include a sector rotator style, which seeks to select the industry that will provide the best short-term return, and a market neutral style, which seeks to neutralize risk and deliver consistent returns independently of general market trends and fluctuations. As you can see, there are many investment styles and combinations. As a result, the process of selecting a manager within a particular discipline can be crucial to assuring that the investor's financial objectives are consistently met. With over 24,000 registered investment managers, this provides a great opportunity to find the best manager who can meet your investment needs, but it also means that you have to sort through extensive data in making your selection.

The Screening Process

With a determination of the initial qualifications for the manager, screening characteristics may include: investment style, minimum account size, location, assets under management, staff size, years in the business, and length of track record. Generally, this initial step will reduce your candidate list to fewer than 100 candidates.

The second step of the process subjects the manager candidates to a series of quantitative screens to identify superior performers. Manager investment performance is measured against an appropriate benchmark and evaluated on the basis of absolute return, risk-adjusted return, volatility, consistency of return, and return in adverse markets. This ideally reduces the potential investment management firms to fewer than 20 final candidates.

The next step is to evaluate the remaining candidates using a series of qualitative screens. This step is more subjective and relies on the experience and judgment of a seasoned investment consultant or investor to identify the likelihood of investment success. Some variables to consider include the following:

1. *Personnel.* What are the experience, depth, and tenure of the firm's investment professionals? What are their professional credentials? Are the key investment professionals who were responsible for past performance still at the firm today?

2. *Investment process and implementation.* Is the firm's stated discipline well articulated? Has it been consistently implemented?

3. *Quality of research.* Evaluate inputs to the firm's investment process.

4. *Business evaluation.* Is the firm viable as an ongoing entity? Is it well managed and prepared for growth?

Keep in mind throughout this process that past performance is no guarantee of future performance. Once all the manager candidates are reviewed, only a few firms will receive superior ratings on all these criteria. At this point, investment manager selection becomes as much of an art as a science. Having successfully survived the rigorous multistep search process, all the finalists should be regarded as acceptable choices, and the selection is then determined by which candidate is best suited to the investor's unique goals and preferences for this component of the investment portfolio. Often, to make this determination an interview with the manager is arranged to grasp some of the intangibles that are critical in making the final cut.

Some considerations are the manager's responsiveness to the investor's inquiries, general knowledge, ability to explain investment options or process, and general rapport with the investor. In many cases, this investor will need to build a team of complementary managers to help meet his or her objectives. Consideration must be given to the value added by a blend or mix of managers rather than just looking at each candidate on a stand-alone basis. To get the best results, selecting the appropriate manager or team of managers requires multiple resources, trained expertise, and extensive experience.

How Should I Monitor My Manager's Performance?

The keys to monitoring the manager's performance are implementing an ongoing, active due diligence process with the investment manager or managers and assessing the portfolio's progress. This involves reviewing how well the manager has performed relative to the firm's stated objectives, the investor's objectives, peer managers, and the appropriate benchmarks. Included in this process is a regular review of the following:

QUALITATIVE

1. *Personnel*—evaluating the quality of the people working for the firm, length of service, turnover, analyst's background, depth and diversity of experience of each key employee.

2. *Investment process*—evaluating how well the firm has developed and articulates its investment philosophy; actively reviewing the manager's criteria on stock/bond selections, asset allocation, and other aspects of active portfolio management.

3. *Investment research*—evaluating the quality and suitability of the firm's information and data resources used for making investment decisions.

4. *Implementation of process*—evaluating the portfolio manager's quality of implementation as it relates to the investment discipline or strategy; actively reviewing how consistently the firm adheres to its sell discipline.

5. *Business evaluation*—monitoring the financial and operating strength of the firm as well as the firm's profitability and capital structure; giving consideration also to the adequacy of the facilities, technology application, administration, and operational support.

6. *Communication and servicing*—evaluating how well the firm meets the needs of the client in terms of responsiveness to requests, expertise of personnel, and customized/accurate account reporting.

QUANTITATIVE

1. *Long-term performance*—evaluating the firm's investment performance over the previous 5-, 7-, and 10-year periods; reviewing performance on a risk-adjusted basis and making comparisons to appropriate benchmarks.

2. *Short-term performance*—evaluating the firm's investment performance over a one- and three-year period relative to appropriate benchmarks and peer managers.

RELIABILITY FACTORS

1. *Dispersion*—evaluating the degree to which all investors' portfolios hold substantially the same securities while adhering to the manager's stated investment discipline, thus resulting in consistent performance for all investors.

2. *Verification/correlation*—verifying the investment performance represented by the manager and how it is computed.

3. *Quality of composite*—reviewing whether the construction of the manager's performance composite is compliant with the actual industry standards (performance composite is the manager's published performance record, and this process identifies what accounts are included in the performance calculations).

This review process begins by monitoring daily activity of each manager and monthly statements to determine if they are consistent with their stated investment discipline. For example, a large-cap growth investment manager should be buying large-cap growth companies, not value stocks or small-cap stocks. The process continues with a more thorough quarterly evaluation, comparing the manager to the appropriate benchmarks. Also on a quarterly basis, regular contact with the manager or the consultant is necessary to review the criteria already discussed. Many resources and much time are needed to perform proper reviews, and it typically requires a team approach utilizing analysts, seasoned investment management consultants, and regular communication to get the best results.

When Should I Consider Firing My Manager?

Most investors will agree that firing a manager is much more difficult than hiring the manager. I think it is best to determine in advance the criteria that would lead you to fire or replace a manager so you can be decisive and objective when necessary. This is where it is helpful to have an investment management consultant to hold the manager accountable to the criteria established at the beginning of the investment process.

This is often a challenging decision, but there are some conditions when it is clear that a relationship should be terminated. Specifically, if the key investment personnel of an investment management firm leave or are unable to perform (health or accident) this is usually a good time for the investor to make a change. This is where active due diligence helps to identify the departure of the key personnel and enables the investor to act quickly. An understanding that the firm must notify you of key changes is suggested, and this is one of the key advantages over mutual funds, which are not required to make any announcements.

The most important consideration should be whether the investor's objectives are being met based on his or her risk/return profile. If the objectives of the investor change or the market environment dramatically changes, then the manager may no longer be suitable. Other criteria are far more subjective. Performance (ideally risk-adjusted) versus a benchmark or peer managers can lead to the decision to terminate a manager. In this case, a reasonable time period must be determined—for some investors it is a market cycle (e.g., three to five years) while for others it's only a year or two. The availability of another investment opportunity better suited to the investment climate or the investor's objectives can also trigger the replacement of a manager.

Conclusion

Professional investment managers and investment consultants can make significant contributions to individual investors' investment experience. This approach allows investors to accurately measure and monitor not only their returns, but also the amount of risk they are taking, and provides much more flexibility in managing the tax consequences of investing. It gives individuals access to the best investment talent on Wall Street with custom-built segregated accounts.

Selecting the appropriate managers requires the investor to identify his or her objectives and systematically filter through the 24,000 investment managers using a quantitative and qualitative screening process. To increase the odds of success, ongoing due diligence should be performed consistently using a similar process to the one used to first select the team of managers. When evaluating managers, the most important measure of success is how well the investor's financial objectives are being accomplished within their defined risk/reward parameters.

Notes

1. The sample set of managers chosen for the survey were selected from a larger universe of managers who were subject to due diligence by the firm. The managers selected had to have a verifiable 10-year record of performance and meet several other qualitative criteria.
2. Morningstar Benchmark Averages as printed in their summary section on May 21, 2000.
3. "Determinants of Portfolio Performance II: An Update," by Gary P. Brinson, Brian D. Singer, and Gilbert L. Beebower, *Financial Analysts Journal*, May–June 1991.

The Impact of Taxes and Other Costs on Total Returns

Larry Swedroe

"Index funds should outperform most other stock-market investors. After all, investors, as a group, can do no better than the market, because collectively they are the market. Most investors trail the market because they are burdened by commissions and fund expenses."
—Jonathan Clements, *Wall Street Journal*, June 17, 1997

"Fees paid for active management are not a good deal for investors, and they are beginning to realize it."
—Michael Kostoff, executive director, The Advisory Board,
a Washington-based market research firm
(*InvestmentNews*, February 8, 1999)

"For all long-term investors there is only one objective—maximum total real return after taxes."
—John Templeton

The value of our portfolio over time will reflect not only the gross returns on our investments, but also the costs incurred. Investment costs can, and typically do, have a substantial effect. The most important cost for taxable accounts is federal taxation. At the time of this writing, short-term capital gains (for investments held less than one year) and dividends are taxed as ordinary income, with a maximum rate of 39.6%, and long-term capital gains (for investments held for one year or more) are taxed at a maximum rate of 20%.

To contradict the proverbial assertion of the inevitability of taxes (and death), at least as far as they relate to investments, capital gains taxes are controllable to some degree. Unfortunately, most individual investors and mutual fund managers pay insufficient attention to the tax impact of their investment decisions.

Other costs can also have a significant impact on investment returns. These include mutual fund and adviser expenses, trading costs, and the "opportunity cost" of cash. The types of investments made and the investment style followed affect each of these.

I will first look at how costs affect the returns of mutual fund managers and other active portfolio managers. Then I will relate these concepts to management of your own stock portfolio, including the use of tax-deferred accounts.

Active Management: A Loser's Game

The debate between academics and practitioners over whether the market is efficient rages on. The vast majority of academics argue that the markets are efficient. This makes active management a loser's game. A loser's game is one in which the odds of winning are so low that it doesn't make sense to play. Practitioners, of course, can't accept that argument. Noted economist Paul Samuelson put it this way: "A respect for evidence compels me to the hypothesis that most portfolio managers should go out of business. Even if this advice to drop dead is good advice, it obviously will not be eagerly followed. Few people will commit suicide without a push."[1]

While the efficient markets theory makes for interesting debates and provides useful insights into how markets work, investors really should be asking themselves this question: Can active managers consistently exploit any market inefficiencies *after* taking into account the costs of their efforts? In other words, are their efforts likely to prove productive or counterproductive?

The Securities and Exchange Commission (SEC) requires mutual fund prospectuses to provide a great deal of information so that investors can make educated decisions. The information required includes investment philosophy, expenses, and past performance. The information on expenses is generally limited to just the operating expense ratio and any 12b-1 charges. Unfortunately, while these expenses are important, they are only a small portion of the many costs imposed on investors by active managers in their pursuit of the Holy Grail of outperformance. There are actually five types of expenses incurred:

1. Operating expenses and distribution fees
2. The "cost of cash"
3. Trading expenses
4. Market impact costs
5. Taxes

As you will see, each of these expense categories creates a hurdle of 1% or more for active managers to leap. For even tax-deferred accounts the collective active management hurdle is at least 4%. Let's examine the impact on returns of the costs mutual fund investors bear in their search for the great fund manager. We will examine the cost issue for both equity and fixed-income funds. We will also examine the implications of another little-understood hurdle, "closet indexing." After doing so, I think you will come to the same conclusion that I did. It is irrelevant whether the markets are efficient. Even if there are inefficiencies, the costs of trying to exploit them are highly likely to exceed the value added. The only way to win the loser's game is not to play! Just own passively managed funds.

Operating Expenses

Operating expenses are about the only expenses that receive investor attention. This is because they are highly visible. Given their visibility, most investors are aware that a fund's operating expenses should be considered prior to making any investment decision. As you will learn, there are other expenses that are hidden—hidden in the sense that, unlike operating costs, they are not reported. Instead, they just show up in reduced returns.

The average operating expense for actively managed funds is 1.53%.[2] For the typical domestic index or passive asset class fund, the expense ratio is between 0.2% and 0.5%. (International funds, both actively and passively managed ones, typically have somewhat higher expense ratios.) Thus, actively managed funds begin the game with a cost hurdle of 1% or more that they must clear in order to add value. This 1% hurdle does not include any 12b-1 expenses or load fees. If a fund imposes any such fees, the hurdle obviously increases. And, while active managers might argue that they add value with certain operating expenses (like research), the only thing that distribution fees (and advertising fees as well) do is reduce returns.

Cost of Cash

While operating expenses are important, unfortunately they are not the only expenses funds incur. Most mutual funds maintain some cash in their portfolios, both awaiting investment and in order to meet investor withdrawals. This cash is typically invested in money market instruments rather than stocks. Therefore, the total return over time is likely to be less than that of a portfolio that is 100% invested in equities.

Let's assume that the typical actively managed fund maintains an average cash position of about 10%. For the 15 years ending in 1998, the S&P 500 index provided total returns of about 18%. During that same period one-month Treasury bills (a good proxy for the return earned on invested cash) yielded about 6%. We can now calculate the "cost of cash" for actively managed funds to be 1.2% per annum [(18% − 6%) × 10%]. For a passively managed fund, which is generally 99% invested, the "cost of cash" is only 0.12%. The "cost of cash" hurdle for actively managed funds is thus in excess of 1%. When added to the operating expense hurdle, the value-added bar has now been raised to in excess of 2% per annum.

Trading Costs

Investors should also consider another hidden cost, trading expenses. The average actively managed fund has turnover of about 80%, and the cost of trading (commissions and bid/offer spreads) is approximately 1% to buy and 1% to sell (for very large-cap stocks the bid/offer spreads are somewhat lower, and for very small-cap stocks the spreads are much wider). The result is that the average actively managed fund incurs trading costs of about 1.6% (1% × 2 × 80%).[3] Depending on the index it is attempting to replicate, the typical passively managed fund will have turnover of between 3% and 25% (lower for passive large-cap funds and higher for passive small-cap funds). If we assume an average turnover of about 15%, then we can estimate the cost of trading at 0.3% (1% × 2 × 15%). For active managers, the hurdle of trading costs is therefore 1.3% (1.6% − 0.3%).

This estimated negative impact of portfolio turnover by active managers is supported by the results of a Morningstar study. Morningstar divided mutual funds into two categories, those with an average holding period greater than five years (less than 20% turnover) and those with an average holding period of less than one year (turnover of greater than 100%). Over a 10-year period Morningstar found that low-turnover funds rose an average of 12.87% per annum, while high-turnover funds gained only 11.29% per annum on average. Trading costs and the impact of trading activity on prices reduced returns of the high-turnover funds by 1.58% per annum—not much different from our estimate of 1.3%.[4]

When we include the costs of trading, the value-added bar has now been raised to well in excess of 3% (in excess of 1% each for operating expenses, "cost of cash," and trading costs). It is worth noting that for international actively managed funds the value-added hurdle is even greater as the operational and trading cost differences (versus passively managed funds) are even greater than they are domestically. Commissions, custodial fees, and bid/offer spreads are generally much higher internationally. In addition, costs such as stamp duties that are not incurred in the United States must be considered.

Market Impact Costs

Unfortunately for active managers, the costs of trading do not end with commissions and bid/offer spreads. Active managers incur market impact costs. Market impact is what occurs when a mutual fund wants to buy or sell a large block of stock. The shares cannot all be sold or bought at once; they must be bought or sold over some short period of time. The fund's purchases or sales will cause the stock price to move lower (sales) or higher (purchases), increasing the cost of trading. Barra Inc., a research organization, recently completed a study on market impact costs. While the cost of market impact will vary depending on many factors (fund size, asset class, turnover, etc.), the cost can be quite substantial. Barra noted that a fairly typical case of a small-cap or mid-cap stock fund with $500 million in assets and an annual turnover rate of between 80% and 100% could lose 3% to 5% per annum to market impact costs—far more than the annual expenses of most funds. In another example, for the period studied, the PBHG Emerging Growth Fund had the highest estimated market impact cost among small-cap or mid-cap funds at 5.73% per annum. Even large-cap funds can have large market impact costs as illustrated by the 8.13% figure estimated for the Phoenix Engemann Aggressive Growth Fund.[5] For the sake of consistency and conservatism, let's assume that market impact costs add an additional 1% hurdle for active managers to climb. That raises the total hurdle to at least 4% per annum.

Before we turn to the last (but certainly not least important) hurdle, taxes, let's look at the impact of costs on fixed-income funds. Keep in mind that the important issue is not whether markets are efficient, but whether active managers can add value after accounting for costs.

Fixed-Income Funds

"Basically, we were guessing on interest rates. . . . What we've come to believe is that no one can guess interest rates."
—Fred Henning, head of fixed-income investing,
Fidelity Investments (*Los Angeles Times*, July 7, 1997)

Mr. Henning may be the only one to admit it, but there is plenty of evidence that the efforts of fixed-income fund managers to guess the direction of rates are counterproductive due to the expenses incurred in the effort.

As with equity markets, if fixed-income markets are not efficient, then one should observe active managers outperforming their benchmarks. If, on the other hand, the markets are efficient, then active managers will be playing a loser's game and will fail to outperform their benchmarks.

A study covering as many as 361 bond funds showed that the average actively managed bond fund underperforms its index by 85 basis points a year.[6] A separate 1994 study found that only 128 (16%) out of 800 fixed-income funds beat their relevant benchmark over the 10-year period covered.[7] A third study, covering the 10-year period ending 1998, found that the average actively managed bond fund returned 8.2%, underperforming the Lehman Brothers Aggregate Bond Index by 0.7% per annum.[8]

John Bogle of Vanguard studied the performance of bond funds and concluded, "Although past absolute returns of bond funds are a flawed predictor of future returns, there is a fairly easy way to predict future relative returns." After he separated the bond funds into their major categories of quality and maturity, he analyzed returns in terms of their expense ratios. Bogle placed funds into four categories: those with expenses of less than 0.5%; those with expenses between 0.5% and 1%; those with expenses between 1% and 1.5%; and those with expenses of over 1.5%. Bogle found: "In every case, and in every category, the superior funds could have been systemically identified based solely on their lower expense ratios. At the extremes, the lower-expense funds outpaced the higher-expense funds by between 1% and 2.2% annually. The ability to predict interest rates played no part in the performance of the bond funds."[9] The only thing that mattered was expense.

Another study found similar results. "Results indicate that bond funds' past performance doesn't predict future performance and that bond fund managers generally are ineffective at increasing risk adjusted returns." The study also found that statistically there was a very strong negative correlation between both fund expenses and returns and fund turnover and returns. The greater the expenses and the greater the turnover, the lower the returns. The authors hypothesized that, because bonds within each investment grade are relatively homogenous investments (have relatively similar risk characteristics), there is little opportunity for fund managers to distinguish themselves. Since different bonds of the same investment grade are good substitutes for one another, costs only reduce returns. This is particularly true of short-term fixed-income investments where little or no value can be added by guessing correctly on the future direction of interest rates.[10]

Investors should also be aware that, since fixed-income returns are lower than equity returns, expenses have a greater relative impact on actively managed fixed-income funds than they do on actively managed equity funds. The average actively managed bond fund has an expense ratio of 1.1%.[11] If bond yields are at 5%, then investors are paying over 20% of the available returns. A fixed-income fund that is passively managed should have an expense ratio of between 0.2% and 0.35%. It is amazing how this difference (1.1% minus 0.2% to 0.35%) is very similar to the size of the underperformance found in the aforementioned studies.

We will now turn to the cost hurdle that is likely to prove to be the greatest for active equity managers to overcome—taxes. This, of course, applies only to taxable accounts.

Taxes

"If index funds look great before taxes, their performance is almost unbeatable after taxes, thanks to their low turnover and thus slow realization of capital gains."
—Jonathan Clements, *Wall Street Journal*, December 22, 1998

Unfortunately for investors, we have not come to the end of the road. In fact, several academic studies have all reached the same conclusion: Taxes on fund distributions are the biggest expense most investors face. Although the effect of paying current income taxes may seem minimal (and therefore insidious) in any one year, it becomes substantial over a protracted period of time.

A study commissioned by Charles Schwab and conducted by John Shoven, a Stanford University professor of economics, and Joel Dickson, a Stanford Ph.D. candidate, demonstrated just how great an impact taxes have on returns. The study measured the performance of 62 equity funds for the 30-year period 1963–1992. It found that, while each dollar invested in this group of funds would have grown to $21.89 in a tax-deferred account, the same amount of money invested in a taxable account would have produced only $9.87 for a high-tax-bracket investor. Amazingly, and painfully, taxes cut returns by 57.5%.[12]

A simulated study covering the 25-year period ending in 1995 examined the effects of expenses and taxes on investor returns. This study assumed that a mutual fund matched the performance of the S&P 500 index (even though, during this period, the average actively managed fund underperformed by almost 2% per annum); had average turnover of 80%; and incurred expenses of 1% (although the average fund today has expenses of about 1.5%).

The study found results that were amazingly similar to those of the Schwab study. It found that the typical investor received only 41% of the pre-expense, pretax returns of the index. The government took 47% of the returns, a figure that would have been even higher if state and local taxes were considered, or if the investor were subject to the highest tax brackets. The fund manager received 12% of the pretax, pre-expense returns. This study also found that reducing operating expenses to as low as 0.3% would have raised the investor's share of returns from 41% to only 45%. The study also examined the effect of reducing the turnover rate, and therefore the amount of realized gains, to the same turnover as the S&P 500 index. By reducing turnover to 3%, the share of returns actually realized by the investor would have increased to 64%, increasing investor returns by 56%.[13]

The investment horizon doesn't have to be 25 to 30 years for the negative impact of taxes to be large. Let's look at several studies that cover progressively shorter time frames. Robert Jeffrey and Robert Arnott studied the performance of 72 actively managed funds for the 10-year period 1982–1991. They found that, while 15 of the 72 funds beat a passively managed fund on a pretax basis, only 5 did so on an after-tax basis.[14]

Morningstar studied the five-year period 1992–1996 and found that diversified U.S. stock funds gained an average of 91.9%. Morningstar then assumed that income and short-term gains were taxed at 39.6% and long-term capital gains at 28%. The result was that after-tax returns dwindled to 71.5%, a loss of 23% of the returns in just five years.[15] A more recent study covering the five-year period ending June 1998 found that the average actively managed fund lost 21% of its pretax return to taxes versus just 9% for an S&P 500 index fund.[16] As these studies demonstrate, while the impact of taxes is great over even short time frames, due to the *black magic of decompounding*, the longer the time frame, the larger the impact of taxes on returns.

To provide one simple illustration of the impact of taxes on returns I looked at the pre- and after-tax performance of one of the few funds that beat the S&P 500 index funds for the three-year period ending in 1997. The Gabelli Growth fund, with a return of 32.95%, outperformed the Dimensional Fund Advisors Large-Cap fund (an S&P 500 index fund), which returned 30.85%. However, these returns are prior to adjusting for the then current long-term capital gains rate. The Gabelli fund lost 15% of its return to taxes, reducing after-tax returns to 28.03%, while the passively managed DFA fund lost only 3.4% to taxes, producing an after-tax return of 29.80%. The impact of taxes turned the Gabelli fund's 6% advantage into a 6% disadvantage.[17]

Perhaps most revealing about the impact of taxes is the following tale. Aronson + Partners is a very successful institutional fund manager. As the plus sign in its name suggests, the fund uses a quantitative approach to stock selection. Its strategy leads to annual turnover of about 100% to 120%. In an interview in the June 15, 1998, issue of *Barron's*, Ted Aronson made some very interesting statements (emphasis mine).

I never forget that the devil sitting on my shoulder are the low cost passive funds. They win because they lose less.

None of my clients are taxable. Because, once you introduce taxes *active management probably has an insurmountable hurdle.* We have been asked to run taxable money—and declined. The costs of active strategies are high enough without paying Uncle Sam.

Capital gains taxes, when combined with transactions costs and fees, *make indexing profoundly advantaged*, I am sorry to say.

All of the partners are in the same situation—our retirement dough (tax-deferred accounts) are here. But not our taxable investments.

If you crunch the numbers turnover has to come down, not low, but to super-low, like 15–20%, or taxes kill you. That's *the real dirty secret in our business.* Because *mutual funds are bought with and sold with virtually no attention to tax efficiency.*

My wife, three children and I have taxable money in index funds.

Investors can learn from Aronson, whose honesty is refreshing in an industry known for its focus on self-interest. Aronson could generate increased fees by just doing what his clients ask him to do—manage their taxable accounts. He refuses to do that because he doesn't believe that for taxable accounts he can outperform passive asset-class funds of similar style. In other words, he is putting his clients' interests ahead of his own.

Tax-Managed Funds

It is important to note that investors now have available to them a wide range of passively managed asset-class or index funds. Not all index funds are the same. Expenses, turnover rates, and how closely they track the index return vary. There is also a variety of tax-managed asset class and index funds available. While their passive strategy keeps turnover and taxes low, tax-managed funds also pursue the following strategies to further improve after-tax returns:

- Attempt to avoid realization of any short-term gains.

- Harvest losses by selling stocks that are below cost, in order to offset gains in other securities.

- Sell the appreciated shares with the highest cost basis.

- Trade around dividend dates, selling before and purchasing after dividends are declared.

- Reduce the costs of short-term buying and selling by investors by charging reimbursement fees payable to the fund (not the fund manager).

A Wolf in Sheep's Clothing—Closet Indexers

A closet index fund is one that looks like an actively managed fund (a wolf), but because the stocks it owns so closely resemble the holdings of an index fund (a sheep), investors are paying large fees for minimal differentiation. How do we measure how closely a fund resembles the index it tracks? The amount of differentiation between a fund and its benchmark (such as the S&P 500 index) is measured by their correlation. The higher the correlation—a fund's "r"—the less the differentiation. The "r-squared" ($r \times r$, or r^2) is commonly used to indicate how much of a mutual fund's price movement is accounted for by the change in the value of the relevant index. For example, Fund A has an r (correlation) of 0.95 with its benchmark, the S&P 500, and therefore an r-squared of 0.90 (0.95×0.95). This means that 90% of Fund A's price movements are explained by the movement of the S&P 500 index (or that 90% of the S&P 500's movements are being reflected in Fund A's price movements). Therefore, the lower the r-squared the less the fund's price movement reflects the movement of the index.

Let's assume that an actively managed fund has operating expenses of 1.2%, or 1% greater than a similar index fund. The average actively managed fund has an r-squared of more than 86%.[18] With a $100,000 portfolio, an investor really has $86,000 in an S&P 500 fund and $14,000 in a differentiated portfolio (and is also paying $1,200 in total fees). The investor could have paid just 0.2% or $172 on the $86,000 in an index fund. The result is that the investor is paying $1,028 in fees on just $14,000 of assets. That translates into a fee of more than 7% on the differentiated portion. Add this large hurdle to the other expenses actively managed funds and their investors incur, and the hurdle becomes virtually insurmountable. Remember that the larger the fund, the more diversified it generally becomes. The more it diversifies the greater becomes its r-squared, and the greater the hurdle the manager must overcome in order to outperform.

The following is evidence of the difficulty of overcoming a high r-squared. For the three years ending August 31, 1999, the five largest funds with r-squareds over 95 returned between 21% and 26.9%. After taxes an investor would have received between 18% and 24.6%. Vanguard's S&P 500 index fund beat them all. It returned 28.5% before taxes and 27.5% after taxes. Of the 80 largest funds with r-squareds over 95, only three managed to beat the Vanguard Index fund and just barely did so. And, none did so after taxes.[19] That is about $400 billion of assets and over $20 billion a year of underperformance.

Summary

The hurdle active managers must overcome in their search for outperformance is very high. It is at least 1% per annum *each* for operating expenses, the cost of cash, transaction costs, market impact costs, and taxes. Closet indexing raises the hurdle even further. We now return to the real question for investors not being whether the markets are efficient. Instead it should be whether active managers add value in excess of the costs of their efforts.

Let's look at the overall record of active managers. For the 16-year period ending in mid-1998 the annual return for all equity funds that survived the period was 16.5%, or just 87% of the 18.9% return of the Wilshire 5000 index. On the other hand, an index fund with operating expenses of about 0.2% would have provided close to 99% of the available returns.[20] In addition, the difference in returns is actually understated due to both survivorship bias (poorly performing funds disappeared from the data) and the impact of taxes on fund distributions. The 2.4% underperformance was due to the impact of costs. This data is supported by Mark Carhart's study, the most comprehensive study ever done on the mutual fund industry. He found that once you account for style factors (small-cap versus large-cap and value versus growth) the average actively managed fund underperformed its benchmark by almost 2% per annum.[21]

Considering the size of the hurdle that active managers face, it appears they were able to exploit market inefficiencies. The only problem is that, since they underperformed their benchmarks (the hurdle proved greater than the inefficiencies), active managers would have been better off if they had never pursued the Holy Grail of outperformance in the first place. They were playing the loser's game. In other words, the hope of outperformance was exceeded by the risk of underperformance.

Given their poor performance, you might ask how actively managed funds get away with charging high fees and incurring large costs. It's simple. They are able to do so because investors let them. First, investors haven't focused on costs, partly because the markets have done so well in recent years. Another reason is that investors don't receive a bill from the fund labeled "management fee" or "trading costs." The money is simply deducted from the fund's total assets, so it never shows up on an account statement. And, investors often make the mistake of ignoring the impact of taxes because the tax payment is often made from an account other than their investment account.

Informed investors know that their main task is to achieve the greatest percentage of the available returns of the asset classes in which they have chosen to invest. Wall Street doesn't want investors to know that the most likely way to achieve that objective is to minimize all fund expenses—not just operating expenses, but trading costs, market impact costs, the cost of cash, and taxes as well.

If all investors knew what you now know, they would stop paying a 1.5% management fee for a poorly performing actively managed fund. Instead, they would pay much lower fees for tax-efficient passively managed funds. Perhaps George Sauter of Vanguard said it best: "When you layer on big fees and high turnover, you're really starting in a deep hole, one that most managers can't dig their way out of. Costs really do matter."[22] And, taxes really matter, too. The winner's strategy, therefore, is to use index and passive asset class funds, and for taxable accounts to use passively managed funds that are also tax-managed.

The following are some general rules to keep in mind when purchasing funds in taxable accounts (especially if the funds are actively managed):

■ Avoid purchasing shortly before distribution date.

■ Avoid purchasing a fund with large net redemptions. These redemptions might trigger large taxable distributions.

■ Avoid purchasing a fund with large unrealized gains that may be realized in the near future.

■ Examine both pretax and after-tax returns. Unfortunately, as with investment returns, historical tax efficiency of active managers is not necessarily a good predictor of future tax efficiency. However, poor historical tax efficiency should set off alarm bells.

■ For actively managed funds, consider not only operating expenses, but turnover rates as well.

Implications for the Individual Investor

Do-it-yourself stock investors are no less affected by these costs than mutual fund investors (with the exception of market impact cost). Terrance Odean and Brad Barber of the University of California at Davis have performed a series of studies analyzing the investment habits of individual investors.[23] Their conclusion: Individuals aren't as bad at investing as people think; they're worse!

First, the stocks individual investors bought trailed the overall market, and stocks they sold beat the market after the sales. The more frequently they traded, they worse they did. For example, the researchers looked at the trading records of a large (unnamed) discount brokerage from February 1991 through December 1996. They divided the 78,000 investor households into two groups, those that averaged four trades per month and those that averaged less. The 20% of households that were in the active trader group produced returns of 10% per annum. This was over one-third less than the return of the less frequent trader group. Unfortunately, even these investors trailed the S&P 500 index with returns of 15.3% per annum compared to 17% per annum for the index. While this study included all trading costs, it did not include the impact of taxes created by the trading activity of these active investors. Obviously, if taxes were considered the pain of trading activity would have been even greater.

Odean and Barber also studied the relative investment performance of men and women. In a study covering 35,000 investors they found that women earn higher investment returns. Before you attribute this feat to a superior genetic makeup, women were not better stock pickers. In fact, the stocks that both men and women sold tended to outperform the ones they bought. The reason men did worse was simple: They traded more often. The increased costs of turnover (both bid/offer spreads and commissions) accounted for the entire difference in investment results.

Another of their studies investigated the performance of 1,500 investors who switched from trading by telephone to e-trading. Those who switched to e-trading substantially increased their trading activity—by 70% during the first month. Two years later, e-traders' turnover was still 80% greater than the turnover of investors who continued to use the telephone. The result of all that trading activity: Before expenses, e-traders managed to match the returns of the market. Unfortunately, after costs were considered (though not taxes) they trailed the market by 3.5% per annum.[24]

The conclusion one should make from these studies: Trading is hazardous to your wealth. Turnover should be kept to a minimum. On average, what you sell will outperform what you buy. Also, the transaction costs and tax consequences of your trades will significantly reduce your return.

Another major cost for individual investors is the opportunity cost of holding cash. Individual investors tend to time the market, holding cash when they think that the market is high. Even when they view the market as undervalued, many hold cash as they are searching for the best investment. As we calculated earlier for mutual fund managers, holding cash reduces returns. Most of the time that cash would increase in value if it were invested in stocks. Some other recommendations for taxable accounts:

- Don't wait until year-end to realize tax losses. Take advantage of opportunities when they arise.

- Use stocks or mutual fund accounts with large capital gains to make donations and gifts to children. (You can tax-deduct the full amount and the charity pays no taxes or your child pays at a reduced rate.)

Tax-Deferred Investing

Many investors do not fully appreciate the benefit of tax-deferred accounts; hence they do not take full advantage of them. Basically there are two advantages to tax-deferred accounts: Investments including dividends and capital gains compound without the IRS taking a cut, and it is expected that your tax rate will be lower when the funds are withdrawn (since your income will be lower in retirement).

Let's compare two investors. The first uses a traditional IRA tax-deferred account, and the second a taxable account. Assume the investors are in the 36% federal tax bracket, and they obtain a steady 9% annual rate of return. Each year the IRA investor puts $2,000 in his or her account. The taxable investor pays 36% income tax first, and invests the remainder ($1,280). He or she also pays taxes each year on dividends and capital gains. The results are given in Figure 18.1. The totals for the IRA investor are after paying 36% income taxes upon withdrawal.

If we look at the real returns of two mutual funds, Fidelity Magellan and Bond Fund of America, 1985 through 1997, the results are just as impressive. In this case we assume an annual income tax rate of 40% and an annual tax-deferred contribution of $1,200 ($720 in the taxable account). At the end of the 12-year period, the tax-deferred investment in the Fidelity Magellan account would have been worth $59,819, and the taxable account $29,910. Upon withdrawal and payment of all taxes due, the tax-deferred account would have been worth $35,893, and the taxable account $27,834. The tax-deferred investment in the Bond Fund of America would have been worth $18,430 after withdrawal and payment of taxes, while the taxable account would have $14,161—23% less.

The other potential benefit of tax-deferred investing is that your bracket may be lower when the money is withdrawn. Your total income will probably be lower in retirement, and the tax rate may be lower. However, we cannot predict how Congress will decide to change tax rates.

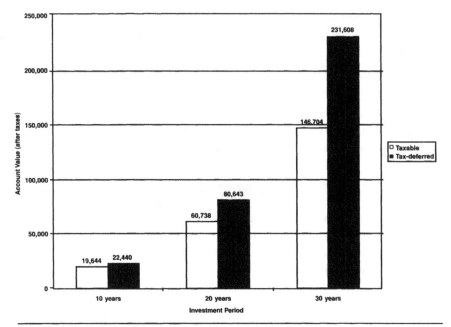

FIGURE 18.1 Tax-Deferred versus Taxable Investing
Data Source: Richard Glass, Investment Horizons, Pittsburgh, PA.

Conclusions

- Pay attention to the tax implications of investing. Taxes are the largest drag on your total return.

- Although the impact of paying current income taxes may be small in any one year, the effect over protracted periods is dramatic.

- Other investment costs can also have a significant impact. They are proportional to your trading frequency.

- In your taxable accounts, buying and holding can help minimize taxes.

- Active managers do not increase return sufficiently to counterbalance their cost.

- The cost of active management includes much more than just the expense ratio. Investors must also consider expenses for which they are not sent a bill. These include transaction costs, market impact costs, the "cost of cash," and, for taxable accounts, the impact of distributions.

- Costs are even higher for less efficient markets (e.g., small-caps and emerging markets), and active managers do no better in them.

- Tax-managed index funds are the best choice for your taxable accounts. Use non-tax-managed index funds for your tax-deferred accounts.

Notes

1. *Journal of Portfolio Management*, Fall 1974.
2. *Business Week*, November 30, 1998.
3. Charles D. Ellis, *Winning the Loser's Game: Timeless Strategies for Successful Investing*, 3rd Edition (New York: McGraw-Hill Professional Publishing,1998).
4. *St. Louis Post Dispatch*, August 12, 1997.
5. *New York Times*, July 11, 1999.
6. John Bogle, *Common Sense on Mutual Funds: New Imperatives for the Intelligent Investor*, New York: John Wiley & Sons, 1999.
7. Mark M. Carhart, "On Persistence in Mutual Fund Performance," doctoral dissertation, University of Chicago, December 1994.
8. CBS MarketWatch, December 16, 1998.
9. Blake, Elton, Gruber, *Journal of Business* 66:1993.
10. *Financial Review*, May 1998.
11. *Investment News*, January 25, 1999.
12. "Ranking Mutual Funds on an After-Tax Basis," Stanford University Center for Economic Policy Research Discussion Paper, 344.
13. James Garland, "The Tax Attraction of Tax-Managed Index Funds," *Journal of Investing*, Spring 1997.
14. "Is Your Alpha Big Enough to Cover Your Taxes?" *Journal of Portfolio Management*, Spring 1993.
15. Bogle, *Common Sense on Mutual Funds*.
16. Ibid.
17. *Barron's*, April 6, 1998.
18. *New York Times*, October 10, 1999.
19. Ibid.
20. Carhart, "On Persistence in Mutual Fund Performance."
21. *Investment News*, January 25, 1999; Bogle, *Common Sense on Mutual Funds*, p. 206.
22. Carhart, "On Persistence in Mutual Fund Performance."
23. Brad Barber and Terrance Odean, "The Courage of Misguided Convictions: The Trading Behavior of Individual Investors," in progress; "The Common Stock Investment Performance of Individual Investors," in progress; "Boys Will Be Boys: Gender, Overconfidence, and Common Stock Investment," in press. All are available at the web site www.gsm.ucdavis.edu/~odean/papers/.
24. *St. Louis Post Dispatch*, September 24, 1999.

Debt in the U.S. Capital Markets

Gerald A. Guild

all Street's reason for existence is to provide capital to governmental and private entities to enable them to carry out their activities. This capital is provided in the form of debt and equity security offerings, which comprise the primary market. The secondary market, which consists of subsequent transactions, usually between dealers or between dealers and investors, exists to support and enable the primary market. After all, no one would invest in a common stock with an infinite maturity unless there were a secondary market to provide liquidity when desired.

The debt portion is far and away the largest component of the U.S. capital markets in terms of issuance and subsequent trading. Debt[1] in the United States currently totals $17 trillion dollars, which, with our current U.S. population of 273 million, translates to over $60,000 per American. Debt is almost twice the size of the gross domestic product, and comprises well over 90% of the U.S. capital markets' new issue offerings. The secondary market is also dominated by debt compared to equity. Still, the financial press overwhelmingly features the equity markets.

Many investors, for example, can readily recall that the Dow Jones Industrial Average fell precipitously 508 points on October 19, 1987, the largest single-day percentage drop in history, 23%. However, very few could tell you what happened to the bond market that day. The $8^7/_8\%$ U.S. Treasury 30-year bonds due August 15, 2017, sold at 85% around 11:30 A.M., which translates into a yield to maturity of 10.529%. Because Treasury obligations became a safe haven and the beneficiary of a flight to safety from equities, bonds rallied dramatically. The next morning as London was closing and the U.S. markets were opening at 8:30 A.M., just a scant 21 hours later, that very same bond traded at $98^1/_2\%$, or a yield to maturity of 9.019%. Imagine a price gain of $13^1/_2$ points or 15.88% in just 21 hours. Incredible!

Debt instruments are also called fixed-income securities, because the cash flow—how much and when it will be received—is specified in advance. Debt has the distinct advantage of the automatic repayment of principal at maturity, if the issuer is financially capable of fulfilling its obligations.

The debt portions of the U.S. capital markets may be broken down into several categories: *U.S. government*, euphemistically called Treasurys, *agencies*, *mortgage-backed securities*, *corporates*, and *municipals*. (See Table 19.1.) These may be further subdivided into two maturity categories: *money market instruments*, maturities of one year or less; and *longer maturities*, maturities longer than one year.

We will first go through some basic information about bonds. Experienced investors may wish to skip the next two sections.

Key Bond Characteristics

Whatever the type of bond, there are a number of variables to look at when investing. First of all, a bond is debt, which is a promise to pay the face amount at maturity, usually with periodic payments along the way.

Interest Rate

Most bonds pay a fixed amount of interest—the coupon rate—on a regular basis until maturity, (called the coupon rate). The interest rate is based on the initial face value of the bond. For example, a $1,000 bond with a 6% interest rate will pay investors $60 a year, usually $30 every six months. The $30 payments will continue for the life of the bond, no matter what happens to interest rates or the resale value of the bond.

TABLE 19.1 Values of Securities Issued, Traded, and Outstanding, 1999

Security Type	Out-standing Value ($ billions)	Percent of Total	Issued Value ($ billions)	Percent of Total	Daily Trading Volume ($ billions)	Percent of Total
U.S. Treasurys	5,766.1	16.37	2,027.8	44.87	186.5	45.74
Agencies	1,450.0	4.12	536.3	11.87	54.6	13.38
Mortgaged-backeds	2,930.0	8.32	686.5	15.19	67.1	16.46
Asset-backeds	719.5	2.04	196.8	4.35	0.0	0.00
Money markets	2,276.8	6.46	0.0	0.00	0.0	0.00
Corporates	2,930.0	8.32	677.0	14.98	10.0	2.45
Municipals	1,518.1	4.31	263.3	5.83	8.5	2.08
Subtotal	17,590.5	49.93	4,387.7	97.09	326.7	80.13
Equities[1]	17,642.7	50.07	131.4	2.91	81.0	19.87
Total	35,233.2	100.00	4,519.1	100.00	407.7	100.00

[1] Common and preferred.
Sources: Federal Reserve *Bulletin*, Bond Market Association, National Association of Securities Dealers *Fact Book*, personal estimates.

A few bonds have adjustable interest rates. Others, called zeros, do not make regular interest payments. Instead the investor receives one payment at maturity that represents the purchase price plus the total interest earned.

Price

The price you pay for a bond is based on a number of factors, including interest rates, credit quality, maturity, tax status, and supply and demand. If interest rates have risen since the bond was issued, the price of the bond will decline. Such bonds are said to be selling at a discount.

Yield

Yield is the return that you earn on the bond. When purchasing a new issue at par (100), the yield is the stated interest rate. However, if you purchase an existing bond and pay more or less than the original principal, the yield changes. There are different measures of yield, which are discussed in more detail later.

Maturity

A bond's maturity is the specific future date on which the investor's principal will be repaid. Maturity can be anywhere from a few days to 40 years.

Redemption Features

A callable bond allows the issuer to repay the investor's principal at a specified date before maturity. Many issues are noncallable, including nearly all Treasurys. Other debt instruments have optional and mandatory redemption provisions that may affect their maturities. Optional features may have a favorable or an unfavorable impact for the investor, according to interest rate and price fluctuations.

Tax Status

An important measure of the efficacy of an investment is its after-tax rate of return. Some bonds are given special tax status by states and/or the federal government. The particular tax advantages and disadvantages of each type of debt security are discussed later.

Credit Quality of the Issuer

Credit quality refers to the likelihood of default, the issuer not being able to make interest payments or repay the principal at maturity. Only Treasurys, issued by the U.S. government, are considered to be credit risk free, so they are the benchmark for all other instruments. The others are tested and rated to assess the probability that the issuer will fulfill its debt obligations.

Risks of Debt Instruments

The paramount rule regarding any type of investment is to determine the risks and the rewards. You must determine whether you are being adequately rewarded for the risks you are taking. Of course, prices and yields are primarily based on perceived risk, which may not be the same as actual risk. What follows is a brief overview of the most common or important types of risks.

Credit Risk

The greatest risk is that the issuer will declare bankruptcy, and you will not receive the promised payments. This is called credit risk. The benchmark, of course, is a Treasury where there is absolutely no credit risk. Except for Treasurys, credit risk may change over the life of the instrument.

Interest Rate Risk

The next most important risk, and probably the most commonly encountered one, is interest rate risk. If interest rates rise after you purchase a bond, the value of the bond will decline, and you will be receiving a lower rate of interest on the bond than could be obtained on new bonds. The greater the maturity, the greater the potential price fluctuation.

Yield Curve Risk

Shifts in the shape of the yield curve can exacerbate both interest rate changes and price fluctuations.

Maturity Risk

The longer the maturity, the greater the risk that economic conditions or the fortunes of the issuer will change.

Liquidity Risk

What will the liquidity (marketability) of the instrument be if you decide to sell? One indicator is its current liquidity. However, liquidity may change for the better or the worse. The most liquid investments are Treasurys, with about $186 billion worth traded daily. Other types of debt instruments are significantly less liquid, and some can be exceedingly illiquid.

Extension Risk

This is the risk that the instrument will pay off significantly earlier or later than expected. Extension risk is more often a consideration in mortgage-backed pass-throughs. Another example might be cushion bonds, bonds that sell at premiums over par, and are expected to be called. If interest rates rise before the call date, the bond may not be called and could extend to the original maturity date, an extension of as much as 25 years.

Covenant Risk

Covenants are special provisions used in some bonds, primarily relating to optional and mandatory redemption features. In sophisticated jargon, the optional and mandatory redemption features are called "embedded options."

Issuer covenants include refunding provisions, optional additional sinking fund provisions, and other call features. Investor-advantaged covenants include put provisions, where the investor has the right to redeem bonds on a specific date or dates at a specific price. Innumerable other provisions exist.

It is imperative to remember that what seems to be an advantage may turn into a disadvantage if prices shift enough. For example, sinking fund provisions may be an advantage for either issuer or investor at various times as prices shift above or below par (100) reflecting interest rate changes.

Opportunity Risk

Opportunity risk is the chance that you will miss some other investment opportunity because your money is tied up in a particular bond investment.

Event Risk

Sudden unexpected changes in the fortunes of an issuer may dramatically change its quality and creditworthiness. Bankruptcy is an extreme sample of a negative event. Takeover by a higher-quality company is a positive event, although it could simultaneously be a negative event for the bondholders of that issuer.

Volatility Risk

Volatility is a risk, because the price may be relatively low when you need to sell. Volatility will be discussed in the section on Treasurys.

Yield Curve Risk

Shifts in the shape of the yield curve can exacerbate interest rate shifts and, therefore, price fluctuations.

Let's now examine the various types of debt instruments.

U.S. Governments (Treasurys)

U.S. governments, also called Treasurys, consist of Treasury bills, notes, and bonds. Treasury bills only pay their principal at maturity, with no interim interest payments. The maximum maturity is 364 days; so all bills are money market instruments. Notes are securities issued with a final maturity of 10 years or less, while bonds have an original maturity of more than 10 years. Notes and bonds pay interest semiannually. Currently the only bonds being issued are 30-year obligations.

Bonds remain bonds even when the time to maturity diminishes to 10 years or less, but notes and bonds evolve into money market instruments at the tail end of their existence, when there is less than a year to maturity.

Treasurys are backed by the full faith and credit of the United States of America. That specifically includes the unlimited taxing authority of the U.S. Congress to assure both the timely payment of interest and principal of its debt. Because of the unparalleled creditworthiness of the U.S. government, Treasurys are considered to be the highest-quality investment in the world.

Treasury bills are available in maturities weekly out to six months, and then monthly out to one year, or 364 days to be exact. There are weekly auctions of three- and six-month bills, and one-year bills are auctioned every three months. Keep in mind that the original one-year bill is reopened as the six-month bill after it has been outstanding for half of its term. Because all six-month bills are reopened again as the three-month bill, the one-year bill is auctioned for the third time three-quarters of the way to maturity.

The minimum denomination is $1,000. Bills are quoted in terms of yield,[2] which is then translated into price. As a result, the bid yield is higher than the asked yield, because the prices are the opposite. Only 2-, 5-, and 10-year notes are currently being offered. Thirty-year bonds are offered only twice a year, February and May. Some fear that they will be eliminated altogether.

Investors may purchase or sell all bills, notes, and bonds through brokers, dealers, and banks and purchase new issues through the auction process up to the maximum allotment ($1 million for bills and $5 million for notes and bonds). The U.S. Treasury has also established the Treasury Direct program to make individual participation in auctions easier for individuals and to provide liquidity in the aftermarket.[3]

Inflation-Indexed Notes and Bonds (TIPS)

Inflation-indexed notes and bonds, Treasury Inflation Protected Securities or TIPS, were introduced in January 1997. Only 10- and 30-year TIPS are offered. TIPS are best suited for tax-deferred and nontaxable accounts. Liquidity is markedly less than that of other Treasury securities, partly due to the limited supply outstanding. Currently TIPS represent less than 2% of the total amount of Treasurys.

While inflation-indexed bonds have been successful in other parts of the world, they are completely inappropriate for many investors. Without explaining the reasons fully, these bonds offer inherent flaws for taxable investors particularly, and in other respects for all investors.

Zeros

A zero coupon bond is one that does not pay regular interest payments. In essence, the interest accumulates and is paid at maturity. All Treasury bills are zero coupon bonds. Additionally, Separate Trading of Registered Interest and Principal of Securities (STRIPS) were enabled in February 1985 by then Secretary of the Treasury Donald Regan. Anyone with access to the Fed Wire has the right to separate the interest coupons and principal payments of all noncallable U.S. government notes and bonds without any maturity restriction.

How are zeros created? A note or bond is broken up into its interest and principal payments. A 30-year bond is divided into 61 separate component parts—60 semiannual interest payments plus the principal payment at maturity. All coupons with the same maturity are interchangeable, regardless of their bond source, but each principal payment is unique with a separate distinct CUSIP number and trades individually.[4]

STRIPS pay only their principal amount, which must be a multiple of $1,000, at maturity. Original issue discount (OID) taxation rules apply to STRIPS. These require the accretion and taxation of phantom income annually, even though it is not received until maturity or sale. Therefore they are best used in tax-deferred and tax-free accounts like inflation-indexed instruments. STRIPS have interesting applications in a variety of investment strategies.

Size of the Treasury Market

The Treasury market is enormous. Over $5.776 trillion is outstanding. Currently the United States has a budget surplus, so the Department of the Treasury must retire some debt. However, even when budget surpluses exist, the Treasury continually issues a mammoth volume of bills, notes, and bonds because of the constant maturing of outstanding debt instruments. In 1999 a total of $2.028 trillion of new bills, notes, and bonds were issued even though a net $76.9 billion was retired because of the budget surplus.

Secondary trading of Treasurys is gargantuan. By way of comparison, even with the geometric rise in equity trading volume in recent years, secondary equity transactions are significantly less than Treasurys, and even less compared to all debt.

Therefore, it follows that the unparalleled quality of Treasurys makes them the benchmark against which all other debt instruments are measured. Other instruments typically have higher returns because their risk is greater and liquidity lower. Only municipals, because of their unique tax advantages, yield less than Treasurys, and only the highest-rated municipals at that.

Volatility

Volatility is a measure of price change over time. The sensitivity of a bond to changes in interest rates varies, and there are different ways of measuring it. These will be discussed in the section on investment strategies.

Volatility in the debt markets is very substantial both over the course of a day and over time. Intraday Treasury price swings range up to three points, or $30 per $1,000 bond, when reported economic statistics deviate from consensus forecasts. Again, the record was the 13$^{1}/_{2}$-point swing within 24 hours, when the Dow Jones Industrial Average dropped 23% on October 19, 1987.

Changes in the yield curve and relative prices of different types of debt instruments may compound volatility. Moreover, volatility in individual issues is much more dynamic than in sectors. This is even true in Treasurys. Since the Long-Term Capital Management hedge fund fiasco, the volatility of Treasurys has increased. The spreads in prices between recent offerings and older outstanding issues with almost the same maturities have widened considerably, largely without justification, creating some opportunities for savvy investors.

The volatility of individual issues in other sectors, like corporates, may be enormous. At the extreme, an unexpected corporate bankruptcy could result in an immediate 40-, 50-, 60-, 70-, or even 80-point decline in the price of its debt!

Agencies

Agencies are obligations issued by agencies of the U.S. government, and are considered the next-highest-quality debt instrument. Some agencies are backed by the full faith and credit of the U.S. government, like the Government National Mortgage Association (GNMA), the General Services Administration (GSA), the Small Business Administration (SBA), and the Washington Metropolitan Area Transit Authority (WMATA). Most are not, like Federal Home Loan Bank (FHLB) or Tennessee Valley Authority (TVA). Some agencies are quasi-government, quasi-public entities like Federal National Mortgage Association (FNMA) and Federal Home Loan Mortgage Corporation (FHLMC), whose stocks are partly privately owned and publicly traded. Most are separate institutions like Federal Home Loan Bank.

A few agencies are exempt from state and local government taxation, like those issued by the Tennessee Valley Authority and the Federal Home Loan Bank, but most are taxable like those issued by the GNMA, FNMA, or FHLMC. All these agencies, like Treasurys, are taxable at the federal level.

The largest segment of agency obligations is mortgage-backed securities discussed in the next section.

In recent years many agencies have issued securities as arbitrage opportunities for dealers and to generate a profit for themselves. This new issuance has mushroomed to over $5 trillion annually in money market instruments and almost $600 billion in long-term instruments.

However, these instruments should probably be purchased only on a buy and hold to maturity basis because they may be illiquid and difficult to trade.

Mortgage-Backed Securities

Mortgage-backed securities exist to fill the demand for mortgages. By the late 1960s the demand for mortgages began growing at a faster pace than savings deposits. The innovative solution was to package existing mortgages into pools and sell them to investors, repaying the savings bank, which could then issue new mortgages. The timely payment of both interest and principal of these mortgage packages was guaranteed by an agency of the U.S. government, the Government National Mortgage Association (GNMA or Ginnie Mae).

Mortgage-Backed Pass-Throughs

A new industry was born that has expanded every year, reaching $2.246 trillion in 1999. Almost 38% of all mortgages outstanding have been transformed into mortgage-backed securities.[5] Each month, on the 15th, the investor receives both the interest and principal paid on the individual mortgages the preceding month, hence their name: *mortgage-backed pass-throughs.*

Since GNMA (chartered in 1968) began the process in 1970, two other agencies have followed suit, the Federal National Mortgage Association (FNMA or Fannie Mae) and the Federal Home Loan Mortgage Corporation (FHLMC, or Freddie Mac).

The most important distinction between these entities is that *only* GNMA is a direct obligation of the U.S. government, while the other two are only agencies of the government and therefore *not* backed by the full faith and credit of the United States. Fortunately, this distinction has never been put to the test, but it is a risk differentiation that should be taken into account. Therefore the market generally offers higher yields on FNMA or FHLMC pass-throughs than on GNMA pass-throughs.[6]

Investment Characteristics of GNMA, FNMA, and FHLMC Mortgage-Backed Securities

Mortgage-backed securities from GNMA, FNMA, and FHLMC offer a unique combination of highest quality and higher yields than corresponding Treasurys. However, there is an imponderable—when will you actually receive your principal back? Unlike Treasurys, which repay the entire principal at maturity, mortgages repay some minimum principal each and every month for the entire term of the mortgage, or until they are prepaid in their entirety. In the case of a 30-year mortgage-backed pass-through, this means 360 separate monthly payments, each consisting of both interest and principal. (However, it should be noted that the monthly payment of interest is a decided positive compared to the semiannual payment of interest on Treasurys, corporates, and municipals.)

Each month the principal portion increases slightly and the interest portion decreases as the mandated payment remains constant. Moreover, the individual mortgagee may make voluntary additional principal payments at any time, or pay off the mortgage entirely when he or she moves, or with refinancing to obtain a lower interest rate. Therefore, *you can never predict the actual yield you will receive on a mortgage-backed security. Only reasoned estimates may be calculated in advance.* For example, while the term of most mortgage-backed pass-throughs is 30 years, history shows us that the average life is about 10 years. That means that 50% of the principal will be returned in 10 years or less, with the remainder spread out over the succeeding 20 years. Individual pools may pay much slower or faster than this average.

There is both risk and opportunity in the uncertainty of principal payments on mortgage-backed securities. Clearly they are best suited for investors who have maturity flexibility, like many institutions, particularly retirement plans. The reward is obvious: highest quality and higher yield. The point is try to find out as much as possible about the makeup of the pool and its prepayment history to date to determine the risks. While the past does not necessarily predict the future, it is a guidepost.

Many investors, including institutions, find the small principal payments every month nettlesome from both a recordkeeping and reinvestment point of view. It is difficult if not impossible to maximize yield when investing small sums of money. They also prefer to concentrate the repayment of principal over a shorter period of time. In addition, different investors want different maturities, some short-term, some intermediate-term, and some long-term.

Collateralized Mortgage Obligations (CMOs)

Wall Street responded by taking mortgage-backed securities and transforming them into collateralized mortgage obligations (CMOs) in 1981. Now over 25% of all mortgage-backed pass-through securities outstanding are CMOs. Essentially the mortgage-backed securities are divided into tranches (from the French *trancher*, to cut) which prioritize repayment of principal.

Initially, all of the principal payments are funneled to the first tranche only, while all tranches receive interest. After the first is completely paid off and retired, subsequent payments are redirected to the next tranche, and so on until all tranches are paid off in turn. Other variations on this theme have also been created as investors have clamored for more certainty in principal prepayments.

In spite of these efforts, the timing of payments is still somewhat unpredictable. Actual repayments on CMOs may be dramatically shorter or longer than estimated at the time of purchase.

Corporates

Corporations issue debt obligations to obtain cash to finance their business activities. The total of new corporate issues, in the latest year available, totaled about $1 trillion versus $2 trillion for Treasurys.

The maturities of corporate obligations cover the entire debt spectrum, from short-term money market instruments to long-term speculations.

Corporate Money Market Instruments

Money market instruments may be either short-term borrowings or older obligations that mature within a year. The most common form of corporate money market instrument is commercial paper. Commercial paper is an unsecured short-term promissory note, usually with a maturity of 270 days or less. Commercial paper is generally rated prime or not prime. Moody's Investors Service divides prime into three subcategories. Many institutional investors restrict their commercial paper purchases to the highest-category prime issuers.

Credit Risk

Creditworthiness is one of the greatest risks in corporates. Will the issuer fulfill its debt obligations on time? There are several agencies that assign ratings to issuers based on their estimate of this risk (Table 19.2). The highest categories of the majors (AAA to Baa or BBB) are investment grade, which means prudent investors could invest in these securities.

Credit risks may change quite significantly over time. The history of General Motors is illustrative. Years ago many in Wall Street believed that when General Motors' 3¼% bonds due in 1975 matured, there would be no debt outstanding at the then world's largest company. The bonds were rated AAA. The fall and subsequent rise of General Motors shows how wrong that prognostication was. General Motors, and its finance subsidiary, General Motors

TABLE **19.2** Credit Ratings of Most Common Agencies

Moody's Investors Service	Standard & Poor's	Fitch	Duff & Phelps
Investment Grade			
Aaa	AAA	Aaa	
Aa1	AA+	Aa+	
Aa2	AA	Aa	
Aa3	AA–	Aa–	
A1	A+	A+	
A2	A	A	
A3	A–	A–	
Baa1	BBB+	BBB+	
Baa2	BBB	BBB	1+
Baa3	BBB–	BBB–	1
Below Investment Grade			
Ba1	BB+	BB+	1–2
Ba2	BB	BB	1–3
Ba3	BB–	BB–	1–4
B1	B+	B+	2–4
B2	B	B	2–5
B3	B–	B–	3–5
Caa	CCC+	CCC	3–6
	CCC		4–6
	CCC–		5–6
Ca	CC	CC	6–7
C	C	C	7–7
	D	D, DD, DDD	8–8

Note: Moody's corporate long-term ratings definitions as well as those of Standard & Poor's and the other rating agencies are similar and easily obtainable on the Internet or elsewhere.

Acceptace Corporation (GMAC), have hundreds of issues outstanding. The fortunes of the company deteriorated as world market forces changed the dynamics of the automobile industry and their ratings slipped all the way down to the bottom range of investment grade, Baa and BBB. Since then General Motors and GMAC have improved to the point that they are currently rated A2 and A by Moody's Investors Service and Standard & Poor's respectively. This is still several categories below the prestigious, and pristine, Aaa/AAA level they once enjoyed. While obvious, it is worth mentioning that one drawback to being rated the highest rating Aaa/AAA is that the best you can do is remain the same. The only possible change is downward.

All of these changes occurred well within the time frame of a long-term corporate bond, 30 to 40 years. (Actually there have been 100-year issues as recently as the 1990s, and at least one perpetual bond, Canadian Pacific 4%, first issued in 1923, but these are aberrations.) The issuer whose debt you buy today may be vastly different from the company that is obligated to pay you the principal at maturity. This new company may be much better or worse off financially.

Credit Enhancement

Lately, insurance companies have been used to upgrade corporate security ratings. The insurance company guarantee is in addition to the issuer's pledge to meet its obligations and becomes in force only if the issuer does not meet its interest or principal payments. The insurance company receives a fee for its service.

To keep risks manageable, usually only a portion of a particular issue will be guaranteed by an insurance company. The rating is increased to Aaa/AAA by the rating agencies. A variation on this theme has been introduced more recently whereby one issuer provides a guarantee to upgrade lower-rated issues to a, medium investment grade. See fuller discussion of insurance wrap in municipals section later in this chapter.

Syndication of Corporates

Before we proceed further I'd like to discuss the issuing process, where your corporate bond originates. The process begins when a corporation perceives that it needs additional capital to continue or expand, and decides to utilize debt to obtain it. Let us assume that the corporation has decided to use long-term debt.

The corporation chooses an investment bank to organize the issuance. The investment bank puts together a group of firms (syndicate), some of which will purchase the securities from the corporation (underwriters), while others will contact potential buyers and sell the securities, usually for a commission (selling group). Papers are filed with the Securities and Exchange Commission in the form of a preliminary prospectus. When the registration process is complete, the company and underwriters hammer out mutually agreeable terms and the offering is made. This is a negotiated syndicate.

The underwriters agree to pay the issuing corporation a price that is slightly lower than the public offering price, and expect to make their profit from the spread between the two. The underwriters, in turn, sell the securities to the selling group, often at a slight discount from the public offering price, and may keep some of the securities themselves.

The key ingredient in the underwriting process is that the syndicate is obliged to pay the issuer the proceeds on a settlement date, regardless of whether the bonds are sold! The underwriters who provide this sort of commitment bear all the risk, since the public may not be willing to buy the entire issue.

There are strict procedures in the underwriting process that are too technical to detail here. Suffice it to say that corporate bonds must be sold at the original price as long as the syndicate remains intact.

Only corporate bonds are subject to the registration process through the SEC. Governments, agencies, mortgage-backed securities of agencies, and municipals are exempt from the registration process. Agencies, municipals, and CMOs issue offering circulars, which offer some information but are usually not as complete as the final prospectus in a corporate bond offering.

When an accredited institution purchases an entire issue the situation can be quite different. This is called a *private placement*, and the buyer has more input into the indenture provisions.

In recent years the process has become streamlined to enable many companies to make offerings at virtually any time. This flexibility is a decided advantage in changing market conditions. A delay in the prospectus review could potentially be quite expensive for the issuer. This "shelf registration" has evolved into medium-term note offerings, which are continuous offerings by major issuers, with or without underwriters. The real disadvantage is the size of various maturities—weekly issues may be quite small and the secondary market quite illiquid.

Liquidity of Corporates

Liquidity of corporate bonds is limited, particularly as compared to Treasurys. The estimated daily volume is around $10 billion out of $3 trillion outstanding. New issuance is substantial, $1 trillion in 1999.

Dealers in the over-the-counter market carry out most of the trading in corporate bonds. However, many corporate bonds are listed on the New York Stock Exchange (in a different location than equity trading). All of it is centered on the NYSE's computerized Automated Bond System (ABS), with 53 members and 225 terminals.

The prices at which these trades are made are published in the financial press. Unfortunately, these listed prices may be significantly different from those in transactions in the larger over-the-counter market. That is one of the significant problems with debt, finding the market price. Governments with their extraordinary volume have price transparency but other segments do not. Price, then, is often an imponderable. Nasdaq started to address this issue with the initiative of the Fixed Income Pricing System (FIPS). A select list of high-yield bonds, updated regularly, require reporting of all transactions to FIPS. How this will broaden to other corporates is only in the development stage.

Liquidity is predominantly provided by the dealer community. The dealer community initially developed secondary trading capacity to support investment banking activities (i.e., underwriting). At the beginning the standard was, "If you bought the security from us, we will make a market in it." It evolved into a more nebulous, "If you bought the security from us, we will make a best-effort basis to find a market for it." Cynics might claim that it is becoming, "If you bought this security, you own it, and it is your problem."

The primary reason for these changes is that the dealers' risk from participation is increasing and their incentives are declining. The field is continuing to evolve, but it appears that greater price transparency will result, a decided plus. However, overall liquidity may shrink if dealers decide to reduce their risk exposure further.

Spread Risk of Corporates

Corporate bonds have higher yields than Treasurys with the same maturity because the corporates have greater credit and liquidity risk. As expected, the difference in yield, or spread, between corporates and Treasurys widens as creditworthiness declines.

Spreads also vary over time. The same year, 1998, that Baa-rated corporates traded as wide as 218 basis points over Treasurys, they also traded as little as 136. Spread changes may occur for a variety of reasons, including: (1) economic cycle changes, perceived or real; (2) industry changes, perceived or real; (3) issuer rating credit watch or rating changes; (4) supply and demand of corporates; (5) supply and demand of Treasurys; and (6) event risk change, including mergers or acquisitions.

High-Yield Securities

High-yield securities are corporates whose credit rating is below investment grade. Often they are disparagingly referred to as *junk bonds*. In dollar terms they represent only about one-fifth of the marketplace. Their yield is relatively high because they have been rated as having higher risks of default. However, if you can identify issues that are not as risky as their ratings suggest, you can obtain high yields with a high certainty of redemption. If you are wrong, however, your capital is at risk.

Unfortunately, accurate assessment of the creditworthiness of these issues is challenging. Ironically, less credit research is available in the high yield arena than in investment grade. Moreover, some of it is suspect or tainted. Other times it is mute; underwriters are prohibited from commenting on a security around the time that the security is coming to market.

There is a perceived conflict of interest when investment bankers report on the credit status of corporations that may be their clients, either past or future. Some also accuse rating agencies of a potential conflict of interest because they derive fees for rating securities. To what extent these potential conflicts affect credit ratings is unclear.

What is the alternative? One choice is to obtain independent research from a disinterested party. One such entity, Duff & Phelps, is a subscription service. You must pay a fee to obtain research or get it secondhand through a subscriber. Duff & Phelp's 1 to 8 ratings are made for both two- and five-year time horizons, which is an interesting approach. Lower-grade ratings are more vulnerable to the business cycle, which could change significantly more over five years than over two years. The business cycle record was broken only recently; February 2000 was the 107th month of economic expansion, eclipsing the former 1961–1969 expansion during the Vietnam War.

Research in high-yield securities is more like equity research than debt research. To determine if the company is likely to be able to pay its interest obligations, you must evaluate the company's present and future cash flow. Study its income statement and balance sheet; determine the capital-to-debt ratios, both current and future projections; and determine the priority of your debt relative to other company debt obligations.

The key to investing in high-yield securities is to spread the risk among issuers in the same industry as well as among various industries. That way, if something does go wrong in one company, your entire portfolio will not be severely impacted.

Emerging Market Debt

There is more than enough risk in high-yield securities for most investors. Emerging market debt involves even greater default risk, as well as additional risks, including political risk.

Third World debt is speculative at best. The pessimistic, but realistic, approach is not to question *if* these loans will go into default but rather ask *who* and *when*. If the price of oil increases, the likeliest defaulters will be oil-importing underdeveloped nations. If the price of oil remains low or declines, the likeliest defaulters will be oil-exporting underdeveloped nations.

It is interesting to note that the International Monetary Fund (IMF) and other Western industrialized nations are considering forgiving a portion of this Third World debt of underdeveloped nations. These countries cannot pay the debt service, interest and principal, and provide the necessary social services. The alternatives of revolution and anarchy are equally intolerable, as we have seen in certain African nations.

Money center U.S. and world banks expanded into this fertile market and grew geometrically. One of the other major reasons for the banking crises in the United States was the losses on emerging market loans. These loans had to be written down and sold, but the market was illiquid at best. Secretary of the Treasury Nicholas F. Brady evolved a creative solution enabling the countries and banks to create securities and sell them in the marketplace. These securities bear his name and are called *Brady bonds*.

In Brady bonds a U.S. government zero-coupon security is used to assure the payment of principal at maturity. However, this does not assure the interest payments, which over time are more important than the principal.

Adding spread risk, political risk, currency risk, and liquidity risk to ordinary economic risks makes emerging market debt unsuitable for most investors.

Other Foreign Debt Securities

Foreign governments or corporations may issue foreign debt in local currency. Some of these foreign corporations may be subsidiaries of major U.S. corporations and guaranteed by the parent. Therefore these securities cover the entire spectrum of credit risk, from virtually none, in the case of a AAA-rated U.S. major corporation, to default.

Let me state I have a prejudice against most investors using foreign currency–denominated securities in their portfolios. Two risks, currency and political, are large enough to outweigh the increase in yield obtained.

Convertible Securities

Convertible bonds are debt instruments that are convertible, at the holder's option, into the common stock of the issuer. A few are convertible into other equities. Convertible preferreds have the same conversion feature but are equity, not debt, and subordinate in the event of dissolution.[7]

Convertible bonds may best be described as "equity with a coupon." Therefore, it follows that you should never buy a convertible bond *unless* you would buy the underlying common stock. There is one exception to this rule, which will be discussed later in this section.

The primary advantage of a convertible bond is the unlimited upside potential of the common stock. Additionally, the current yield is usually higher than the dividend yield on the common.[8] In the event the company encounters difficulties, the convertible bondholder is in the preferential position of a creditor, not an owner.

The disadvantages of a convertible bond are more obscure. First, a convertible bond is usually subordinate to other debt of the same issuer. Second, the coupon is invariably lower than nonconvertible debt of the same issuer. Third, the initial conversion price is substantially higher than the price of the common stock when the convertible bond is issued. This premium has been rising in recent years and now regularly exceeds 25%.

You should examine the merits of a convertible bond in terms of both its upside potential as a common stock and its potential performance as straight debt. What happens if the company's fortunes fall sufficiently to impair its ability to meet its debt obligations? In the worst of times a bondholder may receive something, even as much as all one's money back, while the stockholder receives absolutely nothing.

The downside of a convertible bond, the risk if you will, is its investment value, the value as a straight or nonconvertible bond. This is the floor, but it resembles the floor of an elevator in that it will rise and fall in price inversely as interest rates and spreads over Treasurys gyrate over time.

This "broken" convertible bond that is selling near or at its investment value is the exception to the rule that you should never buy a convertible bond unless you would buy the underlying common stock. Now you are buying it as a bond, not as a convertible debenture.

The best way to evaluate a convertible bond is to complete the convertible bond worksheet (see Figure 19.1).

Issuer: _____   Settlement Date:_____

Bond	**Common Stock**

Symbol: _____   Symbol: _____

Rating: M: _____ S&P:_____ KDP:_____   Rating: S& P: _____

Coupon: _____%   Dividend: $_____

Maturity Date: _____

Price: _____%   Price: $_____

Yield to Maturity: _____%

Current Yield: _____%   Stock Yield: _____%

Conversion Rate:_____Shares

Conversion Price per Share: $_____

Conversion Value: _____% Conversion Rate times Common Stock Price
divided by 10

Bond Investment Value—An Estimation Today

Treasury Note / Bond Yield: _____% add Spread over Treasurys: _____ Basis
Points

Investment Yield to Maturity: _____% convert into Investment Price: _____%

Other Features:

Sinking Fund: Y/N __ ____% Beginning: _____ Amount/Year: _____
Option to Increase: Y/N ___

Call Features: Date: _____ Price: _____%

Other Significant Features like Put/Refunding, etc:_____

Ratios

Conversion Premium: _____%	Calculation is [(Bond Price / Conversion Value) – 1] × 100
Investment Premium: _____%	Calculation is [(Bond Price / Investment Price) – 1] × 100
Yield Pickup: _____%	Calculation is Current Yield of Bond minus Stock Yield
Recapture Period: _____Years	Calculation is Conversion Premium / Yield Pickup

FIGURE 19.1 Convertible Bond Worksheet

Conversion premium should be nil if bond is selling at or above call price.
Investment premium is a measure of the downside risk of a convertible bond.
Recapture period applies only if bond is selling below call price. Also referred to as
"breakeven time," it should be less than 5 years.

*Be sure to include accrued interest in arbitrage calculations. Accrued interest is lost when a
bond is converted into common stock. Therefore, convert on interest payment dates, if
possible.*

Notes for Using Convertible Bond Worksheet

Don't be put off by all the blanks. Most of them are easily obtainable, like terms including coupon, maturity, price, and rating. The same is true of conversion rates and prices. The calculations are self-explanatory.

The only subjective portion is the critical investment value. Here you back into it beginning with the yield on a similar-maturity Treasury today. Add what you think is the appropriate spread above that benchmark to determine the estimated investment yield to maturity of this convertible bond. Then calculate the investment price. This is the value of the convertible bond as straight debt today, the downside, the floor.

Obviously the key word is *today*. The investment value will fluctuate as interest rates change, up or down, or the fortunes of the company change, up or down. There is also serendipity! While it is most unlikely, the company's fortunes could improve sufficiently to drive the price of the common stock high enough to make the conversion feature viable and profitable.

A brief mention of the footnotes on the worksheet. Conversion premium should be nil if the bond is selling at or above call price. It is often in the best interests of an issuer to call its convertible bond if it can force conversion into common stock. The company saves interest expense, increasing pretax income, and improves its debt/equity ratio by reducing debt and increasing equity.

How can a company force conversion? It is really very simple: Call the convertible bond when the conversion value (conversion rate times common stock price) is substantially above the call price. Convertible bondholders will be forced into converting into common stock to maximize value. They will also have to make the choice to keep the stock or sell it. Some will sell, so the price may fall somewhat, and that is why the convertible is usually called when the common stock price is substantially above the conversion price.

Recapture is a nebulous concept. In essence, it is a calculation of the number of years it will take to recover the conversion premium in the higher current yield of the bond over the stock yield. Interest income is taxable as income in federal, state, and local jurisdictions for all but tax-free and tax-deferred accounts. That is not taken into consideration here. You may choose to do so, but that will extend the recapture period.

Finally, one last caveat. Don't forget to factor accrued interest into all calculations. The buyer must pay interest to the seller from the last payment date, or dated date in the case of a new issue, up to but not including settlement date. That is a real cost and may approach up to one-half the coupon rate depending on the settlement date.

For more complete discussion, consult the author's web site: http://guilds. net/gerry.

Municipal Bonds

State and local governments issue municipal securities to finance a wide variety of services. Generally speaking, municipals are either of two varieties: general obligation or revenue. Municipals encompass the entire range of maturities from money market to 40 years.

General obligation municipals are backed by the taxing authority of the issuer. The creditworthiness of the issuer is determined by a rating agency, and is usually one of the top four investment grades at the time of issuance (ratings can change significantly over the life of the bond). Revenue municipals are backed by specific revenues like bridge or turnpike tolls. These revenue sources enable the payment of interest and repayment of principal on the securities, whose proceeds often funded the construction of the facility in the first place.

Municipals enjoy unique tax advantages. The federal government does not impose income taxes on municipals, and state and local municipals are exempt from income taxation by the issuing state or municipality. However, municipal bonds are *not* exempt from capital gain or estate taxes. Finally, municipal bond income is part of the calculation of income in the computation of the federal alternative minimum tax.

Municipal Syndication

The process of municipal bond issuance is similar to that described for corporates. However, municipal syndicates differ from corporate syndicates in several meaningful ways.

First, a preliminary scale may be proposed, which is not necessarily the definite final offering. In essence this is a trial balloon. The orders at those levels are evaluated and the yields are adjusted as necessary to complete the sale.

Secondly, municipal underwriters prioritize orders. The result is that some orders may not be filled because other orders have priority. Exacerbating the problem is the fact that municipal underwriters do not have to offer these bonds at the original price. They may opt to keep them in inventory and reoffer them after the syndicate is closed at the then prevailing market price in the secondary market. Corporate underwriters are required to make a bona fide public offering of all their bonds at the original price. Unsold corporates at the close of a syndicate are still subject to this restriction even if the bonds sell at a premium in the secondary market. If prices are lower, the bonds may be sold at market price.

Municipal bond underwriting may never be the same. For the first time the city of Pittsburgh, Pennsylvania, offered a municipal obligation without underwriters in 1999 through the Internet. Will this prove to be the wave of the future or an aberration? What will be the liquidity of these issues in the secondary market?

In 1999 municipal issuance was approximately $2 billion, and the total outstanding is estimated to be around $1.5 trillion, excluding money market instruments.

Municipal Tax Advantage

The key to understanding municipal bonds is their tax advantage. The relative tax advantage of municipals depends on your tax bracket. The accepted method is to show a mirror image of the tax advantage, the taxable equivalent yield, instead of showing the after-tax equivalent of taxable securities. (See Table 19.3.)

Taxable equivalent yield is merely the reciprocal of your tax bracket. The formula is the municipal bond yield divided by the difference between your marginal tax rate in decimal form (not in %) and 1. If you are in the 50% tax bracket, the taxable bond equivalency is twice the municipal bond yield: municipal bond yield divided by $(1 - .50)$, which equals municipal bond yield

TABLE 19.3 Taxable Equivalent Yield

Municipal Bond Yield	Tax Rate						
	15%	20%	25%	30%	32%	36%	39.6%
3%	3.53%	3.75%	4.00%	4.29%	4.41%	4.69%	4.97%
4%	4.71%	5.00%	5.33%	5.71%	5.88%	6.25%	6.62%
5%	5.88%	6.25%	6.67%	7.14%	7.35%	7.81%	8.28%
6%	7.06%	7.50%	8.00%	8.57%	8.82%	9.38%	9.93%
7%	8.24%	8.75%	9.33%	10.00%	10.29%	10.94%	11.59%
8%	9.41%	10.00%	10.67%	11.43%	11.76%	12.50%	13.25%
9%	10.59%	11.25%	12.00%	12.86%	13.24%	14.06%	14.90%
10%	11.76%	12.50%	13.33%	14.29%	14.71%	15.63%	16.56%

times two. Similarly, if you are in the 33% tax bracket the taxable equivalent yield is 1.5 times the municipal bond yield.

What tax rate should you use? My recommendation is to determine your total tax rate: federal taxes divided by gross income. Others suggest using your marginal tax rate, your rate of taxation on the last dollar of income. I think that overstates your taxable equivalent yield.

Because of their tax advantage, municipals generally sell at a lower yield than Treasurys.[9] Therefore, they are usually quoted as a percentage of Treasurys rather than a spread over Treasurys. In the past decade this percentage has been as low as 77.8% and as high as 98.7% for highest-grade municipals.

Municipal bonds are subject to the same risks as other bonds: credit risk, volatility, interest rate risk, yield curve risk, and liquidity risk. Liquidity in serial issues is more limited than in term bonds because of the smaller sizes and multitude of maturities.

Municipal Secondary Markets

Essentially the only secondary market that exists is a dealer market in the over-the-counter market. Dealers act as principals for their own account and risk. Only a few dollar bonds are quoted in daily newspapers, so following the prices of your municipals is difficult. Municipal prices may be available from *The Blue List*,[10] the original underwriter, or subscription services. Institutions often use brokers to canvass dealers to obtain the best bid or offering available. J. J. Kenny Drake[11] offers a similar service, broadcasting bonds through its wire service or over the Internet to subscribers, looking for bids.

Many bond prices listed on bank and brokerage firm statements are "matrix prices" furnished by independent pricing services. Matrix prices are estimated by comparing one issue to another. If X is here Y should be there.[12] Unfortunately, these estimations may be quite far from reality.

This interim price uncertainty is irrelevant if you plan to hold the issue to maturity. However, if you decide to sell, the difference between the matrix price and a real bid may be a shock.

Zero municipals act largely like other zero debt instruments. If purchased or sold at other than the original or accreted price, the difference will be a short- or long-term capital gain or loss. If the zero were purchased and sold at the same yield, even if it differed from the original yield, there would be no capital gain or loss. All of the difference in price would be tax-exempt accretion. That is exactly what would happen if the zero was purchased at the original offering price (yield), and held to maturity. One other word of caution: If these zeros are purchased at a lower yield (higher price) than the original offering yield, make sure that they are not subject to extraordinary calls. If they are, the zeros are likely to be called at the accreted price. You could end up with a lower yield than you anticipated or even a capital loss.

The relative diminutive size of the municipal market, and its limited liquidity, impede swapping of one municipal into another or sector shifting from one debt sector to another. Limited accurate price information compounds the problem. Hopefully, the price transparency that is currently beginning to expand from highly visible Treasury markets to corporates will also extend to municipals.

Risks of Municipal Securities

Most of the risks of municipals are similar to those of corporates. One aspect of credit risk of municipals needs a little more amplification.

The credit ratings of some municipals are enhanced by insurance to obtain an AAA rating. This insurance "wrap" means that the insurer guarantees the timely payment of interest and principal of the municipal issue if that issuer cannot meet its obligations. AAA insured municipals usually yield more than regular AAA issues (spreads vary over time and coupon range), because the risk is greater. There is a small risk that the insurer will not be able to fulfill its commitment if the issuer fails to meet its obligation. Many insurers guarantee several hundred times their capital, so a prolonged downturn could jeopardize these payments.

Certificates of Deposit

Certificates of deposit (CDs), are available directly from banks or through brokerage firms. Banks must charge a penalty for early withdrawal except if the depositor has died. If the depositor dies, the CD can be redeemed at par plus accrued interest to date. This "death put" provision permits a person with a limited life expectancy to purchase the highest rate available without worrying about the CD's maturity exceeding theirs.

Certificates of deposit are insured up to $100,000 per depositor per institution by the FDIC and directly guaranteed by the United States. The key to remember, here, is that the limit is by institution, not holder. Therefore, an individual can use a variety of accounts to insure many times $100,000.

Market-Linked Certificates of Deposit

These are CDs whose interest payments are linked to a market index, most often a broad index like the Standard & Poor's 500 (the principal is not at risk). In essence, this market-linked CD is a hybrid product consisting of a zero coupon CD plus an option on the underlying index at the starting value at inception.

Unfortunately, the IRS changed the rules on this type of investment in 1996, and the entire issue is taxed as if it were a zero coupon CD. That means every year there is phantom income (original issue discount—OID) attributed to this CD, and taxable income is generated even though no income is actually received. Therefore this instrument is best suited for tax-free or tax-deferred accounts, like retirement accounts. Also, it has limited liquidity, and is therefore suitable only for investors who are willing to hold it to maturity.

Market-linked CDs are a method for cautious investors to put some of their assets into equities while retaining the safety of debt. At maturity they are assured of receiving all their money back.

Preferred Stocks

Preferred stock has attributes of both equity and debt. Like a bond, it promises to pay fixed dividends each year, sometimes in perpetuity. (Typically the dividend rate is fixed, but variable rate preferreds also exist.) It also does not convey voting power. However, like an equity investment, failure to pay the dividend does not precipitate corporate bankruptcy. Instead, unpaid dividends cumulate and must be paid in full before any dividends may be paid to holders of common stock. Also, preferred stock has preference over common stock in dissolution of the corporation, hence the name. It may be issued with provisions similar to those of corporate bonds. Preferred stock may be callable or convertible into common stock.

Preferred stocks are most suitable for investors with a long-term horizon, as the maturity is typically long-term to infinity. Preferred stocks have the advantage of quarterly payments, better than the semiannual coupon payments on most debt instruments.

Derivatives

Derivatives, to my mind, are any securities or investment vehicles derived from other securities or investment vehicles. Derivatives cover the entire gamut of risk and reward, and the entire gamut of investment possibilities. Derivatives are available in most debt sectors, including Treasurys, agencies, mortgage-backeds, corporates, municipals, and preferreds. The most common derivatives on common stocks are put and call options.

By this definition, derivatives include all futures and options, warrants, hybrid securities like convertible bonds, STRIPS, mortgage-backed pass-throughs, and collateralized mortgage obligations, and a wide variety of customized products. There is no limit to the types of derivatives that can be offered.

One vital consideration in any derivative is the ability of the paying party to complete its contractual obligations. Examine the terms of the derivative closely and analyze the permutations as interest rates change over the term of the contract. Many investors, including supposedly sophisticated institutions, have been seriously burned in derivatives. You don't have to look any further than Orange County, California, which nearly went bankrupt, or Procter & Gamble to see major disasters. Their lawsuits alleged "unsophisticated investors," and settlements prevented adjudication of that definition.

Don't be afraid to ask plenty of questions and propose every what-if scenario you can contemplate. If you cannot assess the risks, you certainly cannot determine whether the rewards justify taking the risks.

Debt Mutual Funds

Mutual funds are available that invest in virtually any type of debt instrument. Money invested in debt mutual funds totaled $808.2 billion at the end of 1999. This does not include money market funds, which had assets of $1,612.4 billion.

Money market funds are often used as cash equivalents while investors wait to make longer-term investment decisions. They are discussed in the chapter on cash management.

The major advantages of bond mutual funds are professional management, diversification, and economies of scale. Because their purchases are larger than those of most individuals, funds obtain better price execution. Active management, including swapping, may further enhance performance.

However, my opinion is that the disadvantages outweigh these advantages. I have spent many years directly involved in fixed income investment and I am more comfortable with investors directly owning individual issues. I do not see the need to delegate this function, nor the justification of paying the fees, especially annual management fees on securities held for the long term, perhaps to maturity.

The fatal flaw in debt mutual funds, in my view, is that they take away the major advantage of debt, a definitive maturity date. You must sell debt mutual funds to redeem them, and there is no security of receiving your initial investment if you wait until a future date. When you decide to sell your shares, you may receive a lower price than you paid for them. In contrast, as an individual investor, my mistakes, if creditworthy, mature at par on maturity date. Worse things could happen to an investment than receiving exactly what you expected in the first place, par at maturity. Finally, when managers try to gain advantage by guessing the direction of future interest rate changes, keep in mind they may be wrong as well as right.

When is a debt mutual fund perhaps the best choice? I discourage "junk" bond or emerging market investment in general, because of the potential high loss of principal. However, if you are willing to invest in these speculative areas, consider debt bond funds specializing in these arenas rather than doing it yourself. Professional research and management, wide diversification, and economies of scale usually make funds preferable to individual selection. Active bond swapping is a necessity as industries ebb and flow in changing economic conditions and companies within those industries change dynamically. Close monitoring is essential, since spreads change minute to minute and events such as mergers or bankruptcy can cause price declines of 50% or 80% in milliseconds.

When else should you consider debt bond funds? When *you* want to! Hopefully only after assessing the risks, including all fees. Like with equity mutual funds, it is important to determine front and back-end loads, expenses, and management fees. Examine the management company, its philosophy, its historical record as well as the individuals managing your prospective fund. Past performance is not necessarily a guide to future results. However, taken in context, it is a benchmark of comparison that should be utilized. Individual managers change frequently so consider the management company more than the individual. Look at the latest portfolio to determine where in the range of allowable investments the fund is currently focused. Is this what you would do personally if you were making the decisions for yourself?

Performance is critical, of course, but check first to see if the funds' investment objectives and limitations match your unique investment needs and objectives. That is even more important than performance.

Unit Investment Trusts

Unit investment trusts (UITs) are similar to bond mutual funds in that they represent shares of interest in the entire portfolio. However, UITs have definite maturity dates, and are supervised, not actively managed, so annual fees are typically lower. Investments that deteriorate in quality below the stated standards are sold. All proceeds from sales, redemptions, calls, sinking funds, and so on are distributed to the holders on a pro rata basis.

Liquidity is limited, so the current market value might be lower than net asset value, depending on supply or demand. (Theoretically it could even be higher, but that is highly improbable.) The secondary market is through the original sponsor of the UIT. Be wary of deferred sales charges, and check the terms in advance.

Bond UITs may limit their investments to certain sectors of the debt market, such as corporates, internationals, state and national municipals, Treasurys, or mortgage-backed securities. Bond unit investment trusts are declining in issuance. This may reduce liquidity in the future, as the secondary market relies on other purchasers to continue and that demand may dwindle in a shrinking market.

Interest Rates and Yield Curves

Types of Yield Curves

Essentially there are three types of yield curves: (1) Positively sloped, often called "normal," where rates climb as maturity lengthens; (2) inversely or negatively sloped, often called "inverted," where rates decline as maturity lengthens; and (3) "humpbacked" yield curves, where rates are highest in the intermediate term and lower in both shorter- and longer-term maturities.

The positively sloped yield curve makes the most sense because many risks could occur over a longer term. Widely believed to be the most common, it is not. The negatively sloped, or inverted curve is alleged to portend a coming recession. A humpbacked curve may occur as yield curves shift from positive to inverse, but there is no assurance the shift will be completed.

In June 1996 a study in *Current Issues in Economics and Finance*, published by the Federal Reserve Bank of New York, reported that the relative yields of the three-month bill and the 10-year note predicted the probability of a recession four quarters hence. The results were back-tested to 1960. When the yield of the 10-year note was 80 basis points (–0.80%) lower than the yield on the three-month T-bill (either a humpedbacked or an inverted yield curve), the probability of a recession one year later was 50%!

This relationship became one of 10 component parts of the leading economic indicators in December 1996. Because the equity markets, in theory, forecast nine months in advance, this relationship could have application for the stock market as well, particularly broad indexes such as the Dow Jones Industrials or the Standard & Poor's 500.

Interest Rate Considerations

What Determines Interest Rates?

The simple answer is the inflation rate, but expectation of changes in inflation can also play a role. Investors expect to receive a certain real rate of return, which is defined as the portion of return exceeding the rate of inflation. What the real rate of return should be is subject to debate. Inflation-indexed obligations may provide a benchmark, and in the United States their real return has fluctuated between 3.6% and 4.2%. My personal belief is that the real rate of return should vary, depending on the rate of inflation.

At times bond interest rates are more affected by the expectation of inflation than the current level of inflation. The most notable example was the period 1993–1994 when interest rates rose from 5.79% on October 1993 to a peak of 8.23% in November 1994 despite inflation remaining stagnant at 2.7%. Fear of inflation was the cause. Psychology can be as important a consideration as fact in the bond markets, just like in the equity markets.

Fiscal and Monetary Policy and Interest Rates

Historically, interest rates have been strongly impacted by the federal government's fiscal and monetary policy. Fiscal policy was expansionary from 1960 through 1997, with the federal government running deficits in every year save 1969, when there was a token $2 billion surplus. During that time, by default, monetary policy was the only intentional method of stimulation or retardation of the business cycle.

Monetary policy is determined by the seven Federal Reserve governors appointed by the U.S. president and confirmed by the Senate to 14-year terms. The chairman is the most important governor and serves a four-year term, but may be reappointed. Together with the five Federal Reserve banks' presidents, the Federal Reserve governors determine two key interest rates, the federal funds rate and the discount rate. They attempt to use changes in these rates to control monetary growth, the rate of inflation, and economic growth. These changes in short-term interest rates filter through the system and impact longer-term rates like bond yields and mortgage rates.

Future Considerations

The federal budget surpluses predicted for the foreseeable future portend dramatic change in our capital markets, particularly debt. One forecast suggests that the Social Security surplus will absorb the entire public portion of Treasury debt, $3.3 trillion out of the total federal debt of $5.8 trillion, by 2013.

What does that mean? If true, the entire U.S. government market, the highest-quality, most liquid investment on Earth, will cease to exist! Social Security undoubtedly will have to liquidate its accumulated surplus to pay retirement benefits starting in 2020. Therefore, the Treasury market will disappear in 2013 and have to be restarted in 2020. Imagine! First we eliminate the highest-quality, most liquid investment market on Earth, and then we recreate it all over again less than a decade later.

Because Treasurys are the benchmark against which other debt instruments are compared and traded, what will take its place if that market disappears? Stay tuned for significant changes. One possible negative effect will be the reduced liquidity of all debt markets, which could force a return to the buy and hold to maturity of generations ago. At the very least it clearly demonstrates that liquidity is relative and subject to change, even for Treasurys.

Of course, long-term forecasts are notoriously unreliable. The U.S. economy entered a new record 107th month of expansion on February 1, 2000, and no one knows how long it will last. Predicting it will continue uninterrupted for another decade seems overly optimistic, at least based on history.

Relationship between the Debt and Equity Markets

Low inflation is a key ingredient to a rising debt market, as well as a rising equity market. Declining interest rates mean higher bond prices, as they fluctuate inversely to each other. A generation ago the prevailing wisdom was that equities were an inflation hedge. Investors demanded higher yields—dividends—from equities, because they were riskier investments than debt.

Bond and stock prices have moved together and opposite each other over many years during the past century. Simplistically, bond and stocks moved inversely to each other up to 1966 and more or less in concert thereafter. Significant gyrations between the two have occurred in individual years, like 1994 when stocks had a strong positive rate of return while bonds achieved negative results. The year 1999 was the same, with stock prices up and bond prices down. Both bear markets in bonds were caused by fear of inflation, not inflation itself, although inflation did rise from 1.6% to 2.7% in 1999.

When, not if, bonds and stocks will move in opposite directions over time is unknown.

Fixed-Income Investment Strategies

Should *You* Own Debt Investments?

Everyone should have a portion of his or her portfolio in fixed income. The real question is what percent of your portfolio. The answer: at least some, and perhaps as much as 100%.

The percent depends on your risk tolerances and investment objectives. One guidepost, and only a guidepost, is the concept that *the percent of your portfolio in debt should approximate your age.* That makes sense from the point of view that safety of principal becomes more important as you grow older. Certainly more of your portfolio should shift from equities to debt if you are in or near retirement age. Keep in mind that your needs remain long-term, not a lump sum at age 65.

Moreover, debt investment opportunities range across the entire spectrum to satisfy everyone's needs and objectives. Remember that the Treasury bill maturing next Thursday is the closest thing to a riskless investment. Long-term STRIPS gyrate day to day, as much as futures, options, or other speculative investments. (As an extreme example, recall the 56.88% price appreciation of 30-year STRIPS as yields dropped from 10.50% to 9% as stocks crashed on October 19, 1987.) Speculative debt instruments like below-investment-grade corporates and municipals and emerging market debt offer more risk and reward potential than most common stocks.

Again, be certain to ascertain the risks so that you may determine if the potential rewards justify the investment risk. Do not ever lose sight of this rule.

Basic Strategy

The next decision you must make is whether you are going to manage your own portfolio or hire a manager, even your stockbroker, to do it for you. If you hire a manager, I prefer that you maintain an individual account because it is custom-tailored to your individual needs and objectives.

Let's continue with the notion that you have decided on an individual account. The simplest strategy is to buy and hold to maturity. If implementing this approach, you should match asset maturities to future needs. For most, these needs are long-term. Retirement needs extend well beyond age 65. That is just the beginning of retirement, which hopefully will last 30 or more years.

Even when needs are long-term, short-term trading opportunities could exist. Over an interest rate cycle the possibilities include: (1) invest short-term when interest rates are expected to rise to obtain higher rates later; (2) invest in longer maturities, including longer than needed, to obtain capital appreciation when rates fall and prices increase; and (3) match assets and liabilities when you wish to assure future payments or are unsure of the future direction of rates.

In summary, first match your future assets to your future needs. Then, if you have the stomach for it, trade your positions, shorten and lengthen your maturities, to take advantage of shifts in the yield curve and directions of interest rates.

Infinite variations of these themes exist. Shifting quality and types of investments, including taxable and nontaxable for maximum after-tax rates of return, are examples. Leverage STRIPS on 10% margin and your investment results will be magnified almost nine times on the upside and 11 times on the downside. The difference is the margin interest rate and the length of time held.

You should be willing to own whatever debt instrument you purchase to maturity, if necessary. (An exception would be the trading strategy to purchase longer-term maturities to maximize profit potential when you are certain interest rates are headed lower.) Facetiously, I say my mistakes, if creditworthy, mature at their face value. Except for money market instruments, I don't expect you to hold debt instruments to maturity. Something will change—interest rates themselves, the shape of the yield curve, creditworthiness of the issuer, your investment needs and objectives—to make it prudent to switch instruments prior to maturity.

STRIPS Strategies

Zeros offer additional opportunities and may be used in a wide variety of applications to achieve many investment objectives. While they exist in Treasurys, mortgage-backeds, corporates, and municipals, it is easiest to examine the Treasurys' Separate Trading Registered Interest and Principal of Securities (STRIPS). Remember that STRIPS have the unparalleled creditworthiness of Treasurys. Further, they enjoy the greatest liquidity of all zeros with over $200 billion outstanding. All other zeros have other risks to consider. Municipal and corporate zeros add quality risk and limited liquidity, so they are usually also less suitable in trading strategies.

Zeros can be used in a wide variety of applications to achieve your investment needs and objectives. The discounted prices magnify investment results compared to coupon-paying instruments. Our initial discussion will be about STRIPS, because all other zeros have other risks to consider. Municipal and corporate zeros add quality risk and limited liquidity, so they are usually also less suitable in trading strategies.

Remember, STRIPS are subject to annual assessment of federal income tax, even though there may be no income until as much as 30 years later. Therefore, STRIPS are best suited for tax-deferred and tax-free accounts, but can be used in all types, including taxable.

STRIPS may be used to guarantee the availability of funds needed for a future liability, such as the principal payment of an interest-only balloon mortgage. If they are held to maturity, the investor knows exactly what dollars will be available when, and the precise yield to maturity of the investment, regardless of how interest rates change in the interim. A four-year ladder could assure college tuition and room-and-board payments for a child or grandchild.

STRIPS could also be used in a portfolio with stocks and other bonds to provide a minimum guaranteed return. Investors afraid to purchase common stocks might be comforted by the notion that the STRIPS would assure the return of the original principal at maturity, and the value of the common stocks would be additional.

While investing for retirement, a ladder of STRIPS could be created that would begin to mature at age 65 and continue for as many years as possible. An investor aged 50, for example, could purchase a ladder of STRIPS that would begin to mature 15 years later, when the investor becomes 65, and continue for an additional 15 years until age 80. Future years could be purchased later as they become available.

At current interest rates, 7% yields on long STRIPS, the cost of 15-year STRIPS would be 35.628% or $356.28 per $1,000 principal value; $15,000 face amount would cost $5,344.20. A ladder of STRIPS maturing each year from 15 years through 29 years would cost only $3,449.31 for $1,000 each year, $15,000 in total. That's 64.5% of the cost of the single payment in 15 years.

A lump sum of $250,000 would purchase $701,000 of 15-year STRIPS. The same sum of money could be used to purchase $72,000 of STRIPS each year from 15 through 28 years and the remainder could purchase $84,000 of STRIPS due in 29 years. The total maturity value would be $1,092,000 instead of $701,000, 55.78% more.

Which would turn out better? The answer, of course, depends on where interest rates will be in 15 years. If rates are higher than 7% in 15 years, from one year all the way out to 14 years, then the lump sum reinvested at that time would be best. Since there is no way to predict future interest rates, the ladder of STRIPS, guaranteeing set amounts each year to match retirement needs, might be the better alternative.

This ladder of STRIPS for retirement ought to be considered a benchmark to which you should compare all other investment options in terms of risk and reward. If held to maturity, the investor knows exactly what dollars will be available when, and the exact yield to maturity. In addition, if investment needs or objectives change, the STRIPS may be converted into cash the next business day.

STRIPS are also useful as trading vehicles (equity substitutes), when interest rates are expected to decline. A 25-year STRIPS will appreciate about 35% in one year if interest rates decline 100 basis points (1%). That is much greater than the 12% plus the coupon increase in a 30-year bond. That is the upside potential if rates decline 1%. The downside is that the price will decline about 0.6% in three years if interest rates rise 100 basis points (1%) during that time. Of course, the investor will receive exactly $1,000 for each STRIPS at maturity and exactly the stated yield to maturity. This strategy is best applied by an investor who is willing to hold the STRIPS to maturity, if necessary.

Application of STRIPS is endless, limited only by the investor's imagination.

What's Wrong with Other Ladders?

While I am enamored of ladders of STRIPS, I am opposed to ladders of coupon-paying instruments. The major defect of ladders of coupon-paying instruments is that they lull the investor into a false sense of security, because the principal appears safe. Over time, interest is more important than principal, and that becomes an imponderable.

Municipal Securities Strategy

Finally, the individual investor should consider his or her own investment needs and objectives in using municipals. Liabilities at retirement remain the same: Income at retirement may be reduced and, as a result, alternative investments might be better at that time. That creates challenges. Should you invest in municipals with maturities that match your planned retirement? If you do, you run reinvestment risk at that time, which could be quite costly if interest rates are lower.

Alternately, you could invest longer-term and incur transaction costs switching from one type of debt instrument into another. You also incur the spread risk between municipals and taxables, which could work to your benefit or detriment.

Unfortunately, there is no easy answer to these questions and you must be the judge of what risks you are willing to assume. It is these imponderable external factors that make the assessment of municipals in your portfolio so difficult and imprecise, certainly relative to other debt instruments.

Monthly Distributions

Instruct your broker to send you distributions of dividends and interest monthly. It is easy to set up a plan for monthly distributions from fixed-income securities. Purchase six Treasury, corporate, or municipal securities, or a combination thereof (each of which pays interest semiannually), to enable monthly interest payments. You may stagger maturities if you wish to assume interest-rate reinvestment risk. This is even easier with preferred stocks, as they usually pay quarterly; thus only three issues are necessary to obtain monthly payments. Mortgage-backed securities pay monthly, so you need as little as one to achieve this monthly objective. Be certain to separate interest and principal payments so you don't end up dissipating your principal.

Hedging Techniques

Hedging techniques are used to reduce risk. They are predominantly employed by dealers and institutions, but individuals could use these strategies as well. However, the techniques require some sophistication.

One method would be to employ futures transactions to partially or fully offset long debt positions. Contemplate using hedges for intervals when you expect interest rates to rise. Another solution would be to sell your debt securities and wait for interest rates to climb before repurchasing. Shorting other debt securities is cumbersome. Transaction costs and/or inertia may interfere with the aggressive use of this strategy.

Options, puts, and calls on futures, could also be utilized for hedging. The advantage is that the maximum risk of the option is limited to its cost. However, options are often expensive and a more sophisticated analysis of the time value of options is required to implement this approach.

Transaction Costs

Because almost all debt transactions are done on a principal basis, it is difficult to determine transaction costs, particularly in secondary transactions. (The commission on an agency transaction is separately displayed and readily identified.) The spread is divulged in primary offerings where it is given in the prospectus or offering circular.

Don't be afraid to ask your broker what the commission or markup is on your bond purchase or sale. The response might be illuminating. It may be possible to negotiate the broker's commission as well. You should be willing to pay for advice and service, including the making of secondary markets. As a rule transaction fees are greater, on a per-bond basis, for smaller transactions than for larger transactions.

Conclusion

This chapter is merely an introduction to debt in the U.S. capital markets. I hope I have stimulated your interest in fixed income. Investors should ask:

What are the risks and what are the rewards? Every account should own fixed income. The only question is how much. Let me close by saying: Debt is the answer . . . . Fixed income is the answer![13]

Notes

1. The debt aggregate is the outstanding credit market debt of the domestic nonfinancial sectors—the federal sector (U.S. government, not including government-sponsored enterprises or federally related mortgage pool) and the nonfederal sectors (state and local governments, households, nonprofit organizations, nonfinancial corporate and nonfarm noncorporate businesses and farms). Nonfederal debt consists of mortgages, tax-exempt and corporate bonds, consumer credit, bank loans, commercial paper, and other loans. The data, which are derived from the Federal Reserve Board's flow of funds accounts are breech adjusted (that is, discontinuities in the data have been smoothed into the series) and month-averaged (that is, the data have been derived by averaging adjacent month-ends.)

2. The yield initially is a discount yield, which is converted into a bond equivalent yield (BEY) to enable comparison to semiannual coupon instruments like notes or bonds.

3. See www.publicdebt.ustreas.gov on the Internet for details.

4. The only callable corpus, from the 11³/₄% bond due November 15, 2014, consists of the 10 coupons from May 15, 2010, to November 15, 2014, plus the principal due November 15, 2014. That was the only viable solution because the issue may be called November 15, 2009, or semiannually thereafter. Call seems likely in 2009 unless rates skyrocket from current levels to above 11³/₄% by then, and remain at those lofty levels until 2014.

5. The total of mortgages outstanding, $6 trillion, is greater than the entire outstanding U.S. government debt.

6. FNMA and FHLMC are hybrid entities, quasi-government and quasi-private organizations. Both are partially private investor owned, and their common stocks trade actively on the New York Stock Exchange. All three make profits on their mortgage-backed security programs.

7. Actually, many recent convertible preferred with acronyms like PERCS, DECS, and ELKS have forced conversions into common stock and cap the upside to 50%. These act more like covered call writing on common stock.

8. Dividend divided by common stock price in percent.

9. Actually, Moody's Baa average municipal yield exceeded that of Treasurys twice in 1998, October and December, and three times in 1999, January, September, and November.

10. A subsidiary of Standard & Poors', a division of McGraw-Hill.

11. Also a division of Standard & Poors', a division of McGraw-Hill.

12. *White's Municipal Ratings*, years ago, used this approach. That was back in the days when investors and dealers had to interpolate prices and yields using basis books, tables of prices and yields, because calculators didn't exist, let alone handheld ones. Bonds were rated between 1 and 100, and each point difference in rating equated to a

.05 basis point change. If a bond rated 100 was selling at a 4.00 basis, a bond rated 95 would be expected to yield 4.25 (100 – 95) times .05 or 25 basis points. Perhaps this should be considered the first matrix system. We have certainly progressed a long way even if there is still a great deal of room for improvement.

13. As I wrote this I was reminded of my favorite graffiti in the 86th Street station of the Lexington Avenue subway in New York City many years ago. The New York Bible Society had put up a poster, "God is the Answer." Someone wrote on it, "Would you please repeat the question?"

Real Estate Investment Trusts

Robert Deckey

Why Own Real Estate?

The primary reason to invest in commercial real estate is for diversification. The returns on real estate have relatively low correlation with the returns on other assets. Therefore, putting some share of your portfolio in real estate can reduce the overall risk of your portfolio.

Over the past 25 years, the average returns on real estate have been comparable to those of common stocks. Real estate is also considered to be a better hedge against inflation than are common stocks. During periods of rising interest rates, real estate prices are more likely to hold their value or increase, while common stocks tend to decline in value. For example, during the high-inflation 1970s, real estate returns were considerably higher than those of the broad stock market indexes.

Unfortunately, it is not practical for most individual investors to own commercial property directly. Ownership requires large sums of money and the ability to properly manage the property. Also, private real estate may be more time-consuming to sell, relative to traded shares of stock, while most investors require their investments to be fairly liquid.

What Is a REIT?

Congress created real estate investment trusts in 1960 in order to facilitate public ownership of commercial real estate (Table 20.1). A REIT serves much like a mutual fund for real estate, in that investors obtain the benefit of a diversified portfolio of properties under professional management. Investors can relatively easily purchase and sell shares of the REIT, usually at a stock exchange. Also, very little money is required to participate, since individual shares are fairly inexpensive. Over 90% of current REITs are self-managed. There is not a separate management company whose interests may not coincide with those of the REIT shareholders.

Like a mutual fund, a corporation or trust that qualifies as a REIT typically does not pay federal or state income taxes. According to the law, the trusts are not subject to corporate taxation as long as 95% of their income was passed to the shareholders.

In order for a corporation or trust to qualify as a REIT, it must meet the following requirements:

■ Be a corporation, business trust, or similar association.

■ Be managed by a board of directors or trustees.

■ Have shares that are fully transferable.

TABLE **20.1** Advantages of REITs over Traditional Real Estate Ownership

Liquidity—ability to turn investment into cash readily when necessary

Price established regularly by the marketplace rather than according to appraisals by experts

Low entrance fee and investment size

Regular current income

Professional management

Portfolio diversification, even holding a single REIT

Independent monitoring by a board of directors, independent analysts, outside auditors, and media.

- Have a minimum of 100 shareholders.

- Have not more than 50% of the shares held by five or fewer individuals during the last half of each taxable year.

- Invest at least 75% of the total assets in real estate assets, including mortgages, cash, cash items, and government securities.

- Derive at least 75% of gross income from rents from real property or interest on mortgages on real property.

- Derive no more than 30% of gross income from the sale of real properties held for less than four years, excluding properties acquired through foreclosure, and stock or securities held less than six months.

- Pay dividends of at least 95% of REIT taxable income.

Historically the real estate industry borrowed most of the money needed to purchase properties. It is standard for private companies to obtain loans for 75% of the property value. The owners then focus primarily on capital gains—increases in the value of the property exceeding the cost of the loans. In contrast, REITs are not highly leveraged. Most of the properties are paid for by sales of shares. Instead, they focus on the flow of cash acquired through operation of the real estate properties. With time, the REITs develop track records of relatively predictable income. Shareholders then can be less concerned about the risk of debt, and have a high likelihood of regular distributions of income.

Although it is now 40 years since the law was enacted, REITs are still viewed as being in their infancy. In 1990 there were 56 REITs with a total market capitalization of less than $6 billion. From 1991 to 1997 the number of publicly traded REITs tripled, and the total value of the sector grew twentyfold. In spite of this growth, the total market capitalization of the 200 equity REITs now in existence is less than half that of Microsoft.

It appears that REIT will benefit from increasing interest from institutional investors like pension funds and insurance companies. Regarding REIT, John Neff, the stellar investor who directs the Vanguard Windsor Fund, wrote that he is "banking on exceptional performance when the market shakes off its high-tech stupor."

REIT Structures

UPREIT

An "umbrella partnership REIT" or UPREIT is formed when various existing partnerships, owning multiple properties, come together to form a REIT. The new operating partnership consists of partners from the old existing partnerships and representatives of the newly formed REIT. In exchange for their contributed properties, partners receive portions (units) of the REIT operating partnership. The REIT is typically the general partner and majority owner of the operating partnership units.

The principal owners of the preexisting partnerships can defer the considerable tax liability that would be incurred if the properties were sold to the REIT. After a period of time, often a minimum of one year, the partners can convert all or a portion of their units into cash or shares of the REIT. This enables them to control the timing of their tax liabilities.

A key advantage of the UPREIT structure is that operating partnership units can be used as currency for new acquisitions. Existing UPREITs can absorb additional existing partnerships by issuing additional operating partnership units. The UPREIT benefits by being able to acquire additional assets without having to obtain loans or publicly issue shares, which entails substantial transaction costs.

The principal disadvantage of the UPREIT structure is the potential for conflict of interest. There is a difference between the tax incentives of the original owners, with their relatively low cost basis, and the REIT shareholders, who have considerable higher cost basis. The sale or refinancing of a property could be beneficial to REIT shareholders, but create a substantial tax liability for the original owner, causing him or her to vote against the sale. Therefore, it is critical that decisions regarding property sales by UPREITs be made by the independent members of the board of directors.

DownREIT

A DownREIT is structured much like an UPREIT, but the REIT owns and operates properties other than its interest in a controlled partnership that owns and operates separate properties.

Types of REITs

In addition to structure, REITs can be characterized by the nature of their real estate investments, property type, or geography. REITs may specialize in shopping centers, apartments, warehouses, office buildings, hotels, health-care facilities, or any other type of commercial or residential property. They also can limit their holdings to one region of the country or even a single metropolitan area. Typically, residential and industrial REITs are more conservative than office and retail REITs.

Equity REITs

Equity REITs own income-producing properties. Approximately 87% of the total REIT market capitalization is in equity REITs. A subclassification of REITs is given in Table 20.2.

Mortgage REITs

A mortgage REIT loans money to real estate owners. Its revenue comes principally from interest earned on the mortgage loans. Some mortgage REITs also invest in residuals of mortgage-based securities. Since many mortgage REITs are highly sensitive to changing interest rates, and most use very high leverage, they have been very risky relative to equity REITs.

Hybrid REITs

Hybrid REITs combine the investment strategies of equity REITs and mortgage REITs. Very few hybrid REITs exist.

TABLE 20.2 REIT Sectors

Residential	19.95%	
Apartments		18.25%
Manufactured housing		1.7%
Retail	21.8%	
Community or strip shopping centers		9.7%
Regional malls		9.6%
Freestanding		2.4%
Industrial/office	31.2%	
Office		19.5%
Industrial		6.9%
Mixed		4.8%
Lodging/resorts	5.5%	
Self-storage	3.8%	
Health care	3.8%	
Mortgage	1.6%	
Home financing		.9%
Commercial financing		.7%
Mixed/other	12.4%	

Note: Percentages by market capitalization as of January 31, 2000.
Source: NAREIT.

REITS Are Not Limited Partnerships

Investors frequently confuse REITs and real estate limited partnerships (Table 20.3). Limited partnerships were formed primarily prior to the Tax Reform

TABLE 20.3 REITs versus Limited Partnerships

	REITs	Limited Partnerships
Management	Board of directors elected by shareholders	General partner
Investor control	Yes, but limited in practice	None
Ability to sell your holdings (liquidity)	Yes; most traded on stock exchanges	Usually none
Minimum investment	No minimum	Typically $2,000 to $5,000 (excludes Regulation D private placements)
Investment unit	Shares	Units
Management compensation	Salary, bond, stock options	Variable; may include percentage of capital raised up front, asset management fees, markups when properties are sold to partnership, percentage of distributions
Management/investor conflicts of interest	Possible, but fairly limited outside of the hotel sector	Likely, and frequently considerable
Independent auditing/ tracking	Yes	No
Ability to grow	Can borrow funds or issue stock to acquire new properties	Rarely
IRS classification of income	Portfolio	Passive
Ability to pass tax losses to investors	No	Yes, against passive income

Act of 1986, for their tax benefits. The investment value was relatively low, but the partnerships generated tax losses that saved investors much more in income taxes than they lost on the partnerships. With the loss of these tax incentives, the orientation of limited partnerships has changed, but the demand for them has greatly diminished.

Limited partnerships frequently were highly leveraged, were passively managed, and invested in only one property. Consequently, they performed poorly in the 1980s and as a result, the whole real estate sector acquired a poor reputation. Most REITs tried to address these risk factors with excellent management teams, lower leverage, and large diversified portfolios.

The Industry

Unlike most other investment vehicles, REITs have had a relatively short history. I think that it is worthwhile briefly reviewing this history to understand their current status. Prior to the Tax Reform Act of 1986, seeking a tax shelter was the motivation for many real estate investments. The vast majority of property was owned directly by institutions or by private individuals and real estate companies. After 1986 the tax shelter advantage disappeared, and the industry returned to a more standard business orientation of investment.

In the early 1990s, commercial real estate prices were driven down, largely due to the crisis in the thrift industry. The government-backed Resolution Trust Corporation (RTC) quickly sold off the assets of the failed thrifts, driving prices below half of their replacement costs. Partly for the same reasons, there was also a shortage of lenders for financing these properties. Thus, REITs were formed in order to obtain funds from investors rather than commercial lenders.

Another reason for the establishment of REITs by the major commercial real estate companies was the tax consequences for the owners. The owners of the properties could contribute the properties to a partnership that shared ownership with the public. In this way the owners did not have to realize their capital gains on the properties, and were able to defer payment of taxes. The advantage to current shareholders is that the major real estate companies have large ownership stakes and therefore a vested interest in the performance of the REITs.

Over the past seven years, the RTC liquidation of properties ceased, property prices stabilized, new supply slowed, and a dramatic recovery in property values occurred. This recovery generated artificially high returns for both REIT and private real estate investors. Contributing to this was a tremendous inflow of money into REIT mutual funds. This reached a maximum in January of 1997, and then declined throughout that year. By the end of 1997 property values were back at or near replacement cost. Expected returns on commercial properties were commensurate with historic levels.

However, this was not sufficient to maintain the exceptionally high valuations of REIT stocks. In addition, the flow of new capital slowed. As a result 1998 and 1999 were not good years for REIT stocks, with total returns of negative 17.5% and negative 4.62% respectively. Since January 1998 there have been steady net outflows from REIT mutual funds.

Adjusted for risk, U.S. REITs are currently relatively cheap. There is a high percentage of stable rental income and a high dividend yield on REIT stocks. However, part of the reason for this is that the REIT market is relatively oversaturated. More than half of the current 200 REITs are in low demand. Too many companies came public very quickly, some of the companies have weak management, and the demand for REIT stocks is relatively low.

Investment Characteristics of REITs

Real estate investment trusts (REITs) behave differently from traditional real estate investments. Their investment behavior is similar to stocks and bonds in some aspects, and similar to traditional real estate holdings in others. As with any negotiable asset, their value is established by investors in the marketplace. The long-term performance of an individual REIT is determined primarily by the value of its real estate assets. What investors are willing to pay depends not only on the value of the underlying real estate properties, but also on their anticipated total return over time. Stock price performance reflects the anticipated total return from the stock (including current dividends) and anticipated changes in stock price and dividend yield.

Growth in the value of a REIT can far exceed the increase in rents and the rate of growth in the value of the current properties. This is because REITs are operating companies that can grow through acquisition and development of new properties.

Through strategic planning a REIT is capable of generating value in excess of the value of its assets, and therefore can earn a marketplace valuation in excess of the net asset value of the property portfolio. This premium must be earned through demonstrated earnings growth and a well-conceived strategic plan.[1]

In addition, REITs must compete with other financial assets for investors' dollars. The attractiveness of a REIT is affected by the relationship between the REIT's current dividend yield and the yield of other income-oriented investments such as bonds and utility stocks. Demand for shares and therefore share prices are also affected by the risk, volatility, and liquidity of the REIT shares, how these compare with those of other investment options, general market factors such as interest rates, and investment trends.

In general, since the dividend component of a REIT's total return is so high and certain, overall risk is reduced. This is an advantage over many C corporations with similar growth prospects that do not have any dividends. Therefore it is not necessary to rely on growth to generate the entire return.

The REIT industry has grown to the point that there is a very active analytical community following the companies. The analysts track the companies and markets and provide investors and industry participants with extensive data. The data in Table 20.4 was obtained from the National Association of Real Estate Investment Trusts (NAREIT).

Returns of REITs consist of dividends and share price appreciation. According to NAREIT, the average annual dividend yield between 1988 and 1999

TABLE 20.4 Record of REIT Returns

	Equity REITS				Mortgage REITS			
	Return			Dividend	Return			Dividend
Year	Total	Price	Income	Yield	Total	Price	Income	Yield
1988	13.49	4.77	8.72	8.57	7.30	−5.12	12.42	13.19
1989	8.84	0.58	8.26	8.42	−15.90	−26.19	10.28	13.56
1990	−15.35	−26.45	11.10	10.15	−18.37	−29.18	10.81	13.48
1991	35.70	25.47	10.22	7.85	31.83	13.93	17.91	13.49
1992	14.59	6.40	8.19	7.10	1.92	−10.80	12.72	11.21
1993	19.65	12.95	6.70	6.81	14.55	−0.40	14.95	10.89
1994	3.17	−3.52	6.69	7.67	−24.30	−33.83	9.53	13.52
1995	15.27	6.56	8.71	7.37	63.42	46.80	16.62	9.02
1996	35.27	26.35	8.92	6.05	50.86	37.21	13.65	8.50
1997	20.26	13.33	6.93	5.48	3.82	−3.57	7.40	9.41
1998	−17.50	−22.33	4.83	7.47	−29.22	−34.29	5.07	10.49
1999	−4.62	−12.21	7.59	8.70	−33.22	−40.12	6.90	13.53

Source: NAREIT.

was 7.64%. The average annual price change was +2.66%, and the average total return was 10.73%.

Since 1978, the average excess returns on REITs (the return in excess of the one-month Treasury bill) have been greater than those of long-term government, long-term corporate, and high-yield corporate bonds. However, the standard deviation of returns has been higher as well, but still significantly less than those of large-cap or small-cap stocks. The beta of REITs has been approximately 0.57.

Some financial analysts have recommended REITs as a hedge against inflation. REIT returns are correlated with bond returns and interest rates. However, the correlation between REITs and interest rates is similar to the correlation between the S&P 500 index and interest rates.[2]

According to modern portfolio theory, the main value of REITs to investors lies in how their addition to a mix of assets improves the total risk/reward characteristics.[3] The lower the correlation between REIT returns and those of other portfolio components, the greater the benefit to the portfolio. In recent years the correlation between REIT returns and returns on the S&P 500 has declined from 0.67 (1988–1991) to only 0.35 (1992–1999).

Over their entire history, REIT returns have correlated most with the Wilshire Small Value Index and high-yield corporate bond indexes.[4] In recent years, the relationship has become more complex, with a portion of REIT performance now being explained by the long-term corporate bond index. Using mixtures of these other indexes, it is possible to explain 70% of the variation in REIT returns. Therefore, approximately 30% of the variation in REIT returns is still unexplained by any combination of other assets. This uniqueness contributes to their investment value.

One interesting finding is that historically there has been a significant increase in REIT returns in the month of January. The average REIT trades approximately $2.8 million in stock each day, about 0.3% of its total equity value. By comparison, the average Russell 2000 company has the same market capitalization, but trades $6 million in stock each day, more than twice as much as the REIT.

REIT Valuation

REITs should be easier to evaluate than most other companies due to the relatively simple nature of their business. They own and manage real estate that generates a somewhat stable return.

There are two common approaches to valuing a REIT: *net asset value* and *comparable multiple valuation*. Net asset value attempts to value the underlying real estate the REIT owns. Most research analysts determine net asset value by multiplying the recurring cash flow stream from the assets by a factor called the capitalization rate. Capitalization rates are generally in the 9%–11% range, but vary based on the quality of the assets and their growth characteristics. Therefore, the value of the property is 9 to 11 times the average annual cash flow.

The comparable multiple valuation approach is like comparing price-earnings ratios for corporations. However, unlike most stocks, where earnings are the standard measure of performance, funds from operations (FFO) is the standard measure of REIT performance. With normal accounting techniques the value of properties diminishes with time. This is known as depreciation. However, commercial real estate maintains value to a much greater extent than machinery, computers, or most other property. Also, real estate values may rise or fall, depending on market conditions. For these reasons the REIT industry adopted FFO, which excludes historical depreciation costs from the net income figure. NAREIT defines FFO as net income excluding gains or losses from sales of property or debt restructuring, and adding back depreciation of real estate.[5]

Comparable multiple valuation for REITs, therefore, simply compares the ratio of price to FFO to those of similar REITs. The FFO multiple that a REIT trades at is based on the market's evaluation of the quality of the management team, the quality of the properties, and FFO growth prospects, among other factors. The corporate bond credit ratings provide a helpful benchmark of a REIT's quality.

Considerations When Acquiring Individual REITs

There are several criteria to consider in acquiring individual REITs:

- Management
- Dividend payout ratio
- Size
- Credit rating
- Funds from operations (FFO) multiple and growth rate
- Geographical diversification
- Property type

Management

Most REITs today are internally advised and managed, which best aligns the interests of shareholders and management. In fact, many management teams are large shareholders themselves.

As with any business, the expertise of management is key to a REIT's success. This is difficult for an individual investor to assess, but a couple of indicators may be helpful. The management's total amount of experience and the length of time the management team has worked together are useful signs. The confidence of lenders and other investors are also useful indicators.

In nearly all cases it is better if the REIT performs its own management and administrative functions, rather than contracting them out to a separate adviser. The few REITs that are externally advised or managed are generally not highly regarded. However, if you are considering a REIT that uses a separate adviser, ensure that the advisory relationship is conflict-free, that the fees are reasonable, and that the shareholders benefit from the relationship.

Dividend Payout Ratio

Since most of an investor's total return comes from the dividend a REIT pays, the payout ratio is important to make certain a REIT can continue to make its dividend payments. Lower payout ratios provide a cushion for the REIT, increasing the likelihood that the current level of dividend payments will continue despite market changes.

Therefore, better-quality REITs have lower dividend yields. Generally, a REIT with a dividend yield in excess of 10% is a company with failed operations and perceived by the market as being extremely risky. Therefore, an investor should take caution.

Analysts look at the ratio of dividends to adjusted FFO. Adjusted FFO is FFO reduced by nonrevenue-producing capital expenditures, such as tenant allowances, leasing commissions, and other nonrevenue-producing capital improvements. This ratio is typically lower than the ratio of dividends to net taxable income (which must exceed 95% and can exceed 100%).

Also, some REITs retain a portion of their FFO to invest in their businesses, rather than distribute it as dividends. These retained earnings are a company's cheapest source of capital. For these two reasons, Salomon Smith Barney analysts prefer that REITs pay dividends that are no higher than 85% to 90% of adjusted FFO.

Size

Size has some benefits to an investor. First, larger REITs have better liquidity, higher daily trading averages, better access to capital for growth, and more equity research analysts to provide coverage. Operationally, larger REITs can buy insurance at cheaper rates, hire better people, have greater leverage with tenants, and hopefully generate more revenue and income than an individual property owner. Size can also have some disadvantages. For example, it is more difficult for a large REIT to maintain a high growth rate. However, in general, bigger is better for the REIT investor.

Credit Rating

The rating agencies of S&P, Moody's, and Fitch do a thorough job in reviewing companies' assets and evaluating management teams to determine their corporate credit ratings. Therefore, their ratings provide a good benchmark on the quality of a company. Very few REITs have ratings of A or higher. In general, ratings of BBB– to BBB+ are strong. The ratings also give a REIT better access to capital, which helps it grow without issuing new shares.

FFO Multiple and Growth Rate

In general, you should acquire REITs that have demonstrated a long history of sustained FFO growth. Assuming that the ratio of price to FFO stays fairly constant, a REIT's total return over time will be the sum of its dividend yield and the rate of growth of FFO. Based on this approach, a REIT that has a dividend yield of 7% and has a FFO growth rate of 8% would return to an investor 15%, assuming a constant multiple.

Consequently, many REITs with high growth rates also have high ratios of price to FFO (as rapidly growing companies have high P/E ratios). An investor should be cautious about buying a REIT stock whose multiple is high relative to its historic FFO growth rate. Also, as we all know, multiples change with the overall market and we should try to purchase REITs when the price/FFO multiple is reasonable.

Geographic Diversification

Diversification helps insulate REITs from local economic and real estate market cycles. Real estate values are affected by local business and individual demands for rental space and the available supply. Due to the recovery of the economy in the 1990s and due to the lack of new construction, most regions of the country have enjoyed strong rental rate growth.

Some REITs stay highly focused in specific markets, which allows them to be local sharpshooters and successfully take advantage of the inefficient local real estate market. This strategy can be successful, but it also exposes the REIT to higher risk long-term, since any market can experience unpredicted downturns.

Investors should look for achieving diversification in their portfolio by acquiring either shares of highly diversfied REITs or shares in many market-specific REITs.

Property Type

Most REITs invest in one property type such as apartments, office buildings, industrial space, or shopping centers. Apartments and industrial properties tend to be less cyclical due to their shorter construction time and their lower capital expenditures. Shopping centers, such as those that are grocery-store anchored, are stable because they sell necessity goods. Malls are more risky due to the high capital expenditures required for the common areas and tenant replacement cost with changing fashion. Office buildings are most costly to maintain and construct. Large, well-managed REITs of most property types will generally do well through market cycles.

Other Factors

Other factors to consider are the age of the properties held, since older properties require more capital expenditures to maintain them. Many professional REIT investors calculate cash flow after capital items (cash available for distribution, or CAD) as another measure of a REIT's performance.

One gauge of a REIT's financial flexibility is its ratio of debt to total market capitalization. More precise means of assessing financial flexibility require more complicated analysis, and usually the knowledge and experience of a REIT specialist.

Purchasing Individual REITs versus a REIT Mutual Fund

If you are not willing to spend the time and acquire the knowledge to be able to evaluate REITs yourself, you must rely on expert advice. This can be obtained either through a financial adviser who specializes in REITs or through a REIT mutual fund. There also are REIT index funds, which are unmanaged in that they try to mimic the performance of a REIT index like the NAREIT index, rather than selecting individual REITs that they predict will outperform the average.

The other reason for utilizing a REIT mutual fund is that you gain some diversification within the industry. Individual REITs usually specialize in a specific type of commercial real estate (e.g., shopping centers), or a geographic region. Mutual funds own a variety of REIT types, and the adviser is able to select those that he or she predicts will perform best.

Summary

The real estate market and the REIT sector has now been transformed into what should be a more stable investment class. REITs give the individual investor the opportunity to buy stocks in professionally managed companies. The REIT sector has research analysts, corporate bonds, and competition. The greatest problem facing the sector is liquidity. With low average daily trading volumes, the sector is greatly impacted by the flows of capital in and out of the sector. Let me close by saying: Debt is the answer. . . . Fixed income is the answer![13]

Notes

1. In *Real Estate Investment Trusts: Structure, Analysis and Strategy*, R.T. Garrigan, J. F. C. Parsons, Editors., McGraw-Hill, New York: 1998, p. 161.
2. E. Hemel, S. Sakwa, and R. Bhattacharjee, 1995; "Interest Rates Sensitivity of REITs: Myth and Reality," Morgan Stanley: U.S. Investment Research Paper, "The Historical Behavior of REIT Returns: A Capital Markets Perspective," in Garrigan.
3. T. Cater and K. Pauley, "Opposites Attract: The Diversification Benefits of REITs," *Institutional Real Estate Securities*, 4(5):16–17, 1999.
4. A. B. Sanders, "The Historical Behavior of REIT Returns: A Capital Markets Perspective," in Garrigan.
5. In March 1995 NAREIT approved a "White Paper" on FFO that gives detailed recommendations for accounting and reporting practices.

Venture Capital

David Hillman

What Is Venture Capital?

When most people think of venture capital, the image of a high-technology start-up company in Silicon Valley probably comes to mind. Investments in such companies are certainly part of the asset category known as venture capital, but are only a subset of the total range of activity. Venture capital today encompasses investments in a broad range of businesses, from start-ups to mature companies going through a change of ownership. The broader asset category is often referred to as "private equity," which includes leveraged buyouts as well as venture capital and other illiquid, private investments. For purposes of this chapter, the term "venture capital" will be used to refer to the segment of the private equity asset category that primarily involves investments in relatively young, high-potential companies that need risk capital to finance very rapid expected growth. The other defining characteristic of venture capital is the hands-on, value-added involvement of professionals in this field in their portfolio companies.

Venture capital investing has been around for a long time. The financing of Christopher Columbus's trip to the New World was a venture capital investment with many of the usual characteristics: high risk, long time horizon, the need for more capital than expected, and an outcome much different than what was envisioned in the original plan. For most of the history of the capital markets, investments in new and risky enterprises have been financed by wealthy families with the capacity to absorb significant losses in the hopes of a big payoff. In the second half of the twentieth century, however, a more formal venture capital industry emerged, with full-time professionals organizing pools of capital from a variety of sources. The major expansion of the business began in the early 1980s, with impetus provided by the lowering of capital gains tax rates in 1978, and the revision of pension plan regulations shortly thereafter that permitted a portion of plan assets to be invested in venture capital pools or funds. With the exception of a lull in the late 1980s and early 1990s, the growth of the venture capital industry in the past two decades has been phenomenal, from less than $200 million raised by professional venture capital firms in 1979 to more than $40 billion raised in 1999.

How Venture Capital Is Organized

The venture capital market today is very large and diverse and has four primary groups of participants: "angel" investors, corporate venturing arms, institutional investors, and independent private firms.

Angel Investors

The size of the "angel" market is hard to measure since data is not comprehensively reported, but many observers feel that it is at least as large as the formal, professional venture capital market. Angel investors are individuals who directly fund venture investment opportunities, often at the very earliest stages of a company's development. Angel investors are frequently successful entrepreneurs or businesspeople in the later stages of their careers who enjoy the experience of nurturing or just being associated with younger entrepreneurs. With the number of successful entrepreneurs having multiplied rapidly in the past two decades, angel investors have become a significant force in the venture capital market. However, this type of direct investing is not appropriate for most investors, as it involves significant risk without diversification, and it is difficult to properly assess investment opportunities without specific industry knowledge.

Corporate Venturing Arms

A number of established companies have set up their own in-house venture investing subsidiaries, the purpose of which is often to identify promising young companies that could become future acquisition candidates. Most of participants in this arena are technology companies such as Microsoft, Intel, or Cisco, or major users of new technology in industries such as telecommunications, health care, or finance. For some of these companies, the venture portfolios have become major profit centers and may represent hidden asset value. Corporate venture activity has definitely been on the rise in recent years, as companies scramble to keep up with all the technology being developed by new companies that may represent a competitive threat in the future.

Institutional Investors

Institutional investors such as pension funds, investment management companies, banks, insurance companies, endowment funds, and foundations are the primary suppliers of capital to the venture industry, but most institutions do not invest directly into operating businesses. Instead, most of their investments are channeled through funds managed by professional venture capital firms that specialize in such investments. Some banks, insurance companies, and securities firms do have significant direct investment activities, though, and some have raised outside capital to supplement their own commitments.

Independent Private Firms

Independent private investment firms that raise capital from groups of institutional investors manage the majority of the venture capital being directly invested today. The vehicle of choice for structuring these funds is a limited partnership where the investors are limited partners and the professional managers are general partners. These partnerships generally have a 10-year life, where a series of investments are made in the first three to five years, creating a portfolio of companies to diversify risk. This portfolio is generally liquidated in years four through 10, and the partnership terminates when the last investment has been sold. The general partner has sole discretion with respect to investment selection and disposition, and there are usually significant restrictions on the sale of any limited partnership interests. Also, there are severe penalties for not meeting periodic capital calls. The general partner charges an annual fee on committed capital and usually receives a 20% share of realized profits.

How Have Venture Capital Investments Performed?

The performance of venture capital investments is difficult to gauge with precision, as venture capital funds are not usually publicly traded, and only disclose their results privately to their limited partners. Several publishing firms, investment banks, and consultants that follow the industry do report results on a regular basis, but the universe of managers that each source tracks may vary, and there is no true index of overall industry performance.

The most comprehensive studies of performance that are publicly available are those published by Venture Economics, a subsidiary of Securities Data Publishing. These studies track performance of a large universe of funds over many different time periods and segregate returns by quartiles. Venture Economics reports that for the periods ended September 30, 1999 the average annual returns for venture funds were as follows: 1-year—+62.5%; 3-year—+33.7%; 10-year—+20.8%. For the 10-year period ending December 31, 1998 Venture Economics reported average annual returns of 17.6%. There is significant volatility of returns in venture capital when examined on a quarterly or even annual basis, and there is also a wide variance between top and bottom quartile performance. Returns in the last one- and three-year periods have obviously been much higher than longer-term averages, driven largely by the stock market performance of venture-backed technology and particularly Internet-related companies. It is unlikely that recent outstanding performance can be sustained, however, and annual returns in the high teens are a more reasonable expectation over time.

Who Should Invest in Venture Capital?

Traditionally, venture capital investing has been restricted to very wealthy families and large institutions such as pension funds, banks, insurance companies, endowments, and foundations. This is largely because venture capital funds typically have high minimum investment thresholds (e.g., $5 million or more). In addition, an investment in a single venture capital fund would often not provide the degree of diversification within the category that many investors deem prudent. However, more recently a number of institutions have begun offering a fund-of-funds product to their higher-net-worth client base. A typical fund of funds would invest in a number of different venture funds and pool these funds together in a diversified vehicle that would be sold in smaller increments (e.g., $500,000) to individual investors. Fund-of-funds products have been marketed by a number of larger banks and securities firms, as well as certain fund managers.

Investors considering commitments to venture capital should be aware of the risks and restrictions involved. The biggest hurdle for most investors is the lack of liquidity. Since venture capital funds are invested in a portfolio of private companies that often take many years to mature, returns are achieved gradually over a period of time as each investment is harvested. The full cycle of a venture capital fund may take 10 years or more to complete. The fund in total will be valued by the managers on a quarterly basis, but there is no public market for these funds and no redemption option provided by the managers. In addition to the lack of liquidity, investors should be prepared to see considerable fluctuation in the value of venture funds on a short-term basis.

How Do You Invest in Venture Capital?

As previously mentioned, the venture capital industry has typically not raised capital through publicly traded entities, but rather through private limited partnerships with large minimum investment requirements. The primary exception to this has been the creation of retail-oriented fund-of-funds products by certain large institutions. However, the explosion of investment interest in the Internet has spawned several publicly traded companies that specialize in starting up Internet ventures and trying to guide them toward a public offering as they mature. The most notable among these "Internet incubators" are CMGI, Inc. and Internet Capital Group, although there will undoubtedly be more to follow. Furthermore, the Internet has created a mechanism for many young companies to access potential individual investors far more efficiently than in the past, and a number of Internet-based investment banks such as OffRoad Capital have begun to cater to individual investor interest in direct venture capital investments. In addition, there is at least one well-known venture firm that is preparing to tap the individual investor market with a public closed-end fund, and others are likely to follow. Given these recent trends, it is likely that there will be more opportunities for individuals to participate in venture capital investments than there have been in the past.

Finding and Evaluating Venture Capital Firms

For most investors, finding and evaluating venture capital firms is a challenging task. For institutional investors, this challenge is frequently met by hiring investment consultants who specialize in the evaluation of venture capital and other private equity firms. Such consultants, often referred to as "gatekeepers," subject venture firms to a rigorous analytical and due diligence process, and make recommendations to their clients based on the results of this process. Some institutional investors have the capability to do this sort of screening in-house, and do not use outside consultants. However, for the average individual investor contemplating an investment in venture capital, sorting through the qualifications of the many venture firms seeking capital at any given time is difficult. Most people rely on a trusted intermediary such as a bank or securities firm to do the screening for them, and will select managers based on their style. On occasion, an individual may have personal knowledge about the capabilities of the people managing a venture firm. More frequently, a firm will be known by its reputation in the business community, and some have been able to establish a brand name such as Kleiner, Perkins, Caufield & Byers in venture capital or Kohlberg, Kravis & Robrts (KKR) in the buyout arena.

Portfolio Allocation

The percentage of an investor's portfolio that should be allocated to venture capital depends a great deal on the size of the portfolio and the individual investor's time horizon. Because of the minimum size requirements of most venture capital investment vehicles, it is difficult to commit less than $250,000 to the asset class. If one wished to limit one's venture allocation to 5%, then that would dictate a total portfolio of $5 million. Historically, most investors who participate in venture capital start with an allocation of less than 5% and may gradually move higher as they get comfortable with the asset class. Some institutions with a very long time horizon and a high risk tolerance have gone as high as 40% in private equity, although that is unusual. For most individuals as well as institutional investors, a commitment of 5% to 10% over time would be a more comfortable range. To avoid the risk of being caught in an adverse market cycle, it also makes sense to phase in commitments over a period of time and to stick with a strategy that can be sustained for the long term.

Asset Allocation

Gregory D. Curtis

Asset Allocation in Theory

As with so much in the investment world, there is a huge gulf between the (generally sound) theoretical underpinnings of asset allocation and the (generally problematic) practical application of those theories. Let's first take a look at the theoretical work underlying modern asset allocation strategies. Then we can examine some of the practical difficulties of implementing a sound asset allocation program.

Toward a Modern Understanding of Risk

Before the early 1970s, asset allocation as it is now understood was virtually unknown among individual and institutional investors. Certainly, investors understood the importance of diversifying their holdings among several different securities, as well as between stocks and bonds. But the specific modern understanding of asset allocation—that allocating assets properly among asset classes can actually improve investment returns while reducing investment risks—remained locked within the walls of academe.

Investors have been buying and selling investment assets for thousands of years, of course, but it wasn't until the outcome of choices was understood to be governed by laws of probabilities—as opposed, let's say, to the whim of the gods—that a modern understanding of asset allocation principles could arise. Crucial advances in understanding the nature of risk were made by Pascal and Fermat (in the 1650s), Bernoulli (1730s), and Galton and Poincaré (late nineteenth century).

But the roots of modern asset allocation theory go back no further than the late 1930s, when the American physicist John Von Neumann[1] and his colleague, economist Oskar Morgenstern, developed "game theory." Game theory concerns the rules that govern multiparty interactions, where the behavior of each party is influenced not only by what the other parties do, but by what each party *anticipates* the other party might do.

Game theory was tailor-made for analyzing the investment world. Investors must not only analyze the investment quality of securities objectively, they must also anticipate how other investors are likely to feel about those securities, since it is the actions of those other investors that will ultimately determine pricing. But it was not until after World War II that Harry Markowitz, then at the University of Chicago, began to apply game theory principles to the investment world.

Markowitz's findings[2] were astounding, and they revolutionized the way investment portfolios would be managed—though not, as we have seen, for several more decades.[3] Markowitz discovered that different "asset classes"—groups of securities that tend to act in tandem—performed quite differently from each other, and that by spreading investments appropriately across these asset classes an investor could reduce risk without reducing return (or, put the other way, increase return without increasing risk). These findings represented the beginning of modern portfolio theory, an approach to the management of investment portfolios that now dominates the world of financial management. In 1990, the Nobel Prize in Economic Science was awarded to Markowitz (along with his colleagues Merton Miller and William Sharpe) for his contributions to the development of modern portfolio theory.

Risk as Uncertainty

Central to Markowitz's work was his concept that investment risk is associated with uncertainty, specifically by the variance in returns around an asset's expected return. Imagine an asset (Asset A) that has an expected return of 10%, but for which, two-thirds of the time, the actual range of returns will be −10% to +30%. Its range of expected returns is graphed in Figure 22.1. Compare this asset to one (Asset B) with an expected return of 7% but a range of returns from +1% to +13%, charted in Figure 22.2. According to Markowitz,

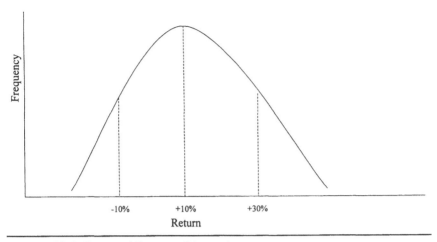

FIGURE 22.1 Expected Return of Asset A

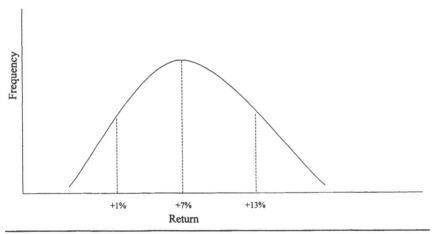

FIGURE 22.2 Expected return of Asset B

the first asset is far riskier than the second, since the variability of its returns is much greater.[4] By superimposing the graphs in Figure 22.1 and Figure 22.2 onto the same scale, as in Figure 22.3, this point is made more graphically.

Although revolutionary at the time, defining risk as the variability in returns makes intuitive sense. Since no one can predict, over the short term, whether the return on Asset A will be –10% or +30%—or somewhere in between—a rational, short-term, risk-averse investor will opt for Asset B. Two-thirds of

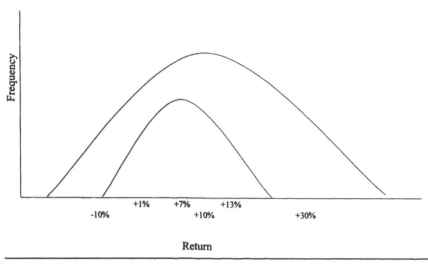

FIGURE 22.3 Expected Returns of Asset A and Asset B

the time, the risk-averse investor will either break even or earn a return between 1% and 13%. On the other hand, a rational long-term investor, who will
not need his or her money for many years, would opt for Asset A, since over
the long term it will generate much higher returns. Along the way, of course,
there will be many peaks and valleys, as implied by the greater short-term
volatility of Asset A.

There is an "iron law" of investment returns that states that, over very long
periods of time, assets that are riskier will also generate higher returns. This
law holds only for broad asset classes. Among individual securities, there will
be crucial exceptions: individual companies can provide stellar returns (GE)
or go bankrupt (Pan Am). Since most investors are risk-averse—we will need
our money sooner rather than later—investors can be tempted to buy riskier
assets only if they are paid to do so: paid in terms of higher returns over the
long run. Hence, longer-term investors will tend to concentrate their portfolios
among riskier assets (stocks), while shorter-term investors will focus on bonds
and cash.

Covariance

If risk is represented by uncertainty—by the wide or narrow variability of investment returns—then reducing risk involves narrowing the area of uncertainty—that is, reducing the variability of returns. But how can this be done?

By definition, asset classes have defined expected returns and defined variabilities around those returns.

Markowitz discovered that asset classes have another crucial characteristic, namely, *covariance*. That is, Asset Class X may rise and fall in value at roughly the same time and at roughly the same rate as Asset Class Y. These two assets classes are, in Markowitz's terms, positively correlated.[5] But Asset Class X may rise when Asset Class Y is falling, and vice versa—these asset classes are negatively correlated. It is covariance that allows investors to create portfolios that maximize return per unit of risk, or minimize risk per unit of return.

Portfolio Optimization

Markowitz discovered that by combining asset classes in various ways, investors could actually control the risk-return profile of their portfolios. To take an extreme hypothetical example, imagine two asset classes—Asset Class X and Asset Class Y—each of which has an expected return of 10%, and an SD of 20, but which have a correlation with each other of −1.0. In such a case, when Asset Class X declines by 5%, Asset Class Y will rise by 5%, and when Asset Class X rises by 12%, Asset Class Y will decline by 12%. As shown in Figure 22.4, an investor whose portfolio consisted of 50% Asset Class X and

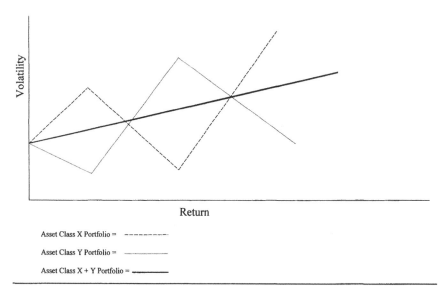

Asset Class X Portfolio =   ─ ─ ─ ─ ─ ─ ─ ─ ·

Asset Class Y Portfolio =   ─────────────

Asset Class X + Y Portfolio = ▬▬▬▬▬

FIGURE 22.4   Expected Returns of Asset Class X, Asset Class Y, and X and Y Combined

50% Asset Class Y would generate an expected return of 10% with no variance in return at all—a high-returning, zero-risk portfolio!

In the real world, alas, perfect negative correlations don't exist. Asset classes tend to be positively correlated, but not perfectly positively correlated. As a result, investors who allocate their assets carefully can maximize returns while minimizing risk. This process is called portfolio optimization, and the calculations required to determine appropriate asset allocation strategies are known as mean variance optimization (MVO) algorithms. The ideal portfolios that result from MVO calculations are known as "efficient" portfolios.

In order to design an efficient portfolio, an investor must determine the expected risks (or volatilities, measured in standard deviation) and returns for each of the many asset classes, as well as the correlations among them. Once these values are known, special software runs through a series of algorithms designed to produce a curve (the "efficient frontier") along which all efficient portfolios fall. In Figure 22.5, for example, cautious investors will select portfolios that fall along the left side of the efficient frontier curve, while more aggressive investors will select portfolios that fall along the right side of the curve.[6]

According to Markowitz, investors who select portfolios—whether cautious or aggressive—that fall below the efficient frontier are behaving irrationally. Portfolios lying below[7] the curve are either generating additional risk without producing additional return or are generating lower returns without

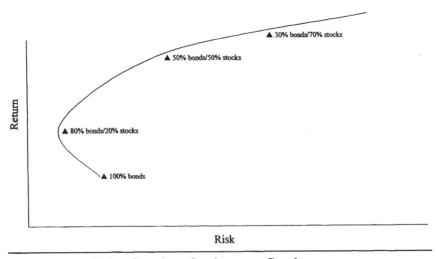

FIGURE 22.5 Efficient Frontier—Stocks versus Bonds

producing lower risk. An investor holding Portfolio B on Figure 22.6, for example, could increase the return without increasing risk by moving the portfolio north to the efficient frontier line, or could achieve the same return at much lower risk by moving the portfolio west to the line.

The more asset classes an investor uses to create a portfolio, the more efficient the portfolio will be. Line A in Figure 22.7 is an efficient portfolio line

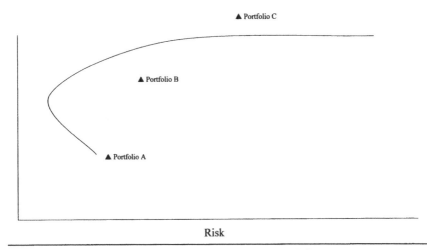

FIGURE 22.6 Efficient Frontier—Portfolios A, B, and C

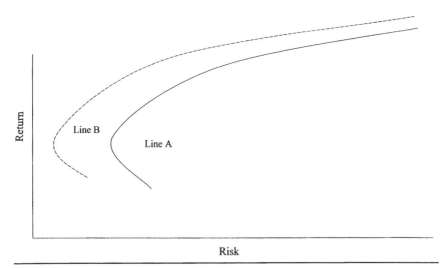

FIGURE 22.7 Efficient Portfolio Lines for a Simple, Two-Asset-Class Portfolio (Line A) and for a Multi-Asset-Class Portfolio (Line B)

for a simple, two-asset-class portfolio (U.S. large-company stocks and U.S. Treasury bonds). Line B is an efficient portfolio line for a multi-asset-class portfolio (U.S. large-company stocks, U.S. small-company stocks, international developed country stocks, emerging markets stocks, U.S. Treasury bonds, U.S. Treasury notes, and cash). Notice that Line B is located to the northwest of Line A—multi-asset-class portfolios tend to be lower in risk than similarly returning simple portfolios and higher in return than similarly risky simple portfolios.

Asset Allocation in Practice

From a theoretical perspective, Markowitz's work represented a revolutionary advance in the management of investment portfolios. Indeed, subsequent investigators determined that investors' asset allocation decisions tended to overwhelm all other decisions they might make—including security selection and manager selection.[8]

But in the real world, the problems involved in establishing and maintaining sensible asset allocation strategies can be overwhelming. In the following paragraphs we will examine some of these challenges.

Rational Theories in an Irrational World

A fundamental problem with efficient portfolio theory is Markowitz's assumption that all investors behave rationally at all times. Like the famous "utility maximizers" so prevalent in economic theory, the assumption of rational investors is a simplification required for theoretical work. But we all know that investors, like individuals in an economy, rarely behave rationally. In the real world investor behavior is much messier than it is in Markowitz's world, and this calls into serious question the relevance of mean variance optimization for real-world investment portfolios. In fact, the pervasive existence of irrational behavior among investors has led to the creation of an entirely new discipline, behavioral finance, which examines in a scientific way how people *actually* behave. This field was launched by Daniel Kahneman and Amos Tversky in the 1970s and 1980s.

Guessing at Inputs

As noted earlier, MVO calculations require an investor to know the expected risks, returns, and covariances of the various asset classes to be used in constructing a portfolio. But where are these values to come from?

We can certainly look backward and calculate *historical* risks, returns, and covariances, but our portfolios will be invested in the future, not the past.

What we need are not historic values for risk, return, and covariance, but *expected* risks, returns, and covariances. Unfortunately, this involves a large element of fortune-telling. Most professionals who use MVO start with the historic numbers, then tweak the results based on their assessments of what the future seems likely to hold. For example, some firms eliminate everything prior to 1970 on the grounds that data prior to that date are irrelevant to the modern investment experience. This seems highly questionable, however. For example, eliminating the stock market crash of 1929 from the historic numbers ensured that MVO calculations based on more recent data could not anticipate the market crash of October 1987.

Other firms use numbers from 1925 but adjust them in various ways. For example, correlations between international developed country equities and U.S. equities seem to have increased in recent years, perhaps due to the globalization of the economy. Some firms therefore adjust for closer correlations between these sectors, dramatically reducing the value of international diversification. Other firms believe that international correlations tend to be cyclical, and that these correlations are likely to decrease in future years.

We know from long experience that investment professionals are far better at identifying sound individual securities than they are at deciding when to get into or out of broad markets.[9] Similarly, economists can rarely agree on the direction of interest rates or the timing of economic boom-and-bust cycles. By analogy, we can expect investment professionals to be fairly lousy at projecting future risks, returns, and covariances.

What's an Asset Class?

If the asset allocation process is to have any meaning, the concept of the asset class must itself be intelligible. In fact, the question whether a particular category of investments amounts to an asset class or is simply subsumed into another asset class can be the subject of debate. The critical determinants of an asset class are (or should be) (1) whether the individual investments in the class behave significantly differently from the investments in other asset classes, and (2) whether the available investments in the class are sufficiently numerous and differentiated to permit diversification of investments within the class. Table 22.1 contains a list of common asset classes and subclasses.

U.S. small-company stocks meet this definition—they are riskier and, over the long term, compound more rapidly, than U.S. large-company stocks, and there are many, many small companies to choose among. Similarly, international stocks are numerous and, as a group, have a different risk-reward profile than U.S. stocks.

From a theoretical perspective, an investor could avoid all nonmarket risk[10]

TABLE 22.1 Asset Classes and Subclasses

Stocks
  Categorized by country
    Domestic
    International
      Developed countries
      Emerging markets
  Categorized by company size
    Large capitalization
    Small capitalization
  Categorized by value (P/E, book/market, etc.)
    Growth
    Value
Bonds
  Categorized by term
    Short term
    Intermediate term
    Long term
  Categorized by yield
    High yield
  Categorized by country
    Domestic
    International
      Developed
      Emerging markets
  Categorized by issuer
    U.S. Treasury
    U.S. government agencies
    State and local municipalities
    Corporations
Real estate
  Categorized by type of real estate
    Commercial buildings
    Apartment buildings
    Homes
  Categorized by method of ownership
    REITs
    Limited partnerships
Precious metals
  Gold, silver, and platinum
  Mining companies
Natural resources
  Energy
  Paper and forest products
  Mining, processing, and supply companies
Cash

by simply owning, proportionally, all the asset classes in the world. But many asset classes (and subclasses) are difficult or impossible to buy. Consider the challenge of buying a proportional interest in sub-Saharan real estate. Most portfolios will therefore consist of "investable" asset classes—a substantially, but by no means perfectly, diversified portfolio. For example, the MSCI EAFE Emerging Markets Free Index excludes emerging markets that, in the opinion of Morgan Stanley Capital International, don't maintain reasonably free-market stock exchanges, rules of contract law, and so on.

But even this subuniverse can be controversial. Some experts don't consider emerging markets to be a separate asset class, but simply a subclass of international assets. Within the past five years or so, many financial services companies have tried to convince investors that midsize companies represent an asset class completely separate from U.S. large and small companies. It remains to be seen whether this is anything more than a marketing ploy.

Constrained Outcomes

As a result, virtually all MVO calculations are constrained in some way. For example, the programmer might require that the final portfolio contain not less than a 30% exposure to U.S. large-cap stocks, and not less than a 20% fixed-income exposure. Constrained algorithms result in much more traditional portfolios, but of course there is nothing remotely efficient about them. Hence the essentially unresolvable dilemma: MVO-designed portfolios will be either efficient but ridiculous or sensible but inefficient.

Unbalanced Portfolios or Unbalanced Investors?

All studies of the importance of asset allocation make a crucial assumption: that the portfolio is religiously rebalanced back to the optimized allocation. Typically, the portfolio will be rebalanced quarterly, although some studies have rebalanced monthly. These studies thereby ensure that the original asset allocation strategy remains in place over time. In addition, rebalancing injects into the portfolio a contrarian element, since the rebalancing exercise by definition requires the sale of recently appreciated securities and the purchase of securities that have performed more poorly.

In the real world, rebalancing rarely occurs in such a clockwork fashion. Part of the trouble is investor behavior: Investors rarely have the courage to sell sectors that are outperforming and buy sectors that have performed poorly, and even if they had the courage, they generally lack the necessary discipline to do so on a regular basis. More fundamentally, rebalancing is usually a costly proposition. For taxable investors, the tax costs of frequent rebalancing will be so high as to outweigh the benefits. For large tax-exempt institutional investors, the costs of rebalancing—typically transaction costs such as commissions, spreads, and market impact—will also be very costly. For investors who hold substantial private investments, rebalancing activities are also constrained by the impossibility of knowing the exact value of the investments at any point prior to liquidation, by the difficulties involved in moving funds into and out of investment vehicles that don't permit daily liquidity, and by the danger of moving funds out of popular managers' vehicles (once out, it may be impossible to get back in).

The result is that most real-world portfolios are rebalanced, if at all, on an annual basis. This saves on tax and transaction costs, but undermines a fundamental value of asset allocation.

Driving via the Rearview Mirror

An unfortunate characteristic of MVO calculations is that they tend to overweight the importance of market sectors that have enjoyed good recent returns. This is not only the opposite of a contrarian approach, but also it almost always leads to portfolio designs that would have worked magnificently in the immediate prior period, but which turn out to be ruinous going forward. This is an important reason for using the longest returns available. Unfortunately, returns for some asset classes—emerging markets, for example—simply aren't available for periods prior to about 1970.

For example, in the early 1980s, MVO-designed portfolios tended to overweight real estate and small caps. The former promptly collapsed after the 1986 Tax Reform Act, and the latter turned out to be hugely overvalued relative to large caps.[11] Similarly, MVO-designed portfolios from the early 1990s tended to have (as noted) oversized allocations to emerging markets—a calamitous sector in the mid-to-late 1990s.[12]

Diversification Never Works When You Need It

Someone has said that, in a financial crisis, all asset class correlations become perfectly positive. And, indeed, careful studies have shown that the remark is only slightly exaggerated.[13] As a result, investors who imagined that a well-diversified portfolio would protect them during difficult market conditions are likely to be sorely disappointed. Diversification works over longer periods of time—that is, it reduces portfolio volatility—but in a crisis all bets are off.

Risk Is in the Eye of the Beholder

The principles behind asset allocation assume that volatility is a sufficient measure of market risk. However, there are in fact as many definitions of risk as there are investors, since risk is experienced subjectively. For example, many investors don't consider *upside* volatility as risk at all.

Consider an investor in emerging markets securities in the years prior to 1994. Certainly that sector was risky in the Markowitz sense: Emerging markets volatility was *three times* the volatility of the S&P 500. But that volatility was mainly on the upside: Between 1990 and 1994, emerging markets investors tripled their money. Now consider those same investors in the period between 1994 and 1999, when emerging markets declined more than 7% per year while the S&P was compounding at 25% per year. From a modern portfolio theory perspective, the periods 1990–1993 and 1994–1999 were wholly unremarkable: Emerging markets were volatile, as expected. But to investors, these periods were as different as day and night.

There are, of course, many more definitions of risk, but the issue is simple: If an investor doesn't perceive reduced portfolio volatility as reduced risk, asset allocation is unlikely to be of appeal.

The Problem of Herd Instincts

Information flows freely in the financial markets, and investors act on that information. When it became widely known that academic research showed a "small-cap effect," namely, that small-company stocks outperformed large-company stocks over time, investors loaded up on small caps. When real estate became "securitized" via real estate investment trusts, investors piled into real estate. When it became possible to invest large sums of money in emerging economies, investors stuffed their portfolios full of emerging markets stocks. As this chapter is being written, hot sectors include U.S. large-company stocks, technology stocks, Internet stocks, and venture capital funds. To the surprise of no one, investors are flocking to those sectors.

The problem, of course, is that when very large sums of money flow into any specific sector, the supply-demand ratio becomes unbalanced. Prices in those sectors have to rise to accommodate the increased demand, and future returns are thereby depressed. MVO calculations, which overweight recent returns, tend to exacerbate the natural herd instincts of investors, and hence asset allocation strategies based on MVO algorithms are often highly suspect.

What's an Investor to Do?

Asset allocation based on modern portfolio theory considerations is the only objective method we have for designing investment portfolios, but, as we have seen, designing sensible asset allocation strategies under real-world conditions can be highly problematic. Indeed, so daunting are the challenges that investors can perhaps be forgiven for deciding to abandon asset allocation altogether. This, however, would be a serious mistake. Designing a portfolio without the tools supplied by Markowitz, et al. would be like designing a skyscraper without blueprints or architectural training. The following paragraphs are designed to help investors find a sensible path through the jungle of asset allocation pitfalls.

Adjust Your Perception of Risk

First, understand that the market doesn't care how you experience risk. Markowitz was right: risk in capital markets is associated with pricing uncertainty, and uncertainty is best measured by price volatility. The fact that to you risk control means never having a down year is irrelevant. The only way to avoid a down year is not to invest at all.[14] The fact that upside volatility isn't risk in your eyes is also irrelevant—volatility is symmetrical, and portfolios that tend to outperform on the upside will tend to underperform on the downside, compounding your losses.

Focus on the Stock/Bond Ratio

Nothing will so dramatically affect your long-term risk and return experience as the decision you make to allocate your assets between stocks and bonds. Over all but the briefest periods of time, a portfolio with 80% of the asset base in stocks and 20% in bonds will dramatically outperform a portfolio with 80% in bonds and 20% in stocks. If your investment time horizon is more than five years, you should probably have at least 60% of your assets in stocks. If your time horizon is more than 10 years (and especially if it is more than 15 years), you should probably have 70% or more of your assets in stocks. On the other hand, very few investors (small children may be an exception) should have more than 80% of their money in stocks: The extra return isn't worth the risk. During very strong bull markets, like the one that prevailed during the mid- and late 1990s, investors tend to ignore this principle, at their peril.

Understand the Performance of the Asset Classes

No matter how attractive a market sector appears to be, you should avoid it like the plague if you don't understand its dynamics. Even relatively sophisticated institutional investors learned this object lesson when they piled into emerging markets in the early 1990s. Emerging markets stocks can be incredibly volatile, and investors who can't stand that heat need to stay well out of that kitchen.

Don't Take More Risk than Necessary

For all but the youngest investors, capital preservation should be an important component of your investment policy. This doesn't mean you should own an extremely cautious portfolio—on the contrary! But it does mean that you should try to structure your portfolio to avoid serious losses, even if those losses are temporary. Consider the math. If a $10,000 portfolio increases in value by 100%, it is worth $20,000. But if it then declines by only 80%, it is worth $4,000. A 100% return followed by a –80% return results in a 60% loss. You can also calculate this unfortunate math the other way around. A $10,000 portfolio that loses 80% will be worth $2,000. If it then increases by 100% it is worth only $4,000. The long and short of this example is that it is much more important to avoid dramatic losses than it is to achieve dramatic gains. Very aggressive portfolios look good during strong bull markets, but they can devastate wealth during bear markets.

Diversify Your Portfolio

Keep your portfolio well diversified and your allocations within the reasonable range. Investors who become enamored of particular market sectors or who hold especially positive or negative views on the future economy tend to hold portfolios that are dangerously concentrated. For example, an investor who suspects economic disaster may be in the offing might put a substantial portion of money in precious metals or gold stocks, while an investor who believes the economy will be strong might hold a 100% stock portfolio heavily concentrated in technology companies. These strategies almost always lead to disaster. Since no one can possibly know for certain what the future holds, sensible investors keep their portfolios well diversified and asset class exposures reasonable. Table 22.2 lists reasonable asset allocation ranges for a longer-term investor.

The longer you expect your assets to be invested, the further toward the high end of the equity exposure range you should be. Children often hold 100% equity portfolios, while young adults should have their retirement funds heavily into stocks—80% equity portfolios are often appropriate.

Even investors just entering retirement are really long-term investors who may have to live on their portfolios for 25 to 30 years. For the recently retired, 65% stock portfolios are not too aggressive. Finally, older investors—those past 75—should maintain healthy equity exposures to avoid the possibility that they will liquidate their assets if they live too long. A 40% stock exposure is not unreasonable for very senior investors.

Rebalance, Rebalance, Rebalance

Hard as it is to do, rebalancing your portfolio religiously is one of the most value-added strategies you can follow. As noted earlier, rebalancing is inherently con-

TABLE 22.2 Asset Class Exposure Ranges

Asset Class	Exposure Range
Stocks	65%–80%
Bonds	20%–35%
Cash[1]	0%–5%
U.S. large-/mid-cap stocks	35%–45%
U.S. small-cap stocks	10%–15%
Specialized assets[2]	5%–10%
International developed country stocks	10%–20%
Emerging markets stocks	0%–5%
Long-term bonds[3]	5%–10%
Intermediate bonds	10%–20%
Short-term bonds	0%–5%

[1]In addition to cash used in the investment portfolio, most investors should keep three to six months of living expenses segregated in an emergency reserve fund.

[2]Specialized assets are those which hold out the promise of sound performance during periods of high unanticipated inflation—probably the worst environment for both stocks and bonds. Such assets include diversified real estate, natural resources, commodities, and inflation-linked bonds.

[3]Long-term, noncallable bonds represent one of the few assets that will perform well in rare but devastating periods of price deflation.

trarian and ensures that you will tend over time to sell highly appreciated securities (capturing some of your gains) and to buy underpriced securities. Taxable accounts should be rebalanced about once a year. Rebalancing more often will tend to generate highly taxed short-term capital gains, rather than more desirable long-term gains. Tax-sheltered accounts can be rebalanced more often, but keep trading costs in mind: Commissions, spreads, and market impact can add up.

Don't Panic

If you invest any significant portion of your assets in equity securities, you can expect at some point in your investment lifetime (and probably at several points) to lose money. It's not easy to watch your capital disappear, but unless you panic and sell out, that capital hasn't really disappeared at all—it will rebound powerfully when the markets recover. The dismal markets of 1973–1974 provided a good example. After many good years in the late 1960s, investors were heavily into stocks. But between January 1973 and August 1974, the U.S. stock market dropped 50% in real terms. Many investors sold out at or near the bottom, then stayed out of the markets (many vowing never to return), missing the huge rebound in 1975 and 1976. Some of these investors had less capital in 1985 than they had had in 1970. Panicky behavior in the stock markets can carry very significant penalties.

Don't Be Greedy

In the late stages of bull markets, investors with soundly diversified portfolios often feel that they are being left out of the riches. Narrow sectors of the markets—typically, technology stocks and mega-cap blue chips—will rise to spectacular heights. Since the main market indexes are all capitalization weighted, the indexes also perform well. For example, the Standard & Poor's 500 index weights the price of General Electric at many times the weight of the smallest stock in the index. Hence, if GE and other big-cap stocks happen to be performing well, the index will be rising rapidly even if a majority of stocks are falling in value. Meanwhile, diversified investors appear to be settling for small gains while their neighbors are getting rich. Unsophisticated investors who find themselves in this situation tend to bail out of their solid portfolios and jump into portfolios concentrated in the skyrocketing sectors. Almost invariably, those sectors promptly collapse, devastating the asset base. For example, between 1929 and 1932, RCA fell 98% in value. Between 1969 and 1970, IBM fell 80%. In 1973–1974, Honeywell and NCR fell 85% to 90%. Even during the modest correction in 1990, Intel fell 46% and Oracle fell 76%.

Get Good Advice

The mere presence of a good adviser can keep you from making a terrible mistake in a panicky moment. The best advisers are those who aren't selling products, since they have no incentive to give you bad advice.

Buy and Hold

One of the simplest and best investment strategies is to buy decent companies at realistic prices and simply hold them for long-term appreciation. You don't have to be a stock-picking genius to make this strategy work. The absence of investment costs—commissions, management fees, and taxes, especially—

will more than make up for any stock-picking mistakes you make. Similar advantages can accrue to investors in index funds and other tax-managed mutual funds that strive for low turnover and long holding periods.

Relax and Enjoy

Whether you experience great or merely modest investment success, you will have the power of compound interest working for you. Over time, even modestly performing investment portfolios will build significant wealth.

Notes

1. Von Neumann was an extraordinary man. In addition to devising game theory, he co-invented quantum mechanics, invented the digital computer, and was instrumental in the design of the atomic and hydrogen bombs.
2. *Journal of Finance* (March 1952).
3. It wasn't until the passage of the Employee Retirement Income Security Act (ERISA) in 1974 that investors began broadly to employ modern asset allocation principles. ERISA in effect codified modern portfolio theory as the approach a "prudent investor" would take to investment management.
4. Variability of returns is measured by Standard Deviation, (SD), the range of returns that will occur two-thirds of the time. For example, the SD of Asset A is 20, while the SD of Asset B is only 6.
5. Technically, the correlation of two asset classes is the covariance of the asset classes divided by the product of their SDs. Correlation coefficients can range from +1 (perfect positive correlation) to −1 (perfect negative correlation).
6. Note that by adding small amounts of diversified stock exposure to a 100% bond portfolio, the portfolio risk actually goes *down* (that is, the efficient frontier line moves up and to the left). Because stocks and bonds have a very low correlation with each other, adding some stock exposure tends to reduce the risk of a bond portfolio, while actually improving the expected return.
7. Portfolios falling *above* the efficient frontier line—like Portfolio C on Figure 22.6— are impossible to achieve.
8. R.G. Ibbotson and R. Sinquefield, *Stocks, Bonds, Bills and Inflation: Year-by-Year Historical Returns (1926–1974)*.
9. To paraphrase the great investor Bernard Baruch, market timing should be avoided because it can be done successfully only by liars.
10. Investors cannot avoid assuming market risk, but can diversify away most other kinds of risks. For example, the risk of owning a specific company or industry sector can be avoided by holding many companies and sectors.
11. Over the 15-year period ended 9/30/99, the Wilshire REIT Index (an index of real estate–related securities) generated a miserable 7.5% annualized return. The Russell 2000 Index (a small-cap index) generated an 11.7% annualized return. The S&P 500 index compounded during this period at 18% per annum.
12. Over the five-year period ended 9/30/99, the MSCI EAFE Emerging Markets Free In-

dex (an index of emerging markets securities) generated a dismal –7.4% annualized return. The S&P 500 Index compounded during this period at 25% per annum.

13. See, for example, Chow, Jacquier, and Kritzman, "Optimal Portfolios in Good Times and Bad," *Financial Economist*, No. 272–1 (December 1998).

14. In fact, it is probably impossible to avoid a down year. Interest rates in Swiss banks in the early 1980s were actually *negative*—depositors had to pay the bank to take their funds. During even modestly inflationary periods, keeping your money under the mattress will ensure that it is worth less next year than it is worth this year.

CHAPTER
23

Retirement Planning

Gary S. Weinstein and Bernard Newman

Introduction

Retirement is the most significant financial hurdle most of us prepare for in our lifetimes. Making it more difficult is that the nature of retirement and retirement planning is changing. The portion of our lives we spend in retirement is increasing. The average American spends about one-third of his or her life in retirement. This is mainly because we are living longer, but also because there has been a trend toward earlier retirement.

Also, job changes are more frequent than in the past, and incomes are less predictable. There is less job security, and many workers are forced into early retirement, second careers, or self-employment. Changes in jobs can reduce pension benefits, because most plans reward long-term employees with larger benefits. Even professionals, such as doctors and lawyers, are facing reduced job security and less predictable income.

These trends make retirement planning more important than ever. Those who fail to plan early may approach retirement with insufficient assets to maintain their lifestyles or to accomplish their goals. Also, failing to start early results in a loss of the opportunity to compound your wealth.

This chapter should help you chart your path to a secure and successful retirement. Spending patterns, financial assumptions, and appropriate investment allocation will be discussed. Finally, computerized investing tools are suggested to help you implement and monitor your plan.

The first task with any plan is to identify your goals. Then you estimate what will be required to reach these goals. You next determine where you are on the path toward these goals. You analyze your current assets and liabilities, and then plot your course. The issues in retirement planning are summarized in Figure 23.1. You determine your retirement goals and what you will need to meet those goals. While the emphasis is on accumulating a pool of funds to meet retirement spending needs, there may be many other considerations. Retirement planning should not be done in isolation—you must take into account your other goals and expenses. A home mortgage, child education expenses, and support for elderly parents are some common issues that must be incorporated into your overall plan.

Planning is a continual process. Your goals may change, or events beyond your control may push you off your plotted course. You should evaluate your progress annually and make necessary adjustments to your plan.

Retirement Planning Process

Determine Your Goals
Do you want to retire?
If you could choose, at what age would you retire?
Would you retire completely, or just work fewer hours or change occupations?
Where would you live?
What kind of lifestyle would you have?

Determine What You Need to Achieve These Goals
What will your living expenses be in retirement?
How much will you spend on housing? Will you stay in your current home, or move to a less expensive home? Will you purchase a second home? Will you own or rent?
What do you need to do to prepare for changes in career?

Determine Your Current Retirement Assets
What is the value of your pension plan(s)?
What can you expect from Social Security?
What earned income do you expect to receive in retirement?
What is the value of your current retirement savings?
What is the value of your home?

FIGURE **23.1** Retirement Planning Process

Estimating Living Expenses in Retirement

After determining your goals, the next step in planning for retirement is to make an estimate of your living expenses in retirement. You start with an accurate assessment of your current living expenses. This can be easily accomplished with software such as Quicken or Microsoft Money. It is often useful to categorize your current expenditures. Basic recurring living expenses include food, clothing, health insurance, other medical bills, other insurance, car payments, car expenses, and telephone bills. Home expenses include mortgage payments, utility bills (gas, water, electricity, and sewage), yard and garden expenses, maintenance costs, property insurance, and real estate taxes. Miscellaneous expenses include travel, recreation, entertainment, dues, gifts, charitable contributions, accounting bills, and disability insurance.

Conventional wisdom dictates that your living expenses will be reduced by approximately 20% when you retire; however, what you spend actually depends on the lifestyle you choose and your personal circumstances. Typically, not working will decrease expenditures for clothing, transportation, disability insurance, and life insurance. You may also qualify for certain senior citizen discounts, and your unearned income will be free of Social Security and Medicare taxation, possibly resulting in more discretionary income to spend. You may no longer have mortgage payments or continue to save for retirement.

However, certain expenses may be higher, particularly medical and prescription costs. You may plan to dine out or travel more extensively, or have expensive hobbies. You may have to pay some costs currently borne by an employer, such as health insurance, automobile lease payments or allowances, automobile insurance, life insurance, telephone expenses, and travel expenses. For some, previously tax-deductible expenses will have to be paid with after-tax dollars.

Other Expenses in Retirement

Moving to a different part of the country or to a smaller home can affect your living expenses. Buying a smaller retirement home will reduce expenses and time and effort spent on maintenance. Moving to an area with lower housing costs and taxes can have a dramatic effect on the standard of living that you can afford. For example, moving to a state without an income tax or without a state tax on pension benefits can significantly increase the money you have to spend. Therefore, it is important to determine the cost of living and state tax laws in potential retirement communities. Different types of retirement income, such as IRA withdrawals, public employer and private employer pension distributions, and annuity payments, are not treated equally by all states. Some states tax tangible property, like automobiles, and others tax intangibles, such as investments.

By moving into a less expensive home, you can turn some of the equity value of your current home into an income-producing asset. There is a $500,000 one-time capital gains tax exclusion on the sale of your home. To be eligible, neither you nor your spouse can have used the exclusion before, and the home must have been your principal residence for at least three of the five years before the sale date. This money can then be invested for income or growth.

Retirees who do not want to leave their homes can tap their home equity using a reverse mortgage loan. The lender makes payments to the homeowner in the form of a loan advance. As the total of the loaned payments and interest on them grow, your equity in the home is gradually reduced. When the residence is sold, the balance of the reverse mortgage loan is repaid to the lender from the proceeds of the sale.

Expected Years in Retirement

The number of years in retirement depends both on your age at retirement and on your life expectancy. You may be surprised at how long a retirement you should plan for. Life expectancy in the United States continues to increase, and it is common to require a retirement income that lasts until you are 90 or even 100 years old! Table 23.1 gives the life expectancies for males and females in the United States in 1996. For planning purposes, most professional advisers recommend adding 10 years to the number of years in the table, since these are averages, and there is a good chance that you will live longer.

What to Expect from Social Security

Anyone with at least 40 quarters of covered employment is eligible for Social Security benefits. The retirement benefit is based on your career earnings (Table 23.2). As you can see, the higher your earnings, the smaller the percentage of your salary that Social Security income will replace.

In the future, changes will have to be made in Social Security benefits. There are fewer workers supporting each retiree with each passing year. To counteract this, the government has increased the age of eligibility for full benefits and increased taxation on the benefits received, particularly for retirees with other sources of income. Most likely, in the future retirement benefits will begin at more advanced ages, and those with higher incomes

TABLE 23.1 Life Expectancy

Age	Average Life Expectancy	
	Males	**Females**
35	40.1	45.4
40	35.6	40.7
45	31.3	36.0
50	27.0	31.4
55	22.9	27.0
60	19.1	22.9
65	15.6	18.9

TABLE 23.2 Approximate Annual Social Security Benefits

Age in 1999	Earnings in 1998				
	$30,000	**$40,000**	**$50,000**	**$60,000**	**$72,600+**
35 or less	$13,104	$15,720	$17,220	$18,720	$20,556
40	$13,104	$15,720	$17,220	$18,720	$20,412
45	$13,104	$15,720	$17,220	$18,720	$20,244
50	$13,104	$15,720	$17,220	$18,696	$20,004

Note: For both husband and wife of same age and with similar lifetime incomes, multiply above amount by 1.5.

will face even greater reductions in benefits and greater rates of taxation on these benefits.

If you would like to determine your expected benefits, you can obtain an estimate from the Social Security Administration. Write the Social Security Administration at 8515A Liberty Road, Randalstown, MD 21133; call 800-772-1213; or look up the web site: www.ssa.gov. Ask them to send you the Request for Earnings and Benefit Estimate Statement (Form SSA-7004-PC).

At present, you will pay a tax on up to 85% of your provisional Social Security income if your income exceeds certain thresholds. The calculations are somewhat complicated, so they will not be reviewed here. You can refer to the following web page: www.irs.ustreas.gov/forms_pubs/pubs/p55403.htm.

Calculating the Nest Egg You'll Need

In order to perform this calculation you need an estimate of your annual living expenses, any other expenses during retirement years, your life expectancy in retirement, the inflation rate, and your tax rate. The first variable needed for your calculations is the projected rate of inflation over the course of your plan. Inflation averaged 4.04% between 1950 and 1998 (arithmetic mean; data from Ibbotson Associates). The annual rate ranged from –0.50% to +13.31%. Over a fairly long financial plan, it is reasonable to estimate an inflation rate of 4%.

It is difficult to predict how tax rates will change, but it is unlikely that taxes will be lower in the future. There is also the possibility that taxation on retirement plans will also increase with time. It is best to apply current tax rates to your retirement income. Remember that you will not have to pay Social Security or Medicare taxes on your investment income.

You should plan on spending some of your principal each year in retirement. It requires much greater assets to meet your living expenses if you depend only on income from the principal. Many retirees are reluctant to spend their principals, partly because they fear that they will outlive their assets or they won't have enough money to meet an emergency. However, not spending your principal in retirement can greatly reduce your standard of living. There are various options for increasing security while spending a portion of your principal, such as setting aside a portion of the principal to invest in cash equivalents and serve as a reserve for unexpected needs.

Once you determine the required annual savings needed to fund your plan, adjustments may be necessary. If you cannot save the indicated amount, you can reduce your retirement income, plan to work longer, plan to work part-time in retirement, or change your asset allocation to increase your returns on your savings. Table 23.3 shows how lowering retirement income or delaying retirement can significantly affect the size of the nest egg required.

Current Retirement Assets

The next step is to determine the value of your current retirement assets. For pension plans, you must ascertain whether these are defined contribution or defined benefit plans. Defined benefit plans will pay a fixed amount at retirement, determined by the plan. The plan managers choose how the money is in-

TABLE 23.3 Effect of Desired Income and
Term of Retirement on Size of Nest Egg Required

Annual	Years in Retirement			
Income	15	20	25	30
$125,000	$1,935,000	$2,470,000	$2,950,000	$3,400,000
$100,000	$1,550,000	$1,975,000	$2,360,000	$2,700,000
$75,000	$1,160,000	$1,480,000	$1,770,000	$2,035,000
$50,000	$775,000	$985,000	$1,180,000	$1,360,000

Note: Assumes 6% annual return on investments, 4% rate of inflation, 15% tax rate, constant after-tax and after-inflation income.

vested. In defined contribution plans, the amount deposited in your account each year is determined, but the payout during retirement depends on the investment performance of the account. The same applies to IRA accounts. Rules for timing of withdrawals and taxes incurred by withdrawn funds differ for each type of tax-deferred plan. These must be taken into consideration in estimating their future value. Non-tax-deductible personal funds earmarked for retirement also should be considered separately, since annual gains on these investments are subject to income tax.

The future value of current tax-deferred and taxable assets can be estimated, based on how those assets are invested, tax rates, the past performance of those types of investments, and the time until retirement. It is important to choose reasonable (conservative) assumptions about your investment returns, in order to make the probability high that you will achieve the goals. If your plan assumptions are overly optimistic or unreasonable, you may end up falling short. You have to select an estimated rate of return for each asset class. The long-term average rates of return (and their standard deviations) for cash instruments, bonds, and stocks are discussed in Chapter 3 "Investment Vehicles." It is probably wise to use the 25th percentile returns, to give a higher chance of achieving the desired goal. Computer programs are available to assist in these calculations. A web site called Financial Engines (www.financialengines.com) will give the range of future values of various asset mixtures. You must take into account the effect of taxes on the growth of taxable savings.

Tax-Deferred Investing

The tax laws have many incentives to encourage saving for retirement. Money placed in approved plans can grow without being taxed until withdrawal. Income and capital gains earned can be reinvested without losing a portion to taxes. Such tax deferral has a cumulative effect, so over many years it can significantly increase the return on your investments. However, Congress has placed many restrictions on these accounts, so they are not available for everyone, and may not be of benefit in all situations.

The most important determinant in deciding whether to contribute to a tax-deferred retirement savings plan is whether the contribution is tax-deductible. In nearly all cases if tax deferral is combined with a tax deduction, you are better off investing. The tax deduction means that you can profit on the gains from the extra money that the government allows you to hold until retirement.

Tax-Deductible Accounts

Individual Retirement Account (IRA)

You and your spouse can invest up to $2,000 each year into a tax-deferred IRA account, if you meet the income requirements. For 1999, if your income is less than $31,000 for an individual or $51,000 for a couple filing a joint tax return, each worker can contribute the full $2,000 to an IRA. If you make more than these amounts, you can take a full IRA deduction only if you are not participating in a retirement plan at work. Even then, the IRA deduction phases out for incomes above $61,000 for a couple and $41,000 for an individual. You have until April 15 of the following year to make your contribution, and you may continue to do so up to the age of $70^{1}/_{2}$.

Employee Savings Plans

The most common employee savings plans are 401(k)s. The employee can contribute up to $10,000 of pretax dollars. (This amount may vary for some plans or employees, and is indexed to inflation.) Approximately 80% of employers will match a percentage of your contribution. Employees of nonprofit organizations are eligible for a similar account, a 403(b).

Self-employed individuals have several retirement plan options, including Keogh plans, Simplified Employee Pensions (SEP-IRAs), and conventional pension plans. There are two different types of Keogh plans, the profit sharing plan and the money purchase plan. The money purchase contribution is mandatory; you must make the same percentage (of salary) contribution each year, whether you have profits or not. The profit sharing contribution can change each year. An individual can have both types of plans, and contribute to each in the same year. The most attractive feature of Keoghs is the high maximum contribution (up to $30,000) they allow.

Individuals who have employment and self-employment income can have a deductible account for each. The maximum contributions are independent, so that you can double your tax deduction.

For a SEP-IRA, the employer contributes up to $30,000 or 15% of each employee's total compensation, whichever is less. The contribution does not reduce salary. With the exception of the higher contribution limits, they are subject to the same rules as a regular IRA.

A defined benefit pension plan is the type that was traditionally provided by employers, but it is becoming progressively less common. The company guarantees a specific monthly benefit to employees, calculated using a formula that typically is based on a percentage of your final salary and years of service. High-income earners who are relatively close to retirement can use this type of plan to rapidly amass a large nest egg. It would require large amounts of capital, since few years are available for tax-free compounding to occur.

If you are self-employed, you should obtain the advice of a professional to help you select the type of plan that best meets your needs and to help with critical Internal Revenue Service compliance. Failure to file the proper forms or meet governmental regulations can place your retirement savings at significant risk.

In general, funds invested in the tax-deferred accounts described here cannot be withdrawn without a 10% penalty until age 59$\frac{1}{2}$, and must start to be withdrawn by age 70$\frac{1}{2}$. You may be able to withdraw your funds earlier if you are disabled. Deciding when and how to withdraw these monies is a complex decision requiring professional advice. Allowing the funds to compound tax-free will result in a larger pension. On the other hand, if you and your spouse leave a large pension plan to your heirs, they will pay ordinary income taxes on the funds as they leave the plan, followed by estate taxes on the remainder. This double taxation can greatly reduce the amount of money left to your heirs.

Non-Tax-Deductible Accounts

If you are not eligible for further tax-deductible contributions, it may be possible to make nondeductible contributions to tax-deferred accounts. If you have already contributed the maximum deductible amount to your employer's retirement plan, it may be possible to make nondeductible contributions. You can then use the employer's plan as a tax-deferred retirement account. Other options include nondeductible contributions to an IRA account, the Roth IRA, and deferred annuities.

Nondeductible IRA

Even if you don't qualify for a tax deduction, you can still contribute up to $2,000 to an IRA. The money will accumulate with deferral of taxes. However, when you withdraw your gains, they are taxed as ordinary income (maximum rate 39.6%).

Roth IRA

A newer type of IRA known as a Roth IRA has greater benefits, if you qualify. At the present time, a single taxpayer needs to have an adjusted gross income of less than $110,000, and a couple must make less than $160,000 annually to participate. The Roth IRA allows you to make a non-tax-deductible contribution of up to $2,000 annually. You may withdraw your money tax-free as long as the funds have been held in the account for at least five years. Furthermore, at the time of death these funds are paid to your beneficiary free of estate taxes. Other advantages of a Roth IRA include the ability to withdraw the money early without the 10% penalty if the funds are being used to pay for a first home ($10,000 limit on withdrawal), college expenses, or disability, and that distributions are never mandatory (you can even pass the assets to your beneficiaries free of income tax).

Deferred Annuity

A retirement savings vehicle that is available to everyone is a deferred annuity sponsored by an insurance company. Nondeductible payments are made to an insurance company and invested in one of several portfolios depending on your tolerance for risk. Variable annuities allow you to choose how to invest your savings. A company may offer different stock and bond mutual funds with different risk profiles. Like an IRA, these funds grow tax deferred and then are taxed as ordinary income upon withdrawal during retirement. These may be used as a supplement to other pension plans, and there is no limit to the amount of money you are allowed to invest. Commissions or loads on your investment, higher investment expenses, the cost of the insurance, and the risk of default of the insurance company holding your annuity may offset these advantages. In addition, depending on your plan, if you die during the accumulation phase, your beneficiary may receive only your original investment.

Other types of insurance programs (e.g., variable or universal life) can also be used as a method of tax deferral. Contributions in excess of the amount necessary to purchase your insurance needs can be invested and accumulate tax-deferred.

Should You Invest in a Nondeductible IRA or Deferred Annuity?

It depends on your tax bracket, your time horizon, and the types of investments you make. Income withdrawn from these accounts during retirement is taxed at ordinary income tax rates (up to 39.6%), even if it resulted from long-term capital gains (otherwise taxed at up to 20%). For example, assume you buy 100 shares of Microsoft, a company that does not pay dividends, for $50 each, and hold on to the shares for 15 years. You then sell the shares for $150 each, for a gain of $10,000, and withdraw the cash from the account. In the tax-deferred plan, you would pay up to $3,960 in taxes, leaving you with $6,040 to spend. In a taxable account, you would pay a maximum of $2,000 in taxes, and have $8,000, or about 25% more, to spend. Therefore, if you are investing in long-term stock holdings or mutual funds with very low turnover (e.g., index funds), you are probably better off using a taxable account.

Another important consideration is the cost of the account. Most IRA accounts incur minimal expenses. Setting up and administering a retirement plan (e.g., Keogh) for a handful of employees can be relatively expensive, because of the additional administration, reporting, and accounting costs. However, in most cases the savings will significantly outweigh the costs. Variable annuities can be a different story.

Variable annuities levy annual fees for investment management and administrative costs, similar to those of a mutual fund. However, in addition, they charge fees to cover the insurance costs. According to Morningstar, Inc., these fees average about 1.3% a year. Therefore, your total cost will average about 2.5% a year, an amount that can significantly depress your accumulation of funds over time.

Money should not be placed in a tax-deferred account if you may need it before age 59$^1/_2$. Withdrawals prior to this age incur a 10% penalty. Most deferred annuities also deduct a surrender charge if money is withdrawn during the first few years after your purchase.

You and your financial adviser will have to determine whether one of these accounts would be worthwhile for you. You should certainly take advantage of all tax-deductible opportunities for retirement investment. If your employer matches part of your contribution, make every effort to get the maximum available match. Whenever possible, make your contributions early in the year, to maximize your total returns over time. If you qualify, a Roth IRA is usually an excellent option. Further nondeductible contributions must be carefully analyzed to estimate their long-term benefit after all costs and taxes are paid.

Investment Selection

Once you have determined how much money you will need, you must decide how to invest your retirement savings. Asset allocation is the single most important determinant of your investment return. If you are too timid and shy away from equity investments, your portfolio is less likely to outpace inflation. If you are too aggressive and lose a large amount of money, it may take years to recoup losses. The solution to this problem is to balance risk and reward over time.

Asset allocation is discussed in a separate chapter; however, some broad guidelines will be discussed here. The classic rule of thumb is to invest 100 to 120 minus your age in equities. This means that a 35-year-old would have 65% to 85% of his or her money in equities, while a 55-year-old will decrease equity exposure to 45% to 65%. Because life expectancies have lengthened considerably, it may make sense to take a more aggressive approach. Many financial planners now feel that 60% to 80% of your portfolio should remain in equities over your lifetime. You can choose a percentage based on your personal risk tolerance. Sample allocations are given in Table 23.4.

The equity portion of your portfolio can be divided between large-company, small-company, and international investments. The remaining portion of your portfolio can be invested in fixed-income instruments such as Treasury notes, corporate bonds, bond mutual funds, tax-free municipal bonds, and money market funds.

The types of investments most suitable for tax-deferred accounts depend on

TABLE 23.4 Total Asset Allocation

	30 Years to Retirement	20 Years to Retirement	10 Years to Retirement	Early Retirement (55–70)	Late Retirement (70+)
Large-cap stocks	30%	35%	35%	30%	25%
Small-cap stocks	30%	20%	15%	10%	5%
Foreign stocks	25%	20%	15%	15%	10%
Fixed income	10%	15%	20%	25%	40%
Cash	5%	10%	15%	20%	20%

Data Source: SmartMoney, August 1999.

the time horizon, total value of savings, and your risk tolerance. In general, you should allocate those investments that are most likely to generate taxable income or capital gains—such as high-turnover mutual funds, high-yielding stocks, taxable bonds, and mortgage-backed securities—to tax-exempt accounts. These accounts generally should not hold real estate investments, collectibles, or investments that are already sheltered from taxation, such as municipal bonds. Annuities are already sheltered from taxes and have higher investment costs. Finally, limited partnerships are illiquid, have high costs, and may be associated with tax deductions that you cannot take advantage of in a tax-deferred account.

Entering Retirement

A series of decisions must be made as you embark on retirement. These are some of the most common ones:

- Many retirement plans offer the choice of an annuity (monthly pension) or a lump-sum distribution.

- If you choose a monthly pension, will you take a higher amount that ends at your death or a lower amount that will continue as long as either you or your spouse is alive?

- If you choose a lump-sum distribution, will you roll over the distribution into another tax-deferred account or pay the taxes immediately (using forward averaging if born before 1936)?

- How much of your savings will you spend each year in retirement?

- How will you invest your retirement funds?

- How will you withdraw funds from your tax-deferred and taxable accounts to meet income needs?

Annuity versus Lump-Sum Distributions

Most company retirement plans allow you to choose between a fixed monthly pension benefit for life and a lump-sum distribution of your plan funds. The pension annuity is based on the current value of your account, your life expectancy, and an assumed rate of investment return, all determined by the plan. The estimated present value of the monthly payments is calculated to be equivalent to the lump-sum distribution.

There are advantages and disadvantages to both a pension annuity and a lump-sum distribution. The main advantage to the lump-sum payout is that you control further investment decisions. You determine the types of investments and the timing of taxable distributions. You can roll over all or part of the distribution into an IRA or purchase an annuity from an insurance company. Any funds remaining will be transferred to your heirs.

A monthly pension can be preferable if you do not want to take responsibility for the investment decisions, if you think that you will live longer than average for your age, or if the employer provides cost-of-living pension adjustments or health benefits for retirees. If you choose a pension annuity and you are married, a joint-and-survivor annuity will provide income for your spouse after your death. This is usually the best option, unless your spouse has his or her own pension income or you expect to live much longer than your spouse.

If you take a lump-sum distribution, the government enables you to pay less than the full income tax rate on the funds. If you are at least $59^{1}/_{2}$ and have been a plan participant for at least five years, you can perform five-year forward averaging. (Ten-year forward averaging is available for taxpayers born before 1936.) You can figure your tax as if the lump sum were distributed over five (or 10) years, using current tax rates. This lowers the tax rate, since it puts you in a lower tax bracket for the distribution than you would be if you were taxed on the income as if it were received all in one year.

The laws governing withdrawal of these funds are constantly evolving, and you should seek professional advice before you start to withdraw the funds.

How Much Will You Spend Each Year?

No matter how much planning you do, your retirement nest egg will not be exactly the amount predicted. Upon entering retirement you must determine how much of your nest egg you will spend each year. Many retirees try to limit their spending to the income from their investment assets. This gives them the psychological security that their principal is left intact for their future needs or to pass on to their heirs. However, there are some significant drawbacks to this philosophy. First, your retirement spending must be much lower if you spend income only. Conversely, in planning, you must prepare for a substantially larger retirement nest egg to provide the desired income if you do not plan on spending some of the principal each year.

If you include spending principal, how much can you afford to spend each year? The answer depends not only on the size of your nest egg, but also on your investment return and your expected life span. Tables 23.5 and 23.6 give mathematical estimates of how long your money will last at different rates of investment return and spending. They assume spending of principal, a constant rate of return, and an annual increase of 4% in spending (to cover cost-

TABLE 23.5 Percentage of Original Amount Withdrawn Each Year at Different Rates of Return

	Percentage Rate of Return					
Years	**4%**	**5%**	**6%**	**7%**	**8%**	**9%**
10	10.0%	10.4%	10.9%	11.3%	11.8%	12.2%
15	6.7%	7.1%	7.6%	8.0%	8.6%	9.1%
20	5.0%	5.5%	6.0%	6.5%	7.0%	7.5%
25	4.0%	4.5%	5.0%	5.5%	6.1%	6.6%
30	3.3%	3.8%	4.3%	4.9%	5.5%	6.1%
35	2.9%	3.3%	3.9%	4.4%	5.1%	5.7%
40	2.5%	3.0%	3.5%	4.1%	4.8%	5.4%

Note: Assumes 4% annual increase in withdrawal to match inflation.

TABLE 23.6 How Long Withdrawals Will Last (in Years)

Percentage of Original Amount Withdrawn Each Year	Percentage Rate of Return					
	4%	**5%**	**6%**	**7%**	**8%**	**9%**
12%	8	8	9	9	10	10
11%	9	9	10	10	11	11
10%	10	10	11	11	12	13
9%	11	12	12	13	14	15
8%	12	13	13	15	16	18
7%	14	15	16	18	20	23
6%	16	18	20	22	25	30
5%	20	22	25	29	35	
4%	25	28	33			

Note: Assumes annual withdrawal is increased by 4% each year to keep up with inflation.

of-living increase). These assumptions may prove incorrect. The rate of return on your investments will vary year to year, and this can have a dramatic effect on the value of your account over time. Similarly, your cost of living may change more or less than expected.

If you have a spending rate in mind, you can determine how long your savings will be able to fund it using Table 23.6. Determine what percentage of your savings your annual spending represents. Then use your expected rate of return on investment to identify in the table the number of years the income will last. If this is not long enough, you will have to cut spending, increase income (part-time job), or attempt to increase investment return. To estimate total savings needed for a given amount of annual income, use the following formula: Divide 100 by the percentage rate of return (from table); multiply result by annual income. Income must be in future dollars (at time of retirement).

Another approach to determining your withdrawal rate is to analyze the success of various withdrawal rates in the past. A study by Cooley, Hubbard, and Walz reviewed portfolios of 15-, 20-, 25-, or 30-year duration from 1925 to 1995. Rather than use an assumed rate of return on investments, the actual return on various proportions of stocks and bonds was applied. Table 23.7 lists the percentages of portfolios in which the withdrawals could be sustained for the entire period. For example: 55 portfolios were established each year from 1925 to 1980, each containing 75% stocks and 25% bonds. Seven percent of the initial portfolio value was withdrawn the first year, and this amount was increased each year according to the cost of living. After 15 years of withdrawals 82% of the portfolios still had money remaining.

Investing in Retirement

Many retirees believe that the safest way to invest their savings is entirely in fixed-income instruments, such as bonds and certificates of deposit. However, this is a myopic view. There are trade-offs between the risks of inflation eroding your purchasing power, the risk of having insufficient current income, and the risk of losing money on your investments. Fixed-income investing places your principal at lower risk, but places your purchasing power at greater risk. It is likely that your principal will not increase enough to keep up with the cost of living. Therefore, the value (or purchasing power) of your income will decline each year. If interest rates are high you will have good income, but inflation is usually proportionally high, and the value of your principal will decline more rapidly.

Investing some of your principal in equities has a much greater likelihood of preserving your standard of living over time. For example, a portfolio that

TABLE 23.7 Portfolio Success Rates with Withdrawals Adjusted for Inflation

Years	% Stocks/ % Bonds	Initial Withdrawal Rate*							
		3%	4%	5%	6%	7%	8%	9%	10%	11%
15	100/0	100	100	100	91	79	70	63	55	43
	75/25	100	100	100	95	82	68	64	46	36
	50/50	100	100	100	89	70	50	32	8	13
	25/75	100	100	100	89	70	50	32	18	13
	0/100	100	100	100	71	39	21	18	16	14
20	100/0	100	100	100	75	63	53	43	33	29
	75/25	100	100	90	75	61	51	37	27	20
	50/50	100	100	82	47	31	16	8	4	0
	25/75	100	100	82	47	31	16	8	4	0
	0/100	100	90	47	20	14	12	10	2	0
25	100/0	100	100	87	70	59	46	35	30	26
	75/25	100	100	85	65	50	37	30	22	7
	50/50	100	93	48	24	15	4	2	0	0
	25/75	100	93	48	24	15	4	2	0	0
	0/100	100	46	17	15	11	2	0	0	0
30	100/0	100	95	85	68	59	41	34	34	27
	75/25	100	98	83	68	49	34	22	7	2
	50/50	100	71	27	20	5	0	0	0	0
	25/75	100	71	27	20	5	0	0	0	0
	0/100	80	20	17	12	0	0	0	0	0

*Percentage of initial portfolio value. Withdrawals increased annually according to change in cost of living index. Highlighted cells are those where 75% or more of past periods supported this withdrawal rate.

This data indicates that withdrawal rate, asset allocation, and investment term affected the odds of success. For long-term retirements (30 years) a 75% chance of success with a withdrawal rate of 4% or 5% was achieved only if 75% or more of the portfolio was in stocks. *Source:* P.L. Cooley, C.M. Hubbard, and D.T. Walz, "Retirement Savings: Choosing a Withdrawal Rate That Is Sustainable," *AAII Journal*, February 1998. Percentage of periods between 1925 and 1995 of indicated length that withdrawal could be sustained. The S&P 500 index was used to represent stocks, and long-term, high-grade corporate bonds were used to represent bonds. The study did not adjust for taxes or transaction costs.

is 100% in money market and bond funds returned an average of 7.3% between 1970 and 1998, while a portfolio with 40% in equities and 60% in bond or money market funds returned 10.84%. In the worst years, the fixed income portfolio returned 0.28%, and the 40% stock portfolio lost 6.54%.

One compromise for people very concerned about the potential loss of principal in stock investments involves using zero coupon bonds. You purchase zero coupon bonds that will come due in each of the next 5 or 10 years and provide sufficient income to meet your spending needs. The remainder of your assets is then invested more aggressively, mainly in a diversified stock portfolio. The odds of obtaining a favorable return on your stock investment over a 10-year period are excellent, and meanwhile you are assured of meeting your spending needs for the next 10 years.

It makes sense for most people to set aside a reserve fund for personal or medical emergencies. Most advisers recommend having at least six months of living expenses in cash or cash equivalents.

Withdrawal of Funds to Meet Spending Needs

You will have to decide from which account you will withdraw funds first.

The main considerations are taxation and estate planning. If you have a qualified pension plan, you will have to start withdrawing assets at age $70^{1}/_{2}$. Leaving funds in tax-deferred accounts as long as possible will maximize the effect of tax-deferred compounding. However, whatever funds remain in the account at the time of your death will be subject to onerous taxation. The assets in the account are first taxed as ordinary income, and the remainder is then subject to estate taxes, which can be as high as 55%. The best solution may be to evaluate your health and life expectancy, and then try to balance tax-deferred compounding against the possibility of high levels of death taxes.

In order to maintain your desired asset allocation, you may need to sell both fixed-income and equity investments to provide retirement income. Maintaining a fixed allocation will require selling more equities when stock prices are high, and more fixed-income investments when stock prices are low. This is like reverse *dollar cost averaging*, namely selling more shares of a stock when prices are high and selling fewer shares when prices are low.

To summarize, you will want to evaluate your income needs, probable life expectancy, and the projected size of your estate. You should then plan rates of withdrawal from your qualified pension plans, and dovetail this with your taxable portfolio in a way that preserves your asset base for as long as possible and maintains an asset allocation and risk level that you are comfortable with.

Tracking Your Progress

Once you have developed a plan, it is important to track your progress over time and adjust your savings or spending as necessary. In the past, individuals were forced to rely on financial professionals, tables in books, or sophisticated business calculators. Most individuals will still want to consult a certified financial planner or other professional for assistance. However, those who are so inclined may choose to use software on their home computer.

Many individuals currently track their income and spending with financial packages such as Quicken or Microsoft Money. These are both excellent programs with financial planning modules that can help you determine how much money you spend each year, and what size nest egg will be required to support your lifestyle. More extensive retirement planning packages, such as Vanguard Navigator, are readily available. These programs ask you to input your spending, current savings, and projected investment returns. The programs will help you to determine if you are on track to meet your financial goals. Packages from brokerage companies like Vanguard may make specific fund recommendations.

However, the commercially available programs may not accurately project your unique financial needs and investments. As an example, Quicken Financial Planner allows qualified retirement accounts to grow as long as possible, with distributions occurring at the end of your life. This obviously can result in a significant estate planning problem.

Those who would like to perform these calculations on their own and want a truly personalized approach to planning for retirement can utilize customized spreadsheet models that take into account the specifics of their own spending patterns and investments. One of the authors (GSW) has taken the following approach: A spreadsheet model was developed to assess spending both before and after retirement. Conservative assumptions have been utilized to err on the side of leaving a substantial estate, rather than falling short of retirement income. Examples of individualization include assuming that adult children will remain at home into their mid-20s, and that travel will occur primarily between the ages of retirement and 80. The amount of investment income required rises each year to keep pace with inflation. This model provides a relatively accurate assessment of income needs in retirement.

The next spreadsheet takes each asset class and projects conservative rates of return. The qualified retirement plans are slowly drained of funds over the lifetime of the retiree and the surviving spouse. Dividend and investment incomes are expended to cover living expenses, and assets are sold as needed to cover shortfalls when spending outpaces investment income. Each asset class can be graphed to visually observe the success of the plan. A variation of this spreadsheet is to assume different bear markets and evaluate each scenario to see how much downside protection the plan has. The numbers in the plan are adjusted annually to reflect changes in the investment portfolio. The goal of this planning is to allow a comfortable retirement and to assist with intelligent estate planning.

Conclusion

Ultimately, your success in retirement planning will correlate strongly with the habits you establish early. If you can moderate your living expenses, you will free up discretionary income that can be invested for growth. The earlier you begin saving, the faster your funds will grow. If you allocate assets properly, your returns will outpace inflation, and the magic of compound interest will multiply your investments. If you understand your needs and your assumptions are conservative, you stand an excellent chance of exceeding your financial goals. You can use commercially available software packages and spreadsheet models to monitor your progress and assist with lifestyle changes and estate planning decisions. It is never too early to start planning properly for this significant financial hurdle.

Estate Planning

Harold I. Apolinsky

Summary of Estate, Gift, and Generation-Skipping Tax Laws

In 1921 Congress passed laws imposing taxes on the privilege of passing assets to beneficiaries during life (gift) and at death (estate). Unlike the income tax laws, which required a constitutional amendment (Sixteenth) in 1913, transfer taxes exist simply at the whim of Congress. Currently, the effective transfer tax rate begins at 37% and grows rapidly to 55%. In addition, in 1988 Congress imposed an extra 55% tax on gifts or bequests to grandchildren or beneficiaries two generations younger, in excess of a $1 million exemption amount. The generation-skipping transfer tax exemption is indexed to the cost of living starting in 1999 and will move up in increments of $10,000 (approximately 1%).

In the year 2000, $675,000 can be left or given tax-free. This amount is expressed as a credit of $220,550 against the tax that effectively eliminates the lower tax rates of 18% to 37%. This amount will change in uneven increments as indicated in Table 24.1. All assets given or left to a spouse are deductible. Thus, the estate or death tax can be postponed until the last to die of the husband and wife.

TABLE 24.1 Maximum Estate Tax Exclusions

Year	Applicable Exclusion Amount	Applicable Credit Amount
2000	$675,000	$220,550
2001	$675,000	$220,550
2002	$700,000	$229,800
2003	$700,000	$229,800
2004	$850,000	$287,300
2005	$950,000	$326,300
2006	$1,000,000	$345,800

How to Calculate the Death Tax

The starting point is the gross estate. A person's gross estate is the sum of the market value of all assets owned, including stocks, bonds, businesses, real estate, life insurance, qualified or retirement plans, deferred compensation, and so on. When a person dies owning assets equal to or greater in value than the tax-free amount, the estate planning attorney is called upon to assist the family in completing an estate tax return, which is essentially an inventory with supporting appraisals. This must be furnished to the Internal Revenue Service within nine months after death. (Filing of the estate tax return can be extended for another six months for a total of 15 months after death, where appropriate.)

Prior to calculating the estate tax, three amounts can be deducted from the gross estate. The first is the total of all debts and expenses. The second deduction is for property left to a surviving spouse. This marital share can be unlimited, although it is not wise to leave everything outright to a surviving spouse, as we will review in planning approaches. The third deduction is for assets left to charity. This, like the marital deduction, is unlimited. However, while the marital deduction only postpones the tax until the last spouse dies, the charitable deduction can eliminate the death tax entirely.

Once the three deductions are taken, the result is referred to as "the taxable estate." To this are added all taxable gifts made since January 1, 1977. These are gifts over and above the $10,000 annual gifts (indexed to the cost of living in 1999), plus tuition expenses (if paid to a school) and medical expenses (if paid to the provider or insurance company) that each taxpayer can give to any donee, whether in the family or not. A single taxpayer can give $10,000 in present interest gifts per donee each year that are not considered taxable gifts. A married couple can each give $10,000, or a married individual can give $20,000 and simply have the spouse sign the gift tax return. Any future-interest gifts of any amount are added back in the estate tax return at death. Congress simply wants to know what you have given your beneficiaries during life and what you are leaving them at death other than the excluded gift amount.

The sum of the taxable estate and taxable gifts equals total transfers against which the appropriate tax rate is applied. The tax rate begins at 18% and the maximum is 55%. Each taxpayer has a credit equal to the death tax or gift tax on the amount given in Table 24.1. Once the credit is used, the effective tax rate begins at 37% and grows to 55%.

There is an extra 55% tax for assets left to the grandchildren or someone in that generation or below. This is referred to as the generation-skipping tax. For 2000 the first $1,010,000 left to grandchildren or more remote generation beneficiaries is exempt from estate taxes. This amount rises annually according to the rate of change in the cost-of-living index. It is hard to understand what Congress had against grandchildren.

A simple way to estimate the minimum death tax after the death of the second of a married couple is to (1) add up the fair market value of all assets owned by husband and wife; (2) subtract debts; (3) subtract $2,000,000 from that sum; (4) multiply the result by 0.5 (50% estimated tax). This assumes both spouses fully utilized their credit amounts and that both husband and wife will live at least to 2006, and is somewhat conservative since the maximum rate is 55%.

It is important to understand what happens to remaining balances in qualified and nonqualified retirement plans and deferred compensation programs when the second spouse dies. The assets are first subject to an income tax of up to almost 40%. The remaining funds are then subject to the 55% death tax. There are some offsetting deductions, but the total amount of tax is approximately 77%. This leaves only 23% to children.

Estate Planning Ideas to Reduce Estate, Gift, and Generation-Skipping Taxes

The first approach is to try to secure for the client's family two full credits or tax-free amounts. In the years 2000 and 2001 this would allow a total of $1,350,000 to pass to beneficiaries tax free. There are only two requirements to achieve this. The first requirement is a properly worded estate-planning document, whether it is a will, a revocable trust, or some combination of these. The second requirement is that the first to die have *separate* title to assets with a fair market value equal to the tax-free amount (e.g., $675,000 in 2000). If you cannot predict with certainty which spouse will die first, both should have separate title to assets equal to the tax-free amount. Jointly owned assets are common, but represent the worst form of ownership for estate planning purposes. Assets in qualified or nonqualified retirement accounts or deferred compensation plans should not be considered in these calculations. Life insurance in the spouse's name can also be used to provide these assets.

The tax-free amount is generally "set aside" at the first death. It can be set aside for, or left to, children, if there are enough other assets for the surviving spouse. It can also be set aside to provide living expenses for the surviving spouse, in what is referred to frequently as a family trust or bypass trust. While living, the spouse can receive income and principal as needed to maintain one's standard of living. Upon the spouse's death, the remainder passes on to the designated beneficiaries without incurring estate tax. The spouse can be the sole trustee; however, he or she cannot have a general power of appointment over the principal or corpus, or else the trust will be considered part of the spouse's estate.

QTIP Trust

The estate or death tax can be postponed until the last to die of the husband and wife. This is accomplished by leaving any amount in excess of the tax-free amount that was directed to the family trust or bypass trust to the surviving spouse. Some or all of this can be placed in a *qualified terminable interest property (QTIP) trust*. The QTIP provides income at least annually to the spouse. The spouse can be the sole trustee or can be a cotrustee. The trustee can be authorized to spend the principal to maintain the standard of living or to meet emergency needs for the spouse, but that is not required to qualify this trust for the marital deduction. However, the trustee must not be able to distribute any of the assets to anyone other than the surviving spouse. Upon the death of the spouse, the balance in the QTIP is included in the spouse's estate, and estate or death taxes are levied. However, unlike an outright bequest to a spouse that would be disposed of by the spouse's will, the remainder in the QTIP will be controlled by and disposed of according to the the terms dicated by the first spouse to die as expressed in the QTIP.

Generation-Skipping Trusts

Generation-skipping trusts work great for client's children and client's parents. A couple can designate that, at the last to die of the two of them,

$2,020,000 (to be increased each year according to the rise in the cost of living) will be set aside in trusts for children in such a form that these trusts will not be subject to the 55% death tax at the death of the children. It does not save any estate taxes for the parents, but avoids estate tax on this amount at the death of the children, increasing what goes to grandchildren. Although the amount of the generation-skipping trust is limited at the outset, there is no limit to which it can grow through wise investments.

The trust can be designed in a number of ways. The simplest way is to allow the adult child to manage his or her trust. The child can be given the privilege to choose how the funds will be divided among his or her children upon the adult child's death. The options can be expanded to include the adult child's surviving spouse for life, nieces and nephews, or charities. This can be a very effective way to have intergenerational transfer of wealth without the 55% death tax at each death. If the child becomes tired of having a separate investment account, taxpayer identification number, and tax returns for the trust, it can be shut down. The Internal Revenue Service will then happily sweep all of the trust assets into the child's estate, for taxation at the child's death.

Irrevocable Life Insurance Trust

Life insurance is frequently best owned by an irrevocable trust. An irrevocable trust is one where the donor no longer has any right of ownership to its contents. (Funds in a revocable trust can be reclaimed by the donor.) One or both spouses gift enough money to the trust to purchase the life insurance each year. New life insurance should be applied for, owned by, and payable to the irrevocable trust. Then it will be owned by the trust and not be part of the estate of the insured (under the current law). Thus, this can be an effective way to avoid all death tax on life insurance benefits.

If life insurance already in existence is given to an irrevocable trust, the donor must live for three years. If death occurs within three years, the amount of the life insurance is brought back into the gross estate of the donor.

It is possible to combine life insurance and the irrevocable life insurance trust designed in a generation-skipping form. For example, combining a $1 million life insurance policy in an irrevocable trust with a generation-skipping design may save $16 million in death taxes for great-grandchildren (6% growth in wealth accumulation or dynasty trust—compounded over 60 years). An annual gift tax return is required.

Qualified Personal Residence Trust

A *qualified personal residence trust* (*QPRT*) is an effective way to gift a primary home and/or a vacation home to children. The home is gifted (deeded) to a trust. The donor can be the trustee. The donor retains the right to live in the house for a stated number of years. The longer the term of the right to live in the house, the smaller the calculated value of the gift. Such a trust may reduce the value of gifted properties to 20% or 10% of their market value, and freeze (for tax purposes) the value of the home. The house must be appraised and, to make the transaction simpler, it should be free of a mortgage. For the technique to work, the donor must live at least one day longer than the term of years selected. However, if the donor dies even one day too soon, the transaction reverses itself with no harm done, except the payment of legal fees.

Family Limited Partnership (FLP) or Family Limited Liability Company (FLLC)

The Internal Revenue Service published a ruling in 1993 recognizing discounts for gifts of minority interests in limited partnerships and limited liability companies in family situations. Gifts of interests in either of these types of entities may produce discounts, for tax purposes, of from 30% to 70%. Partnerships, LLPs, and LLCs have been created for active businesses, real estate, stocks and bonds, plus combinations of various assets. Often, in addition to the tax benefits, effective management and possibly asset protection can result.

Annual gifts are the simplest way to transfer wealth to the next generation without paying the 55% death tax. A single donor may give $10,000 per donee per calendar year, and a husband and wife may give $20,000 to each donee without incurring any gift tax. In addition, tuition can be paid as an add-on. Tuition paid directly to the school is not considered a gift, nor are medical expenses or medical insurance paid directly to the provider or the insurance company.

By way of example, gifts can be made in December of one year, January of the next year, and January of the following year. Thus, in 13 months the amount of annual giving basically can be tripled. It is frequently advisable to make gifts in January in case someone does not survive the calendar year.

The lifetime applicable exclusion amount or tax-free amount can be used for gifts. In the year 2000, husband and wife could give $1,350,000 of gifts over and above the nontaxable annual exclusion gifts. At the time of death these gifts would be added back into the calculated estate. However, the value used when adding such taxable gifts back to the estate at death is the fair market value of the gifts *when they were made*. The value of the gifted assets may have grown significantly, but any growth would escape the transfer tax. Thus, it may be advisable to use the lifetime tax-free amount for gift purposes instead of waiting for death.

Gifts of amounts above the annual exclusion, with payment of taxes due, can provide a 60% discount compared to transfer taxes. By way of example, consider a situation where an individual leaves $2,220,000 at death to his daughter. After paying an estate tax of $1,220,000 the net to the daughter would be $1 million. This assumes that the individual has used the lifetime giving amount beforehand. By contrast, suppose the individual gave $1 million during his lifetime to his daughter. The gift tax would be $550,000. The daughter receives $1 million in both cases, but in the first situation the government takes a death tax of $1,220,000, and in the second case the government collects a gift tax of $550,000. There is a tax savings from gifts of $670,000 or approximately 60%.

The law provides that any gift taxes paid within three years of death are pulled back into the estate. Thus, to get the 60% discount, the gift tax would have to be paid more than three years before death.

Grantor Retained Annuity Trust (GRAT) or Grantor Retained Unitrust (GRUT)

A *grantor retained annuity trust* (*GRAT*) or a *grantor retained unitrust* (*GRUT*) may be a tax-effective way to make gifts. Basically, these involve transferring an asset to a trust. The grantor or donor retains an income interest or an annuity for a certain term of years. At the end of the term, the income stream or annuity may go to a surviving spouse for life and then the remainder will go to children. The value of the gift, which is the remainder interest at the end of the term, is valued at the time the trust is established. Thus, it is frozen in value. There is no tax at the time the trust is collapsed.

For the technique to work, the donor or grantor must live at least one day longer than the term selected. If death occurs even one day too soon, the transaction reverses. Once again, if this occurs, the only harm is the wasted legal fees. The technique is best used for stock in an S corporation, for limited partnership interests, or for LLC interests. It is best used with an entity that is taxed only once, unlike a regular or C corporation.

Family-Owned Business

Individuals owning a privately held company or a major position in a public company should consider a sale to an intentionally defective grantor trust if it is felt that the stock will grow in value. Such a trust is ignored for federal income tax purposes, but results in a completed gift.

The grantor would sell a block of stock and receive in return a note, usually a term note. The purchasing trust is a defective grantor trust. The interest the defective grantor trust pays on the note is set at the applicable federal rate and is payable each year. The principal is payable at the end of the term. It is important to have the debt retired before the death of the grantor, so the term of the note should be carefully considered.

The selling shareholder would not owe federal income tax on either the gain on sale or the interest received. Since it is a grantor trust, if the trust sold the stock to a third party, the grantor would owe the income tax on the capital gains, not the trust or its beneficiaries. This can be an additional way to transfer value to children if they are beneficiaries of the trust since they would ultimately receive the corpus (principal) undiminished by income taxes. Grandchildren can be the beneficiaries of this trust as well. It may be possible to establish this trust in one of the states such as Delaware, Alaska, or South Dakota that have repealed their rule against perpetuities and thus allow trusts to remain in existence in perpetuity. This would allow the corpus of the trust, whether an operating business or passive investments, to continue for generations without a 55% death tax hit at the death of each generation.

Anyone with farm or timberland should explore the possibility of qualifying for what is known as the "2032A exclusion." This allows the exclusion of up to $750,000 of the value of qualified real property, or $1,500,000 for a couple. It is an extremely complex provision of the estate tax law. It requires active family participation in management and that such participation be documented. In addition, the family must continue to operate the farm for 10 years after the death of the owner. If the farm is sold within the 10-year period, the additional estate taxes are due.

There is a similar provision, Section 2057, that provides for a deduction of up to $675,000 for qualified family-owned businesses. This is an even more complicated provision than the 2032A exclusion, but should be reviewed for every family-owned business to see if it qualifies for the deduction.

Charitable Bequests

Charitable bequests can eliminate estate taxes altogether. The charitable estate tax deduction is unlimited. If you were considering a bequest to charity, it would be best to leave that amount to your spouse, with language expressing a hope or wish that the charitable gift be made. The surviving spouse would then not be legally bound to make the gift, but implicit would be the feeling that if the surviving spouse did not do so, the deceased spouse would come back and haunt the widow or widower. If the surviving spouse makes the gift during his or her lifetime, he or she will get a charitable *income* tax deduction. Thus the funds pass to the spouse without paying estate taxes because of the marital deduction and the spouse uses them to earn an income tax deduction. In a sense, there are two deductions for the same amount.

A *charitable remainder trust* (*CRT*) may increase cash flow five to eight times. Basically, non-income-producing and/or appreciated assets are transferred to a trust. The CRT can sell the assets without paying any income tax, and invest in income-producing assets. Although the assets are owned by the trust, the donor can continue to receive income from the assets or trust. Generally, the trust remains in existence for a fixed term of up to 20 years, or for the life of the donor and the donor's spouse. Even children can be named as noncharitable beneficiaries where appropriate. At the end of this period the asset goes either to a public charity or to a private charitable foundation established by the donor. The donor-grantor can be the trustee, or a professional trustee can be chosen.

Good assets to choose for a CRT are stock holdings that have a low cost basis and that pay few, if any, dividends, and undeveloped real estate with a low cost basis. The donor will receive an income tax deduction for the full value of the charitable contribution, equal to the calculated value of the remainder interest (at the end of the trust term). Since the assets go to charity at the termination of the trust, the trust is tax-exempt. Thus, the trust can sell the appreciated stock, real estate, or business and purchase income-producing assets without incurring income tax obligations (unlike the donor, who would have had to pay income tax on the capital gains). The assets placed in the CRT will be excluded from the estate of the donor and therefore not be subject to the 55% death tax. Of course, the recipient(s) will have to pay tax on the income received each year from the CRT.

A CRT is a good way to benefit charity without reducing current income, an excellent way to increase cash flow, and a very good way to diversify a portfolio without paying capital gains taxes.

A charitable bank account (either a private, family, or supporting foundation) can be fun for children. The net cost (after income tax and estate tax savings) may be recovered manyfold as the charitable bank account makes charitable gifts for the donor, donor's children, grandchildren, and so on. The foundation can last forever. Most communities have community foundations for those who do not want to incur the legal expense or annual upkeep costs for a private foundation. One current study showed 50,000 private charitable foundations in the country with approximately $200 billion of assets. Unlike supporting foundations for public charities (which have to give substantially all of their net income to the charities they support), private foundations only have to give 5% of their prior year's balance to charity as a minimum. The entire amount, of course, can be given depending on the wishes of the trustees or directors of the charitable foundation.

Qualified and nonqualified retirement plans are perfect assets to leave to charity or a family private charitable foundation. Recall that any assets remaining in these accounts at the time of the death of the second spouse are subject to both income tax and death taxes, leaving the family with only about

23% of the original amount. By leaving the balances to charity, you ensure that your gift is more or less matched with a gift from the government: The full amount goes to charity, with it costing the family 23%, and the Internal Revenue Service 77%. The family charitable foundation can be a great way to bring children together. It works much more effectively than mixing active and inactive children in running family businesses, which typically creates significant problems.

A *charitable lead annuity trust (CLAT)* can be an effective means of transferring significant wealth to grandchildren. This was the type of trust used in Jacqueline Kennedy Onassis's will. Basically, she arranged that the trust would transfer a 10% stream of income (10% of the trust assets at the establishment of the trust) each year, for 20 years, to charity. (Another option would be to make this 8% each year for 25 years.) When the 20 years had passed, any remaining funds would go to the grandchildren. Therefore, if the trust can earn 10% annual returns, the initial amount will still be in the trust at the end of this period. However, under the then IRS valuation tables, the stream of income to charity represented virtually 100% of the assets, and thus provided a very significant charitable deduction offsetting any tax. It would be important to calculate the amount of generation-skipping tax due at the time the trust collapses. Even though there may be generation-skipping taxes, it would be one tax instead of the normal two, and leave a significant amount of wealth for grandchildren.

Protecting Assets from Potential Creditors

A part of estate planning an individual should consider is asset protection. Techniques have been developed to move assets offshore, and hopefully beyond the reach of creditors (Cook Island trusts and trusts in the Isle of Man). In addition, both Delaware and Alaska have changed their trust laws to permit the creation of a trust with the grantor as a permitted beneficiary that will not be subject to claims of creditors. (In the other 48 states, anytime the grantor might benefit from a trust the amount in the trust would be subject to creditors.) These laws have not been tested, however. Asset protection is something to be considered from the standpoint of lawsuits, marriage, problems children might encounter, and so forth.

Other Arrangements for Passing a Business to Heirs

If a person is blessed with a profitable family business or professional practice, a written succession plan is most appropriate. Statistics show that only 30% of family businesses make it through the second generation, and only

13% through the third generation. A combination of the onerous impact of the 55% death tax and mistakes made by new management contribute to these dismal statistics. However, family disputes over ownership and control of the business can be deadly. Proper planning with written instructions and a clear succession plan can avoid many problems. Also, children can be taught how to read financial statements and how to resolve problems by focusing on facts and opportunities and not blaming each other, as siblings may be wont to do. In addition, it may be advisable to recruit some nonfamily members to serve on a board of directors to better guide the family.

Conclusion

If any of these estate-planning ideas are new to the reader, the reader should engage the services of an experienced estate planning attorney. Lawyers specialize much as doctors. In some 40 states, they are not permitted to advertise their specialties. Only 10 states currently permit that, though more are considering changing the rules. Check the web site of the National Association of Estate Planners and Counsel; consult a listing of estate planners in your community; talk to a seasoned trust officer; and, finally, verify by asking the attorney what part of his or her practice is in estate planning. If it is less than 80%, seek help elsewhere, for estate planning is a dynamic and constantly changing area of practice. After all, there have been 16 major tax laws in the past 18 years.

Insurance

Peter Katt

This insurance chapter deals primarily with life insurance with significantly smaller sections on disability income and long-term care insurance. I am avoiding health insurance altogether. At various points I will reference articles I have written that will better explain a particular issue. These referenced articles can be found on my web site (www.peterkatt .com). If you don't have Internet access you can contact me and I will forward them to you. (See my May 2000 *Journal of Financial Planning* column for my dreaming about a rational approach to health insurance and health care.)

Uses of Life Insurance

The life insurance planning process must start with determining whether life insurance is objectively needed. There are four major categories for the use of life insurance: (1) family protection, (2) tax-deferred savings or investing, (3) business planning, and (4) estate planning.

Family Protection

The major reason to have life insurance is to provide protection in the event the primary family income earner has the bad judgment to die. Family protection life insurance is usually associated with the period of time children are being raised, but it could also apply to protecting other family members who are financially dependent regardless of ages. That noted, the remaining comments about family protection life insurance focus on the more typical situation of raising children.

The starting point in family protection life insurance planning is determining how much is needed. There are many different methods for determining how much life insurance should be purchased, and all of them are estimates. The easiest method of estimating how much life insurance is appropriate is to multiply the primary family earner's income by, say, 14. That is, if the primary family income earner earns $100,000, life insurance in the amount of $1.4 million might be appropriate. The method I prefer is a bit more sophisticated.

My preferred method starts by asking how much monthly income is desired to provide for the family in the event the primary family income earner dies. If the desired amount is $7,500 per month (pretax), the annual survivors' income goal is $90,000. From the survivors' income goal subtract income the surviving spouse (if there is one) could earn, but keeping in mind that if a two-parent family is down to one parent it might make sense to provide financing so the survivor can stay at home with the children. For this example, this family decides to provide enough resources so a surviving spouse can stay home with no offset to the $90,000 annual goal.

The next step is to determine the amount of principal needed to provide $90,000 a year without using principal. If a yield of 5.5% is assumed, the principal amount is calculated by dividing 0.055 into $90,000, or $1,636,000 of principal needed. From this principal amount subtract the value of invested assets presently owned, including current life insurance. Let's say there is $150,000 in pension assets, $86,000 of other investments, and $400,000 of life insurance, for a total of $636,000 in assets that are available at present to meet the principal goal. The amount of additional life insurance to satisify this family's survivors' income goal of $90,000 annually is $1 million.

The amount of family protection life insurance will not remain constant. If invested assets increase as the children grow up, the amount needed may decline; therefore, periodic monitoring is a good idea. Finally, always err on the side of having too much life insurance to meet the survivors' income goal. While I have observed instances of community fund-raisers being held after the death of a parent in order to generate money for the surviving family, I have never experienced a surviving family complaining that they received too much life insurance cash.

Once the amount of family protection life insurance is decided, the type of life insurance needs to be considered. (The next section describes types of life insurance.) Let us assume that our primary income earner desiring an additional $1 million life insurance is a 40-year-old nonsmoker in good health. If he or she can qualify for a preferred rating (one step below super-preferred), the annual premium for a 20-year level term policy is approximately $1,200. If the family's cash flow is tight, term insurance is the ideal purchase because there isn't sufficient income to have the benefits of permanent forms of life insurance. However, if the family is able to invest more than they are allowed to in tax-deferred plans such as 401(k)s and IRAs, then purchasing a portion or all of their family protection life insurance for the dual purposes of protection and tax-deferred investing is an astute thing to do.

Tax-Deferred Investing

Permanent life insurance has certain favorable tax considerations. They are: (1) increasing cash values are not subject to income taxes; (2) cash values can be withdrawn tax-free until withdrawals equal a policy's cost basis; (3) policy loans are not taxable; and (4) the death benefits are not considered income or gain. Thirty-, 40-, and 50-something persons purchasing life insurance for family protection who have strong cash flow should consider buying *super-funded* universal life (UL) or variable universal life (VUL) policies as part of their total life insurance and financial planning. Considering life insurance for its tax-deferred saving and investing advantages is not favored by many in the financial planning and investment management areas, but it is my opinion that their disapproval is due to a lack of knowledge and insight into the matter. (See *Journal of Financial Planning* January 1995.)

Super-funded refers to a policy design where the maximum annual premium is paid relative to the minimum initial increasing death benefits in order to emphasize the tax-deferred accumulations of the policy's cash values. That is, the death benefits purchased in a super-funded UL or VUL are objectively needed for family protection and would be paid for in a term insurance policy anyway, so the death benefits of the super-funded policy aren't just extra cost. Over time the super-funded policy's cash values can be withdrawn tax-free as long as they don't exceed the amount paid in premiums.

Withdrawals prior to retirement might be used for educational costs, down payment on a vacation home, or extended travel. And policy cash values can be used on a systematic basis to supplement retirement income. Once cash value withdrawals exceed the amount paid in premiums they are fully taxable.

Or, current law allows insurance companies to effectively offer policy loans having a net zero cost to borrow, and policy loans are not considered taxable. However, caution is warranted when using net-zero-cost loans. Net-zero-cost loans aren't guaranteed. This could be a real problem if after accumulating a large loan balance the company began charging interest. And a policy that inadvertently terminates with large policy loans will cause income to be recognized without the cash to pay the resultant taxes. (See *AAII Journal* November 1995 and July 2000 articles for case studies and more detail of tax-deferred investing using super-funded life insurance.)

Business Planning

There are two primary reasons to use life insurance in the business setting. One is to protect the business in the event a key employee were to die. Two examples will better explain so-called key-man insurance. Joe develops an idea for a business venture and convinces Sam to invest in this venture. Other than as an investor, Sam will have nothing to do with the business. If Joe were to die while getting the business up and running, Sam would be out his investment. Therefore, it would be wise for Sam to purchase term insurance on Joe's life in the amount of the investment. Once their business venture has succeeded, the company's stock is publicly traded, and a full management team is in place, Sam no longer needs key-man insurance on Joe. However, the company now has three regional sales representatives whose presence is absolutely necessary to the company's high level of profits. The company would be wise to insure these sales representatives with key-man insurance.

The other primary reason to use life insurance in the business setting is to provide funding for buy-sell agreements. Buy-sell agreements are very important for the continuance of closely held corporations and partnerships, because there is no market for the sale of a shareholder or partner's business interest. Therefore, how a business interest will be handled in the event of a partner's demise or permanent disability should be planned for in advance within an agreement binding all parties. A buy-sell agreement can be between the business entity and its partners, known as an entity-purchase, or between the partners themselves, known as a cross-purchase. If the buy-sell agreement is an entity-purchase, the life insurance and disability buyout (DBO) insurance are owned by and payable to the business. Upon a partner's death or permanent disability, the business will use the life insurance or DBO insurance proceeds to redeem his or her business interest, thereby increasing the percentages owned by the other partners. If a cross-purchase agreement is used, the partners own life insurance and DBO insurance on each other's lives. Upon a partner's death or permanent disability the other partners use the life insurance proceeds or DBO insurance to buy the deceased or permanently disabled partner's business interest. The price paid for a deceased or permanently disabled partner's business interest increases the surviving partners' cost basis by the amount paid.

If retirement dates are rather firmly established so that partners' interest in the entity have a known ending date, term insurance is appropriate. On the other hand, if partners intend to more or less continue their interest in the entity until death, term insurance should be avoided and whole-life or UL insurance should be used.

Business continuation planning is complicated because there are usually interesting differences encountered from case to case that should be understood and accommodated. (See *AAII Journal* April and August 1997 articles and *Journal of Financial Planning* February 2000 article for more detail and case studies.)

Estate Planning

Although estate planning is most often thought of when an individual or couple's assets are sufficient to be subject to estate taxes, estate planning really refers to the disposition of assets regardless of whether their value will trigger the estate tax. However, for the purposes of this chapter I will associate my remarks about estate planning with life insurance planning that has been coordinated to address the probable payment of estate taxes upon the estate owners' deaths.

The obligation of an estate to pay estate taxes before assets reach heirs is a welcome problem because it means estate owners have created significant wealth during their lifetimes (or at least haven't completely wasted an inheritance). Estate taxes of between 39% and 55% are imposed on estate values above $675,000 (increasing incrementally to $1 million by 2006) for a single taxpayer and $1,350,000 (increasing incrementally to $2 million by 2006) for a couple who have done appropriate estate tax planning. Life insurance is often promoted as a way of paying estate taxes as if every estate was in dire need of liquidity. This mind-set causes many planning professionals to completely miss some rather obvious estate planning distinctions, notably that the kind of estate assets and family relations are far greater determinants for life insurance recommendations than is the one-dimensional question of net worth. You should be alert to this one-insurance-plan-fits-all mentality and insist that distinctions with respect to the kind of assets, the family relations, and the estate owner's specific intentions be made.

It is my experience that there are three very common estate/life insurance planning situations: liquidity, equalization of inheritance for heirs, and wealth transfer—with wealth transfer being by far the most common situation I experience in my practice.

Liquidity refers to providing much-needed cash to an estate that has few readily marketable assets (such as real estate) or for an estate that has assets that need to be retained (such as a family business). The goal of estate liquidity is to provide the maximum death benefits for the least cost. Under this design, if the insured lives too long the economic performance of the life insurance will be very poor, but this can't be avoided because the need for the liquidity is so acute. (See *AAII Journal* November 1999 article for a detailed discussion of how properly to fund such a permanent life insurance policy.)

The need to equalize inheritances generally occurs in two types of situations. One is where a family owns a closely held business in which some children work in the business while other children have chosen separate careers. Closely held businesses usually don't pay dividends, and their equity isn't publicly traded; therefore, children who have an equity interest but do not work in the family business obtain little or no financial benefits unless the business is sold. In contrast, children running the business attain all of their income and perks from the business. This difference is almost certain to cause significant intrafamily conflict and is why it is wise to leave the family business to those children who actually work there while equalizing the inheritance for children who don't work in the family business. If other family assets are not enough to provide this equalization of inheritance and pay estate taxes, life insurance is ideal for making up this deficit. (See *AAII Journal* August 1997 article, the Sam and Pranab case study.)

Another common inheritance equalization situation occurs when the estate owner has been married twice, and there are children from both marriages with a large gap in ages between the first and second set of children. Since it is common when there is another set of children for the second wife to be considerably younger, it is very poor planning to have the older children wait around for an inheritance until the younger second wife dies (she may live until the older children are in their 60s or 70s). This can be avoided by having life insurance for the exclusive benefit of the older children.

For example, Don is 55 with two children ages 22 and 20 from his first marriage and two children ages 4 and 2 from his second marriage to a woman 38. Don, a physician, has a current net worth of $2.5 million. Don decides to provide an inheritance for his two children from the first marriage at his death regardless of whether his second wife survives him. He does this by acquiring a new life insurance policy for, say, $500,000 that is owned by and payable to an irrevocable trust with his two older children as the primary beneficiaries. He also provides that upon his second wife's death their estate will be divided among all four of his children, with the present value of the life insurance proceeds received upon his death subtracted from the older children's shares. That is, if the second wife lives 25 years longer than Don, at 6% the present value of the initial inheritances of $250,000 (each) for the two older children have a present value of slightly more than $1 million each. If the net estate value (after taxes) is $10 million upon the second wife's death, the two younger children receive $3 million each and the two older children receive $2 million because they must count the present value of the life insurance proceeds received upon their father's death 25 years earlier.

The other common use of life insurance associated with estate planning is to fund a wealth-transfer strategy. Wealth transfer is an estate planning strategy used when the majority of estate assets are marketable securities. The goal is to moderate an estate's future maximum growth by making gifts. That is, estate owners with assets of, say, $10 million who have the income and resources to continue saving and investing may come to the conclusion that dying with an estate value of, say, $30 million isn't desirable and so, among other estate-moderation strategies, they begin making cash gifts. Such gifts can be given directly to children for their immediate use and enjoyment or they can be made to an irrevocable trust to be invested and accumulated for distribution to children at the second parent's death, or a combination of these two can be done. Cash gifts to an irrevocable trust can qualify for the annual gift tax exclusion, they can be part of the estate tax credits, or they can be taxable gifts.

Life insurance is the ideal wealth-transfer asset because the proceeds are entirely income tax free and also avoid capital gains taxes. Further, when the life insurance purchase features minimum initial death benefits that are projected to increase during the insureds' lifetimes, the long-term rate of return (premiums to death benefits) will mirror the underlying investments rather than dramatically dropping in the long term, which is the fate of a maximum level death benefit design. By its nature wealth-transfer life insurance designs sacrifice larger benefits in the short and medium term in order to maximize the benefits for the long term. Wealth-transfer life insurance can be whole or universal life whose investment component is primarily fixed-income instruments, or variable life can be used so the policy owner can make asset allocation decisions from the subaccount funds, including equities. (See August 1996 and July 2000 *AAII Journal* articles about wealth-transfer life insurance.)

Congress passed a phased-out repeal of estate taxes, but this legislation was vetoed. This issue continues to be in play politically and has generated optimism that an end to estate taxes is in sight. If estate taxes were ended, this would affect the estate planning life insurance, but in ways that may not be obvious to civilians, and life insurance should not be reflexively terminated while estate owners are still under the influence of adult celebratory beverages. (See April 2000 *AAII Journal* article.)

Types of Life Insurance

Term Insurance

Term insurance provides a death benefit and nothing more. Almost all of its premium is the cost-of-insurance (COI) that is based on the chances an insured has of dying during that year. As an insured gets older the chances of dying increase; therefore, the premium increases. Some term insurance policies allow an insured to continue the policy to age 100, but an insurance company encouraging a potential insured to think he or she will keep a term policy until age 100 is being disingenuous, because the cost would be prohibitive. For example, the cumulative premiums for a $1 million term policy from age 85 to age 100 are over $3 million. Term insurance is *if-I-die* coverage and is usually used for definable periods of time. It is ideal for family protection coverage because the need for large amounts of term coverage will usually continue until children are raised or the insured has accumulated assets that offset the need for life insurance.

Five, 10-, 15-, 20-, and even 30-year level term policies are now the most common term purchases. The *level* designation means the cost remains constant for the period of time specified. Many level term policies' premiums have been guaranteed for the period of time specified. These guaranteed term prices have been in free fall for about a decade due to competition brought on by heavy advertising that has essentially turned level term insurance into a commodity. Level term prices had become so low that the National Association of Insurance Commissioners (NAIC) promulgated model regulations, which came to be known as Triple X, because of concern that insurance companies were not properly reserving for their guaranteed level term liabilities. The NAIC hopes that Triple X will cause either long-term level guaranteed premiums to increase or the guarantee period to be reduced to no more than five years. That is, 20-year level term policies will still be available with a specified premium, but the premium will be guaranteed for only five years, after which it could change if the insurance company's actual investment and mortality experience could not support the estimated original premiums. Or, 20-year level term premiums can be guaranteed for the full 20 years but at a higher cost than was available before Triple X. My view is that Triple X is a good thing because it may prevent insurance companies from committing financial suicide that might have resulted if they had continued to drop guaranteed prices to maintain or increase market share from competitors. However, until we see how Triple X affects the design of all level term policies it won't be certain if the regulations are actually doing what is intended; a clever interpretation of Triple X by only several companies that results in very low premiums continuing to be guaranteed for 10, 20, and 30 years will cause many companies to stampede back into very low guaranteed level premiums and cause the regulators to go back to the drawing board.

Many level term policies can be renewed at competitive rates after the specified period of time is over, usually to a maximum age of 70, but proof of continued good health is required. If an insured cannot prove he or she is still in good health, the term rates become very high. Renewal premiums won't be known in advance because companies change them at their discretion. Many policies can be converted, without proof of continued good health, to permanent (whole, universal, and/or variable life) policies the company so designates.

Even with Triple X's effects on level term pricing, term costs are dramatically lower than they were 10 years ago. Besides improvements in overall mortality, these very low term costs are achieved by separating potential insureds into three categories: super-preferred, preferred, and standard (all requiring no tobacco use). Generally, a super-preferred rating is earned by having good to excellent height/weight ratio, blood values, health history, personal habits, and family health history. The lesser preferred rating is earned when one or two of the areas needed for super-preferred are a little bit weaker. A standard rating is given to insureds who have greater weaknesses in any of the important underwriting areas.

Also available are annual renewal term (ART) policies, whose costs go up incrementally each year. ART is appropriate when the coverage is needed for less than five years, and the ART costs are less than five-year level term costs. For example, a creditor may require insurance to protect a loan or line of credit for a short period of time.

Finding a source for low-cost term is as easy as searching the words "term insurance" on the Internet. Two of the more popular sites are SelectQuote.com and Quotesmith.com. You can buy term insurance from these sites. Or if you want information from a source that doesn't actually sell insurance you can contact Insurance Information at 800-472-5800. Insurance Information, for a fee of $50, will send you the names of the insurance companies with the best rates for any individual case.

Permanent Insurance

Permanent insurance has much higher initial premiums than term insurance. These initially higher premiums generate the policy's cash values. Permanent life insurance has two major pricing components: mortality costs that go up each year, and an investment component.

Permanent or cash-value life insurance is variously known as participating whole-life (WL [par]), interest-sensitive whole-life (WL [int-sen]), universal life (UL), and variable universal life (VUL). WL (par), WL (int-sen) and UL policies' primary investment component is bonds held for yield. Therefore their investment performance will track with interest rates and be quite predictable. VUL policies allow policy owners to select from various subaccount funds, including equities. As such, VUL's investment performance will track with the investment categories selected for the cash values. When cash values are invested in equity funds, performance will be unpredictable and volatile. To follow is a brief explanation of each type of permanent insurance.

WL (par) has fixed premiums and guaranteed cash values and death benefits. The pricing components are set very conservatively so that the fixed premiums are very high. To make WL (par) policies competitive they receive nonguaranteed dividend distributions whenever the actual mortality, investment, and expense results are better than have been guaranteed. WL (par) policies have consistently paid dividends that enhance the policy either by adding additional benefits while continuing to pay the fixed premiums or by reducing fixed premiums while the policy values remain constant. Since the amount of dividends isn't known in advance, the amount of increase in policy values above the guarantees is not predictable, nor is the amount of reductions in the fixed premiums. Since the 1980s WL (par) has added a dizzying array of premium payment options in order to be as flexible as universal life. WL (par) policies sold by Northwestern Mutual, Guardian, and MassMutual have significantly outperformed WL (int-sen) and UL.

WL (int-sen) is similar to WL (par) in that it has fixed premiums, guaranteed cash values, and death benefits, but unlike WL (par) whose fixed premiums, cash values, and death benefits are based on very conservative pricing assumptions that are adjusted to current conditions by the distributions of dividends, WL (int-sen) fixed premiums, cash values, and death benefits are based on current pricing assumptions that are periodically changed as pricing conditions change. For example, if interest rates decline after an interest-sensitive whole-life policy has been purchased, the policy owner will be given a choice of either an increase in premiums in order to continue with the original cash values and death benefits, or a reduction in death benefits in order to keep the premium the same.

Although WL (int-sen) could be worthy of consideration for certain situations, I won't bother to cover them because I don't know of a company whose WL (int-sen) policy I would recommend.

Universal life insurance has been referred to as *unbundled* permanent insurance because cost-of-insurance (COI) and interest crediting are distinct and published pricing factors. UL has considerable premium flexibility because as long as there are enough policy cash values to cover COI charges the policy will continue without the necessity of paying a premium and without a policy loan being created. Another difference is the ability to change death benefit amounts, either up (subject to underwriting) or down. UL's flexibility is a two-edged sword. In the hands of an insurance professional this flexibility can be a significant benefit. However, UL's flexibility is also the cause of significant problems when UL policies are not monitored and managed. Unattended, UL policies can become substantially underfunded due to declining interest rates, or overfunded in an increasing interest rate environment.

I recommend UL when policy flexibility is important. The two companies with excellent actual performance during the previous years are: Ameritas Life Insurance Corporation (800-552-3553) and USAA Life Insurance Company (800-531-8000).

WL and UL policies' premiums flow into an insurance company's general account. The policy owner has no say as to how the general account assets are invested. Typically, life insurance company general accounts are invested primarily in bonds held for yield. Therefore, the investment component of WL and UL will track with interest rates, subject to a minimum guarantee. Variable universal life, on the other hand, directly involves the policy owner in policy investment decisions because each VUL policy has around 10 subaccount funds from which a policy owner can choose for the investment of his or her policy's cash values. The range of available mutual funds runs from aggressive stock portfolios to a fixed-income account. Investing policy cash values in equity or equity combination funds necessarily will cause investment results to be volatile, unlike the far more predictable results with WL and UL. And unlike WL and UL that have guaranteed yields, VUL policies invested in funds other than the fixed-income account have no yield guarantees and can suffer year-to-year losses.

Unfortunately, the reality that VUL will produce volatile results is completely hidden from advisers and consumers because life insurance companies are required to show sales illustrations with a constant investment yield. Showing a constant investment return, even if it is very low, completely misses the point in considering VUL. VUL policies that are designed to have level-to-maturity death benefits will alternately become underfunded and overfunded with policy termination a real possibility due to volatile and unpredictable equity returns. Indeed, I offer VUL as an option in only two types of life insurance designs. One is deferred savings combined with family protection planning. The other is wealth transfer associated with estate planning. That is, I recommend VUL only in situations where the premium commitment is large relative to the initial death benefits so that the inherent investment volatility is very unlikely to cause the policy to terminate because of negative investment results. (See *AAII Journal* July 1999 and July 2000 articles.)

The VUL policies I recommend are: Northwestern Mutual (that can be purchased from a local Northwestern Mutual agent); Ameritas that can be purchased directly (800-552-3553); and USAA (800-531-8000).

Second-to-Die Insurance

In contrast to life insurance policies insuring one life, second-to-die (STD) life insurance insures two lives and pays its benefits at the second death. There are three common uses of STD life insurance. The first common use is for estate liquidity. Under current estate tax laws, estate assets can be arranged so that no estate taxes are due until the second spouse's death. Therefore, life insurance proceeds being used to provide cash for the payment of estate taxes aren't needed until the second death, making STD an ideal choice because the benefits appear when needed, and STD premium costs are lower on an annual basis than single-life premiums. (However, a lower annual premium shouldn't be understood to mean that STD is cheaper or a better value than single-life insurance. STD insures a different risk—two lives rather than one. The lower annual cost of STD should be understood in the same way as the annual cost for a 30-year mortgage is lower than for a 15-year mortgage. This doesn't mean that a 30-year mortgage is a better value.)

A second common use of STD is for wealth-transfer estate planning. Recall that wealth transfer is a policy design featuring the maximum premiums to the minimum initial death benefits. The wealth-transfer design sacrifices better values in the short and medium term for much better benefits long-term. Since STD doesn't pay its benefits until the second death, the longer the insurance is in force under the wealth-transfer design the better. (See *AAII Journal* July 2000 article.)

The third potential use for STD life insurance is in families with children where there are two principal income earners whose individual incomes are large enough to provide the family with financial security even if one spouse were to die. That is, STD life insurance is family protection coverage for the contingency that both income-earning spouses die. While the use of STD life insurance in the two-earner family is logical, I hardly ever see it purchased in such situations because although the loss of one income would not create financial problems for the family it would reduce family expectations. Therefore, coverage on both spouses is almost always used.

Permanent STD life insurance can be WL, UL, or VUL. The WL STD policies I recommend are the same as recommended for single-life permanent policies—Northwestern Mutual, Guardian, and MassMutual. The UL STD policy I recommend is Ameritas (800-552-3553). The VUL STD policies I recommend are Northwestern Mutual and Ameritas.

Managing Existing Life Insurance Policies

Life insurance policies should not be folded up and put in a drawer and forgotten. They need to be periodically monitored and managed. The first issue that should be addressed is whether the reason for the life insurance coverage is still relevant. For example, if the life insurance was purchased to protect a growing family and now the children are financially independent, is the coverage still needed in its present form? That is, should it be simply terminated or should it be restructured? Or, if the coverage was purchased to cover estate taxes because estate assets were very difficult to market, but have since been sold with the proceeds now invested in marketable securities, should the insurance coverage be terminated or restructured to provide wealth transfer?

If the coverage is still needed, other issues that need attention are: What is the insurance company's financial strength? Is the policy's pricing competitive? Is the policy properly funded? With respect to financial strength you can contact the insurance company and ask to be sent its financial strength ratings from A. M. Best, Standard & Poor's, Moody's, Duff & Phelps, and Weiss. Sometimes an insurance company's financial strength ratings can tip you off to trouble, but not always.

Checking pricing competitiveness is relatively simple for term insurance. Compare a policy's premiums with premium costs obtained from Insurance Information (800-472-5800). Just be sure that the comparison uses the same rating category, like super-preferred, preferred, and standard.

Comparing a permanent policy's pricing is much more difficult and can lead to false information. Perhaps the best way to check pricing is to obtain what I refer to as an in-force illustration for the existing policy. The in-force illustration will project the policy's future cash values and death benefits based on a specified premium amount for 20 or more years into the future using the company's current pricing factors. With this in-force illustration you can contact Ameritas and ask the company to prepare a sales illustration as a replacement policy for comparative purposes. To do this, fax Ameritas the in-force illustration you received for the existing policy. If the Ameritas replacement policy illustration shows considerably better projected values, say better by more than 15%, then a replacement might be considered. Alternatively, contact a local Northwestern

Mutual agent and ask the agent to make this comparison. I recommend Ameritas and Northwestern Mutual for this comparison because both companies' pricing has been fair and legitimate. I can't say this of all companies.

Please note that if a policy replacement occurs, a death claim within two years would be investigated for material misrepresentations and denied if death were due to suicide. Put another way, if an insured does not intend to falsify the application or to commit suicide, a replacement will pose no problem.

After being satisfied that policy pricing is okay, on a regular basis check the policy's funding. Contact the company, asking for various in-force illustrations to be run that confirm that the current premiums are sufficient to properly fund the policy, or show new levels of premium that may be needed.

Finally, there are numerous policy management issues that need attention that can't be covered in this work, except for noting one very common policy mismanagement problem—the continuance of policy loans. Either the loan should be paid back, or ask the company how the policy can be restructured to eliminate the loan.

Managing existing life insurance is complicated, and I debated whether even to include it in this chapter. For a broader insight into policy management issues, please refer to the following articles on my web site:

- November 1999 *AAII Journal*

- April 1999 *Journal of Financial Planning*

- August 1998 *AAII Journal*

- February 1998 *AAII Journal*

- October 1996 *Journal of Financial Planning*

Disability Income Insurance

Disability income (DI) insurance benefits replace occupational income lost as the result of a disabling accident or sickness. The object of DI insurance is to give the disabled insured an income stream to replace wages lost due to the disability. Anyone who can't replace occupational income from invested assets in the event of disability should investigate DI insurance options. There are group and individual DI insurance policies. Group DI insurance is coverage associated with employment or professional associations and unions. Group DI insurance can be short-term, usually lasting less than one year, or long-term, lasting from two years to lifetime benefits. Individual DI insurance usually has broader benefits and long-term coverage. Those jobs most likely to cause a disability (e.g., construction, farming, factory work) are the least likely to have long-term group benefits or any individual DI insurance available to them. Long-term group and individual DI insurance is mostly reserved for white-collar jobs and especially for professionals with high incomes.

With respect to group DI insurance, some companies provide group long-term DI insurance to middle and upper management personnel as a no-cost benefit. Other companies and some professional associations offer group DI insurance as a voluntary purchase that is paid for by the insured, usually requiring proof of good health. Obviously, if an employer is providing group DI insurance at no cost, the starting point is to investigate individual DI insurance options that might enhance the group benefits since there is no question the group coverage will be continued. However, if the group coverage is optional, it should be compared with individual coverage. Usually group coverage is less expensive per unit of benefit, while the individual coverage is better.

To follow is a brief explanation of the major long-term DI policy characteristics and options that should be understood:

- *Benefit period.* This is the time duration the insurance company must pay disability benefits, ranging from two years to lifetime benefits.

- *Waiting period.* This is the time between when the disability begins and first benefit payment, ranging from 30 days to two years. The waiting period can coordinate with the length of time an insured can comfortably self-insure, with a 90-day waiting period usually being the most cost-effective.

- *Benefit integration.* Many group and some individual DI policies reduce benefits if other disability benefits, like Social Security, are being received.

- *Residual benefit.* This pays a partial benefit based on a percentage of income lost due to the disability. I believe this is very important because it encourages insureds to return to interesting work without the loss of proportionate benefits.

- *Own occupation.* A total benefit is paid even if the insured is working in another occupation. My opinion is that this is an expensive policy characteristic or option that probably isn't needed if the policy has a good residual benefit that doesn't force an insured into another occupation, but provides financial incentives if the insured does decide to take a job compatible with one's abilities while disabled. However, many buyers of DI insurance consider this the most important aspect of DI insurance.

- *Noncancellable premium.* This really means the premium is guaranteed.

Throughout the 1980s and early 1990s, competition in the professional market caused some companies to offer extravagant benefits at modest guaranteed costs. Since the early 1990s there has been a significant retrenchment in benefits and options, especially for DI policies sold in states with year-round entertainment, like California and Florida. Therefore, existing DI policies should be retained, not replaced, if they have have better benefits and costs. For a more complete discussion of DI insurance, please see my November 1992 *AAII Journal* and June 1997 *Journal of Financial Planning* columns. Note that because of certain events that occurred from 1992 to 1997 my 1992 recommendation to purchase DI policies from UNUM and Paul Revere (no longer a separate company) has changed as explained in my 1997 article. For professionals seeking individual DI insurance I recommend Northwestern Mutual, MassMutual, and Guardian.

Long-Term Care Insurance

Long-term care (LTC) insurance is a relatively new risk management concept, at least on a broad marketing scale. Typically LTC insurance will cover some or all of the costs associated with nursing home care, home care, or adult day care. Generally LTC insurance benefits are triggered when an insured is no longer able to perform two or three common activities of daily living (ADL—i.e., dressing, eating, bathing, toileting, mobility, and taking medicine) or has a cognitive impairment or a medical necessity. The amount of benefit, the length of time it is paid, inflation protection, and the waiting period before benefits commence after a triggering event are variables that each insured selects for oneself.

Long-term care refers to custodial care due to chronic infirmities and should not be confused with full-time or intermittent skilled nursing care associated with acute medical episodes. Skilled nursing care, whether in a facility or at home, is covered in part by Medicare. Medicare supplement (Medigap) insurance covers some of the gaps in Medicare coverage, but neither covers LTC costs. Some studies indicate that many Americans are confused about this issue, believing that Medicare will pay some long-term care costs. It doesn't. Medicaid, on the other hand, may pay for some or most long-term care costs if the claimant's income and assets place him or her at or near the poverty level.

I believe potential LTC needs ideally should be evaluated around age 50, a time when it is likely that retirement resources can be reasonably estimated. If a preretiree is particularly vulnerable to the financial consequences of LTC (either afraid of running out of money or reluctant to spend too much of heirs' inheritances) an LTC policy should be purchased. However, if retirement assets are so substantial that there will be no problem paying LTC costs and providing the level of inheritance desired, LTC insurance should be avoided.

To follow is a brief explanation of the major LTC policy characteristics and options:

- *Benefit amount.* The usual range is between $100 and $300 per day ($3,000 to $9,000 per month). The benefit amount should be directly related to the cost for nursing home care in the area of retirement.

- *Waiting period.* The usual range is zero days to one year.

- *Benefit period.* The range is one year to lifetime. The longer the benefit period, the higher the cost.

- *Inflation protection.* The usual inflation factor is 5%. Some policies figure this as simple interest, and others figure it as compound interest. The inflation protector increases the benefit from the first day of the policy, not from the first day that benefits are received.

LTC insurance premiums are not guaranteed, and can be raised (or lowered) on a company-wide basis. For many companies it is my suspicion that LTC buyers will see significant increases in their premiums because of competition to sell policies based on price and the fact that there is so little actuarial experience to set pricing rationally. LTC insurance should be purchased based on the quality of the company, not who has the lowest current premiums. At present, the only company I recommend for LTC insurance is Northwestern Mutual. (See my December 1998 *Journal of Financial Planning* and November 1997 *AAII Journal* columns for more LTC details.)

Glossary

abnormal returns the component of the return that is not due to systematic influences (movement of the overall market).

accrued interest interest earned but not yet paid to the investor.

agency security security issued by corporations or agencies created by the U.S. government, such as the Federal Home Loan Mortgage Corporation (Freddie Mac), Federal National Mortgage Association (Fannie Mae), or Government National Mortgage Association (Ginnie Mae).

aggressive growth funds mutual funds that seek maximum capital gains, often by investing in shares of companies with earnings and profits that grow at a rapid rate. Higher than average risk.

alpha a statistical measure of a security's price volatility caused by factors other than the stock market as a whole; often used to measure the value added by a money manager's security selection skill.

American depositary receipt (ADR) a security issued by a U.S. bank representing foreign shares held in trust by that bank; used to facilitate the purchase and sale of foreign shares by U.S. investors.

amortization the liquidation of an obligation through regular payments, which include both interest and principal reductions. Amortization comes from the Latin *ad mort*, which means "to death." Thus the obligation is "killed" as it is paid off.

annuitant an investor who is receiving annuity payments.

annuity   a series of equal payments made at fixed times.

arbitrage   an investment technique employed to take advantage of differences in price for the same security on different exchanges. For example, if XYZ stock is selling for $50 a share on the New York Stock Exchange and for $49 a share on the London exchange, an arbitrageur could buy XYZ in London and sell it in New York and make a riskless profit of $1 per share, less expenses.

ask (ask price)   the lowest price an investor will accept to sell a stock. In effect, it is the quoted price at which an investor can buy shares of stock.

asset allocation   dividing your investment portfolio among the many types of investment alternatives (asset classes). Major asset classes include stocks, bonds, and cash.

balanced mutual fund   a mutual fund that invests in a mixture of asset types, mainly stocks and bonds.

balloon payment   the common name for a loan in which the full amount of principal and interest due must be paid in a lump sum at the end of the term of the loan.

basis point   one-hundredth of 1% (50 basis points = one-half of 1%).

bear market   an extended decline in stock prices.

benchmark   the performance of a predetermined set of securities, used for comparison purposes. Such sets are typically based on published indexes, but can be customized to suit an investment strategy.

beta   a measure of the volatility of the price of a stock or mutual fund relative to the overall volatility of the market. A beta of 1.0 indicates that the stock's volatility is equal to that of the market.

bid   the price at which a buyer is willing to purchase a security.

blue-chip stock   stock of a large company with a sound financial history, good management, and steady growth prospects.

bond   a security representing debt owed to investors, which pays a stated rate of interest and returns the face value to the investor on the maturity date.

book value   the net liquidation value of a corporation on a per-share basis.

broker   an investment broker is a person who represents a firm that is a member of an exchange and can handle orders to buy and sell securities.

bull market   an extended rise in stock prices.

business cycle   the recurring periods of growth and decline in economic activity.

call   in banking, a demand for immediate payment of a loan.

call option   a type of option that entitles the owner to purchase a specified amount of shares of a stock on or before a specified date. Calls are purchased if the investor expects the stock to rise in price.

callable bond   bond that is redeemable by the issuer prior to the maturity date at a specified price.

capital   the amount of money invested in a business.

capital asset pricing model (CAPM)   an economic theory that describes the relationship between risk and expected return and serves as a model for the pricing of risky securities. According to the CAPM, the expected return of a security is equal to the return of a risk-free security plus a risk premium.

capital gains   the profits from the sale of investment assets.

capital stock   the permanent investments made in a corporation by its owners, either at the formation of the company or subsequently.

capitalization   the total value of securities issued by a corporation; includes common stock, preferred stock, bonds, and debentures.

cash flow   the difference between cash received and cash disbursed.

cash-management account (CMA)   a multiservice account offered by many brokerage houses and banks under which a customer can have a checking account, an investment account, a credit card, and a personal line of credit.

cash-surrender value   the amount a policyholder receives if he or she cashes in a cash-value life insurance policy.

certificate of deposit (CD)   short-term investment issued by banks. Pays fixed principal and interest over a specified period of time. Insured by the FDIC for up to $100,000. CDs are subject to early withdrawal penalties.

charitable lead trust   a trust that allows a charity to receive income during the grantor's life, and the remaining income passes to designated family members upon the grantor's death. The gift to the trust must be irrevocable.

charitable remainder trust   a trust that pays income to a designated person or persons until the grantor's death, when the income is passed on to a designated charity. The gift to the trust must be irrevocable.

churning the illegal and unfortunately frequent broker practice of recommending buying and selling of securities in order to earn extra commissions.

closed-end fund a type of mutual fund in which there are a fixed number of shares, and funds are invested for a fixed time period. After the initial offering existing shares can be bought only from existing shareholders.

collateralized mortgage obligation (CMO) a fixed-income security backed by a pool of pass-through mortgages, structured so that there are several classes of investors with varying maturities, called tranches.

commercial paper debt instruments issued by well-established companies to meet short-term financing needs. The instruments are not secured and have a maximum maturity of 270 days.

commission the fee paid to an agent or broker.

commodities products of trade, such as sugar, pork bellies, soybeans, coffee, gold, and silver.

common stock securities that represent ownership in a company; also called equity. An investor is entitled to a share of the company's profits and can vote on such matters as the election of directors.

compound interest interest earned on interest.

convertible a security that can be exchanged for another (e.g., a convertible bond may be exchanged for stock).

coupon the part of a bearer bond that indicates the amount of interest due, and where and when payments will be made. Bearer coupons are presented to the issuer's designated paying agent for collection. With registered bonds, physical coupons do not exist, and payments are mailed directly to the registered holder.

coupon rate the interest payment as a percentage of the initial bond value.

current asset an asset that is expected to be converted to cash within a year.

current yield the annual income from an investment, expressed as a percentage of the market price of the bond.

day order an order given to a broker to buy or sell stock that expires at the end of the business day, if the transaction has not been made.

debenture an unsecured long-term debt obligation; usually a corporate bond for which no specific collateral is pledged.

deferred annuity an annuity that does not begin until after a certain period, or until the annuitant reaches a certain age.

deflation a decrease in the cost of living, which increases the purchasing power of the dollar.

demand deposit funds on deposit that the owner may withdraw on demand, without prior notification.

depreciation the loss in value of property over time.

derivative security a financial security, such as an option or future, whose value is derived in part from the value and characteristics of another security.

discount rate the interest, expressed as a percentage, charged by the Federal Reserve, for loans made to its member banks.

discounted cash flow future cash flows reduced by an estimated inflation rate to obtain their present value.

discretionary trust a trust that gives the administrator the right to decide how much of the funds to disburse to the beneficiary and when.

diversification spreading investments among different types of investment holdings to reduce the risk of loss.

dividends a portion of earnings paid to stockholders.

dollar cost averaging an investment technique of buying shares of a security at fixed intervals with fixed dollar amounts.

Dow Jones averages indexes created by the Dow Jones Corporation to track the performance of the stock market. The Dow Jones Industrial Average (DJIA) is based on the stock prices of 30 of the largest companies; the utilities average is based on 15 public utility stocks; the transportation average is based on 20 companies in the transportation industry.

duration the weighted maturity of a fixed-income investment's cash flows, used in the estimation of the price sensitivity of fixed-income securities to changes in interest rates.

dynamic asset allocation a strategy of changing asset allocation in response to changing market conditions and anticipated market performance.

earnings per share the total amount of a corporation's earnings (minus preferred dividends) divided by the number of outstanding shares of company stock.

earnings yield the ratio of earnings to stock price (E/P). The reciprocal of the price-earnings ratio.

equity (1) a common stock; (2) the difference between the value of a property and any liability or outstanding debt.

equity fund a mutual fund that invests in common stocks.

equity investment the purchase of a portion of the ownership of a corporation through buying shares (e.g., common stocks).

escrow a written agreement setting aside funds to be held by a second party to eventually benefit a third party. The most common use is an account maintained by a mortgage lender to accumulate funds to pay property taxes and homeowners insurance.

estate all property owned by a person at the time of his or her death.

ex-coupon bond a bond sold with the coupon for the interest currently due removed, and its value deducted from the price of the bond.

executor a person named in a will to administer the estate after the maker of the will has died.

expense ratio a mutual fund's expense ratio is the percentage of assets used to pay certain costs, including administrative fees, fees paid to investment advisers, and operating costs. It does not include transaction costs.

face value same as par value, the principal amount of a bond or note (appears on the "face" of the bond).

Fannie Mae (Federal National Mortgage Association) a private corporation, chartered by the federal government to help mortgage lenders obtain funds for home purchasers. The FNMA purchases mortgages from the lenders and resells them as debentures.

Federal Deposit Insurance Corporation (FDIC) a government-sponsored agency that insures deposits in affiliated institutions (e.g., national and state banks) up to $100,000.

federal funds rate interest rate at which banks that are members of the Federal Reserve may borrow from the excess reserves of other member banks. The rate charged for these loans is used as an early indicator of inflationary trends.

Federal Reserve banks the operating arms of the Federal Reserve Board, whose main function is to control the nation's money supply. They issue currency and control the discount rate, the interest rate that banks must pay to borrow from the Federal Reserve.

Federal Savings and Loan Insurance Corporation (FSLIC) an agency of the Federal Home Loan Bank that insures all accounts maintained in insured savings institutions up to the limit mandated by federal law.

fiscal year   a company's accounting year, which may be different from the calendar year.

Freddie Mac (Federal Home Loan Mortgage Corporation)   a government agency designed to help members of the Federal Home Loan Bank obtain funds for mortgage loans. The FHLMC purchases mortgages from the lenders and resells them as bonds.

fundamental analysis   the use of fundamental financial factors, such as company earnings, growth, sales, hard assets, and expenses to determine a company's value.

future value   the amount that a sum of money today will be worth on a specific future date.

futures exchange   a place where commodity futures are traded.

general-obligation debentures   bonds that are not secured by specific property, but only by the overall financial condition of the issuer.

Ginnie Mae (Government National Mortgage Association)   an agency in the U.S. Department of Housing and Urban Development that buys mortgages insured by the Federal Housing Administration and the Veterans Administration from banks and lenders, and resells them as bonds. The bonds are pass-through certificates; interest is paid to the bondholders monthly as income is received.

growth fund   a mutual fund that invests primarily in companies whose stock is expected to rise in price.

growth stock   stock that is expected to rise in price due to growth in company earnings.

hedge   to offset the risk of one investment by making another investment. An example would be to use put options as a hedge against a stock declining dramatically in price.

hedge fund   a type of mutual fund run like a limited partnership (i.e., with a limited number of shareholders and reduced liquidity). The fund may employ a variety of techniques to enhance returns such as using derivatives, and both buying and shorting stocks.

hidden assets   things of value owned by a company, but not identified on its balance sheet.

holding company   a company that owns the stock of another company.

horizon analysis   analysis of total return over some specific investment period (horizon).

illiquid asset   a fixed asset; one that cannot readily be converted into cash.

income fund   a mutual fund whose holdings are selected in order to provide current income rather than price appreciation.

income stock   a stock that pays regular and relatively high dividends.

index   statistical composite that measures changes in the economy or in financial markets. Certain indexes measure the ups and downs of stock, bond, and commodity markets. The constituents that make up an index and the weighting (e.g., equal or according to size) vary.

index fund   a mutual fund that aims to approximate the return of a particular index of stocks or bonds.

individual retirement account (IRA)   a type of account, authorized by Congress, in which individuals are allowed to deposit and accumulate funds on a tax-deferred basis for retirement.

inflation   an increase in the cost of living over time; a decrease in the buying power of a dollar.

initial public offering (IPO)   the first sale of company stock to the public, most commonly by small companies seeking outside capital for development. Investors must be prepared to accept large risks for the possibility of large gains.

installment loan   a loan on which both interest and principal are repaid in regular, equal installments.

interest   the price paid to the lender for use of the borrowed money, expressed as a percentage of the sum borrowed per time period (e.g., 6% per annum).

interest rate risk   the risk that a security's value will decline due to a change in interest rates. For example, a bond's price drops as interest rates rise.

international fund   a mutual fund that can invest only outside the United States.

inverted yield curve   short-term interest rates are higher than long-term rates.

investment grade bond   a bond that is assigned a rating in one of the top categories by commercial credit rating companies.

investment manager   the person who manages a portfolio of investments for an individual or a mutual fund company; also called a money manager.

junk bond   a bond rated below investment grade. They are usually rated BB and lower, and have a higher default risk than investment grade bonds. The interest paid is greater because of the increased risk.

Keogh plan   a tax-deferred retirement plan for the self-employed.

ladder of bonds   a portfolio of bonds of every maturity within a given range. Typically equal amounts are invested or the values at maturity are equal.

level premium term insurance   a life insurance policy with a fixed face value and fixed premiums each year for a defined number of years.

leverage   the use of credit to increase potential profits; also increases potential loss. For example, money is borrowed to purchase additional shares of a stock, with the expectation that the stock price will rise more than the cost of the loan.

liability   money owed, such as a loan, unpaid bills, interest due, and other financial obligations.

lien   a claim on property against an outstanding debt.

life annuity   an annuity that provides an income for life and then ceases.

limited partner   a partner with limited legal liability for the financial obligations of the partnership.

liquid asset   property that can readily be converted into cash, such as a bank account, mutual fund shares, stocks, and government bonds.

liquidity   when referring to an asset, the ability to sell the asset and convert its value into cash. When referring to a market, a high level of trading activity, allowing buying and selling rapidly and with minimum price disturbance.

load   a charge made on a securities transaction (e.g., mutual fund purchase). A front-end load is paid when the security is bought.

long position   owning shares of common stock with the expectation that they will increase in value.

low-load   a mutual fund sales fee that is lower than average.

lump-sum payment   payment in full made at one time.

margin   the down payment made by an investor when purchasing securities on credit. The Federal Reserve sets a minimum initial margin rate.

margin account   a brokerage account in which the holder is able to buy stocks on credit.

margin call a demand by a broker for an investor to put up additional equity to back his or her purchase of stocks on credit (margin).

market maker an intermediary who keeps over-the-counter stocks available for purchase and sale by a broker, and charges a percentage in exchange.

market risk the risk that the value of a security will decline.

market value the current price at which a financial asset could be sold.

mature to become payable.

maturity the date on which the principal amount of a security becomes payable.

mid-cap company whose total stock value is in the middle range, usually between $1 billion and $5 billion.

modern portfolio theory academic understanding of the principles underlying the analysis and evaluation of portfolio choices, based on risk-return trade-offs and cross-correlation between assets.

money market short-term debt instruments, usually one year or less in maturity, such as Treasury bills, commercial paper, and certificates of deposit.

money market mutual fund a mutual fund that purchases short-term money market investments, such as Treasury bills.

money purchase plan a retirement plan in which the annual contribution is defined (rather than the amount withdrawn in retirement). Typically the participant contributes some part and the firm contributes at the same or a different rate.

mortgage-backed securities securities backed by a pool of mortgage loans. The pass-through issuer or servicer collects payments on the loans and "passes through" the principal and interest to the security holders.

municipal bond a bond issued by a state or smaller political subdivision in order to meet spending needs. The interest paid on municipal bonds is exempt from federal income taxes and state and local income taxes within the state of issue.

Nasdaq a computerized system of trading over-the-counter stocks, originally an acronym for National Association of Securities Dealers Automated Quotations system.

negotiable a property is negotiable if the ownership may be transferred from one person to another.

net money remaining after certain deductions have been made.

net asset value the amount each shareholder in a mutual fund would receive if its assets were sold and all bills paid.

net capital net worth minus illiquid assets: assets less liabilities less any assets that cannot be quickly converted into cash.

net earnings gross earnings less gross operating expenses less taxes.

net income profit after all costs and expenses have been paid and allowances for depreciation and losses have been set aside.

net present value (NPV) the present value of the expected future cash flows minus the cost.

net profit profit after deducting all expenses.

net worth total assets less total liabilities.

net yield the profit or loss from an investment, calculated by deducting all costs from all income.

no-load the absence of a charge for investing in a mutual fund.

note the written, legally binding evidence of a debt. Treasury notes are those with initial maturities of more than one year and less than 10 years.

offering price the price at which new issues of stock are placed on sale.

opportunity cost the extra cost of a good or service due to the loss of an investment opportunity (e.g., delaying purchase of a stock rising in price; spending money to purchase a new car rather than investing the money).

option the privilege to buy or sell a financial asset.

over-the-counter (OTC) stock a security not listed or traded on a stock exchange, but rather bought and sold through dealers who make a market in such stocks.

par value the principal amount of a bond or note due at maturity, typically $1,000 per bond.

passive portfolio strategy a strategy that involves minimal expectational input, and instead relies on diversification and asset allocation to optimize portfolio performance. A passive strategy assumes that the marketplace will reflect all available information in the price paid for securities and therefore does not attempt to find mispriced securities or other assets.

performance attribution analysis the decomposition of an investment manager's results to explain why those results were achieved. This analysis determines the relative contributions of security selection, market timing, asset allocation, and market performance.

point   in the case of shares of stock, a point means $1. For bonds, a point means $10.

policy asset allocation   an asset allocation method in which the investor determines the appropriate long-term optimum asset mix, based on risk and return predictions, and does not alter the allocation based on short-term past performance or predictions of short-term future performance.

portfolio   a collection of investments, real and/or financial.

positive yield curve   short-term yields are lower than long-term yields.

preferred stock   preferred stock entitles holders to precedence over common stockholders on dividends and in the event of company default. However, holders of preferred stock have no right to vote on corporate affairs.

premium   the amount by which the price of a security exceeds its principal amount.

present value   the equivalent value today of an amount of money to be received at some future date.

price-book ratio   compares a stock's market price to the value of total assets less total liabilities (book value). Also called market-to-book. The inverse, book-to-market, is often used in academic finance.

price-earnings ratio   the current price of a share of stock divided by the annual earnings per share; an indication of the value of a stock and the market's expectations for growth.

prime rate   the interest rate charged by a bank to its commercial borrowers with the best credit ratings.

principal   (1) a major party to a business transaction; (2) the amount invested, not counting interest or earnings.

profit   the amount of income remaining after all bills have been paid.

prospectus   a written offer to sell a security that provides the information an investor must have to make an informed decision.

proxy   a limited power of attorney given by a stockholder that authorizes someone else to vote his or her stock on issues at a corporate meeting.

public offering   the issue of corporate stock shares for public purchase.

put option   gives the holder the right to sell a number of shares of stock at a certain price by a set date. Put options are purchased in anticipation that a stock will drop in price.

qualified plan a retirement plan or annuity into which tax-deductible contributions are made and invested; for example, IRA, Keogh, 401(k).

quantitative research use of advanced econometric and mathematical valuation models to identify companies with the best investment potential.

random walk a theory that assumes that the future price movement of a security cannot be predicted from past price movement and that prices move in a random pattern.

real earnings income that has been adjusted to allow for the effect of inflation.

real estate investment trust (REIT) an organization holding real estate investments and distributing nearly all of its income to shareholders.

real rate of return the percentage return that has been adjusted to allow for the effect of inflation.

realty real estate.

registered bond a bond whose owner is registered with the issuer or its agent. Transfer of ownership requires endorsement by the registered owner.

reinvestment risk the risk that proceeds received in the future will have to be reinvested at a lower interest rate.

relative strength a stock's price movement over the past year as compared to a market index (like the S&P 500).

renewable term life insurance a term life insurance policy that allows the holder to renew the policy if desired at the end of the term.

repurchase agreement a person "lends" a bank money for a short period, usually less than 90 days, and the bank promises to repay the money plus interest when the "repo" matures.

return on equity (ROE) an indicator of profitability and management skill, calculated by dividing net income for the past 12 months by common stockholder equity (adjusted for stock splits); result is shown as a percentage.

revocable trust a trust that may be altered as many times as desired and in which income-producing property passes directly to the beneficiaries at the time of the grantor's death. Since the arrangement can be altered at any time, the assets are considered part of the grantor's estate, and they are taxed as such.

risk-adjusted return the rate of return is compared to the return of other assets with similar risk. An investment manager's return may be due to assuming greater risk rather than more skillful security selection.

risk-reward ratio   a method of comparing the relative attractiveness of investment options; calculated by dividing the expected return by the standard deviation of past returns.

Sallie Mae (Student Loan Marketing Association)   a private corporation sponsored by the federal government that purchases student loans from banks and other lenders and resells them as bonds.

secondary market   the market that exists for resales of a financial instrument after its initial distribution to the public.

security   any document representing a holding of assets, such as stocks, bonds, or notes.

Sharpe ratio   a measure of a portfolio's return relative to its total variability (volatility). Named after William Sharpe, Nobel laureate. Calculated as the portfolio's average performance minus the benchmark portfolio's performance, divided by the standard deviation of the portfolio.

short   to sell a stock with an agreement to repurchase it at a later date, in anticipation of a drop in its price.

simple interest   interest calculated as a simple percentage of the original principal amount (in contrast to compound interest).

simplified employee pension (SEP)   a retirement plan similar to an IRA, to which both the employee and the employer contribute; funds accumulate tax deferred.

spread   (1) in stocks, the difference between the bid and ask prices; (2) in commodities trading, the purchase of a futures contract for delivery in one month, and the sale of a futures contract in the same commodity in another month; (3) in options trading, writing a call and buying a call on the same stock.

strike price   the price at which an option may be exercised.

subordinated debenture   a debenture that has a secondary claim to payment if the company fails, and therefore offers a higher rate of return.

systematic risk   also called undiversifiable risk or market risk.

tactical asset allocation   portfolio strategy in which the relative allocation of funds among assets is altered based on rigorous objective measures of value. It involves forecasting asset returns, volatilities, and correlations.

tax-equivalent yield   the pretax yield required from a taxable bond in order to equal the tax-free yield of a municipal bond.

technical analysis   security analysis that seeks to predict future stock prices by detection and interpretation of patterns of past security prices.

tender offer   (1) an offer by a corporation to purchase its own stocks or bonds; (2) a bid by a person or corporation to buy controlling interest in another company.

term life insurance   a life insurance policy that provides a death benefit if the insured dies during a fixed period, but no cash buildup or investment component.

term loan   a loan with a fixed maturity, as opposed to a demand loan, which is payable at any time.

Treasury bills (T-bills)   obligations of the U.S. government having 13-, 26-, or 52-week maturities. They are purchased at a discount, and pay face value at maturity.

Treasury bonds (T-bonds)   U.S. government obligations with maturities of more than seven years. They pay interest semiannually.

Treasury notes (T-notes)   U.S. government obligations with maturities of one to seven years. They pay interest semiannually.

trust   a fiduciary relationship whereby a trustee holds the title to assets for the benefit of the beneficiary.

turnover ratio   a measure of a mutual fund's trading activity during the previous year, expressed as a percentage of the average total assets of the fund. A turnover ratio of 75% means that the value of trades represented three-fourths of the assets of the fund.

unearned interest   loan interest prepaid but not yet earned.

unit investment trust   a type of investment company in which a portfolio is purchased and held with little or no change in the investments; commonly used with municipal bond investments.

universal life   a type of cash-value life insurance (whole-life) in which the cash value earns a competitive rate of interest.

value manager   an investment manager who seeks to purchase stocks that are selling at a discount to their fair market value (underpriced) and to sell them at their fair market value or a greater price.

variable annuity   an annuity whose return varies depending on the result of the return of principal invested. Usually a substantial portion of the principal is invested in common stocks.

variable life insurance policy a type of cash-value life insurance (whole-life) in which the policyholder can invest the cash value in stocks.

venture capital money invested in a new undertaking.

volatility variation in price of an asset, usually expressed as standard deviation; a measure of risk.

whole-life insurance a contract with both insurance and investment components. The insured pays premiums in excess of those necessary to purchase current insurance needs, and the excess accumulates as a cash value that the policyholder can redeem or borrow against.

working capital cash or other current assets available for the day-to-day operation of a business.

yield the rate of return on an investment, usually expressed as an annual percentage.

yield curve a graphical depiction of the relationship between yield and maturity. Usually the average yields on Treasury securities of maturities of 3 months to 30 years are used.

yield to call the rate of return on a security, assuming that the security will be redeemed at the call date and price.

yield to maturity the annual rate of return on a bond if it is held to maturity.

zero coupon bond a bond sold at a substantial discount and which does not pay periodic interest. Its value rises as the time to maturity shortens.

Index

Printed and bound by CPI Group (UK) Ltd, Croydon, CR0 4YY

16/04/2025

14658455-0003